American Musicological Society-Music Library Association Reprint Series

The American Musicological Society and the Music Library Association have undertaken to sponsor the republication of a series of scholarly works now out of print, translations of important studies, essays, etc. An editorial committee representing both organizations has been appointed to plan and supervise the series, in cooperation with Dover Publications, Inc., of New York.

Sir John Hawkins, *A General History of the Science and Practice of Music*
W. H., A. F., and A. E. Hill, *Antonio Stradivari, His Life and Work*
Curt Sachs, *Real-Lexikon der Musikinstrumente,* new revised, enlarged edition
The Complete Works of Franz Schubert (19 volumes), the Breitkopf & Härtel Critical Edition of 1884-1897 *(Franz Schubert's Werke. Kritisch durchgesehene Gesammtausgabe.)*
Charles Read Baskervill, *The Elizabethan Jig and Related Song Drama*
George Ashdown Audsley, *The Art of Organ-Building,* corrected edition
Emanuel Winternitz, *Musical Autographs from Monteverdi to Hindemith,* corrected edition
William Chappell, *Popular Music of the Olden Time,* 1859 edition
The Breitkopf Thematic Catalogue
Otto Kinkeldey, *The Organ and Clavier in the Music of the 16th Century*
Andreas Ornithoparcus, *Musice active micrologus,* together with John Dowland's translation, *A. O. his Micrologus, or Introduction, Containing the Art of Singing*
O. G. T. Sonneck, *Early Concert-life in America (1731-1800)*
Giambattista Mancini, *Practical Reflections on the Figurative Art of Singing* (translation by Pietro Buzzi)
F. T. Arnold, *The Art of Accompaniment from a Thorough-Bass as Practised in the 17th and 18th Centuries*

A.M.S. - M.L.A. JOINT REPRINT COMMITTEE

Sydney Beck, The New York Public Library, Chairman
Barry S. Brook, Queens College
Hans Lenneberg, University of Chicago
Walter Gerboth, Brooklyn College
Gustave Reese, New York University

THE ART OF
ACCOMPANIMENT
FROM A
THOROUGH-BASS

AS PRACTISED IN THE
XVIIth & XVIIIth CENTURIES

By F. T. ARNOLD, M.A. (Cantab.)

WITH A NEW INTRODUCTION BY

DENIS STEVENS

IN TWO VOLUMES

Volume II

DOVER PUBLICATIONS, INC., NEW YORK

Copyright © 1965 by Dover Publications, Inc.

All rights reserved under Pan American and International Copyright Conventions.

This Dover edition, first published in 1965, is an unabridged and unaltered republication of the work first published by Oxford University Press in 1931. The work, originally in one volume, has been divided into two volumes in this edition.

A new Introduction has been written specially for this edition by Denis Stevens.

Library of Congress Catalog Card Number: 65-24022

Manufactured in the United States of America

Dover Publications, Inc.
180 Varick Street
New York, N. Y. 10014

TABLE OF CONTENTS

VOLUME II

CHAPTER V. FORBIDDEN PROGRESSIONS 483
    § 1. Introductory 484
    § 2. The fewer the parts, the greater the strictness demanded . . 484
    § 3. Marpurg's rules adopted as the basis of the present chapter . 485
    § 4. Octaves 485
    § 5. Hidden Octaves 487
    § 6. Fifths 489
    § 7. Hidden Fifths 495
    § 8. Consecutive (perfect) Fifths by contrary motion . . 496

CHAPTER VI. THE TRIAD OR COMMON CHORD . . . 497
    § 1. The constitution of the chord 498
    § 2. *Trias harmonica aucta* 498
    § 3. Duplication of 5, or 3 498
    § 4. Rules for duplication of the 3 499
    § 5. Progression of the 3 of dominant Triad . . . 499
    § 6. Figuring 500
    § 7. Three-part harmony 502
    § 8. Two-part harmony 502
    § 9. Repetition of figure 3 over quick notes in the Bass . . 502
    § 10. The same, with one part sustained . . . 502
    § 11. Examples of Triads from Ph. Em. Bach's *Versuch* . . 503

CHAPTER VII. THE DIMINISHED TRIAD 505
    § 1. The constitution of the chord. Its seat in the major mode . 506
    § 2. In the minor mode 507
    § 3. Duplication of intervals in four-part harmony . . 508

CHAPTER VIII. THE AUGMENTED TRIAD . . . 511
    § 1. The constitution of the chord 512
    §§ 2, 3. Its seat on the third degree of the minor scale . . 512
    § 4. Chromatic alteration of the major Triad . . . 513

CHAPTER IX. CHORDS OF THE SIXTH 515
    I. *The chord of the Sixth*:
      A. As the first inversion of a perfect Triad:
      § 1. Constitution of the chord as the first inversion of a major Triad . 516
      § 2. Duplication of intervals 516
      § 3. Constitution of the chord as the first inversion of a minor Triad.
        Duplication of intervals 518
      § 4. Figuring 518
      B. As the first inversion of a diminished Triad:
        (*a*) On the leading note of the major and minor scales:
      § 5. Constitution and figuring of the chord . . . 519
      § 6. The 6 not to be doubled 519
      § 7. Duplication of the 3, or the Bass . . . 520
      § 8. Progression of the 3 520

vi   CONTENTS

§ 9. Progression of the 6 521
    (b) On the second degree of the minor scale:
§ 10. Constitution and seat of the chord. Duplication of intervals . . 523
§ 11. Progression 523
    C. As the first inversion of an augmented Triad:
§ 12. Treatment in four-part harmony 525
II. *Chords of the Sixth in sequence and otherwise*:
§ 1. Succession of Sixths in three parts 525
§ 2. Difficulties arising in four-part harmony 526
§§ 3, 4. Extracts from Ph. Em. Bach's *Versuch* . . . 527, 530

CHAPTER X. $^6_4$ CHORDS 535

A. $^6_4$ as the second inversion of a perfect Triad:
§ 1. Constitution of the chord. Duplication. Figuring . . . 536
§ 2. Distinction between the strict and free styles in the employment of the chord 536
§ 3. Unprepared cadential $^6_4$, *in arsi*, in the strict style . . . 537
§ 4. Other uses of $^6_4$ *in arsi* 537
B. $^6_4$ as the second inversion of a diminished Triad:
§ 5. The employment of the chord illustrated . . . 537
C. $^6_4$ as the second inversion of an augmented Triad:
§ 6. The employment of the chord illustrated 538
D. Retardations:
§ 7. Examples of $^{6\ -}_{4\ 3}$, $^{6\ 5♭}_{4\ 3}$ 539

CHAPTER XI. SEVENTHS 541

I. Introductory:
§ 1. Definitions of an essential discord 542
§ 2. Cases in which a Seventh can be taken unprepared . . . 544
II. Essential Sevenths:
§ 1. Constituents and figuring 547
§ 2. Progression of the 7th 548
§ 3. Progression of the 3rd 549
§ 4. Progression of the 5th 550
§ 5. Progression of the Bass 553
III. Other progressions of the Bass:
§ 1. A Seventh on the Dominant resolving on a Bass rising (a) a tone, (b) a semitone 558
§ 2. A Seventh on the leading note resolving on a Bass rising a semitone . 559
§ 3. Other Sevenths resolving on a Bass rising a degree . . . 563
§ 4. A Seventh on the Dominant resolving on another Seventh on a Bass falling a tone, or a semitone 564
IV. Suspended Sevenths:
§ 1. On a single Bass note 569
§ 2. The inclusion of the Fifth 571
§ 3. The progression of the perfect Fifth 573
§ 4. The progression of the augmented Fifth 576
§ 5. The progression of the imperfect (diminished) Fifth . . . 578
§ 6. Sequences of 7 6 suspensions on a falling Bass . . . 579
§ 7. Sequences of 7 6 suspensions on a rising Bass . . . 583
§ 8. The status of the 5 in a 7 6 suspension 590
V. Unresolving Sevenths:
§ 1. Stationary Seventh between a Triad and its first inversion . . 593
§ 2. Ditto between a Triad and a $^6_5$ 595

§ 3. Ditto between a Seventh $\binom{8}{7}{3}$ and its first inversion . . . 597
§ 4. Irregular unresolving Sevenths 597

CHAPTER XII. $^6_5$ CHORDS 601
  § 1. Constitution of chord, figuring, preparation 602
  § 2. $^6_5$ as the first inversion of a Seventh resolving on a Bass rising a Fourth
       (or falling a Fifth) 602
       (a) As the inversion of a Seventh resolving on (1) a Triad, (2) another Seventh, individually, or in a sequence, 603. (b) Delayed resolution, 605. (c) $^6_5$ on Subdominant resolving on $^4_3$ on Supertonic, 605. (d) Cadential $^{\flat 6}_{5}$ on Subdominant ('Neapolitan' $^{\flat 6}_{5}$), 606. (e) Cases in which the real resolution is disguised, 609. (f) Transferred resolution, 611.
  § 3. $^6_5$ as the inversion of dominant Seventh resolving on Triad on Submediant 611
  § 4. $^6_5$ as the inversion of Seventh on leading note, or sharpened Subdominant 611
  § 5. $^6_5$ as the inversion: I, of Seventh on Subdominant resolving on dominant Triad or Seventh; II, of Seventh on other degrees of the Scale resolving on Bass rising a degree to a Triad 612
  § 6. $^6_5$ as the inversion of suspended Seventh which (1) does not include the 5, (2) includes the 5 614
  § 7. $^6_5$ as the inversion of a Seventh resolving on another Seventh on a Bass falling a Third 618
  § 8. $^6_5$ chords in which the 5 does not resolve 621
  § 9. Unessential (passing) $^6_5$ chords 625
  § 10. $^6_{5'}$ as the inversion of retarded major Seventh on the Tonic . 626

CHAPTER XIII. $^4_3$ CHORDS 627
  § 1. Constitution of the chord, figuring, preparation . . . 628
  § 2. $^6_{4_3}$ as the second inversion of $^7_{5_3}$ resolving on a Bass rising a Fourth (or falling a Fifth) 628
       (a) $^4_3$ as the inversion of a Seventh resolving: I, upon a Triad; II, upon another Seventh 632–4
       (b) Delayed resolution of $^4_3$ on the Submediant . . . 634
       (c) $^{\flat 4}_{3}$ on the Submediant as the inversion of a Seventh on the flattened Supertonic ('Neapolitan' $^{\flat 4}_{3}$) 635
       (d) Cases in which the resolution is disguised . . . 637
  § 3. (a) $^4_3$ on the Subdominant as the second inversion of $^7_{5_3}$ on the leading note resolving on the tonic Triad 638
       (b) $^{4\sharp}_{3}$ on the Subdominant as the inversion of a diminished Seventh on the leading note resolving on $^6_5$ on the same Bass . . 639
  § 4. $^4_3$ on the Tonic as the inversion of a Seventh on the Subdominant resolving on a Seventh on the Dominant . . . 641
  § 5. $^4_3$ as the inversion of a suspended Seventh which includes either the perfect or augmented Fifth 643
  § 6. $^4_3$ with stationary 3 644
  § 7. Unessential (passing) $^4_3$ chords 644

CHAPTER XIV. $^6_{4_2}$ CHORDS 647
  § 1. Constitution and figuring of chord 648
  § 2. $^6_{4_2}$ as 3rd inversion of Seventh resolving on a Bass rising a 4th (or falling a 5th) 648

CONTENTS

(a) As the inversion of a Seventh resolving on I, a Triad, II, another Seventh, 652–3. (b) Cases in which the real resolution is disguised by: (1) suspension of one (or more) of the intervals, 654; (2) *anticipatio transitus*, 654; (3) ellipse of resolution, 655.

§ 3. $\smash{{}^6_{\substack{4\\2}}}$ as the inversion of a Seventh on leading note (or sharpened Subdominant): (1) of a minor Seventh; (2) of a diminished Seventh ... 655–6

§ 4. $\smash{{}^6_{\substack{4\\2}}}$ as the inversion of a Seventh on the Subdominant resolving on a dominant Seventh 659

§ 5. $\smash{{}^6_{\substack{4\\2}}}$ as the inversion of a suspended Seventh which includes the 5 . 660

§ 6. $\smash{{}^6_{\substack{4\\2}}}$ on a passing Bass falling a degree to a Triad or $\smash{{}^7_{\substack{5\\3}}}$ . . . 664

§ 7. $\smash{{}^4_2}\left(={}^{\widehat{6}}_{\substack{4\\2}}\text{ or }{}^8_{\substack{4\\2}}\right)$ as inversion of a stationary Seventh . . . 665

§ 8. The same disguised by the progression of the Bass . . 667

§ 9. $\smash{{}^6_{\substack{4\\2}}}$ on leading note, with resolution in Bass . . . 668

§ 10. $\smash{{}^6_{\substack{4\\2}}}\left({}^6_{\substack{2}},{}^6_{\substack{4}}\right)$ resolving on Triad over stationary Bass . . . 668

§ 11. Instances of the wrong use of the figuring 4 ♮4 (Ex. from Leclair, Op. 4) 669

§ 12. Certain special cases mentioned by Ph. Em. Bach . . . 671

CHAPTER XV. MAJOR SEVENTHS RESOLVING UPWARDS OVER THE SAME BASS 673

§ 1. $\smash{{}^7_{\substack{4\\2}}}$ on the Tonic as a retardation of the resolution of a preceding dominant Seventh $\smash{{}^7_{\substack{5\\3}}}$ 674

§ 2. The same following $\smash{{}^6_3}$ on the Supertonic . . . 675

§ 3. $\smash{{}^7_{\substack{5\\4}}}\left({}^7_{\substack{4\\2}}{}^7\right)$ on the Tonic following $\smash{{}^8_{\substack{7\\3}}}$ on the Dominant, or $\smash{{}^4_3}$ on the Supertonic 675

§ 4. $\smash{{}^7_2}\left(={}^7_{\substack{5\\2}}\right)$ and $\smash{{}^7_{\substack{4\\2}}}$ on the Tonic following a Triad on the Dominant . 677

§ 5. $\smash{{}^{78}_{\substack{5\text{-}\\3\text{-}}}}$ on the Tonic 677

§ 6. $\smash{{}^7_{\substack{4\\2}}}$ as a passing chord over stationary Bass . . . 677

§ 7. $\smash{{}^{77}_{\substack{66\\44\\22}}}$ on the Tonic, as a retardation of $\smash{{}^{99}_{\substack{77\\55\\3♯}}}$ on the Dominant, 678; $\smash{{}^{77}_{\substack{66\\44\\2}}}$, with unprepared 6, on the Tonic of the minor key, 679; $\smash{{}^{77}_{\substack{66\\44\\24}}}$ on the Dominant of the minor key, 679. 678

§ 8. $\smash{{}^7_{\substack{6\\4\\2}}}$ taken unprepared over stationary Bass . . . 680

§ 9. Retardation of one or more intervals of $\smash{{}^7_{\substack{6\\4\\2}}}$ over stationary Bass . 680

§ 10. Special instances from Ph. Em. Bach 681

CHAPTER XVI. CHORDS WITH AN AUGMENTED SIXTH . 683

§ 1. Three chords containing an augmented Sixth. Probable origin of the latter 684
§ 2. The "Italian" Sixth 684
§ 3. The "French" Sixth 685
§ 4. The "German" Sixth 685
§ 5. "Inversions" 687

CONTENTS

CHAPTER XVII. HARMONIES DUE TO THE RETARDATION OR ANTICIPATION OF ONE OR MORE INTERVALS . . 691

§ 1. Introductory 692

§ 2. $\frac{9}{5}$ 693
3

§ 3. $\frac{8}{5}$ 694
4

§ 4. $\frac{9}{5}$ 697
4

§ 5. $\frac{9}{6}$ 698
3

§ 6. $\frac{9}{7}$ 699
3

§ 7. $\frac{7}{6}$ and $\frac{7}{6}$ 701
34

§ 8. $\frac{8}{7}$ and $\frac{7}{5}$ 703
44

§ 9. Retardations of the Bass 708

(a) $\frac{7}{4}$, 708. (b) $\frac{5}{2}$, 708. (c) $\frac{7}{5}$, 709. (d) Alternative method of figuring, 710.
22

(e) $\frac{5}{3}$ (5), $\frac{7}{6}$ ($\frac{7}{5}$), 710. (f) $\frac{5}{4}$, 711. (g) $\frac{5}{3}$, 713.
3322

CHAPTER XVIII. QUICK NOTES IN THE BASS . . . 715

§ 1. Different forms of passing note 716
(a) Difficulty of recognizing passing notes as such, 716. (b) The wider sense of the term, 716. (c) *Transitus regularis*, 716. (d) *Transitus irregularis*, 717. (e) Intervals larger than a Third bridged by passing notes, 719. (f) Passing notes between (and a degree above or below) two notes of the same denomination, 720. (g) Passing notes (1) approached and quitted by leap, (2) approached by leap and quitted by step (in direction opposite to leap), (3) vice versâ, 721. (h) An interval of the chord last struck as passing note, 722. (i) Bass of Triad falls a Third, giving rise to passing $\frac{7}{5}$ chord, 722. (k) Passing notes representing an anticipation of the following harmony, 722. (l) Bass leaps downwards to passing note which rises a degree to following harmony note, 723. (m) Ellipse of passing note peculiar to *Allabreve* (Fux's *nota cambita*), 725.

§ 2. Repercussion and modification of the harmony over passing notes. (Examples from Ph. Em. Bach) 725
(a) (1) Repercussion dictated by considerations of taste; (2) Modification sometimes necessary, in order to avoid consecutives, 725. (b) Examples of repercussion, 726. (c) Modification of harmony to avoid consecutives, 727. (d) Modification of harmony necessary for preparation of subsequent discord, 728. (e) Example of an old vocal tradition, 729. (f) Examples illustrating ambiguities arising in connexion with passing notes through lack of adequate indication, 730.

§ 3. Heinichen's Rules 731
(a) Introductory—Ph. Em. Bach on the difficulty of recognizing passing notes, 731. (b) Crotchets in true common time, 732. (c) Quavers in common time, 733. (d) Semiquavers in common time. Five cases distinguished, 736. (e–m) Triple Time: (e) Introductory, 748. (f) The unit of the measure, 749. (g) The half-unit, 752. (h) Further rules, 754. (i) Five half-units preceded by rest, 757. (k) Composite groups, 758. (l) Certain figures in very quick time in which four half-units (quavers or semiquavers) pass under the harmony of the preceding unit, 760. (m) Quavers as quarter-units, 762. (n–p) *Allabreve*: (n) The true *Allabreve*, 764. (o) Two spurious varieties, 766. (p) The true *Alla-Semibreve* (*Semi-Allabreve*), 768. (q, r) Overture Time: (q) Slow Introduction, 769.

CONTENTS

    (r) Quicker measure following Introduction, 771. (s) Conclusion, 774.
§ 4. Repeated notes 774
    (a) Introductory, 774. (b) Heinichen, 774. (c) Ph. Em. Bach, 776.

CHAPTER XIX. THE FIGURING OF TRANSITIONAL NOTES . 779
§ 1. Introductory 780
§ 2. Figuring of the major scale under sustained tonic chord . . 781
§ 3. $\genfrac{}{}{0pt}{}{7}{5}\binom{9}{7}\genfrac{}{}{0pt}{}{}{2}$ and $\genfrac{}{}{0pt}{}{7}{4}\binom{9}{7}\genfrac{}{}{0pt}{}{}{2}$ representing 6 $\left(=\genfrac{}{}{0pt}{}{8}{6}\genfrac{}{}{0pt}{}{}{3}\right)$ on the Supertonic when preceded
    by an accented passing note, (1) falling, and (2) rising . . 782
§ 4. $\genfrac{}{}{0pt}{}{5}{2}$ and $\genfrac{}{}{0pt}{}{7}{4}$ on accented passing notes 783
§ 5. Different methods of indicating *transitus irregularis* in the Bass . 783
§ 6. Summary of the figurings of changing notes in the Bass . . 786
§ 7. Further illustrations 787
§ 8. Figurings arising through the combination of a transitional note in the
    Bass with one in an upper part 792
§ 9. Necessary precautions 793

CHAPTER XX. PEDAL POINTS 797
§ 1. Introductory 798
§ 2. Difficulties presented by the figuring 799
§ 3. Careful study of principal parts necessary 799
§ 4. Examples 799

CHAPTER XXI. INCOMPLETE FIGURING 803
I. The omission of accidentals:
§ 1. Diminished Thirds, Fourths, and Sixths, even though in accordance
    with the key-signature, require to be specially indicated in the figuring 804
§ 2. Fifths assumed to be perfect, in the earlier figured Basses, unless the
    contrary is indicated 805
§ 3. The sharpening of the leading note in closes (in the minor key, and in
    cases of modulation) not indicated in the earlier Basses . . 806
§ 4. Accidentals often omitted in stereotyped progressions, where the key
    is clear 809
II. Accepted optional interpretations of the figuring:
§ 1. $6 = \genfrac{}{}{0pt}{}{6}{4}\genfrac{}{}{0pt}{}{}{3}$ 810
§ 2. $6 = \genfrac{}{}{0pt}{}{6}{4\sharp}\genfrac{}{}{0pt}{}{}{3}$ 813
§ 3. $\overline{6} = \genfrac{}{}{0pt}{}{\sharp 6}{4\sharp}\genfrac{}{}{0pt}{}{}{3}$ 814
§ 4. $\overline{6} = \genfrac{}{}{0pt}{}{\sharp 6}{5}\genfrac{}{}{0pt}{}{}{3}$ 814
§ 5. 7 taken, without indication, in closes 815
§ 6. $\genfrac{}{}{0pt}{}{6}{5}$ taken, without indication, on the Subdominant . . . 816
III. Special cases in which figures are sometimes omitted:
§ 1. When the figure omitted denotes an interval required for the preparation
    of a subsequent discord 816
§ 2. When the figure omitted denotes an interval required for the resolution
    of an antecedent discord 817
§ 3. When the resolution of an antecedent discord falls upon a passing note
    of the Bass, and the intervals held over from the previous chord are
    left unfigured 817
§ 4. Certain cases, for the most part especially characteristic of the Italians:
    (1) The omission of 6 or $\genfrac{}{}{0pt}{}{6}{5}$ over the leading note, and (2) of 6 on
    another bass note rising a semitone to a Triad; (3) the omission to
    figure the resolution of a suspension resolving over a different bass
    note, or (4) over a rest 818

IV. Incomplete figurings not recognized (in some cases condemned) by the authorities:
§ 1. Such figurings due, in many cases, to thinking in three parts . . 819
§ 2. Over changing notes, appoggiaturas, &c.: $\frac{4}{2}$ (or 2) $=\frac{7}{4\,2},\frac{5}{2\,4}$ and $\frac{4}{2}=\frac{5}{2\,4},\frac{6}{2\,4}=\frac{7}{4}$ 819
§ 3. Over other notes: $\frac{7}{3}=\frac{7}{6\,3},\frac{7}{2}$ and $\frac{7}{4}=\frac{7}{4\,2}$ 824
§ 4. $\frac{6}{4}=\frac{6}{4\,2}$ 826
§ 5. $\frac{6}{4}=\frac{6}{4\,3}$ 830
§ 6. $\frac{7}{4}=$ either $\frac{7}{5\,4}$ or $\frac{8}{7\,4},\frac{7}{4}=\frac{7}{4\,3}$ 830
V. Condensed *formulae*, &c.:
§ 1. In cadences 831
§ 2. 3 2 $=$ 6 $\frac{4}{2}$ 832
§ 3. A stroke over two or more bass notes indicating, not the retention of the entire chord under the right hand, but a different inversion of the same harmony 833

CHAPTER XXII. INVERSION AND TRANSFERENCE OF DISCORD. TRANSFERENCE OF RESOLUTION. *ANTICIPATIO TRANSITUS. CATACHRESIS* 837
§ 1. Free treatment of discords a special characteristic of the Free Style . 838
§ 2. Inversion and transference of discord 838
§ 3. Transference of resolution 840
§ 4. Cases in which a Seventh may rise 842
§ 5. Successive Sevenths resolving on a Bass falling a Third . . 849
§ 6. Examples from different composers of Sevenths so resolving . . 850
§ 7. *Anticipatio transitus* 855
§ 8. Ellipse of the resolution, or *Catachresis* 857

CHAPTER XXIII. VARIETIES OF FIGURING . . . 861
§§ 1–4. Use of the figures 1, 2, 3, 4 862
§ 5. (1) 5, ♭5, 5̸ (a) = ♭$\frac{6}{5}$ (b) = imperfect Triad. (2) 5⁺ = 5 accidentally sharpened 862
§ 6. Exceptional uses of 5 866
§ 7. Normal uses of 6 867
§ 8. Leclair's use of 6̸ = $\frac{6}{4\,3}$ 868
§ 9. Ditto continued 870
§ 10. 7 872
§ 11. Special use of ♮7 873
§ 12. 8 873
§ 13. 9 874
§ 14. 9 as an alternative to 2. I. In the figuring of changing notes. II. In retardations 874
§ 15. 10, 11, 12, &c. in the earliest figured Basses . . . 877
§ 16. Later use of double figures 878
§ 17. 'Enharmonic' figuring 879
§ 18. Retrospective figuring 880
§ 19. Telemann's sign ⌢ and other special devices . . . 881

CHAPTER XXIV. VARIETIES OF NOTATION . . . 883
§ 1. Key-signatures 884
§ 2. Accidentals: (a) Earlier usages, (b) Leclair's usage . . 884
§ 3. Notation of double sharps and flats 886
§ 4. Clefs 888
§ 5. The *Custos* 889

CHAPTER XXV. PRACTICAL HINTS 891
§ 1. Introductory 892
§ 2–4. Development of 'finger instinct' 892
§ 5. Practice with sequential passages, gradually elaborated . . 894
§ 6. Practice in figuring Basses 897
§ 7. Ph. Em. Bach's method 898

APPENDIX TO CHAPTER I 899
I. The Tenbury *Syntagma* 899
II. *Basso seguente* 899
III. Saint-Lambert's mythical *Traité* of 1680 . . . 900

APPENDIX TO CHAPTER V 901
A. Corelli's consecutive 5ths 901
B. An archaic usage of J. S. Bach 902
C. Further rules of Marpurg 903

APPENDIX TO CHAPTER XVIII 903
Treatment of quavers in $\frac{4}{4}$ time 903

CHAPTER V
FORBIDDEN PROGRESSIONS

V

FORBIDDEN PROGRESSIONS

§ 1. Before embarking on any details, it will be well to warn the beginner that it is in a succession of two or more concords, and particularly Triads, that the greatest danger of consecutives lies. In the case of discords, the fixed progression of the dissonant interval serves, to a large extent, as a guide to the progression of the remaining intervals of the harmony; in the case of concords this guidance is lacking, and it must be remembered that, in every progression of two parts, *by similar motion*, to a perfect concord (Fifth or Octave), there are bound to be hidden, if not apparent, consecutives. It follows, therefore, that the greatest safeguard against faults of this kind is the use, so far as is consistent with elegant progression, of *contrary motion*.[1]

§ 2. In this matter of avoiding consecutives, the greatest strictness of all is demanded in the transparent texture of two-part harmony, with which the accompanist is not very often concerned. The greater the number of parts, the more licence is allowed, and Marpurg expressly states that somewhat less strictness is demanded in an accompaniment from a Thorough-Bass than in a composition. Least strict of all is the form of accompaniment in which full chords are played with the left hand, as well as with the right, without adhering to any definite number of parts. In this, as we have seen,[2] Heinichen boldly laid down the axiom that, as long as the extreme parts were perfectly correct in their relation to each other, and as long as the hands were kept close together, no heed need be taken of consecutives.

The beginner, however, will be well advised to avoid all liberties, and to adhere to three- or four-part harmony (mainly the latter), till correctness of progression has become instinctive. He must remember, further, that such instinct is not to be acquired by setting out figured Basses on paper, though this, too, is a valuable exercise, and cannot be dispensed with, as it helps to impress the progressions on the mind.[3] But, in playing from a figured Bass,

---

[1] Ph. Em. Bach, in his chapter on Triads (*Versuch &c.*, Part II, 1762, Ch. 2, II, § 1), writes as follows: "One must constantly insist with one's pupils on contrary motion, even when it is not especially necessary (*höchstnöthig*). In the examples for practice, let all possible kinds of insidious progressions (*alle mögliche verführerische Gänge*) be presented to them to that end, in order to show them clearly the mistakes which are liable to occur therein. HERE, THE SETTING OUT OF THE THOROUGH-BASS DOES PARTICULARLY GOOD SERVICE."   [2] Cf. Ch. iii, § 3, II.

[3] Ph. Em. Bach's instructions, based on his own extraordinarily wide experience, and possibly on memories of his great father's methods as well, are too valuable to be passed over here. He writes (*Versuch &c.*, Part II, 1762, Introd. §§ 32-6): "One must let one's pupils FIRST PLAY that which is set before them, and then SET IT OUT on two staves. In this way, eye and ear learn clearly to distinguish the true from the false.

"One must not, however, stop there, but must criticize BOTH PERFORMANCES with them; one must, as it were, demand an account of every note; objections should be made, which they must invalidate by reasons why e.g. this or that note must be where it is, SO and NOT OTHERWISE.

"It is fitting to begin with four-part accompaniment and to take it as a basis. Whoever learns this thoroughly, can also handle the other kinds with ease.

"One should go through all the chords (*Aufgaben*) with one's pupils in all positions, especially in four-part accompaniment, in order that they may become familiar with them. As this is, here, the sole object in view, we cannot, it is true, prevent inelegant progressions from slipping in occasionally, or avoid the occurrence of positions which are not the best. In this way, however, pupils learn, nevertheless, to distinguish the

there is no time for mental calculations: the accompanist must develop a mind in his fingers, and that can only be done at the keyboard.

§ 3. We have already seen that sensitiveness in the matter of consecutives had considerably increased by the beginning of the second half of the eighteenth century, and that many things were no longer tolerated by the best masters, in an accompaniment from a Thorough-Bass, which would easily have passed muster in earlier days.[4]

By far the most detailed exposition of the rules in question is given by Marpurg in his *Handbuch bey dem Generalbasse*, at the end of the First Part (1755, 2nd ed. 1762) and the beginning of the Second Part (1757). Apparent consecutives are dealt with at great length in the former place, and hidden ones, much more briefly, partly in the one and partly in the other.

It is from Marpurg, then, that the following rules and examples are taken.[5]

§ 4. *Octaves.*

(*a*) Two parts may not proceed by similar motion from one Octave, or Unison, to another.

(*b*) Octaves are not saved by the intervention of an imperfect consonance (Third or Sixth) in contrary motion, whether the interval in question appears as such (Ex. 1 *a*), or is bridged by an intermediate note (Ex. 1 *b*):

Ex. 1 [bad]

This rule does not, however, apply in the case of harmony in three or more parts, if the time is not too quick, and another harmony intervenes,[6] whereby the other parts acquire a good progression (Ex. 2):

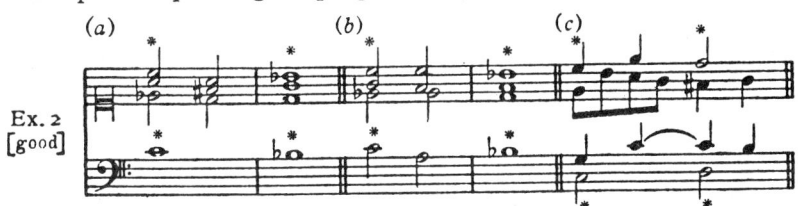

Ex. 2 [good]

best progressions and positions from the bad ones; but one must, as occasion arises, clearly point out the inelegancies (*das Ungeschickte*) and, at the same time, the way to remedy them.

"But, although these progressions may be inelegant, they must, nevertheless, not be incorrect: there must be no mistake about the necessary preparation and resolution, and prohibited Fifths and Octaves must be most rigorously avoided."

[4] Cf. Ch. iii, § 10.

[5] Not all of Marpurg's rules are given here, most of those which apply mainly, if not entirely, to composition (as opposed to accompaniment) being omitted. As the original text has been, for the most part, freely paraphrased, rather than translated, inverted commas are not used (even where the original text is closely followed) except in one or two instances in which it seemed especially important to let Marpurg speak for himself.

[6] Older composers—Marpurg quotes Battiferri (born early in the seventeenth

486 FORBIDDEN PROGRESSIONS V § 4 (c)

(c) Octaves are saved by the intervention of a Fourth or Fifth, though it is better when the harmony is in three or more parts (Ex. 3 a and b) than when it is in two (Ex. 3 c):

Ex. 3

[It will be observed that in (b) another harmony intervenes, so that the progression is doubly justified.]

(d) It is important to distinguish carefully between Octaves of the type shown in Ex. 4 (which Marpurg calls *nachschlagende Octaven*), and also Octaves in *arpeggios* (Ex. 5), on the one hand, and those of the type shown in Ex. 6 (which Marpurg calls *durchgehende Octaven*), on the other. The former are all good, if reasonably used, while the latter are totally unjustifiable. [It will be observed that, in the latter case, the Octaves are immediately consecutive, while in the former they occur on alternate, *unaccented*, notes.]

Ex. 4 [good]

Ex. 5 [good]

Ex. 6 [bad]

century) as the author of the following examples—used this progression even without the intervention of another harmony:

V § 4 (e)   FORBIDDEN PROGRESSIONS   487

(e) A type of progression which is very liable to be erroneously regarded as involving prohibited consecutives arises when, of two parts at an interval of an Octave (or in unison), one moves by oblique motion, and is subsequently followed by the other in such a way that the original interval between them is re-established. This was known by some authors as *praevenire Octavam (vel Quintam)*. Such progressions can be used with good effect in imitations against the beat (*Nachahmung im widrigen Tacttheile*), but involves the employment of more than the two parts in question, as the effect would otherwise be poor. The second series of examples (Ex. 8), in which all the dots and slurs shown in Ex. 7 are removed, clearly shows the nature of these "mock Octaves" (*Scheinoctaven*):[7]

[There is one limitation to the above rule, which Marpurg very possibly considered too obvious to be worth mentioning: the oblique motion, mentioned above, must not be of such a kind as arises when one of the two parts in question is *retarded*, as, otherwise, e.g. the preparation of a Ninth by the Octave of the Bass, which Marpurg himself stigmatizes as "an ugly breach of the rule against Octaves",[8] would be justified, as would also be the progression shown in Ex. 6 e, in which the Octave f in the Alto is retarded by what is, in fact, an Appoggiatura, though it is not noted as such.]

§ 5. Hidden Octaves.

Hidden Octaves arise when two parts proceed by similar motion from any interval whatever to an Octave (or Unison).

(a) In the progression from a Fifth to an Octave the only case in which

---

[7] It will be observed that the second crotchet of each pair in Ex. 8 is a passing note; without such passing notes the example would appear as follows:

[8] e.g. (cf. Ch. iii, § 10 a).

hidden Octaves are sanctioned in two-part harmony, or *between extreme parts*, is when the upper part falls a Second, and the lower falls a Fifth, as:

Ex. 9

Except under these conditions hidden Octaves are legitimate only between middle parts, or between a middle and an extreme part, although (as Marpurg tells us) such Octaves between extreme parts as those in the following example "are often found in the works of very good authors":

Ex. 10

(*b*) In the progression by similar motion from a Third, major or minor, to an Octave (or Unison) it is only when the upper part rises a degree, and the lower a Fourth, as in Ex. 11, that hidden Octaves between extreme parts are allowed:

Ex. 11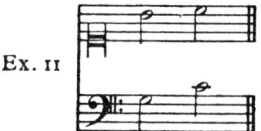

Apart from this case, they cannot be avoided, with full harmony, in the middle parts.

Prinz allows the progression shown in Ex. 12 between extreme parts, with full harmony. In such a case, however, (Marpurg tells us) there must be contrary motion between one of the middle parts and the Bass (Ex. 12 *b*):

Ex. 12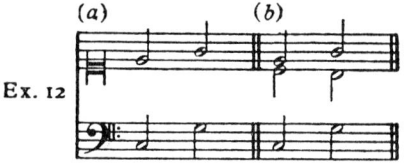

(*c*) In the progression by similar motion from a Sixth, major or minor, to an Octave, hidden Octaves are not, strictly speaking, allowed except in the middle parts. Nevertheless, with full harmony, those shown in Ex. 13, between extreme parts, are admissible, their ill effect being counteracted by the contrary motion of the middle parts:

Ex. 13

(d) The resolution of a Seventh on the Octave of the Bass, when the latter falls a Third, involves prohibited hidden Octaves. It is, nevertheless, permitted, when the harmony is in more than two parts, in certain progressions belonging to the free style [9] (Ex. 14), and, at a pinch, in a $\smash{{}^9_7}$ chord (Ex. 15):

[It may be mentioned here that hidden Octaves of the kind described above, arising between Treble and *Tenor*, as in the resolution of a suspended Seventh (generally one of a series) over the same Bass, were considered quite unobjectionable, as may be inferred from their occurrence in examples given by Ph. Em. Bach (cf. Ch. xi, "Sevenths", IV, § 6, Ex. 2 *a*, *b*).]

§ 6. *Fifths*.

(*a*) Two parts may not proceed by similar motion from one perfect Fifth to another.

(*b*) Fifths are saved by the procedure, known by some writers as *praevenire quintam* (cf. § 4 *e*), by which one part progresses by oblique motion, and is followed by the other in such a way that they are again separated by the interval of a Fifth, as in the following examples:

This device is particularly useful in connexion with the middle parts.[10]

(*c*) [That the above does not apply to a *downward* progression *by step* will be seen from the following rule, which, however, concerns the composer more than the accompanist. It shall be given in Marpurg's own words, freely translated:]

"However good the rising progression of alternate Fifths and Sixths in Fig. 9 [=Ex. 17] may be, whether syncopated or not, the corresponding downward progression in Fig. 10 [=Ex. 18] is no less bad and faulty, and is therefore to be avoided."

[9] *in gewissen galanten Gängen.*
[10] The following type of cadence affords a familiar instance of its employment:

Marpurg does not expressly say so, but it is to be assumed, as in the case of the corresponding anticipation of the Octave (§ 4 *e*), that the harmony should not be in less than three parts.

490   FORBIDDEN PROGRESSIONS   V § 6 (c)

(d) [The authorities were not agreed as to whether Fifths are to be regarded as saved by the interposition of a Third. Marpurg's opinion, which is characteristic of his eminently sane attitude in the matter of consecutives, shall again be quoted in his own words. He writes:]

"The Third, even if accompanied by subsidiary notes (*und wenn dieselbe auch mit Nebennoten vermehret wird*), does not correct the mistake of the two Fifths. That is the teaching of Fux among others; Tevo teaches the opposite, and claims that the Third makes good the mistake of the Fifths. Whom is one to believe? The most reasonable attitude is, doubtless, to choose the middle course and, as regards two-part harmony, especially if the movement be somewhat quick, to accept the view of Fux. But as soon as the harmony is in several [i.e. not less than three] parts, and the movement not too quick, especially in the case of the middle parts, and with dissonant harmonies, I do not see the smallest reason why one should not share the opinion of Tevo. Fux has more than once used such progressions, contrary to his own rule. We will therefore pronounce the examples in Fig. 25 [=Ex. 19] to be incorrect (*unächt*), but those in Fig. 26 [=Ex. 20] to be, not, it is true, correct, but, at least, admissible:

"An exactly parallel case to that of the Thirds is that of a Seventh following a preceding Fifth as a passing note (*im Durchgange*), bad examples of which are found in Fig. 27 [=Ex. 21], and admissible ones in Fig. 28 [=Ex. 22]:

V § 6 (d)   FORBIDDEN PROGRESSIONS   491

Ex. 22 [possible]

"I said 'as a passing note', for in a main note (*im Anschlage*), as in Fig. 29 [=Ex. 23], it is questioned by nobody:

Ex. 23 [good]

"This much, however, is certain, that one must be very sparing of such progressions [i.e. as those in Exx. 21 and 22], as long as one has better ones at command."

[Marpurg is here using the term *im Durchgang* very loosely; for the Sevenths in Ex. 22 b cannot, even in the widest sense of the term, be called "passing" notes. His meaning would appear to be that, in order to save the Fifths beyond dispute, the intervening Seventh must *bear a stronger accent than they*.]

(*e*) Fifths are saved by an intervening leap of a Fourth, Fifth, or Sixth, as in Ex. 24; but it is better that the harmony should be in more than two parts:

Ex. 24

[In the above series of examples the following points will be noticed:

(1) The Fifths, which in all the examples except (*f*) are between extreme parts, are in every case on the strong beats of the bar.

(2) In (*a*) and (*b*), in which the leap is one of a Fourth, and in (*c*) and (*d*), in which the leap is one of a Sixth, it is connected with the note which forms the following Fifth with the Bass by an intervening passing note, while in (*e*) and (*f*), in which there is a leap of a Fifth into a weak quaver, there are *two* intervening quavers. This, though not essential, emphasizes the contrary motion which is such an important factor in similar cases; in (*e*) the contrary motion between the extreme parts is further emphasized by the progression of the middle part.

(3) Being in less than three parts, (*c*) is the least good of all the examples.

(*f*) A careful distinction must be drawn between *immediately* consecutive

Fifths due to an unaccented note in one of the two parts in question (*durchgehende Quinten*) and Fifths, not immediately consecutive, arising on alternative (unaccented) notes (*nachschlagende Quinten*).[11]

The former, as shown in Ex. 25, are all bad:[12]

The latter are permitted under the following circumstances:
(1) When the Fifth is preceded by a Third, as in Ex. 26:

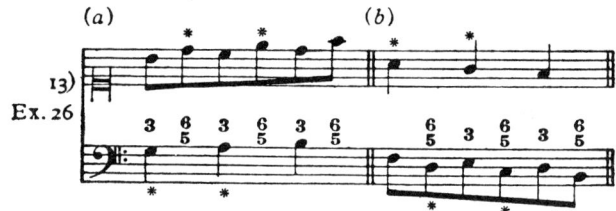

(2) When the Fifth is preceded by a Sixth (Ex. 27 *a*); so, too, according to Telemann, even if the Fifth is dotted (Ex. 27 *b*):

---

[11] Cf. § 4 *d*.
[12] Türk, however, tells us that Fifths due to either a passing or a changing (i.e. accented passing) note, in either case one extraneous to the harmony, can be tolerated "in case of extreme necessity, especially if the movement be somewhat quick". He gives the following examples (*Kurze Anweisung &c.*, 1791, § 50):

In (*a*) and (*c*) the Fifths are due to a changing, in (*b*) to a passing, note. Those in (*a*), though between extreme parts, are somewhat mitigated by the contrary motion between Tenor and Bass.

[13] Ex. 26 (*a*) concerns the composer rather than the accompanist, who would not ordinarily take the 5 of the $^6_5$ chord, indicated by Marpurg's figures, unprepared, as in the example.

V § 6 (*f*) FORBIDDEN PROGRESSIONS 493

If, however, the progression in both parts is by step, it is only with a *rising* progression, as in Ex. 28, that the Fifths on a succession of unaccented notes are permitted:[14]

Such Fifths, therefore, as those in Ex. 29 *a* are to be regarded as forbidden consecutives, though, under certain circumstances, similar Fifths may be justified by the harmony, as in Ex. 29 *b*:

(3) In harmony of three or more parts, when a middle part falls a degree, thus changing the interval between itself and the part above from a Fourth to a Fifth, as in the next example:

(*g*) Fifths between main notes are not saved by the interposition of either a Sixth or a Fourth formed by a *passing* note, as in Exx. 31 and 32:

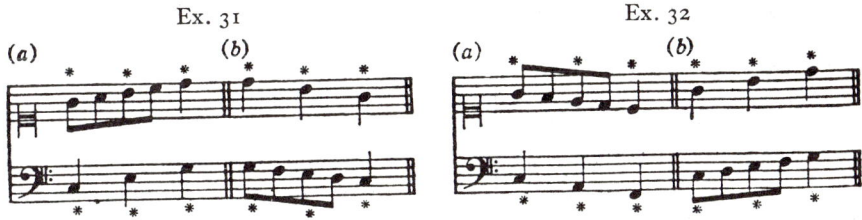

(*h*) On the other hand, in harmony of three or more parts, Fifths between main notes may be saved by the interposition of a Fourth formed by an

---

[14] It will be remembered that a similar rule applies to the progression in which a Fifth on an accented note is followed by a Sixth on an unaccented one (cf. Exx. 17 and 18).

[15] In the original (at all events in the 2nd edition, 1762) the upper part of Ex. 29 (*a*) is given a degree lower on the stave. This should either be corrected as above, or else *the clef should be changed* from Soprano to Tenor:

unaccented *harmony* note (*nachschlagende Quarte*), which, as Marpurg expresses it, "can only occur comfortably in the upper part", as in the following example:

16)
Ex. 33

[By way of illustrating the above statement, Marpurg adds, without comment, the following remarkable example in four parts, in which the Fifths occur simultaneously (1) between the extreme parts and (2) between the Alto and Tenor, while the "Nachschlag", i.e. the fall of one part from a Fifth to a Fourth above a lower part, occurs in the Alto as well as in the Treble:]

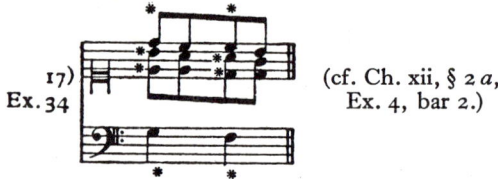

17)
Ex. 34

(cf. Ch. xii, § 2 *a*, Ex. 4, bar 2.)

(*i*) All Fifths occurring in arpeggios (*Brechungen*) are permissible, as:

(*a*) (*b*)
Ex. 35

(*k*) In certain progressions consecutive Fifths between middle parts are rendered tolerable by the dissonant nature of the harmony, which diverts attention from the fault in question.

[This, however, is a point in regard to which there was a considerable difference of opinion, for an account of which the reader is referred to Ch. iii, "The general character", &c., § 10 *e*.]

---

[16] It will be observed that the progression in the above example (a 7 6 suspension and resolution, repeated over a falling Bass) is exactly the same, except for the relative position of the upper parts, as that shown in Ex. 30.

[17] The above example illustrates that particular form of *catachresis* (i.e. incorrect or irregular progression) known as *anticipatio transitus per ellipsin* (cf. Ch. xxii,

"Inversion", &c., §§ 7, 8). The normal progression is as follows:

The upward progression of the first and third quaver of this Bass (necessary to the full resolution of the $^6_5$ chord) is omitted—this is the *ellipsis*—and each of the two bass notes in Marpurg's example anticipates, as it were, its own recurrence as a passing note (as it might have recurred, but for the *ellipsis*). The following, then, is the

complete form of Marpurg's progression: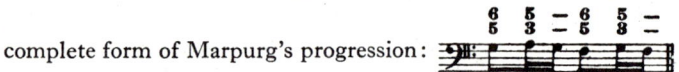

§ 7. *Hidden Fifths.*

Hidden Fifths arise when two parts proceed by similar motion from any interval whatsoever to a Fifth.

(*a*) In the progression from an Octave to a Fifth, the only case in which hidden Fifths are permitted in two-part harmony, or in fuller harmony, between extreme parts, is when the upper part rises a Second, and the lower, a Fifth, as:

Ex. 36

Even apart from these conditions, however, the progression from an Octave to a Fifth, by similar motion, between extreme parts, can be used with good effect if the harmony is full enough, and the progression of the inner parts good [i.e. in contrary motion], as:

Ex. 37

(*b*) In the progression from a Third, major or minor, to a Fifth, hidden Fifths between extreme parts are allowed only when the upper part falls a Second, and the lower, a Fourth, as:

Ex. 38

Such progressions, however, as those shown in the following example are excusable, at a pinch, on account of the contrary motion of an inner part:

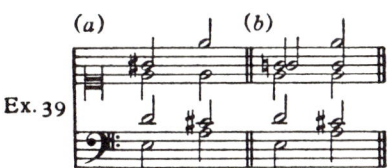

Ex. 39

(*c*) In the progression from a Sixth, major or minor, to a Fifth, hidden Fifths between extreme parts are sanctioned when the Bass rises a Third, and the upper part a Second, as:

Ex. 40

Such examples as the following must depend for their justification on the progression of the inner parts:

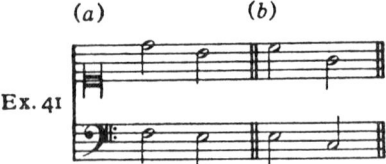

Ex. 41

(d) The resolution of a Fourth upon a Fifth, when the Bass falls a Third, is condemned by some on account of the hidden Fifths; the presence of a third part, however, as in the following example, is enough to make them unobjectionable:

Ex. 42

§ 8. *Consecutive (perfect) Fifths by contrary motion.*

In four-part harmony this progression is permissible, even when the time is slow, as in the following example:

Ex. 43

In two-part harmony the time must be quick, and it is better that the first of the two Fifths should be a passing note [i.e. another interval of the same harmony, struck over the same Bass], as in Ex. 44 (a), than that both should be main notes [i.e. intervals belonging to different harmonies], as in Ex. 44 (b), though the latter is tolerated: [18]

Ex. 44

[18] It is best to give this rule in Marpurg's own words: "Zwo QUINTEN können in der widrigen Bewegung auf einander folgen. In einem vierstimmigen Satze kann es langsam und mit anschlagenden Quinten geschehen, Fig. 28 [=Ex. 43]. In einem zweystimmigen Satze muss es geschwinde geschehen, und es ist besser, dass die erste [Quinte] durchgeht, Fig. 29 (a) [=Ex. 44 (a)] als dass alle beyde anschlagen, (b), ob dieses letzte gleich auch geduldet wird."

CHAPTER VI
THE TRIAD OR COMMON CHORD

VI
THE TRIAD OR COMMON CHORD

§ 1. The Triad (*trias harmonica*) consists, besides the Bass, of the major or minor Third and the perfect Fifth. According to the quality of the Third, the Triad itself is called major or minor.

§ 2. In four-part harmony the most usual form of the chord is with the addition of the Octave of the Bass [1] (*trias harmonica aucta*), as in the following example: [2]

Ex. 1 from Türk (*Kurze Anweisung &c.*, 1791, § 83, p. 105).

§ 3. It may, however, be necessary, in order to avoid consecutives, or the forbidden progression of an augmented interval, or for other reasons, to omit the Octave of the Bass and, in its stead, to double either the Fifth or the Third, whether in the Octave or the Unison.

In Ex. 2 (*a*) consecutive Octaves, and in (*b*) consecutive Fifths, are avoided by doubling the 5 of the Triad:

Ex. 2

from Türk, l.c.

The following example, common (in all essentials) to many text-books, illustrates a most important rule: When two bass notes rising or falling a *semitone* bear two successive major Triads, the only way in which mistakes (either consecutives or the progression of an augmented Second) can be avoided is by doubling the 3 of the Triad on the *higher* of the two bass notes, as:

Ex. 3

[1] Türk gives a rule to the effect that, except at the end of a piece (or of a period), the position of the chord with the Octave of the Bass in the upper part is to be *avoided as much as possible* (*Kurze Anweisung &c.*, 1791, § 86, p. 109).

[2] In passing from one Triad to another two main principles are to be kept in mind:

§ 4. The *minor* Third of a Triad can be doubled freely.
The *major* Third, on the other hand, cannot be doubled:
(1) in the Dominant chord, in which it is the leading note of the key;
(2) when, by being accidentally sharpened, it becomes the leading note of a new key;
(3) in the Tonic chord when it becomes a leading note in virtue of the progression of the Bass, the latter rising a Fourth, or falling a Fifth, to a Triad.[3]

In the Triad on the Subdominant the major Third can be doubled freely,[4] and, *except under the circumstances described above*, in that on the Tonic also.

Such was the teaching of Kirnberger,[5] and, at an even earlier date, Heinichen had emphatically dissociated himself from the ancient prejudice against the duplication, under any circumstances, of the major Third of a Triad.[6]

§ 5. Although the proper progression of the major Third of the Dominant

(1) the avoidance of unnecessary skips by retaining in each successive chord (with or without repercussion, according to the circumstances) any interval or intervals common to it and the preceding chord, and (2) the employment of contrary, or oblique, rather than of similar motion.

[3] The same obviously applies when the Bass, instead of rising a Fourth (or falling a Fifth) to a Triad, falls a Third to its first inversion, as: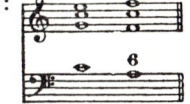

[4] Except, of course, when the Triad on the Subdominant is followed by one on the *accidentally flattened* seventh degree of the scale, or its first inversion, as:

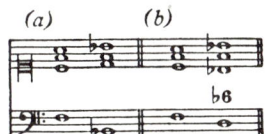

[5] Cf. *Die Kunst des reinen Satzes*, Part I, 1771, pp. 35 sq.; also *Grundsätze des Generalbasses*, 1781, § 154, p. 61.
[6] Cf. *General-Bass &c.*, 1728, pp. 940 sq., where he writes as follows: "With the duplication of the accidental major 3rd, in music written in few parts, ... I have, it is true, not cared to have anything to do; but, as to the duplication of the natural major 3rd, I avoid it, in my latest works, as little as do other practitioners of to-day. That I was formerly afraid of any duplication of the major Third is, however, undoubtedly true, because I had, from youth upwards, been indoctrinated with this idea. It is a case of *Consuetudo altera natura*: by long habit prejudices are acquired of which one cannot all at once get rid. For this very reason I am the more inclined to pardon the older composers of our times, who have been thus accustomed from youth upwards and abhor all other instances of apparent harshness (*sonst alle anscheinende Härtigkeiten*), for their fear of the duplication of the major 3rd; but one would hardly imagine such an absurdity as that there should be composers, quite fresh from their travels (*neugereiset*) to whom the doubling of all major 3rds alike (however perfectly they may be tuned) appears harsh and intolerable; whereas, on the other hand, the diminished 3rd, the diminished 8ve, and even, in certain cases, the major and minor 6ths struck simultaneously, seem to them quite endurable and curious (*sonderbahr*). Nay, there are examples in Recitative in which the accompanist has to strike the diminished 5th, the diminished 3rd, and the diminished 8ve, all three together in a single chord, with the voice; and all that is not repellent to their ears: it is only the duplication of the major 3rd that seems to them so harsh."

chord, when the latter is followed by that of the Tonic, is a semitone upwards, nevertheless, in a four-part accompaniment, it may, *when not in the upper part*, fall to the 5 of the Tonic chord.[7] If, however, the accompaniment is in three parts only, the Third in question must rise, thus leaving the Tonic chord incomplete.

Ph. Em. Bach gives the following examples (*Versuch &c.*, Part II, 1762, Ch. 2, II, §§ 6, 7):[8]

§ 6. A Triad may be figured $\frac{8}{5}$, $\frac{5}{3}$, $\frac{8}{3}$, 8, 5, 3, or not at all. *Every unfigured bass note, other than a passing note*,[9] is understood to bear a Triad. Except, therefore, under certain circumstances no figuring is employed.

Such circumstances arise:

(1) When the 3 of the chord is accidentally sharpened or flattened, in which case the Bass is figured: ♯, ♭, ♮ (or, more rarely, ♯3, ♭3, ♮3), in accordance with the key-signature, as:

[7] This progression of the leading note, under the conditions mentioned above, besides being generally recognized as a permissible liberty on a keyed instrument, was, as is well known, freely employed by J. S. Bach himself in his harmonization of Chorales, where it is particularly easily apprehended by the ear. It is, therefore, somewhat remarkable that Türk appears to regard it as something to be avoided as far as possible, even in accompanying from a Thorough-Bass. Of the progressions:

which occur in the course of an extended example, in which mistakes are purposely introduced, he writes:

". . . the leading note does not, as it properly should do, rise a degree. However, this progression in a middle part might perhaps pass in playing from a Thorough-Bass." But (in the course of a footnote) he adds: "However, I certainly advise even the player from a Thorough-Bass against employing similar liberties, as a habit disadvantageous to the future composer may be easily and imperceptibly acquired thereby. My point was merely that there are progressions which can be pardoned in the player from a Thorough-Bass rather than in a composer" (*Kurze Anweisung &c.*, 1791, § 90, p. 114).

It must, however, be remembered that Türk was avowedly writing for beginners, and was therefore right in advocating a strictness which he would probably not have observed in his own practice.

[8] It must be mentioned that Ph. Em. Bach makes no mention, either in connexion with the above examples, or elsewhere, of "Dominant", "Tonic", or "leading note": he merely gives general rules to the effect that the major Third of a Triad, more especially if *accidentally sharpened*, tends to rise.

[9] The term is here used in its widest sense, to indicate any note not bearing an harmony of its own. For the means of distinguishing between passing and harmony notes the reader is referred to Ch. xviii, on "Quick notes in the Bass", § 1.

(2) When the 5, *but not the 3 as well*, is accidentally sharpened, as in the second chord of Ex. 7. When the 3 is accidentally sharpened as well as the 5 (as in the last chord of the example), the sharpened 5 is not usually indicated, as, when the Third is major, the Fifth is generally assumed to be perfect. Some composers, however, think it necessary to indicate the sharpened 5 as well as the sharpened 3, as shown beneath the example:

Similarly, when the Bass is accidentally flattened, the Fifth is assumed to be perfect, and no special indication is necessary:

(3) When the Triad is preceded, or followed, by another harmony over the same Bass, or its Octave. In such cases it is usual to figure only those intervals of the Triad which are affected by the change of harmony:

(4) When a note which would otherwise be treated as a passing note is intended to bear a Triad:

§ 7. In three-part harmony the interval most commonly omitted is the Octave of the Bass (Ex. 11 *a*). It may, however, be better, in order to avoid skips, or the *duplication of the melody of the principal part*, to omit the 5 instead (Ex. 11 *b*); very often the fixed progression of a leading note makes it necessary to do so (Ex. 11 *c*). The 3 must *never* be omitted:

Ex. 11

§ 8. In the rare cases in which a two-part accompaniment is employed, it may be necessary, as Türk points out,[10] to omit the Third (Ex. 12 *a*), in order to avoid faulty progressions in the upper part (Ex. 12 *b*):

Ex. 12

§ 9. The repetition of the figure 3 over a series of quick notes, moving by step, indicates that only Thirds (or Tenths) are to be played with them. Türk (l.c., see note 10) gives the following examples, in which it will be noted that the full harmony enters on the *last*, and not (as might perhaps have been expected) on the penultimate, crotchet of the bar:[12]

Ex. 13

§ 10. The method of figuring seen in the following examples,[13] indicating three-part harmony in which one part is sustained, while the other follows

---

[10] *Kurze Anweisung &c.*, 1791, § 87, pp. 110 sq.

[11] The only possible alternative (which Türk does not, however, mention) by which one or both of the Thirds might be retained would be to substitute a *diminished* interval for one, or both, of the augmented ones:

[12] From this we may infer that if a chord had been intended on the penultimate crotchet, it would have been necessary to figure it *differently* from the preceding series of quick notes, i.e. $\genfrac{}{}{0pt}{}{8}{5}$, $\genfrac{}{}{0pt}{}{5}{3}$, 8, 5, or not at all.

[13] From Türk, o. c., § 87 *h*, and § 91, bars 13 sq. of the extended example there given.

VI § 10   THE TRIAD OR COMMON CHORD   503

the Bass in Thirds (or Tenths), is mentioned by Türk as being "now [1791] fairly common in certain districts":

Ex. 14

§ 11. The following short example of Triads, from Ph. Em. Bach,[14] will be useful to beginners. It will be observed that, even in the cadences where the Bass falls a Fifth, one of the instances in which hidden Octaves are generally held to be excused (cf. Ch. v, § 5, Ex. 9), Bach is at pains to avoid them:

Ex. 15

[14] *Versuch &c.*, Part II, 1762, Ch. 2, II, § 11. In the original the Bass only is given, and the figures above it show which interval is to be taken in the upper part. The chords have here been added.

[15] In the original the fourth crotchet, c, in Ex. 15 (a) is figured 3; it is, of course, possible that Bach intended the 3 to be doubled, and the 8ve of the Bass omitted, $\frac{3}{5}$; but it is much more probable that the 3 is due to a misprint and that 8 (as given above) was intended. The same applies to the first crotchet, c, in Ex. 15 (c). In Ex. 15 (f) the second crotchet, d, is figured 5; here the misprint is certain.

CHAPTER VII
THE DIMINISHED TRIAD

VII
THE DIMINISHED TRIAD

§ 1. The diminished Triad consists, besides the Bass, of the minor Third and the diminished Fifth.

It may be figured 5, $\widehat{5}$,[1] $\widehat{5\flat}$, or not at all.

It may occur on the seventh degree of the major scale:

(1) in the repetition of a sequence; in four-part harmony with the Octave of the Bass as a fourth part:

Ex. 1

(from Kirnberger's *Grundsätze des Generalbasses &c.*, 1781, volume of examples, Part II, Fig. XXV).

(2) as an incomplete form (lacking the Sixth) of the first inversion of the chord of the Dominant Seventh, when the progression of the Bass and of the diminished Fifth is subject to the same rules as the corresponding intervals (the Third and Seventh) of the complete chord (cf. Ch. xi, "Sevenths", II, §§ 3 and 2), i.e. the Bass must rise, and the diminished Fifth fall,[2] a semitone.

Its most natural use is, then, in three-part harmony:

Ex. 2

In four-part harmony the only interval of the chord which can be doubled is the 3, as in the following examples from Ph. Em. Bach:[3]

---

[1] For the significance of the semicircle ⌒ over the figure, see Ch. xxiii, "Varieties of figuring", § 5, 1 b ad fin.

[2] Except in the pattern of a sequence (a), or in a modulation (b), when the diminished Fifth is free to rise:

[3] *Versuch &c.*, Part II, 1762, Ch. 8, II, § 4. In the original the examples are given on a single stave, and an Octave lower than here.

§ 2. (1) In the minor key the diminished Triad may occur on the sharpened seventh degree of the scale under exactly the same conditions as those illustrated in Ex. 3.

Ph. Em. Bach gives the following example,[5] showing the same progression in two different positions:

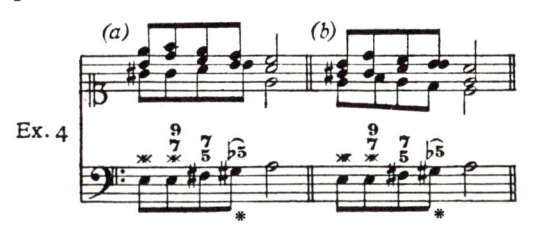

He explains that the diminished Triad is to be used in this instance, rather than the more usual $^6_5$ chord, in order to "preserve a good melodic progression (*einen guten Gesang*)" [i.e. by avoiding the downward leap of a Fourth from *a* in the third chord to *e* in the following one, a leap which, though not serious in itself, would in this instance disturb the symmetry of the whole progression].

(2) The seat of the true diminished Triad (as opposed to the incomplete $^6_5$ chord described above) is on the second degree of the minor scale.

Its most usual progression is to the chord of the Dominant—either directly (Ex. 5), or with an intervening $^6_4$ chord (Ex. 6)—or to its first inversion (Ex. 7):[6]

---

[4] In (*a*), as Bach explains, the chord at * is taken in its incomplete form (without the 6) in order to avoid the ugly progression of two consecutive Seconds [or, in another position, Sevenths and Fifths], and in (*b*), in order to avoid the consecutive Fifths which would otherwise arise between Tenor and Bass.

For the method of figuring in (*b*) (oblique dashes on the accented passing notes), see Ch. xix, "Figuring of transitional notes", § 5.

[5] Cf. note 3.

[6] Exx. 5 and 7 are from Ph. Em. Bach, who gives the Bass only (*Versuch &c.*, Part II, 1762, Ch. 4, § 4); Ex. 6 is from Türk (*Kurze Anweisung &c.*, 1791, § 107, p. 142).

[Ex. 7 musical example]

In the following example from Ph. Em. Bach[7] the fourth part is furnished by the doubled Third, instead of by the Octave of the Bass (as in Exx. 5–7):

[Ex. 8 musical example]

§ 3. (1) With regard to the duplication of one or other interval of the diminished Triad on the second degree of the minor scale, Ph. Em. Bach[9] and Türk[10] are agreed that the duplication of the Bass produces a harsher effect than that of the Third, and also that, if the Octave of the Bass is employed, it should, if possible, *not appear in the upper part*.

[7] *Versuch &c.*, Part II, 1762, Ch. 4, § 6.
[8] In the original the example is given on a single stave, and an Octave lower.
[9] Bach writes as follows (*Versuch &c.*, Part II, 1762, Ch. 4, § 5): "... Our Triad sounds well in three parts, but somewhat empty in four. If, instead of taking the Octave, the Third is doubled, all the middle parts are consonant with each other, and this makes the chord more tolerable; but if the Octave is in the upper part, it sounds worst of all. The choice of position depends upon a cautious accompanist more than does the duplication [i.e. the choice between the duplication of the Third and of the Bass]. The resolution of a discord may sometimes hinder the latter [i.e. prevent the doubled Third from being chosen]:

[musical example]

[10] Türk writes as follows (*Kurze Anweisung &c.*, 1791, § 108, p. 143): "As it is not advisable to double the false Fifth in the diminished Triad, there remains, in four-part harmony, nothing but the doubled Third, or perhaps the Octave. The latter makes the diminished Triad perceptibly harsher—for it forms an augmented Fourth with the [diminished] Fifth when this is below it—therefore, in this chord, the doubled Third is decidedly to be preferred to the Octave. ... In any case, when the Octave becomes indispensable, one must seek to avoid it, if possible, in the upper part. But, that this position cannot always be avoided without mistakes is clear, among others, from the [following] example at + :

[musical example]

[N.B.—Türk exaggerates, as far as the present instance is concerned, when he talks of "avoiding mistakes": the nearest approach to a mistake that could occur would be

VII § 3 (1) THE DIMINISHED TRIAD 509

Apart, however, from the instances (illustrated in notes 9 and 10) in which the resolution of a 9 on the second degree of the minor scale involves the employment of the 8ve of the Bass, there is a far commoner case in which the duplication of the Third is inconvenient, namely, when the diminished Triad in question is immediately followed by the Dominant chord—whether Triad or Seventh.

The following example from Kirnberger [11] will suffice to make this clear:

Ex. 9

In (a) we have the forbidden progression of a consecutive Second in the Alto, and in (b), which is otherwise correct, a very undesirable skip in the upper part.[12]

(2) Ph. Em. Bach still clings to the ancient superstition which forbids the employment of the Octave of an accidentally sharpened bass note, irrespective of whether it thereby becomes a leading note or not. Concerning the following example, which is obviously in the key of E minor, though there is no ♯ in the signature, he writes: [13]

"When the Bass of our Triad is preceded by an accidental which raises it [♯ or ♮], the Octave is omitted and the Third doubled:

Ex. 10
14)

the inelegant progression of a diminished Fifth descending to a perfect one, if the diminished Seventh on ♯G were taken in the upper part:

On the other hand, if the remaining position were selected, the melodic progression of the upper part—the "guter Gesang" on which Ph. Em. Bach always lays such stress—would be much less good than in the position selected by Türk.]

[11] *Grundsätze des Generalbasses &c.*, 1781, § 51, p. 25; ibid., volume of examples, Part I, Figs. 35 and 36.

[12] A better progression is obtained by choosing the positions in which the Third is doubled in the unison, as: , but the doubling of the Bass, as: , remains far preferable.

[13] *Versuch &c.*, Part II, 1762, Ch. 4, § 6.   [14] Cf. note 8.

Türk, on the other hand, though paying due deference to the accepted doctrine, as the following example [15] shows, is careful to explain its fallacy.

Ex. 11

Concerning the chord at * in the above example, he writes in a footnote: "The duplication of the Third in the unison (and the consequent skip in the Alto) is here necessary because, as some teach, the Octave of the accidentally sharpened Bass note must on no account be employed. However, I should ... without hesitation permit this duplication of the Bass in case of need, because, in E minor, ♯F is not in point of fact accidental. For the 𝄪 has no influence on the effect. The case is quite different when a modulation to another key is effected by such an interval [i.e. an accidentally sharpened Bass], or when it occurs for the first time; [16] for in the latter case the tartness (that which challenges the attention) resides in the unaccustomedness, because the sharpened interval is, so to speak, still strange. Only it is a matter of course that leading notes occurring in the Bass are not included in the above permissible duplication."

[15] *Kurze Anweisung &c.*, 1791, § 118, p. 155, bars 5–7 of the extended example there given.

[16] In the above excerpt from Türk's example (in which the author would certainly have sanctioned the doubling of the Bass of the chord in question) it will be seen that the key of E minor is already well established in the course of the preceding bar and a half.

CHAPTER VIII
THE AUGMENTED TRIAD

VIII
THE AUGMENTED TRIAD

§ 1. The augmented Triad consists, besides the Bass, of the major Third and the augmented Fifth. The latter interval has a fixed progression of a semitone upwards and can under no circumstances be doubled.

The chord is figured ♯5 (5♯), 5̸, ♮5 (5♮).

§ 2. Its seat is, primarily, on the third degree of the minor scale. Here it occurs most frequently as a retardation of the chord of the Sixth. The augmented Fifth must then be prepared. In four-part harmony either the Third may be doubled (Ex. 1 b) or the Bass (c and d); but the Octave of the Bass must not appear in the upper part (bb) if it can be avoided:[1]

Ex. 1

It will be observed that (c) is a repetition of (b), but in a different position, in which the employment of the Octave of the Bass c is on the whole more natural (and gives a fuller harmony) than the doubling of the Third in the unison.

In (d) the doubling of the Bass ♭e is indicated by the fixed downward progression of the 3 (the dissonant note) of the preceding $^6_4{}_3$ chord, though the upward progression of the said 3, the 'mistake' to which Türk alludes (cf. note 1), might be defended on the ground of the transference of the resolution to the Bass (cf. Ch. xxii, "Inversion", &c., § 3).

§ 3. An augmented Triad on the third degree of the minor scale may also arise through the retardation of the Bass (Ex. 2 a and b), in which case the latter must be prepared, and cannot, of course, be doubled. In (c) and (d) the Third is retarded as well as the Bass, and duly prepared:

---

[1] (1) Türk, from whom Ex. 1 a and d are taken, writes as follows (*Kurze Anweisung &c.*, 1791, § 112, p. 150): "In a four-part accompaniment the best interval to double is the Third. But if this duplication is not possible without mistakes, as in (cc) [=Ex. 1 d above], the Octave of the Bass must be chosen; but it must never, particularly in this chord, be taken in the upper part without the most pressing necessity. For the Octave c in the Treble at (d) [cf. Ex. 1 (bb) above] forms a diminished Fourth with the ♯g below it and makes this chord, which is already somewhat harsh, more unpleasant still."

(2) Ph. Em. Bach does not expressly condemn the employment of the Octave in the upper part, but referring to Ex. 1 b above, which he gives on a single stave with the upper parts an Octave lower (*Versuch &c.*, Part II, 1762, Ch. 5, § 4), he writes as follows: "The DUPLICATION OF THE THIRD, omitting the Octave, has not a bad effect in our Triad, as the middle parts [i.e. the three upper parts] are then all consonant with each other."

THE AUGMENTED TRIAD

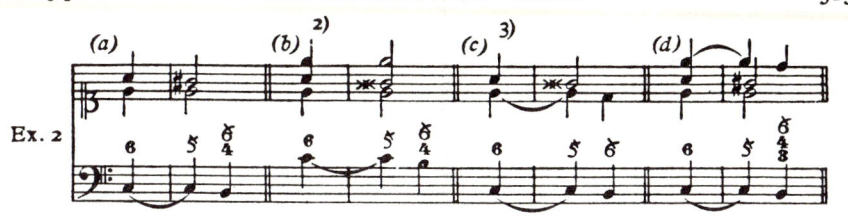

Ex. 2

§ 4. An augmented Triad may further arise through the chromatic alteration of the Fifth of a major Triad. In four-part harmony the nature of the progression will determine whether the Bass or the Third is to be doubled:

Ex. 3

Ph. Em. Bach gives the following example,[4] concerning which he writes: "A SLOW PROGRESSION by semitones, in which our [augmented] Fifth occurs, is best accompanied in three parts. Such semitones in the principal part are not well suited to a quick measure; should they, however, occur, they are not included in the accompaniment:[5]

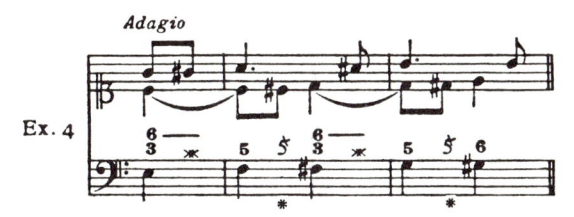

Ex. 4

---

[2] From Schröter, *Deutliche Anweisung &c.*, 1772, § 237, p. 127.
[3] From Türk, ibid., p. 151.
[4] *Versuch &c.*, Part II, 1762, Ch. 5, § 6. In the original the example is given on a single stave, an Octave lower than above.
[5] It will be observed that this injunction applies to the composer (or whoever figures the Bass) rather than to the accompanist.

CHAPTER IX
CHORDS OF THE SIXTH

IX
CHORDS OF THE SIXTH

Section I. The chord of the Sixth:

A. As the first inversion of a perfect Triad:

§ 1. As the first inversion of the major Triad the chord of the Sixth consists, besides the Bass, of a minor Third and minor Sixth; as that of the minor Triad, of a major Third and major Sixth.

§ 2. In four-part harmony either the Sixth may be doubled, in the 8ve or in the unison (Ex. 1 *a*, *b*, *c*), or the Third (*d*, *e*, *f*), or the Octave of the Bass may be included (*g*, *h*, *i*):

Ex. 1

N.B.—The above example may be applied *mutatis mutandis* to the first inversion of the minor Triad.

In the absence of some reason to the contrary (cf. II, § 4 *ad init.*), the duplication of either the Sixth or the Third is generally preferable to the inclusion of the Octave of the Bass.[1] When included, the latter should, if possible, not appear in the upper part.[2]

It will be realized that the duplication of the 6, the 3, and the Bass of a chord of the Sixth is exactly parallel with that of the Bass, the 5, and the 3, respectively, of the corresponding Triad. We have already seen that in certain cases the major Third of a Triad cannot be doubled (cf. Ch. vi, § 4). Accordingly, when the Bass of a chord of the Sixth is the leading note of the key [3]

---

[1] Cf. Ph. Em. Bach, *Versuch &c.*, Part II, 1762, Ch. 3, I, § 5.
[2] Ibid., § 12.
[3] (*a*) It will be remembered that the idea of the sanctity of the leading note, *as such*, quite apart from any accidental sharpening, was of gradual growth. Writing in 1728, Heinichen stated categorically that ♯c might be doubled in the key of D major, where it is 'natural', but not in D minor, where it is 'accidental' (cf. Ch. ii, § 5, III (*a*) *ad fin.*). Again, Mattheson, writing in 1735, did not hesitate to give examples of such a progression as the following: (cf. Ch. ii, § 7 *d*, Ex. 1).

Ph. Em. Bach himself, writing in 1762 (and also in a later edition of Part II of the *Versuch*, "with corrections and additions by the author"), seems to share to a large extent the point of view of his predecessors, for he gives two examples (two *only*, as for as the present writer is aware) in which the Bass of a chord of the Sixth on the

(Ex. 2 *a–cc*), or becomes a virtual leading note by its progression a semitone upwards to the Bass of a Triad, whether it be accidentally sharpened [4]

seventh degree of the *major* scale (where the bass note in question is therefore "natural") is doubled. In the first of the two examples (see II, § 3, Ex. 8 *b*), moreover, the leading note rises a semitone to the Tonic Triad; in the second (see II, § 4, Ex. 13 *c*), the progression (which is not completed) might either be as above, or to a chord of the Sixth on the Tonic, in which case the duplication of the seventh degree of the scale would be less remarkable. In the chord of the Seventh, on the other hand, when the Seventh is minor and the Third major (i.e. the Dominant Seventh), Ph. Em. Bach forbids the duplication of the Third (i.e. the leading note), "even though it be natural". This is, however, not so illogical as it might, at first sight, appear, for in the chord of the Seventh the 3 becomes quasi-dissonant in relation to the 7, which forms a diminished Fifth above it (or an augmented Fourth below, according to the position in which the chord is taken), whereas the 3 of the Dominant Triad and the Bass of its first inversion (with which latter we are at present concerned) are alike consonant with the other intervals of the chord.

(*b*) With regard to the practice to be observed by the beginner, he will be well advised (in spite of the examples quoted above) to avoid doubling the seventh degree of either scale when employed as a leading note, that is to say, when rising to the Tonic chord. When *not* so employed, there is no logical reason against its duplication as in the following examples (especially Ex. 1 *a*, in which the Bass *falls*):

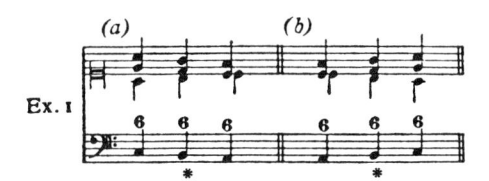

Ex. 1

Care must, however, be taken to avoid the progression of an augmented Fourth, as:

(*aa*) bad (*bb*) bad

Kirnberger himself gives the following example, of which he writes (*Grundsätze des Generalbasses &c.*, 1781, § 74, p. 37):

"At the second bass note, contrary to the injunction to double either the Sixth or the Third, the Octave of the Bass is taken. But in the sequel it will often be found that many rules suffer an exception on certain occasions. This is exactly a case in point, because then a sequence of harmonious chords results."

N.B.—Kirnberger points out later on (o. c., § 75) that, instead of taking the Octave of the Bass *B*, the 6 may be doubled (*b*):

Ex. 2

(o. c., volume of examples, Part I, Fig. 59, Ex. 5, and Fig. 61.)

---

[4] Mention has already been made of Ph. Em. Bach's failure to discriminate between the cases in which an accidentally sharpened bass note thereby becomes a leading note and those in which it does not (cf. Ch. vii, § 3, 2). A case in point is the sharpened

(*d, dd*), or diatonic (*e–ff*), its Octave cannot be included in the chord, and the 6 or 3 must be doubled instead:

Ex. 2

(N.B.—All the possible duplications of the Sixth and Third in the *unison* are shown in Exx. *a–bbb*, and need not be repeated in the other examples.)

§ 3. As the first inversion of a minor Triad, the chord of the Sixth consists (besides the Bass, which corresponds to the minor Third of the Triad) of a major Third and major Sixth, corresponding, respectively, to the Fifth and the Bass of the Triad. Any one of these intervals may be doubled; but here, too, it is better that the Octave of the Bass should not appear in the upper part.

§ 4. Chords of the Sixth are usually figured with the single figure 6,

sixth degree of the melodic minor scale. He gives (on a single stave and an 8ve lower) the two following examples (ibid., Ch. 3, II, § 3 *e* and § 8):

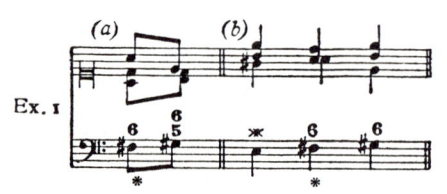

Ex. 1

Of the first of these he says: "An accidental, *which may not be doubled*, is sometimes responsible for the duplication of the Third." [The italics are not Bach's.] It is plain that the sharpened sixth degree of the melodic minor scale is as essentially diatonic in character as the leading note itself, although both require an accidental; there is therefore no valid reason against treating the above progressions as follows:

Ex. 2

N.B.—The position shown in (*aa*) and (*bb*) is less good than the others on account of the Octave of the Bass of the Sixth on ♯F being in the upper part. In the second example a third position is impossible because of the consecutive Fifths which would arise.

preceded or followed by a ♯ (♯6, 6♯), or else crossed (6̸), if accidentally sharpened,[5] and accompanied by a ♭ (♭6, 6♭) if accidentally flattened. The Third does not usually appear in the figuring unless accidentally altered, in which case ♯ or ♭, either alone or, more rarely, accompanied by the figure 3 (♯3, ♭3), appears below the 6.

A fuller figuring is, however, often necessary in order to indicate the progression of a preceding harmony, as:

Ex. 3

B. As the first inversion of a diminished Triad:
  (a) On the leading note of the major and minor scales.

§ 5. The chord of the Sixth, corresponding to the diminished Triad on the leading note of either scale, is characterized by the combination of a minor Third and major Sixth. Its seat is on the second degree of the scale, and in the minor scale, where the leading note requires an accidental, it is figured accordingly: ♯6 (6♯), 6̸, ♮6 (6♮). Where the minor Third is not in accordance with the key-signature, this must, of course, be indicated by a ♭ or ♮ (as the case may be), with or without the figure 3, below the 6.

§ 6. The 6, being the leading note, cannot be doubled except, possibly,[7]

---

[5] N.B.—In chords of the *augmented* Sixth, to be considered in a later chapter, the 6 is usually crossed or accompanied by a ♯, whether accidentally sharpened or not, in order to prevent misunderstanding.

[6] From Ph. Em. Bach, ibid., Ch. 19, § 4, and Ch. 20, § 4, only the Basses being given.

[7] Ph. Em. Bach uncompromisingly forbids the doubling of a major Sixth when associated with a minor Third, quite irrespective of the fundamental difference of character between the chord of the Sixth on the second degree of either scale and the same chord (as far as the actual intervals are concerned) on the Subdominant of the minor scale. He simply says: "Neither the natural, nor the accidentally sharpened major Sixth, is doubled when associated with the minor Third" (ibid., Ch. 3, 1, § 7).

Christoph Gottlieb Schröter, Ph. Em. Bach's senior by fifteen years, writes of the chord of the Sixth on the second degree of the major scale (and the same applies, of course, to the minor): "Chorda II has the essential [i.e. natural] major 6 and minor 3; but never the doubled Sixth: otherwise the leading note (*Character Modi Tonici*) would be doubled, which is contrary to all nature, and would be just the same as if this hemisphere had two suns."

He gives the chord (1) with the Octave of the Bass, and (2) with the 3 doubled, as follows:

[The semiquaver *B* denotes the 'fundamental' Bass.]

Türk, on the other hand, tells us that "some people permit" the doubling of the major Sixth, not only on the Subdominant of the minor scale (with which we are not at present concerned), but on the second degree of the major scale when the chord

under the same conditions as the Bass of the corresponding Triad, namely, in the repetition of a sequence (cf. Ch. vii, Ex. 1), as:

Ex. 4

§ 7. The 3 corresponds to the 5 of the diminished Triad, and it might therefore have been expected that it would as little be doubled as the latter. Such, however, is not the case; the reason being, no doubt, that, in the chord of the Sixth with doubled 3, the quasi-discordant interval of a diminished Fifth is found between the upper and a *middle* part (Ex. 5 a), instead of between extreme parts, as would be the case if the 5 of a diminished Triad were doubled in the Octave (Ex. 5 b): [8]

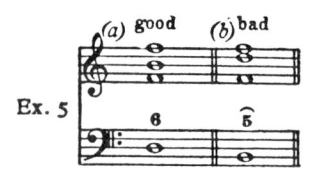

Ex. 5 (a) good (b) bad

The intervals, therefore, that may be doubled are the Bass, corresponding to the Third of the diminished Triad, and the 3.

§ 8. The progression of the 3, as might be expected from the above, is considerably more free than that of the corresponding interval of the Triad. Marpurg writes as follows (*Handbuch &c.*, 2nd ed. 1762, p. 39): "The Third of this chord tends (*verlangt*), like the diminished Fifth of the parent chord, to fall, in the following progression: Tab. II, fig. 21 (*f*) [=Ex. 6 a]. However, it is not only permitted in certain cases, like the parent Fifth,[9] to rise, e.g. in (*d*) and (*e*) of Fig. 21 quoted above [=Ex. 6 b and c], but, when doubled, is compelled to do so in one part, e.g. $\begin{smallmatrix} f & e \\ b & c \\ f & g \\ d & c \end{smallmatrix}$, Tab. III, Fig. 1 [=Ex. 6 d]."

in question is *not* followed by a Tonic chord (either Triad or first inversion), but by a Triad on the Mediant, "when the Sixth which precedes it is, therefore, not to be regarded as a leading note", as in the following example:

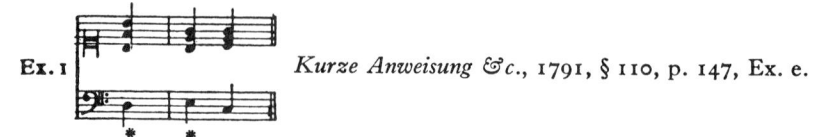

Ex. 1   *Kurze Anweisung &c.*, 1791, § 110, p. 147, Ex. e.

But he adds: "However, even under these circumstances, *I* should countenance the doubled Sixth only as a last resort (*im Nothfalle*), for to *me* it seems somewhat harsh in itself. Better, in any case, is the accompaniment with the Octave of the Bass. . . ."

[8] Cf. Türk, who writes (ibid., l.c.): ". . . the duplication of the Third is by no means uncommon. And, indeed, the dissonance of the false Fifth in the fundamental chord (concerning which, moreover, the opinions of theorists differ) becomes still less noticeable by inversion. For now the *f* is no longer dissonant with the Bass itself, as in the diminished Triad, but only with a middle part."

[9] The instances given by Marpurg (o. c., Tab. II), concerning which he says (o. c.,

CHORDS OF THE SIXTH

Ex. 6

Apart from the examples given by Marpurg (Ex. 6 *a–d*), it is evident that, when the chord in question is followed, not by the Tonic Triad, but by its first inversion, the 3, even though not doubled, must rise (Ex. 6 *e*), while, if it is doubled, one 3 rises and the other falls (Ex. 6 *f, g*), as in Marpurg's example.

§ 9. The 6 must invariably rise when in an upper part. When in a middle part it may upon occasion, like the 3 of the Dominant Triad when the latter is followed by that of the Tonic (Ch. vi, § 5), and of the Dominant Seventh (cf. Ch. xi, "Sevenths", II, § 3), fall a Third, as in the following example from Schröter (*Deutliche Anweisung &c.*, 1772, § 114, p. 58, Ex. *b*):

10) Ex. 7

Ph. Em. Bach expresses himself with regard to this matter as follows: "The major Sixth, when associated with the minor Third, inclines upwards; in the following example, therefore, the second form of accompaniment is to be preferred to the first one. This observation is more necessary than ever when the Sixth is in the upper part."

11) Ex. 8

2nd ed., 1762, p. 38) that they are "justified by the authority (*Ansehen*) of great composers", are:

[10] Only the upper part and Bass are given by Schröter, but there can be no doubt that he intended the middle parts to be as given above. Wherever the reader may be supposed to be in doubt, he gives the chord in full, and would assuredly have done so in the present case had anything different been intended.

[11] *Versuch &c.*, Part II, 1762, Ch. 3, II, § 9, where the example is given on a single stave, an Octave lower than above.

It must be admitted, with all due respect to Philip Emanuel, that the example is not very well chosen, inasmuch as, where a keyed instrument is concerned, the difference between the two progressions exists only on paper.[12]

[12] The question as to how Ph. Em. Bach would have treated the first bar of Ex. 7 is, perhaps, not a very important one, but it is not devoid of interest. The position in which the first chord is there taken is the one least favourable to a good subsequent progression, but it must be remembered that an accompanist is sometimes tied to a composed upper part (e.g. in the Chorale "O Lamm Gottes unschuldig" in the first chorus of the St. Matthew Passion), and in such cases the simplest chords, having to be taken in unfavourable positions, often present difficulties. There are, then, several alternatives. One, with which we are not at present concerned, would be to take the second chord of Ex. 7, not in strict accordance with the figuring as $\substack{6\\3}$, but as $\substack{6\\4\\3}$:

(cf. Ch. xxi, "Incomplete figuring", II, § 1).

Apart from this there are the following:
(1) The chord in question might be taken with doubled 3, thus involving one of those skips (in the Tenor, not to mention the one in the Alto) which Ph. Em. Bach so particularly disliked:

Ex. A

(2) The skips may be avoided by any one able to stretch a Tenth (or on the Organ by using the pedals) by taking the first chord in extended harmony:

Ex. B

(3) The third chord (6 on *c*) might be taken in an incomplete form, minus the 3:

Ex. C

(4) This most undesirable omission might be avoided by taking the second chord with a fifth part, after which the harmony would automatically revert to four parts:

Ex. D (cf. Ch. iii, § 4, II).

Of these alternatives there is little doubt that Ph. Em. Bach would have preferred the second, for he constantly recommends the occasional use of what he calls a "divided accompaniment", i.e. extended four-part harmony divided between the two hands, either for a continuance or in one or two chords only. Failing this, the present writer is inclined to think that he would have favoured the temporary adoption of a fifth part (Ex. D). In a somewhat similar case (namely, in order to avoid the downward progression, not, it is true, of a major Sixth with a minor Third, but of an augmented Fourth) he recommends this device (see Ch. iii, § 4, II, Ex. 6 of the present work).

In one respect, however, the case in question is not quite parallel to that shown in Ex. D above, inasmuch as, in the latter, the introduction of the extra part a Fifth below the lowest inner part of the preceding chord produces on the ear nearly (though not quite) the same effect as the objectionable skip in Ex. A.

In conclusion, the reader is reminded that on the Harpsichord, though not (at least not to anything like the same extent) on the Organ, such problems were often much simplified by the employment of a "filled-in" accompaniment, in which consecutives, *except between extreme parts*, were disregarded, and less strictness was observed in the

(b) On the second degree of the minor scale:

§ 10. The chord of the Sixth, which is the first inversion of a diminished Triad on the second degree of the minor scale, and has its seat on the Subdominant of the latter, has the same intervals as the one just described, but differs widely from it in its function. Any interval of the chord (Bass, 3, or 6) may be freely doubled, though in actual practice it is seldom convenient to double the 3, since the result is an awkward progression to the Dominant harmony, as will be seen by the following examples from Kirnberger (*Grundsätze &c.*, 1781, volume of examples, Part I, Fig. 58). In (a) the 6 is doubled, in (b) the 3:

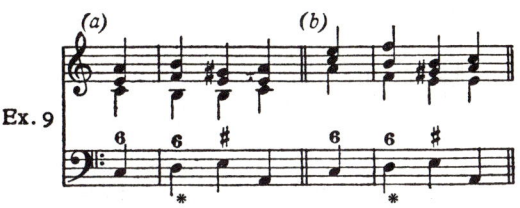

Ex. 9

With regard to the doubling of the 6, which Ph. Em. Bach, as we have seen, disallowed (cf. § 6, note 7), and which Türk, though he did not actually forbid it, apparently did not like, Kirnberger writes as follows (o. c., § 147, footnote, p. 57):

After stating that the major Sixth on the second degree of the scale must never be doubled, "because it is the *ton sensible* [i.e. leading note], which bears no duplication", he continues: "But from this it by no means follows as a fundamental rule (*Grundregel*) that the major Sixth, when associated with the minor Third, may never be doubled, for, whenever the major Sixth is not *ton sensible* of the Tonic, it can be doubled without hesitation, as in Fig. XLVIII [the same progression as that shown in Ex. 9 (a) above]; this is at once clear from the sequence [of the harmony], since, instead of [the Bass] falling a degree [as in Ex. 6 a–d above], it here rises a degree to a Triad."

§ 11. The normal progression of the chord is to the Dominant harmony, either the Triad (Exx. 9, 10), or its first inversion (Ex. 11), or the Dominant Seventh (Ex. 12), or its inversions (Exx. 13–15):

Ex. 10

progression of the individual parts (cf. Ch. iii, § 3, 11, from § 32 of the quotation from Heinichen onwards, and III).

Treated thus, the first bar of Schröter's example would appear more or less as follows:

Ex. E

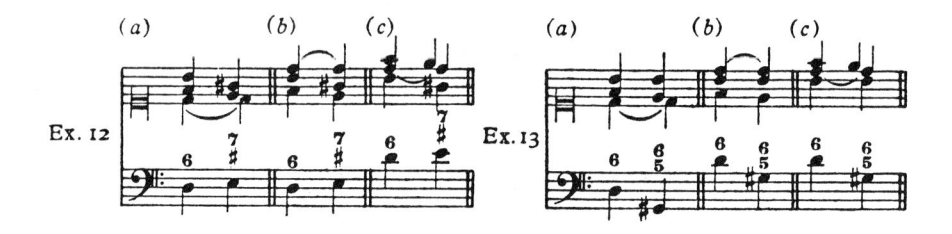

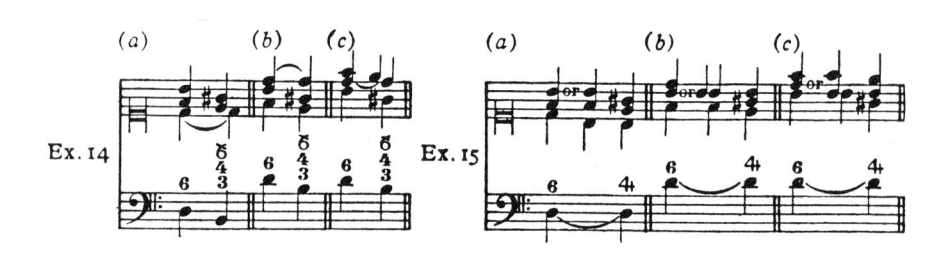

It will be observed that, when the progression is to the chord of the Dominant Seventh, or to its first or second inversion, the chord of the Sixth must include the Octave of the Bass if the subsequent discord is to be prepared, as is necessary in the strict style, in which, moreover, the discord must fall upon a strong beat of the bar.

Also, if the chord of the Seventh is to include the 5, the chord of the Sixth must be taken with the doubled 6 as a fifth part, which can afterwards be dropped as soon as convenient (Ex. 16 a), as otherwise the forbidden progression of an augmented Second would result (Ex. 16 b), unless, indeed, the Seventh be taken unprepared in a manner unusual even in the free style [13] (Ex. 17):

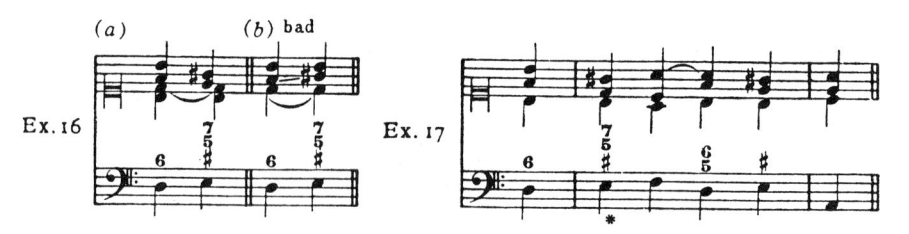

---

[13] Cf. Ch. xi, "Sevenths", 1, § 2.

CHORDS OF THE SIXTH

C. As the first inversion of an augmented Triad.

§ 12. Just as, in an augmented Triad (on the third degree of the minor scale), the retarded interval may be either the augmented Fifth or the Bass (cf. Ch. viii, §§ 2, 3), so, in its first inversion, a chord of the Sixth with a major Third and minor Sixth (on the Dominant of the minor scale), the retarded interval may be either the major Third or the minor Sixth, as corresponding, respectively, to the above-mentioned intervals of the Triad.

In the first case the Octave of the Bass is most commonly and naturally included as the fourth part (Ex. 18), more rarely the doubled 6 (Ex. 19); in the second case the 6, as the retarded interval, cannot be doubled, but only the Bass (Ex. 20). The major Third, as leading note, can under no circumstances be doubled.

Ex 18

Ex. 19

Ex. 20

If Ex. 20 *b* is compared with Ex. 2 *d* in Ch. viii, § 3, it will be seen that the progressions are identical.

Section II. Chords of the Sixth in sequence and otherwise.

§ 1. There is perhaps no progression which offers so many traps for the unwary as a succession of Sixths in four-part harmony.

When played in three parts there is comparatively little danger: it is obvious that the interval of a Fourth between the 3 and the 6 becomes a Fifth by inversion and that, therefore, the 3 cannot be in the upper part in two successive chords. When the Bass moves by step, it is clearly best to keep the 6 in the upper part throughout (Ex. 1 *a*), as, otherwise, ugly skips (involving, moreover, hidden Fifths) would result (Ex. 1 *b*). The same applies to a Bass moving by Thirds (Ex. 2). On the other hand, when the Bass moves by leap of a Fourth (or its inversion, a Fifth), the best progression is obtained by alternating between the 6 and the 3 in the upper part, as there is in every case one part common to the two chords (Ex. 3).

The leap of a Sixth or Seventh is to be regarded as equivalent to that of a Third or Second, respectively.

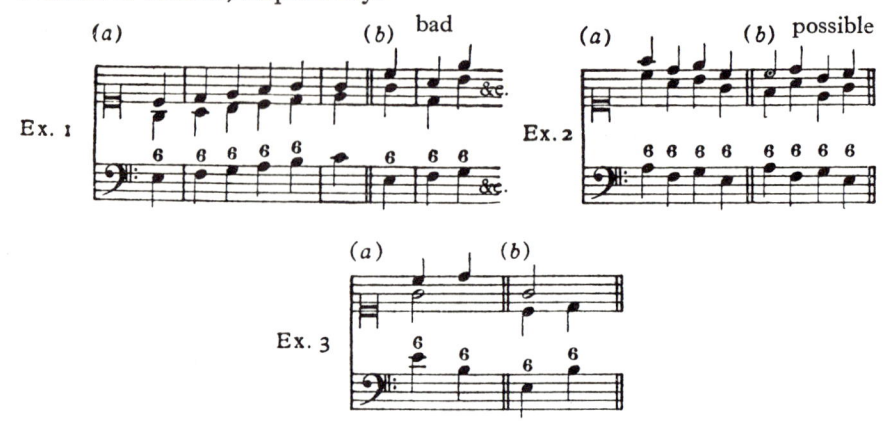

In all successions of Sixths in which the 6 is uniformly in the upper part (as in Ex. 1 *a* and Ex. 2 *a*) the chief point to be borne in mind is that the two upper parts must not be allowed to be too far (certainly not more than a Tenth and Thirteenth respectively) above the Bass, as, otherwise, the succession of Fourths strikes the ear unpleasantly.

§ 2. In four-part harmony there is more freedom as regards the position in which the chords are taken,[1] but there are also many more chances of making mistakes. Apart from the consecutives which are liable to arise through the duplication of the same interval (3, 6, or Bass) in two successive chords,[2] the mistakes most likely to occur are: (1) wrong duplications (as of the leading note or, in a 5 6 sequence, of the diminished Fifth), and (2) forbidden progressions by augmented intervals (Second and Fourth).

It is therefore of the utmost importance to a beginner to master thoroughly the different possibilities (in the matter both of the position in which the chords are to be taken and also of the duplication of one or other of their

---

[1] By alternately including the Octave of the Bass and doubling the 3 it is even possible, at the expense of great clumsiness, to keep the 3 in the upper part indefinitely. Kirnberger gives the following example of the procedure to be adopted, if the accompanist "gets into the embarrassing predicament of being obliged to have the Third in the upper part" (*Grundsätze des Generalbasses &c.*, 1781, § 73 *ad fin.*; volume of examples, Part I, Fig. 59, Ex. 5):

[2] As:

intervals) which arise in the various progressions of Sixths. These matters are treated in great detail, and with abundant illustration, by Ph. Em. Bach in the course of the two sections of one of his longest chapters (*Versuch &c.*, Part II, 1762, Ch. 3). It is therefore proposed to quote *in extenso* as much of this chapter as bears upon the points above mentioned, and certain other interesting questions of detail. In § 3 will be given the extracts taken from the first section (*Abschnitt*) of Bach's chapter, and in § 4 those from the second. They are taken from the 1797 reprint of the second edition.

The numbering of Bach's paragraphs is given in brackets.

In the notation of his examples the same liberty is taken as in other parts of the present work.[3]

§ 3. Extracts from Ph. Em. Bach (o. c., Ch. 3, II):

("§ 10") "If many Sixths occur in succession on bass notes moving by step, or by leap of a Third, duplication [4] [i.e. of the Third or Sixth] is employed on alternate notes (*wechselsweise*) to avoid Octaves:

[Ex. 4]

[Ex. 5]

"Although the need for duplication is greater with the bass notes which move by step than with those moving by leap, nevertheless one is inclined to double (*verdoppelt man doch gerne*) with the latter for the sake of the good melodic progression of the upper part."[5]

---

[3] Those of Bach's examples which are noted in full on a single stave are here, with two exceptions (§ 4, Exx. 14 and 18), noted on two staves, an Octave higher than in the original. Where Bach gives the Bass only (or, in one or two instances, the Bass and principal part), the harmony has been supplied in small notes, and, in such cases, the position in which the chords are taken is, of course, arbitrary.

[4] Ph. Em. Bach, like many other German writers, uses the term "duplication" (*Verdoppelung*) only of the upper parts of a chord (3, 5, &c.); the doubling of the Bass he nearly always describes as "taking the Octave" (*die Octave nehmen*).

[5] The possible alternatives in the case of Ex. 5 would be:

("§ 11") "These passages are best accompanied in three parts when the time is quick. There is then only one good position; with the other the Fourths become Fifths. The Sixth must therefore always be uppermost; even with a four-part accompaniment this is the most tuneful, and the safest position."

("§ 12") "When the Octave [of the Bass] is taken with the chord of the Sixth, one avoids taking it in the upper part (*so greift man die letztere nicht gerne in der Oberstimme*)."

("§ 13") "The unmelodic progressions (x) [in c and d] are avoided by duplication:

[Ex. 6]

N.B.—The "unmelodic progression" (augmented Fourth) in the last example could be avoided without doubling either Third or Sixth of the first chord, as follows:

("§ 14") "When the 6 is immediately followed by a 5, one proceeds from the Sixth to the Fifth in the same part, and holds the other parts. This progression often occurs several times in succession. All three ways of accompanying the Sixth [6] can be employed, provided that the rules for duplication, given above, are observed. If the following examples are translated into the remaining positions, duplication in the unison will also occur. In a couple of examples with doubled Third [Ex. 7 d and Ex. 8 d] we find that the Third sometimes leaps to the Fifth (*die Quinte ergreift*), the Sixth being held; skips are thus avoided, and one can keep in the same position (*sich in der Lage erhalten*), which, without this device, is hardly possible, if this progression occurs only once."[7]

[Ex. 7]

[Ex. 8]

[6] i.e. with doubled 6, doubled 3, or the Octave of the Bass. When the 6 is doubled, the result (as may be seen in Exx. 7 and 8 a) is a passing $^6_5$ chord; this is also the case when the 3 is doubled and one of the two leaps to the 5 (Exx. 7 and 8 d).

[7] It will be seen that, in Ex. 8 c, the right hand gets into a lower position (as compared with Ex. 8 d) after each 6 5.

CHORDS OF THE SIXTH

("§ 15") "When a [bass] note is figured 5 6, the Triad is to be struck together with the note, the Fifth then proceeding to the Sixth. The other parts are held;[8] but if this progression occurs many times in succession, a three-part accompaniment, with the Third only, is the easiest and, with quick notes, in pieces which do not anyhow require a heavy accompaniment, the best."

("§ 16") "If the accompaniment of this progression is to be in four parts, an easy way of avoiding mistakes is by duplication, because the entire harmony

[Ex. 9]

[a] [b] [c] [d] [e] [f] [ff] "wrong" "right"
[g] [gg] [h] [hh] "wrong" "right"
[i]

---

[8] This applies (as will be seen from the next example) only when the progression in question does *not* occur in sequence.

consists of consonances. The examples in which both kinds of duplication [9] alternate are the best. From this duplication the dissonant false [i.e. diminished] Fifths, which may occur, are to be excluded [Ex. 9 *f*]; likewise the skip of an augmented Fourth is to be avoided [Ex. 9 *g*]. The accompaniment with skips, with or without duplication [Ex. 9 *h* and *hh*] is not wrong, but is not always beautiful. At (*d*) [=Ex. 9 *i*] we see an example with divided accompaniment [i.e. extended harmony, divided between the two hands]."

("§ 17") "In the free style (*in der galanten Schreibart*) $^8_6$ sometimes occurs. This is a three-part harmony (*Satz*), and must be carefully distinguished from the same figuring which demands four parts. It would here be a good thing to fix upon a distinguishing sign, as the cases in which this figuring occurs are often ambiguous. This $^8_6$ is found over bass notes when it would be impossible, without great harshness, to take as a fourth part, sometimes the Third (*a*), sometimes the Fourth (*b*), sometimes any other part whatever (*c*), if one were not obliged to adhere to three parts:

[Ex. 10]

("§ 18") "But when the accompaniment has to be in four parts, the figures [in question] are found when there is a RESOLUTION of preceding dissonances (*a*), and, APART FROM THAT, when one wants to mark clearly the progression of a part (*b*). Now since the latter consideration exists in the case of the three-part progression as well, and as there is no distinguishing mark, no better advice can be given than to LISTEN and USE JUDGEMENT:

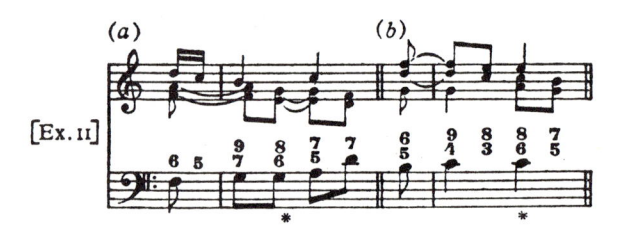

[Ex. 11]

§ 4. Extracts from Ph. Em. Bach continued (o.c., Ch. 3, II).

("§ 3") "When a bass note bearing the chord of the Sixth rises a degree, and the latter note is figured $^6_5$, it is safest to take the Octave [of the bass] with the Sixth, IF IT IS POSSIBLE. This progression of the parts is best (*a*). When the Third is doubled, a skip occurs in one of the three parts (*b*). With however good a right a composer sometimes, for good reasons, introduces skips in the middle parts, on equally sufficient grounds does an accompanist avoid them as much as possible. The doubled Sixth may easily occasion Fifths [as] in our example (*c*); if they are to be avoided, skips must be made in two parts (*d*). I purposely said above: IF IT IS POSSIBLE, because one is

---

[9] Cf. § 3, note 4.

occasionally compelled to double either the Sixth or the Third. An accidental, which may not be doubled,[10] is sometimes responsible for the duplication of the Third (*e*); the duplication of the Sixth may be occasioned by dissonances which must be properly resolved, as we see by the Seventh and augmented Fifth at (*f*):

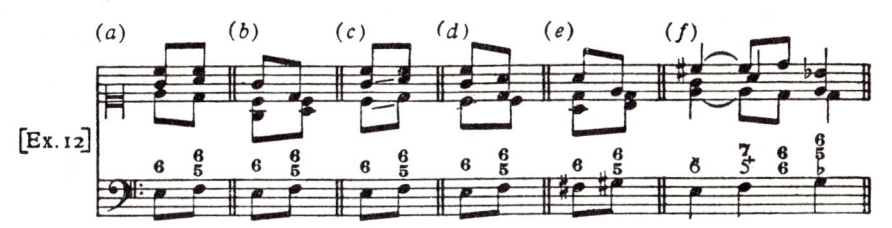

("§ 4") "If a number of Sixths occur in succession on a Bass rising or falling by step, and passing notes [11] intervene, the necessity for duplication, in a four-part accompaniment, is not thereby avoided:

("§ 5") "That, in certain positions, even contrary motion does not always suffice for the avoidance of Fifths is seen from the following examples. These mistakes are corrected by duplication [*aa, bb*].[12] In [*c, d*] contrary motion answers in all positions without duplication; only the position shown at [*e*] will not do:

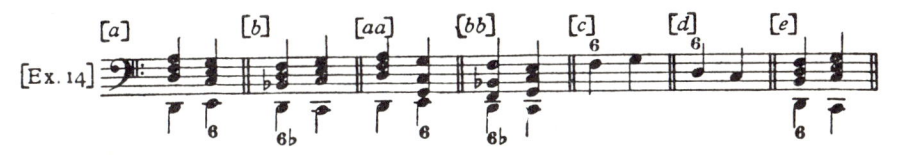

("§ 6") "Duplication in the unison makes for a good melodic progression (*einen guten Gesang*) in the upper part, secures a compacter position (*hält die Lage besser zusammen*) than that in the Octave, and is therefore often preferable, as we see from the following examples:

---

[10] Cf. I, § 2, note 4.
[11] i.e. unaccented notes representing an interval of the harmony struck with the preceding accented note (cf. Ch. xviii, "Quick notes in the Bass", § 1 *h*).
[12] It will be observed, with regard to [*aa*], that a much better progression is obtained by partially dispensing with contrary motion:

[Ex. 15]

"not so good"

("§ 7") "If one fails to keep a sharp look-out on what follows, and to arrange the chord of the Sixth accordingly, it will be lucky if one is able narrowly to escape mistakes. In the first of the following examples the Octave [of the Bass] must be resumed[13] on the passing note,[14] to prepare the following Seventh [Ex. 16 a].... However, such an emergency measure (*Nothhülfe*) will never constitute an adornment (*zur Schönheit werden*). In the second example, the Third which accompanies the major Sixth must be doubled [b], or, if the Octave [of the Bass] has already been struck with the Sixth, recourse must be had to extended harmony [15] [bb], because the Fourth must remain stationary; for the same reason, in the last example, the Sixth in the $^6_4$ chord × must either be doubled [ccc], or else the duplication of the Sixth must be abandoned on the second half of the following note, *A*, and the Octave taken instead, in order that the Seventh may be prepared [c, cc]:

[Ex. 16]

("§ 8") "In the first of the following examples, in which there must be two duplications in succession,[16] we see the necessity for alternating between the kinds of duplication,[17] in order that no Octaves may occur. In the later example this necessity increases on account of the greater number of duplications. In this way one keeps in the [right] position and avoids unnecessary skips:

[13] i.e. after being taken in the preceding chord.
[14] i.e. the unaccented quaver.
[15] "Man muss ... das getheilte Accompagnement wählen."
[16] Cf. I, § 2, note 4.
[17] i.e. of the Sixth and of the Third (cf. II, § 3, note 4).

CHORDS OF THE SIXTH

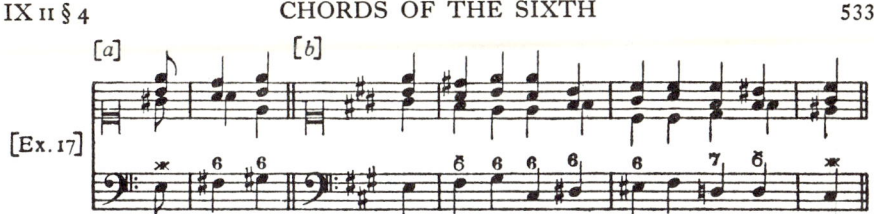

[Ex. 17]

("§ 14") "It has been mentioned more than once that, in the accompaniment, the progression of an augmented Second is to be avoided. But, as this progression, in the melody, is none the less ... often an adornment, there arise, therefore, certain cases in which it is not only used without scruple [in the accompaniment], but in which the melodic progression would be spoiled, as we see in [Ex. 18 c], if the accompaniment were arranged differently. Otherwise, this progression is rightly avoided:

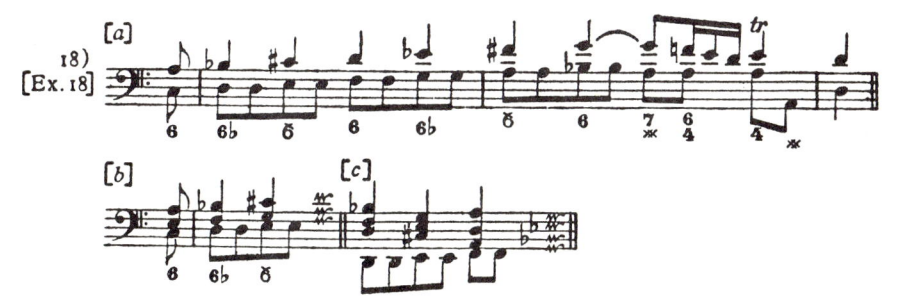

18)
[Ex. 18]

[18] In the first example [a] we see the principal part and the Bass, in the second [b], the accompaniment as we are told it should be. This is to be specially noted as an instance in which (unless a two-part accompaniment, Bass and Thirds only, is preferred) the upper part of the accompaniment is *bound to coincide with the principal part*, a coincidence usually to be avoided.

CHAPTER X
$^6_4$ CHORDS

X
$^6_4$ CHORDS

A. $^6_4$ as the second inversion of a perfect Triad.

§ 1. As the second inversion of a perfect Triad a $^6_4$ chord consists, besides the Bass, which corresponds to the Fifth of the Triad, of a perfect Fourth and major or minor Sixth, corresponding, respectively, to the Bass and the major or minor Third of the Triad. In four-part harmony the Octave of the Bass is normally included as the fourth part, though, under certain circumstances, the 6, or even the 4, may be doubled instead (cf. Ex. 4).

The figuring[1] is $^6_4$. If an interval of the chord is not in accordance with the key-signature, this must be indicated by the appropriate accidental affixed to the figure in question: $^{\flat 6}_{\ 4}$ ($^{6\flat}_{\ 4}$), $^{\ 6}_{\flat 4}$ ($^{6}_{4\flat}$), $^{6}_{4}$♯, &c.

§ 2. In the strict style (*stylus gravis*), when a $^6_4$ chord occurs *in thesi* (i.e. on a strong beat), as in a cadence, the 4 becomes invested with the qualities of a discord in so far as to require (1) preparation, and (2) resolution a degree downwards, as:

Ex. 1

But in the free style, the 4 of even a cadential $^6_4$ is taken unprepared, as in the following examples, and may even resolve upwards (Ex. 2 *d*):

Ex. 2 [2]

---

[1] The resolution of a preceding suspended discord may necessitate the inclusion of 8 in the figuring, as in the following example from Türk (*Kurze Anweisung &c.*, 1791, § 101, p. 132):

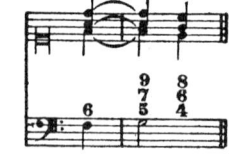

[2] Exx. *a–c* are from Ph. Em. Bach (*Versuch &c.*, Part II, 1762, Ch. 6, 1, § 15, where they are given on a single stave, an 8ve lower than here). Ex. *d* is from Türk (o. c., § 102, p. 133).

$\frac{6}{4}$ CHORDS

§ 3. Even in the strict style, and in a cadence, a $\frac{6}{4}$ chord may be taken without preparation *in arsi* (i.e. on a weak beat), after another chord on the same Bass, as in the following example from Marpurg:[3]

Ex. 3

Under these circumstances the Octave of the Bass is liable to be omitted and either the 4 (Ex. 4 *a*), or the 6 (Ex. 4 *b*), doubled instead:

Ex. 4

§ 4. Apart from the usage described above, a $\frac{6}{4}$ chord is liable to occur, on a weak beat, either (1) preceded and followed by the same harmony in its root position or first inversion (Ex. 5 *a*), or (2) with the 4 stationary, i.e. present in the preceding and following chord (Ex. 5 *b, c*), or (3) as a passing chord (Ex. 5 *d–f*):

Ex. 5

B. $\frac{6}{4}$ as the second inversion of a diminished Triad.

§ 5. As the second inversion of a diminished Triad, a $\frac{6}{4}$ chord with augmented Fourth and major Sixth may occur on the Submediant of a minor key, being preceded and followed by a diminished Triad on the Supertonic,

---

[3] *Handbuch &c.*, 2nd ed. 1762, p. 35. The example is not given in musical notation, but in letter tablature, with no indication of the time-value of the notes.

538 — ⁶₄ CHORDS — X § 5

or its first inversion. It is then better to double the 6 (corresponding to the 3 of the diminished Triad) than to include the Octave of the Bass:

Ex. 6

A chord with the same intervals may also occur as a passing chord:

Ex. 7

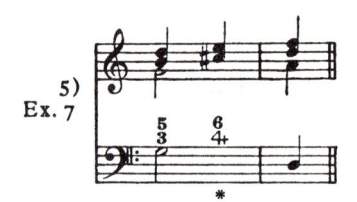

Ph. Em. Bach gives the following interesting example in which, as he explains, the augmented Fourth on f is due to the anticipation of a passing note (*anticipatio transitus*);[6] the real progression is shown in (*b*):

Ex. 8

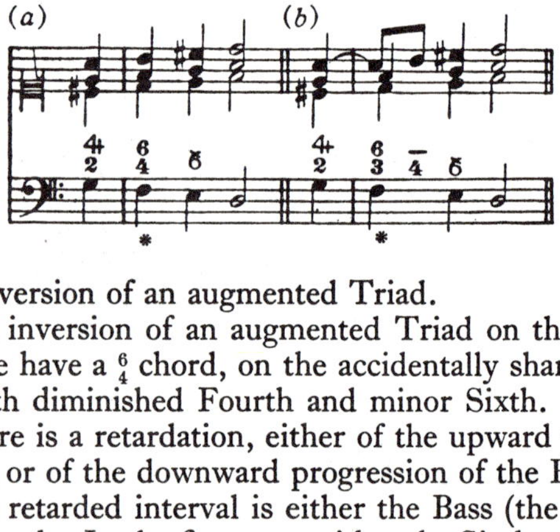

C. ⁶₄ as the second inversion of an augmented Triad.

§ 6. As the second inversion of an augmented Triad on the third degree of the minor scale, we have a ⁶₄ chord, on the accidentally sharpened leading note of the same, with diminished Fourth and minor Sixth. Just as in the augmented Triad there is a retardation, either of the upward progression of the augmented Fifth, or of the downward progression of the Bass,[7] so, in its second inversion, the retarded interval is either the Bass (the leading note), or the diminished Fourth. In the first case, either the Sixth may be doubled (Ex. 9 *a*), or the diminished Fourth (*b*); in the second case, the only interval that can be doubled is the Sixth (*c*):

[4] Ex. 6 (*a*) and (*b*) are from Türk (o. c., § 112, p. 148). The first bar of (*c*) is from Ph. Em. Bach (ibid., § 13); he gives the Bass only, but writes: "the Sixth can be doubled over the *f*, if the Third of *b* [i.e. of the first chord] is in the upper part; this position is here the best."
[5] This example and the next are also from Ph. Em. Bach (l.c.), who gives them on a single stave, an 8ve lower than here.
[6] Cf. Ch. xxii, "Inversion", &c., § 7.
[7] Cf. Ch. viii, §§ 2, 3.

$^6_4$ CHORDS

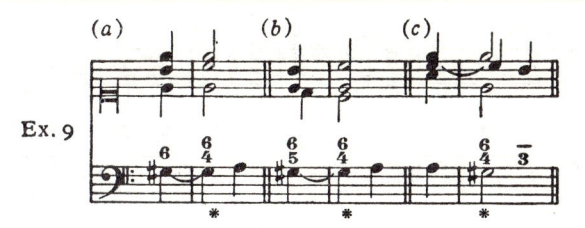

Ex. 9

The chord in question may also appear, in three parts only, as a passing chord. Türk gives the following example:[8]

Ex. 10

D. Retardations: $\overset{\wedge}{6}\,\overset{-}{3},\,\overset{\wedge}{6}\,5^{\flat}$.

§ 7. The figuring $^6_{4\,3}$ represents a chord of the Sixth with the 3 retarded. According to Ph. Em. Bach, this is best taken in three parts only; but if a fourth part is desired, the 6 must be doubled, and the Octave of the Bass omitted.[9] Bach adopted the following sign ∧ as a guide to beginners:

Ex. 11

In the following examples we have a $^6_5$ chord with both the 5 and the 3 retarded:

---

[8] o. c., § 114, p. 152.
[9] Cf. *Versuch &c.*, Part II, 1762, Ch. 6, 1, § 9. Türk points out, however (o. c., § 154, p. 211), that it is sometimes more natural to include the Octave of the Bass than to double the Sixth, as in the following example (a), in which, if the Sixth were doubled, consecutive Fifths would only be saved by the retardation (b):

540      $^6_4$ CHORDS   X § 7

[10) Ex. 12 — musical notation with examples labeled (a), (aa), (b), (bb), each figured $^6_4$ $^{5\flat}_3$]

[10] In a four-part accompaniment the position shown above, (*aa*) and (*bb*), is the best. If the Sixth is doubled in the unison, the position shown in A and B of the following examples is the better:

[musical notation with examples labeled A, AA, B, BB, each figured $^6_4$ $^{5\flat}_3$]

CHAPTER XI
SEVENTHS

XI
SEVENTHS

I. *Introductory*.

§ 1. A chord of the Seventh may be either essential or non-essential.

The term 'non-essential' is here to be understood to apply to the chord as a whole, rather than to a single interval, and to include, on the one hand, those cases in which the 7th itself is not an integral part of the chord in which it occurs, but an interval belonging to the preceding harmony, and delayed by suspension, as: **Ex. 1** and, on the other, those in which it is not the 7th which is non-essential, but other components of the chord in which it occurs, as in the case of the 'Stationary Seventh' (V), and the $\frac{7}{5}$ on the Subdominant which sometimes follows a $\frac{7}{3}$ on the Dominant (III, § 4).

Suspended 7ths are frequently disguised, and assume the appearance of an essential discord owing to the omission or ellipse of the resolution, as:

Ex. 2

For this ellipse of the resolution, or 'Catachresis', see Ch. xxii, § 8, and for the rising of the 7th in the above example, ibid., §§ 4 and 5.

It is important to note that the terms 'essential' and 'non-essential' were applied in different senses by different writers.

Kirnberger, *Kunst des reinen Satzes*, &c. ('The art of a pure style in musical composition'), *Abschnitt* (Section) IV. 4, p. 63, says in connexion with the 7th (minor or diminished) on the leading note:

"One can take it as a general rule that, after every essential Seventh, the Bass rises four degrees, or falls five, and has a Triad [1] as its harmony, unless an inversion of this chord be taken."

In the same connexion, in his *Grundsätze des Generalbasses* ('Principles of Thoroughbass'), 1781, § 172, Kirnberger says:

"It can very easily be recognized whether the chord of the Seventh over a note is an 'essential' one, or one in which the discord is 'accidental', by examining the Bass; if it rises four degrees or falls five, it is an essential Seventh. If however the Bass rises a semitone, from *b* to *c*, or from ♯*g* to *a*, it is a non-essential (lit. 'accidental') one."

Marpurg in his *Versuch über die musikalische Temperatur nebst einem Anhang über den Rameau- und Kirnbergerschen Grundbass* ('Essay on the tempering of

---

[1] By 'Triad' Kirnberger does not, of course, mean to exclude the cases in which the 3rd of the first chord remains as a 7th in the next one.

XI 1 § 1   SEVENTHS   543

the scale with an Appendix on the fundamental Bass of Rameau and Kirnberger'), 1776, §§ 254–5, gives a widely different definition: "Every discord which is used merely for the sake of the melody, and which, as far as the harmony is concerned, might just as well be present as absent [sic], is called an accidental discord. Of such nature are all passing and changing notes, or, as it is also expressed, regular and irregular passing notes. Thus the passing notes in Fig. 20, and the changing, or irregular passing notes in Fig. 21, are accidental discords. Every discord which is there for the sake of both melody and harmony is called an essential discord. Of such nature are: (1) such discords as result from suspension, as in Figs. 22 and 23; (2) such as result from the anticipation of a regular [i.e. unaccented] passing note [2] ('des regulären Durchgangs') as in Figs. 24, 25, 26, and 27."

No views could, at first sight, seem more diametrically opposed than those above quoted of Kirnberger and Marpurg. Nevertheless, the difference is more one of terminology than of principle.

Kirnberger's view was a perfectly consistent one, as will be seen later on in the present chapter, when the cases are considered in which a 7th resolves otherwise than on a Bass rising a 4th or falling a 5th.

It is therefore in Kirnberger's sense that the terms 'essential' and 'accidental', or 'non-essential', are to be understood here.

Note.—It may be noted in this connexion that a chord may be taken, to all

---

[2] *Transitus regularis* and *irregularis* were the terms used in the older German treatises to indicate passing and changing (or accented passing) notes; thus the taking of a passing note before its time, as in 24 and 25 of Marpurg's Examples, or, as in 26 and 27, with ellipse of the main note from which it was supposed to pass, was known as *anticipatio transitus*, or *anticipatio transitus per ellipsin*, as the case might be (cf. Ch. x ii, § 7).

appearances, as an essential discord and quitted as a suspension, in which case the resolution of the suspension will of course fall on the weaker beat, according to rule.

In both examples, judging by the progression of the Bass which rises a 4th from *g*, the last crotchet of the first bar, the Seventh on *c* (which in Ex. A is the Subdominant, and in Ex. B the Tonic) would seem to be an essential one with *c* as its root; but the resolution on 6 over the same Bass points to *a* as the root.

The root progression in the two examples is therefore

The 7 on *g* in both cases can be explained as an example of *anticipatio transitus per ellipsin* (Ch. xxii, 'Inversion &c.', § 7), the true progression being

but in this instance it would perhaps be truer to say that it owes its presence to what, for want of a better name, might be termed 'sequential attraction'.

§ 2. In the strict style, *every Seventh must be prepared* by being present as a concord, in the same part, in the preceding harmony. The preparation falls on the weak beat of the bar, and the 7th itself on the strong, Ex. 1 :

except in a chain of prepared 7ths, in which, however, the first 7th falls on the strong beat, Ex. 2 :

Moreover, the note of preparation must not be of shorter duration than the discord which it prepares (cf. Kirnberger, *K. d. r. S. &c.*, Abschnitt [section] V, i. 2, p. 81).

In the free style the two latter restrictions are not observed, and there are cases in which the 7th may be taken unprepared, which Marpurg formulates in the two following extracts.

In his *Handbuch &c.*, Pt. I, 2nd ed. 1762, Abschnitt (section) I, Absatz (subsection) IV, § 42, pp. 55 sq., he says: "There are two cases in which the Seventh may appear unprepared. The first is *when one discord resolves on another*. This, however, takes place only in the free style. See the following examples: [1]

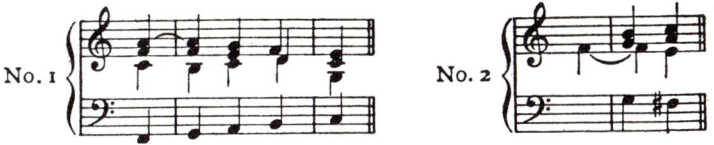

"In No. 1 not only does the Ninth (with which we are not at the moment concerned) fall to a Seventh, but the Seventh to an imperfect Fifth as well. This case can best be explained by the suppression or omission [2] of a subsequent harmony on the same bass note ('einer nachschlagenden Harmonie') on which the Ninth and Seventh ought to resolve, as we see in Scheme No. 3.

"In the case of No. 2 the Seventh falls to another Seventh. Here the same explanation holds good, as we see by No. 4, though one can also regard the matter as in No. 5. In the latter case the Seventh ♯*f e* in No. 2 is an anticipation.[3]

"The second case of unprepared discords occurs only in the case of certain Sevenths and their derivatives [i.e. inversions] in the free style (*galanten Schreibart*).

"These Sevenths are: firstly that on the Dominant, e.g. *g b d f* in C major; and secondly and thirdly the minor and diminished Sevenths combined with the imperfect Triad, e.g. *b d f a* and ♯*g, b, d, f*.

"In the strict style (*in der gearbeiteten Schreibart*), on the other hand, all these Sevenths must be duly prepared, and, even in the free style, it is advisable in certain progressions [4] that, even if the upper extreme of the Seventh is not prepared, at least the lower one should precede.

---

[1] The examples are given, not in musical notation, but in the letters of the alphabet, without figuring.
[2] Cf. Ch. xxii, § 8.　　　　　　　　　　[3] Ibid., § 7.
[4] This is somewhat vague. By 'certain progressions' Marpurg probably means such as involve the dominant 7th, as the recommendation obviously does not apply to minor or diminished 7ths on the leading note or sharpened Subdominant, still less to such cases as Exx. 3 and 4, mentioned in a subsequent extract. He applies the same treatment to all three inversions of the dominant 7th, namely, that if the discord is not prepared, the Dominant itself should be present in the previous chord; but

"Meanwhile, the liberty to use the above-mentioned Sevenths unprepared by no means cancels the obligation to resolve them; and in many cases the usage in question can be explained as the anticipation of a Seventh following as a passing note over the same Bass (*einer nachschlagenden Septime*). Thus, for instance, the example in Tabula III, fig. 34 must be understood as in fig. 35."

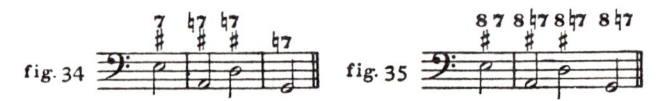

"Those persons are wrong who claim to find preparation for these Sevenths, taken as chords of simple percussion (*in dem freyen Anschlag dieser Septimen*), by having regard, e.g. in the progression $\sharp^c_a \mid \natural^c_d$, to the degree of the scale to which c and $\sharp c$ belong, and not to the magnitude of the interval which that degree represents. As long as c and $\sharp c$ are not the same, but differ by a semitone, so long can c not be prepared by $\sharp c$. If $\sharp c$ can stand for c, then $a \sharp c \, e$ would perforce be used in place of $a \, c \, e$ and so forth."

whether it should be present *in the same part* in both chords, as in the subjoined example he does not specify.

Ex. A

Ph. Em. Bach, in speaking of the 2nd inversion of the dominant 7th, *Versuch &c.*, Part II, Ch. 7, § 5, says: "Either the Fourth or Third must *be prepared*"—i.e. remain as a tied note from the previous chord.

But it is pretty certain that neither he nor Marpurg would have objected to such progressions as Ex. B (*a*) (*aa*) (*b*) (*c*) as opposed to (*d*) (*e*) (*f*):

Ex. B

except on the ground of the general rule that, in passing from one chord to another, as many notes as possible should be retained from the previous chord, and skips, especially in the top part, avoided. It is obvious, however, that this rule is liable to be broken whenever it is desired to secure a particular melody in the top part, as for instance, in accompanying a single instrument or voice, when the solo part has a rest of several bars.

Marpurg suggests that unprepared 7ths can, in many cases, be regarded as the anticipation of a passing note, and it will be observed that this applies to either version, (*a*) (*aa*) (*b*) (*c*) or (*d*) (*e*) (*f*), of Ex. B above; (*a*) and (*d*) can be regarded as originating in   and   respectively, and so with the rest.

We may therefore venture to formulate Marpurg's rule somewhat more explicitly, as follows: "When the dominant 7th, either in root position or in any of its inversions, is taken unprepared, it is desirable that the Dominant itself should be present in the previous chord, and either remain stationary, or fall a degree to the discord."

Later on in the same work, Pt. 2, Abschnitt (section) II, Absatz (subsection) V, § 1, p. 153, Marpurg adds two further instances in which, in the free style, 7ths may be taken unprepared, *either by step or by leap*, namely, the minor 7th on the Supertonic, and that on the sharp Submediant of the minor scale, as at * * in Exx. 3 and 4.

Ex. 3

Ex. 4

In Ex. 3 the 7ths are taken by step, and in Ex. 4 by leap. Marpurg himself does not furnish an example.

II. *Essential Sevenths*.

§ 1. An essential chord of the Seventh may consist of either: (1) the 7th, 5th, and 3rd, or (2) the 7th, 3rd, and 8ve, or (3) the 7th and doubled 3rd; it may be found upon every degree of the major scale, though it is only in the repetition of a sequence that a 7th on the leading note will be found to resolve on a Bass rising a 4th, or falling a 5th. A similar progression is found in the case of the flat 7th of the minor scale, but not in that of the leading note.

The usual figuring of the chord is $^7_5$ or 7 † with the necessary ♯ ♭ ♮ prefixed, or their equivalents in the shape of strokes through the head or tail of the figure (see Ch. xxiii).

† In most of the following examples the chord is fully figured, but in actual practice the figuring frequently fails to distinguish between $^7_5_3$ and $^8_7_3$ (or $^7_3$); this is especially the case in chains of 7ths which are, more often than not, figured 7 throughout. Roughly speaking, the figuring $^7_5$ demands the inclusion of the 5th, while 7 leaves the composition of the chord undetermined. The figuring $^7_3$ is used by some composers to indicate that the 5th is not wanted, but the figuring ♯3^7 ♭3^7 ♮3^7 (in which the presence of the ♯ ♭ ♮ is necessary to indicate the sharpening or flattening of the 3rd) is not necessarily prohibitive of the 5th.

If it be desired that every chord in a chain of 7ths should contain the 5th, it must, of course, be played in five parts:

whereas in 3-part harmony the 5th is necessarily excluded:

The 3rd is not usually specified in the figuring, unless it be to indicate that it is accidentally sharpened or flattened, or to contradict a previous accidental: $\smash{{}^{7}_{\#3}}{}^{7}_{\flat3}{}^{7}_{\natural3}$ or $\smash{{}^{\#7}_{3}}{}^{\flat7}_{3}{}^{\natural7}_{3}$. In such case the figure 3 itself is more commonly omitted: ${}^{7}_{5}$, &c.

§ 2. *The progression of the 7th.*

The normal progression of the 7th is one degree downwards. The following exceptions are, however, to be noted.

(1) Instead of resolving, the 7th on the Dominant may become concordant, remaining as the 6th on the Submediant:

Ex. 1

(2) Instead of resolving on the tonic Triad, it may resolve on its first inversion, in which case the Bass falls a 3rd (or rises a 6th).

The 7th may then either: (1) fall a degree to the 8ve of the Bass, Ex. 2; in which case hidden 8ves may be avoided, either by contrary motion (*a*), or an ornamental resolution (*b*); or (2) become free in its progression, either rising a degree, Ex. 3, or falling a 4th, Ex. 4.†

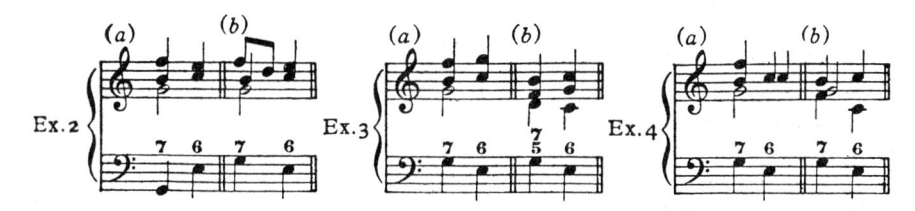

Ex. 2   Ex. 3   Ex. 4

(3) The 7th on the Supertonic, instead of resolving on the dominant Seventh in its root position, may resolve on its first inversion, ${}^{6}_{5}$ on the leading note. In this case the 7th rises a degree, the resolution (as in Exx. 3, 4) being regarded as transferred to the Bass.

Ex. 5

For F. W. Marpurg's strong condemnation of this progression see Ch. xxii, § 4.

† This freedom does not appear to have been recognized in theoretical treatises till well on in the eighteenth century (see Ch. xxii, § 4).

§ 3. *The progression of the 3rd.*
As we see from the following table, the 3rd may be either major or minor:

The progression of the minor 3rd is free. It may either remain as the 7th of the following chord, Ex. 1; or rise to the 8ve, Ex. 2; or fall to the 5th, Ex. 3. It may likewise be doubled, in which case there is a twofold preparation for a subsequent 7th, Ex. 4.

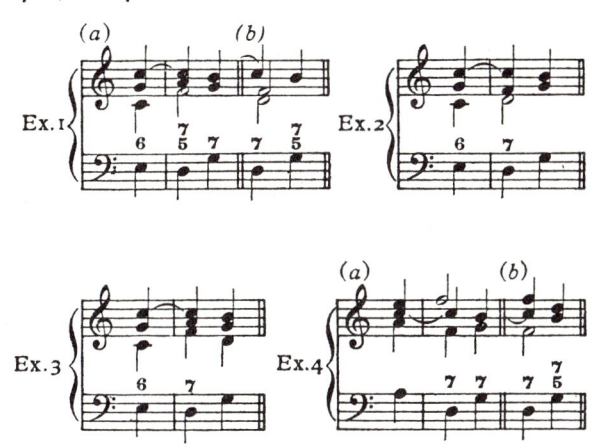

The major 3rd in conjunction with the major 7th, as on the Tonic and Subdominant, is likewise free in its progression and can be doubled.

In conjunction with a minor 7th on the Dominant, it must, in a diatonic progression, either remain as the 7th of the following chord,[1] Ex. 5; or rise a semitone, Ex. 6; and must on no account be doubled.

When in an inner part, but never otherwise, it may drop to the 5th of the tonic chord, Ex. 7.

---

[1] In the minor scale, in a succession of Sevenths, it cannot remain as the 7th of the following chord without being chromatically flattened, A; for otherwise the forbidden progression of an augmented 2nd, b ♮a, would result. Moreover, the chord c ♭e g ♮b, or any inversion of it, is only possible when the ♮b is an upward resolving suspension or retardation, B:

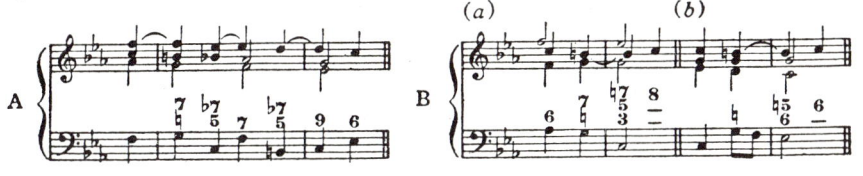

550 SEVENTHS XI II § 3

Where the dominant Seventh is followed by modulation to a flatter key (Ex. 8), or where the major 3rd is chromatic (Ex. 9), it may fall a semitone.[2]

Ex. 8

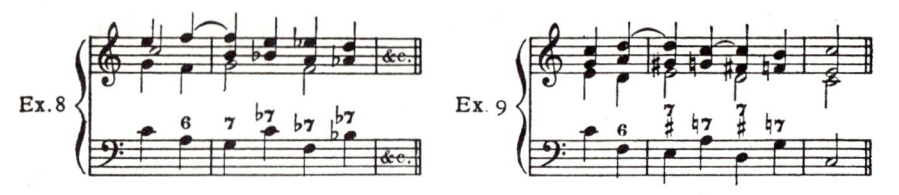

Ex. 9

§ 4. *The progression of the 5th.*

By referring back to the table of essential Sevenths, § 3, it will be seen that the 5th is perfect except in the following cases:

(1) on the 7th degree of the major scale (cf. §§ 1 and 5);
(2) on the 2nd degree of the minor scale;
(3) on the major ('Dorian') 6th of the minor scale: when it is imperfect;
(4) on the 3rd degree of the minor scale: when it may be augmented.

The inclusion of the imperfect 5th in chords of the Seventh is one of the points on which the authorities differed.

Gasparini, the author of a well-known work, *L'armonico pratico al cimbalo, di Francesco Gasparini Lucchese. In Venetia MDCCVIII appresso Antonio Bortoli*, does not include the imperfect 5th except under conditions which exclude it altogether from essential chords of the Seventh, in the sense in which the term is used in the present work, namely: (1) that the imperfect 5th, as well as the 7th, should be prepared, and (2) that it should resolve a degree downwards *on the 3rd of a Bass rising one degree*, Ex. 1 (*a*) (*b*) (*c*).

In (*d*) (*e*) (*f*) (*g*) (*h*) the progression of the Bass is a 4th upwards or a 5th downwards, and in (*g*) (*h*) the imperfect 5th is unprepared as well; all these examples would therefore be disallowed by Gasparini.

Heinichen, from whom these examples are taken, sanctions them all (*G-B. &c.*, 1728, Pt. 1, Ch. 3, § 41, p. 186). He quotes Gasparini, denying the necessity for the preparation of the imperfect 5th, and expressing himself satisfied with its resolution a degree downwards irrespective of the progression of the Bass. Even this he does not particularly insist upon, saying that "any one whose conscience is not sufficiently elastic may avoid the imperfect 5th in such Examples as (*i*) (*k*)"; he adds, moreover (p. 187, note *s*): "I do not, however, blame any accompanist if he always plays it [the imperfect 5th] along with the 7th, whether it be specially indicated in the figuring or not."

Ex. 1 (*a*) (*b*) (*c*) 1) (*d*) (*e*)

[2] The minor 7ths on the fourth and sixth crotchets of Exx. 8 and 9, like that on the third crotchet of Ex. A in note 1, are not to be regarded as 'prepared' by the major 3rd of the previous chord, but as an instance of *anticipatio transitus per ellipsin* (see Ch. xxii, §§ 7 and 8; cf. also the extract from Marpurg in 1, § 2 of the present chapter).   [1] For note see p. 551.

Stricter harmonists, however, as Ph. Em. Bach (*Versuch &c.*, Part 2, 1762, Ch. 13, 1, §§ 10, 11, 12, 15, 17 *et passim*), insist upon the proper resolution of the imperfect 5th a degree downwards as an absolute condition of its inclusion in chords of the Seventh.

It is therefore only in following the pattern of a sequence that it may be allowed to rise to the 3rd of the following chord, as in Exx. 2, 3, 4.

It is chiefly when it is desired to enliven the upper part of the accompaniment, as, for instance, during the pauses of the principal part in an instrumental or vocal solo, that such licences are in place. In such cases auxiliary notes may often be introduced with advantage, as in Ex. 4 *b*, more especially when a melodic or rhythmic figure used in the principal part (or parts) is thereby imitated.

In the chord of the 7th on the 3rd degree of the minor scale the augmented 5th, if present, must be prepared, and must rise a degree, Ex. 5 *a*. The full figuring of the chord is $^{7}_{5\natural}$, $^{7}_{5\sharp}$, or $^{7}_{5}$ (cf. Ch. xxiii, § 5), but the figuring 7 does not exclude the augmented 5th if it is duly prepared. By the licence which permits the leading note, when not in the top part, to drop to the Dominant, Ex. 5 can be treated as (*b*) (*c*).

[1] Ph. Em. Bach (*Versuch &c.*, Part II, Ch. 3, 11, § 10), like Heinichen in Ex. 1 (*c*), allows the doubling *in the unison* of 'a 3rd accidentally sharpened' as preferable to (1) a perfect 5th following an imperfect one, or (2) a leap of a 5th downwards:

Kirnberger, on the other hand, prefers the skip to the doubling (even in the unison) of a leading note (cf. III, § 2).

[Ex. 5: musical example with sections (a), (b), (c), or]

In Ex. 6 the preparation of the subsequent discord makes it necessary to change from $\substack{8\\7\\3}$ to $\substack{7\\5\\3}$ on the same Bass.

[Ex. 6: musical example]

J. S. Bach, Sonata for 2 Flutes and Bass, Presto *ad fin.* *B-G.*, ed. IX (K-M. I.), p. 273.

[Ex. 7: musical example] Ph. Em. Bach, *Versuch &c.*, Part II, Ch. 13, II, § 4 (i).

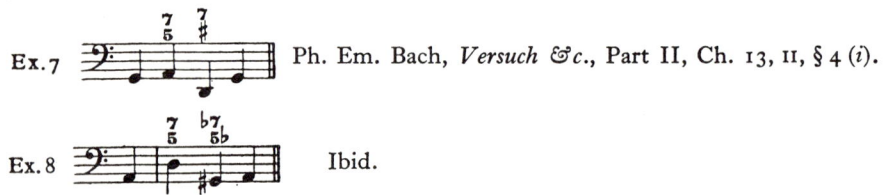

[Ex. 8: musical example] Ibid.

Of these two examples Ph. Em. Bach says: "We have here two examples that I have found, extraordinary on account of their figuring. They should properly be figured: [musical example]

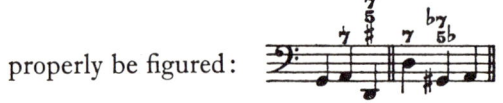

In the other case, none but the divided accompaniment [i.e. taking some of the chords in extended harmony] is possible without mistakes and without taking in a fifth part."

[(Ex. 7): musical example with (a), (b)] [(Ex. 8): musical example with (a), (b)[2]]

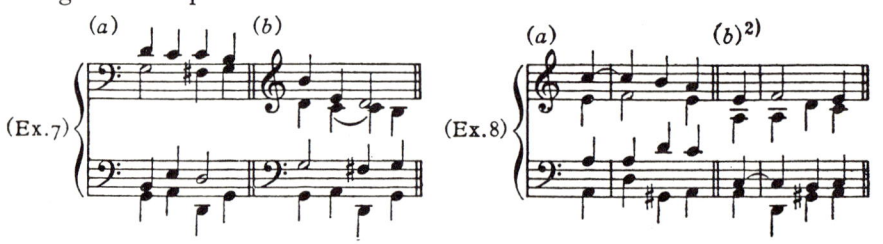

The mistakes to which Bach alludes would, in the case of Ex. 7, of course be consecutive 5ths with the Bass [musical example] while, in the case of Ex. 8,

[2] In Ex. 8 (b) the *d* in the Bass has to be taken in the lower 8ve.

XI II § 4   SEVENTHS   553

the diminished 7th on the leading note would be taken unprepared in a way not usual even in the free style:

The temporary adoption of a fifth part is, in both cases, a rough-and-ready way out of the difficulty.

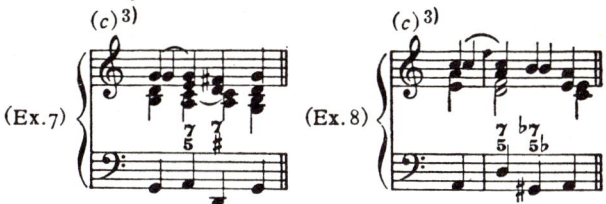

(Ex. 7)   (c)³)   (Ex. 8)   (c)³)

§ 5. *Progression of the Bass.*

In considering the progression of the Bass (as of the other intervals) it is important to bear in mind that chords of the Seventh occur (1) individually, and (2) in sequences.

The root progression of the Bass of all essential Sevenths is a 4th upwards (or 5th downwards).

Individually, such Sevenths may occur upon every degree of the scale, major or minor, except the leading note, Exx. 1 and 2.

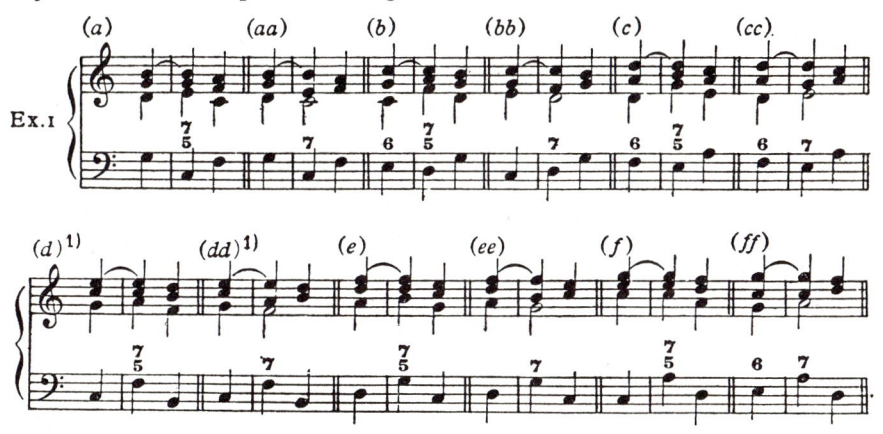

Ex. 1 (a) (aa) (b) (bb) (c) (cc)
       (d)¹⁾ (dd)¹⁾ (e) (ee) (f) (ff)

[3] For the sake of clearness the above examples are set out as though in 5-part harmony throughout. In such cases, however, the assumption is that the fifth part enters when required, as though after a rest, and disappears when its purpose is served.

[1] The progression (d) (dd) is little likely to occur, except in a sequence, unless modulation follows, as:

In the repetition of a sequence, however, a Seventh on the leading note of the major scale may resolve on a Bass rising a 4th (or falling a 5th), and in such case the leading note may be doubled; the chord may therefore be taken either as $\frac{7}{5}$ or $\frac{8}{7}$, Exx. 3 and 4; or as $\frac{7}{3}$, Ex. 5.

[2] This progression is, of course, identical with a final cadence in the key of ♭E major; but it can be used without suggestion of major tonality, either individually, A, or sequentially, B.

Ex. 4

Ex. 5

Note.—In playing over the above (and other) examples in the other positions, it must be remembered that, in actual practice, it is usually desirable to avoid a close on the Tonic with the 5th in the upper part (Ch. iii, § 5 B I c). This limitation is, however, of comparatively late origin: neither Niedt nor G. P. Telemann observed it (Ch. i, § 25 III, 8 c ad fin., and Ch. ii, § 8 c 6). The accompanist must, therefore, regulate his practice accordingly.

In a chain of 7ths in which every alternate chord includes the 5, a close on the Fifth is automatically avoided *when the $\frac{7}{5}$ falls on the weak beat of the bar*; for, in 4-part harmony, the dominant chord will not then contain the 8ve, which would otherwise remain as the 5th of the tonic chord, and the leading note cannot fall to the Dominant except when in an inner part. The tonic chord will therefore have either the 8ve or the 3rd on the top, Exx. (a) (b) (c):

(a)   (b)   (c)

When, however, the $\frac{7}{5}$ falls on the strong beat of the bar, with the 5th in the upper part, the tonic chord will also have its 5th in the upper part, Ex. (d):

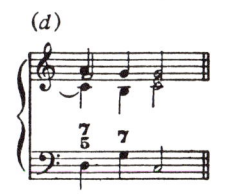

(d)

---

[3] Note the extra part taken in the final chord in order that it may not lack the 5th. The alternative is to double the 3rd instead of the Bass in the penultimate Seventh:

[4] In such a progression, when the 5ths are in the upper part, it is better to let the Bass rise a 4th (instead of falling a 5th) from the $\frac{7}{3}$ to the $\frac{7}{5}$ chord, in order to avoid hidden 5ths between extreme parts (cf. § 4, Exx. 2, 3, 4).

This can be best avoided by breaking the pattern of the sequence and taking the antepenultimate Seventh as $\genfrac{}{}{0pt}{}{7}{3}$ instead of $\genfrac{}{}{0pt}{}{8}{7}{3}$, and using the upper instead of the lower 3rd to prepare the following 7th, whereby a higher position is gained, Ex. (*e*).

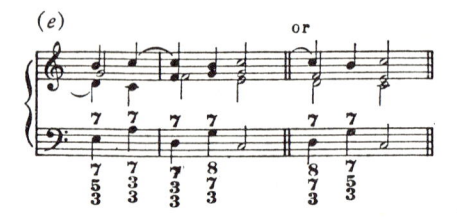

In default of this precaution, the last 7th can, at a pinch, be taken as a passing note, Ex. (*f*).

The full figuring is given below the Bass in Ex. (*e*) and the usual one above.

Instead of resolving upon a chord in its root position, a Seventh may, in certain cases, resolve upon one of its inversions.

Examples have already been given of a Seventh on the Dominant resolving on the 1st inversion of the tonic Triad, and of a Seventh on the Supertonic resolving on a $\genfrac{}{}{0pt}{}{6}{5}$ chord on the leading note (§ 2 above, Exx. 2–5).

An essential Seventh may also resolve on a $\genfrac{}{}{0pt}{}{6}{4}{3}$ on the same Bass, that is to say, on the 2nd inversion of a Seventh on a Bass a 4th higher or a 5th lower.

This progression is most often to be found on the Supertonic, Ex. 6, and on the Submediant of the minor scale, Ex. 7.[5]

In Ex. 8 it is seen on three degrees of the major scale, and in Ex. 9 on four degrees of the minor.

In all four examples 6 stands for $\genfrac{}{}{0pt}{}{6}{4}{3}$ in accordance with Leclair's practice in the first book (only) of his *Sonatas for Violin and Bass* (Ch. xxiii, 'Varieties of figuring', § 8).

Ex. 6

Leclair, *Sonatas for Violin and Bass*, Bk. 1, Sonata VII, Giga, 2nd section, 6th bar from end.

---

[5] The convention by which the accompanist is at liberty in these two cases to treat 6 as $\genfrac{}{}{0pt}{}{6}{4}{3}$ (Ch. xxi, 'Incomplete figuring', II, §§ 1, 2) makes it, in most cases, impossible to determine whether $\genfrac{}{}{0pt}{}{7}{5}{3}\genfrac{}{}{0pt}{}{6}{4}{-}$, or a simple 7 6 suspension was intended, as composers were

Ex. 7

Ibid., Sonata I, Adagio *ad fin.*

Ex. 8

Ex. 9

Ibid., Sonata IV, Andante, bars 13-18.

Ibid., Sonata XII, Allegro ma non tropo (*sic*), bars 53-6.
For ♭ (prefixed to note or figure) =♮, and × (prefixed to figure) =♯, see Ch. xxiv, 'Variety of Notation', § 2, note 1.

generally content to leave the choice to the accompanist. After Leclair abandoned the use of $\tfrac{6}{6} = \tfrac{6}{4}$, as seen in Exx. 6-9, he seldom troubled to use the full figuring in passages exactly parallel to those in which, in Bk. 1, he invariably used 6.

III. *Other progressions of the Bass.*

§ 1. A Seventh on the Dominant may resolve on a Bass rising: (1) a tone to a minor Triad, Ex. 1; (2) a semitone to a major Triad, Ex. 2.

In both cases the 3 rises a semitone to the 3 of the following chord, though in the first case it may, according to Kirnberger (*Grundsätze des Generalbasses*, § 101), fall a tone to the 8, as a preparation for a subsequent discord, Ex. 3. Kirnberger does not himself furnish an example.

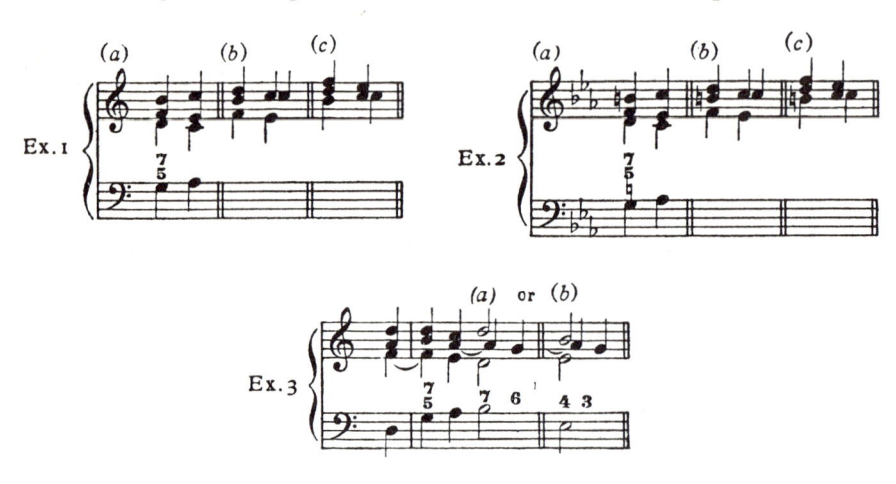

The figuring is as above, or 7 7♮ 7♯, or sometimes [music example] as a warning against [music example] Cf. ii, § 2, Ex. 1.

The progression probably originated in the anticipation of a passing note linking the Triad on the Submediant to that on the Dominant, Ex. 4 (cf. Ch. xxii, § 7, Ex. 4); the Seventh should therefore, except in 3-part harmony, include the 5.

In practice, however, it may sometimes be convenient to take it as $\frac{8}{7}$, Ex. 5; in this case the positions (*a*) (*b*) are preferable to (*c*).

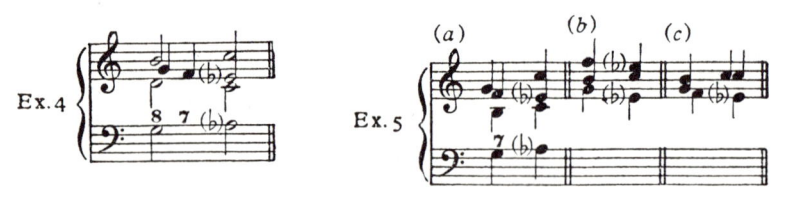

Note.—Kirnberger's view of the progression [music example] is a remarkable one. In his anxiety to prove that the Seventh is not essential, and therefore an exception to his rule for the progression of the Bass of essential discords (I, § 1), he overlooks the simple explanation suggested above and explains the 7 as really the 9 of an incomplete chord on the Mediant, and consequently the $\genfrac{}{}{0pt}{}{7}{\genfrac{}{}{0pt}{}{5}{3}}$ on *g* as the 1st inversion of $\genfrac{}{}{0pt}{}{9}{\genfrac{}{}{0pt}{}{\genfrac{}{}{0pt}{}{7}{5}}{3}}$ on *e* (*Kunst des reinen Satzes*, 1771, Abschnitt (section) IV, § 4, p. 62).

In common with all the earlier theorists Kirnberger regarded the 9th only as a suspension and thus, from his point of view, an 'accidental' (i.e. unessential) discord. According to him, therefore, the root progression is [music] and in its

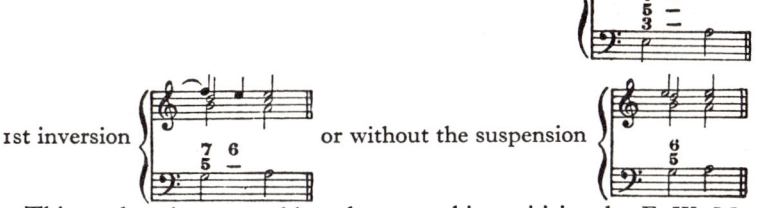

1st inversion [music] or without the suspension [music]

This explanation was subjected to a scathing criticism by F. W. Marpurg in his *Versuch über die musikalische Temperatur &c.*, § 288, pp. 266–7.

With regard to the progression [music] Kirnberger offers no explanation.

One of the most obvious objections to his theory (apart from the difficulty of applying it to the progression [music]) is the fact that if [music] really stands for [music] one would have expected the progression to be [music]

instead of [music]

Kirnberger would probably have answered this objection by saying that the delayed resolution of the suspended 7 modified the progression of the 3 by causing the augmented 4th [music] of which the natural resolution was [music] to be present in the chord. Similarly, when the 7 is in the top part, the 3 must rise to avoid the bad progression of an imperfect 5th falling to a perfect one [music]. These considerations do not, however, suffice to recommend his theory.

But we shall see that the same explanation, though artificial and improbable in the case of the progression just discussed, can be applied quite naturally to the one which forms the subject of the next paragraph, a $\genfrac{}{}{0pt}{}{7}{5}$ on the leading note resolving on the tonic Triad.

§ 2. A Seventh on the leading note (or sharpened Subdominant) of the major or minor scale resolves, either (1) directly on a Bass rising a semitone, Ex. 1 (*a*) (*aa*), or (2) on a $\genfrac{}{}{0pt}{}{6}{5}$ chord on the same Bass, (*b*) (*bb*); or (3) an inversion of the harmony may precede the final resolution (*c*) (*cc*).

The 7th (minor or diminished) is always accompanied by the imperfect

5th, the chord being, in its origin, a $\smash{{}^6_5}$ (1st inversion of the dominant Seventh) with the 6 delayed by suspension; the 3 (rather than the 5) is therefore omitted in 3-part harmony.

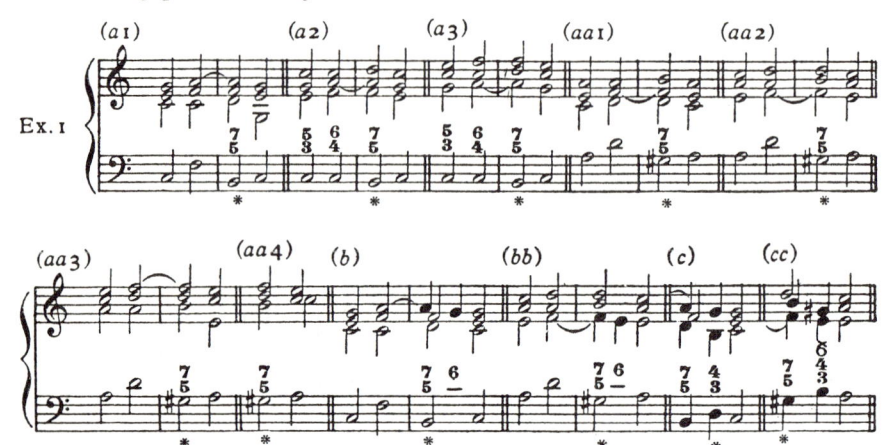

Ex. 1

Kirnberger, *Grundsätze des Generalbasses*, 1781, from which the above examples, except (c) (cc), are taken, § 172, p. 79, says:

"It is fundamentally wrong to call this Seventh on *b* an essential Seventh, as it is nothing but the first inversion, $\smash{{}^7_5{}_3}$ on *b*, of $\smash{{}^9_7{}_3}$ on *g*; and, as the 9th is an accidental [i.e. unessential] discord with *g* as its root (*Grundton*), so also the 7 on *b* is the 6 of a $\smash{{}^6_5}$ chord delayed by suspension—an accidental discord, whether it resolves on the 6 over the same Bass (*b*) (*bb*), or whether the resolution is delayed till the following bass note, when it becomes the 5 of the Bass *c* (*a*) (*aa*).

"In the example in the minor key (*aa* 3) the 5th is doubled, as well as in the major (*a* 1), for the benefit of those who are too conscientious to let a perfect 5th follow an imperfect one; but the progression (*aa* 4) is best, as the minor 3rd can be doubled without offending the ear, whereas the doubling of the major 3rd, especially when accidental [i.e. raised by ♯ or ♮], is unpleasant."

On the latter point Ph. Em. Bach differs from Kirnberger. He prefers the doubling of the major 3rd *in the unison* to the leap of a 5th, and would therefore treat Ex. 1 (*a* 1) as follows: as can be inferred from *Versuch &c.*, Part II, Ch. 3, II, § 10, where he says:

"The doubling of an interval in the unison allows more liberty than that in the octave. In the former case an accidentally sharpened interval can upon occasion (*allenfalls*) be doubled, as for instance, to avoid skips:[1]

Ex. 2

[1] For note see opposite page.

"As composers sometimes do this in inner parts, though in such cases the doubled interval can be heard as two distinct sounds, players on keyed instruments (*Clavieristen*) should the more readily be allowed the liberty, since, upon their instrument, the striking of only a single note is heard."

This is a characteristic instance of the eminently practical spirit in which Ph. Em. Bach approaches his subject.

It will be noticed: (1) that the 'accidentally sharpened interval' is, in both Bach's examples, a leading note, and (2) that in (*b*) the duplication in question is regarded as preferable to an imperfect 5th falling to a perfect one.

Kirnberger's *Grundsätze*, quoted above, was published nineteen years later than Part II of the *Versuch*; it may therefore well have been Ph. Em. Bach whom Kirnberger had in mind when he spoke of 'those who are too conscientious to let a perfect 5th follow an imperfect one'.

In Ex. 1 the 7 is, in every case, prepared, and falls on a strong beat, in conformity with the requirements of the strict style (1, § 2).

In the free style, however, in spite of its origin as a suspension, it is taken unprepared—especially the diminished 7th—and is used on a weak beat. In the case of the Seventh on the sharpened Subdominant the resolution is frequently delayed by a $^6_4$ chord, Ex. 3:

Ex. 3

With regard to the position in which the chord is to be taken there is a difference between the earlier and later practice. In the case of the diminished 7th the position has always been optional, but later text-books prescribe that, in the major key, the minor 7th on the leading note (or sharpened Subdominant) should always be in the upper part, and so also in the 1st and 2nd inversions of the chord; earlier authorities, however, seem to have known no such rule.

In Ex. 4, the only example which Heinichen gives of the chord (*G-B. &c.*, 1728, Ch. 3, § 41, p. 187), the 3 is in the upper part.

Ex. 4

It will be noticed that Heinichen prepares the 7, as also does Mattheson

---

[1] The skip cannot, of course, be avoided when the resolution of the 5 is delayed by suspension as:

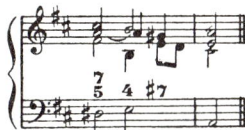

in the following example (*Kleine General-Bass-Schule*, 1735, Höherer Classe, 4te Aufgabe [Higher Grade, Lesson 4], § 6):

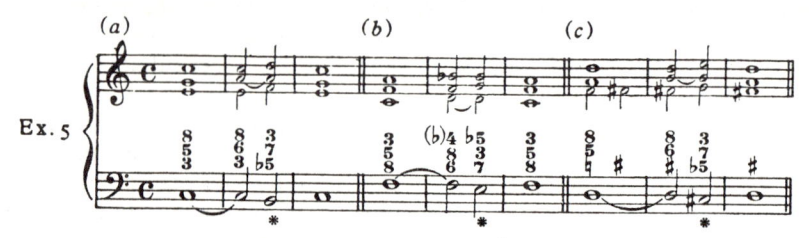

Ex. 5

Mattheson gives the Bass only, but figures it in such a way as to show the position in which the chords are to be taken. In (*a*) and (*c*), which are practically identical, the 3 is on the top, and in (*b*) the 5.

Ph. Em. Bach, *Versuch &c.*, Part II, Ch. 13, II, § 3, says:

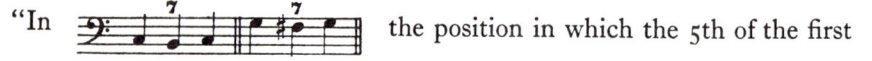

"In [music example] the position in which the 5th of the first [bass] note is on the top is no good." [2]

C. G. Schröter, on the other hand (*Deutliche Anweisung zum General-Bass*, § 152, *a*), writing some years before the publication of Part II of Ph. Em. Bach's *Versuch*—his book was completed (all but the introduction) December 30, 1754, though not published till 1772—in giving examples of the unprepared Seventh on the leading note of the major scale, "without the 3 because of consecutive Fifths" (Ex. 6), says:

Ex. 6

"As this 7 must always be in the top part, careful composers, as is only reasonable, are in the habit of indicating so special a chord as follows: $\frac{7}{5}$."

N.B.—Schröter figures all other Sevenths with a 7 only—never $\frac{7}{5}$ unless the 5

---

[2] The consecutive 5ths [music example] are of course the objection. The difficulty might have been got over, either by the doubling in the unison of the 3 (cf. Ex. 2) of the first (as well as the third) chord [music example], though this would have resulted in a weak chord (three sounding parts) on the strongest beat of the bar, or else by the doubling of the 5 in the octave, in spite of the undesirable skip: [music example] The significant point is that Ph. Em. Bach evidently attached no importance to keeping the 7 in the top part. With regard to the 2nd inversion of the same chord, however, he says (ibid., Ch. 7, 1, § 8): "The position in which the Fourth and Third are separated [i.e. with the 3 on the top] always sounds best [i.e. in all $\frac{6}{4}$ chords], but especially so with this kind of $\frac{4}{3}$ chord."

requires an accidental. Generally speaking, the figuring $^7_5$ would give no indication whatsoever of the position in which the chord was to be taken.[3]

§ 3. Sevenths on the remaining degrees of the scale occur on a strong beat (*in thesi*), resolving on a Bass rising one degree (1) to a Triad, Ex. 1 (*a*) (*b*) (*c*) (*d*) (*f*), or (2), in the case of the Subdominant, to another Seventh, (*e*) (*ee*). In the latter case the first Seventh must include the 8 as preparation for the second.

Ex. 1

Kirnberger's explanation of the Seventh on the leading note (see preceding section) can be applied to all the above examples, in which case the chord * in (*a*) (*b*) (*c*) (*d*) (*e*) (*f*) is essentially a $^6_5$ [4)], and in (*ee*) a 6.

[3] Not so, however, in the case of the 1st and 2nd inversions of the chord in question, which Schröter figures $^5_6$, $^3_4$ respectively, instead of the usual $^6_5$, $^4_3$:

With regard to the 1st inversion Schröter remarks (ibid., § 174, note): "I remember a former composer in Westphalia who indicated this special case with $^{12}_6$, which irreproachable method of figuring has, however, not yet come into general use."

[4] In every case the 5, as well as the 7, is prepared, as it is only on the leading note that the 5 in a $^6_5$ may be taken unprepared, except as a passing note

If therefore the 7 in Ex. 1 *c* were prepared as follows: &c. it could

not be regarded as standing for $^7_5\,^6_-$, as the progression is irregular.

On the other hand, in some cases at any rate, the explanation suggested in the case of the resolution of the dominant Seventh on the Submediant, namely, the anticipation of a passing note (III, § 1), may apply.

In Ex. 1 (*a*) for instance, the progression can be regarded as originating in

whereas, in (*f*), the Seventh on *a* is obviously a sequential imitation of the preceding one on the leading note.

In most instances, probably, a progression, established in the case of the Dominant and leading note, was extended, consciously or unconsciously, to other degrees of the scale.

It is quite possible for two composers to arrive independently at the same harmonic innovation *by quite different mental processes*; the same progression need not, therefore, in every case have the same origin.

A Seventh on the Subdominant followed, either directly Ex. 2 (*a*), or with an intervening $_4^6$ chord or 4 3 suspension (*b*) (*c*), by a Triad on the Dominant, is also found on a weak beat (*in arsi*).

Such a Seventh can, like those in Ex. 1, be explained as essentially a $_5^6$ with delayed resolution of the suspended 7:

In other cases it may have arisen through the anticipation of a passing note (*anticipatio transitus*, Ch. xxii, 'Inversion &c.', § 7) in the Bass * and an upper part * moving in Thirds therewith:

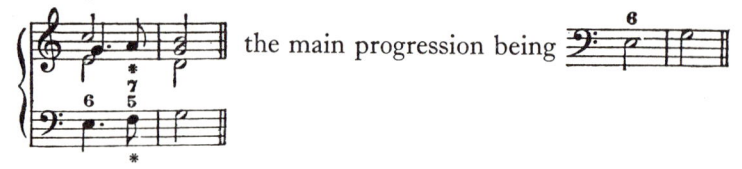

the main progression being

Examples of the Seventh on the Subdominant have been given above in the major key only, but examples in the minor will be found in the following chapter, § 5 (1), Ex. 1 *bb*, Ex. 2 *bb*, *bbb*, and Ex. 3 *bb*.

§ 4. A Seventh on the Dominant may resolve on a Bass falling either:
(1) a tone, to a Seventh (major or minor according to the key) on the Subdominant, which Seventh in its turn resolves on a dominant chord, the

resolution being generally delayed by, either suspension, Ex. 1 (a) (b), or by the intervention of another harmony (c), or:

(2) a semitone, to a Seventh (either minor, Ex. 2 (a), or diminished (b) (c)) on the sharpened Subdominant.

Ex. 1

Ex. 2

The figuring [score] is preferable to [score] (though the latter often occurs) as in 4-part harmony the second Seventh would lack the 3 if the first one included the 5 instead of the 8 [score]

The alternative would be a wrong progression of the leading note, and, when the 7 is in the upper part, an imperfect 5th descending to a perfect one as well: [score]. In 3-part harmony the 3 (rather than the 5) must be omitted from the second Seventh:

The reason why the 3 of the dominant Seventh must have the progression proper to the leading note, although it does not immediately lead to a tonic chord, will become apparent when the true nature of the progression is considered.

There are two possible explanations.[2]

---

[1] Ex. 1 (c) is from Ph. Em. Bach, *Versuch &c.*, Part II, Ch. 13, II, § 2 (f), the Bass only being given.

[2] Compare Marpurg's analysis of No. 2 of his examples in the extract quoted in I, § 2.

It may originate in an auxiliary passing note, first in the Bass, and then in its octave as well, the three stages being:

Ex.3

In this case it is an example of *anticipatio transitus* (Ch. xxii, § 7), the main progression being

It may, however, also be due to the suppression of the resolution of the Seventh on the same bass note (cf. Ch. xxii, § 8), Ex. 4:

Ex.4

The $^7_5$ on f (or $\sharp f$) is then, in its turn, really a $^6_5$ with delayed resolution of the suspended 7 (cf. § 3), the main progression being

The one explanation does not necessarily exclude the other, as there is no reason why the progression should not have a double origin (cf. § 3).

In the case of Ex. 1 *c* the first alternative is certainly preferable, as

is a better progression than

In Ex. 2 *b* the contrary is the case, since   is consistent with the major tonality of the example, whereas [music] would stamp it as minor.

Ex. 1 *a, b* and Ex. 2 *a, c* can be regarded either way.

The following examples are of special interest:

Ex. 5 [music] Antonio Vivaldi, Opera Prima, 12 Sonatas for 2 Violins and Bass, Sonata II, Grave, bar 17.

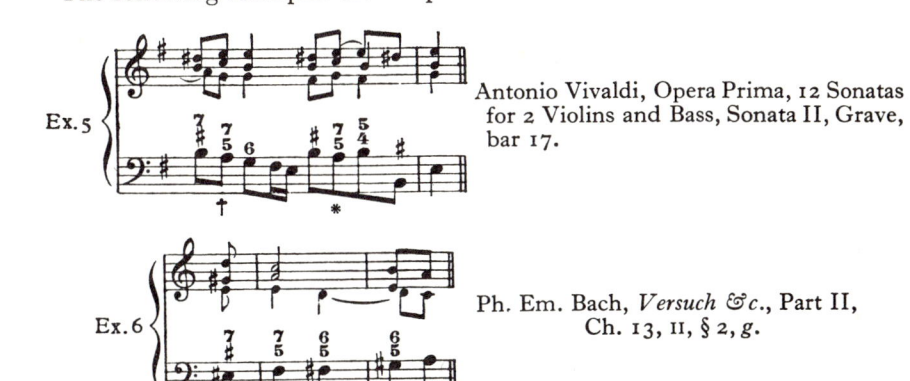

Ex. 6 [music] Ph. Em. Bach, *Versuch &c.*, Part II, Ch. 13, II, § 2, *g*.

In Ex. 5 we have, in the second half of the bar, the same progression (in the minor key) as in Ex. 1 *b*, except that the chord * is preceded by a Triad instead of a Seventh. At † we have the same chord, but the 7 remains as a concordant note in the tonic harmony.[3]

The real progression is [music] or [music] the *a* in the Bass (Ex. 5 †) being a passing note, while the *c* in the upper parts—likewise a passing note—follows the Bass in 3rds.

The accompaniment can, if preferred, be treated as follows:

[music]

Ex. 6 really belongs to the next chapter, on $^6_5$ chords, but is more conveniently treated in the present connexion. In it we have the dominant Seventh followed—not by a Seventh on the Subdominant—but by its 1st

---

[3] This case must not be confused with that in Ex. 1 *a* in which the Seventh is followed by the 2nd inversion of the tonic chord *as a suspension, on the strong beat of the bar.*

inversion, $^6_5$ on the Submediant, the latter being sharpened as its progression to the leading note demands.

The main progression is [musical notation] and is modified by the chromatic Bass and the suspended 7 over *f*.

The progression from the dominant Seventh to $^6_5$ on the Submediant—like that to the Seventh on the Subdominant—may easily have arisen, either (1) through passing auxiliary notes:

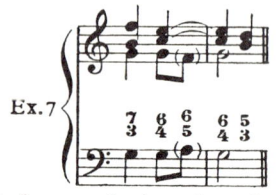

Ex. 7 [musical notation]

or (2) through ellipse of the resolution (on the same bass note) of the dominant Seventh: [musical notation] in which case the 5 on *a* (like

Ex. 8 [musical notation]

the 7 on *f* in Ex. 4) is an unresolved suspension, the chord being essentially a $^4_3$, the 2nd inversion of a Seventh on *d*:

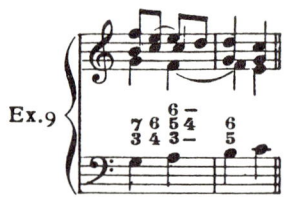

Ex. 9 [musical notation]

The 6 on the Submediant may also be delayed by suspension, either (1) resolving together with the 5:

Ex. 10 [musical notation]

or (2) (as in Ex. 6) leaving the 5 unresolved:

Ex. 11 [musical notation]

the root progression being in every case [musical notation]

In Ex. 6 the dominant Seventh is on a short unaccented note, but it must be remembered that a progression, when once established, is likely to occur under conditions quite different from those under which it probably originated.

§ 5. For Sevenths resolving on a Bass falling a 3rd to another Seventh, see Ch. xxii, § 5.

IV. *Suspended Sevenths.*

§ 1. In a Seventh resolving on $^6_3$ on the same bass note either the Bass or the 3 must, in 4-part harmony, be doubled, except when the 5 is included, § 2.

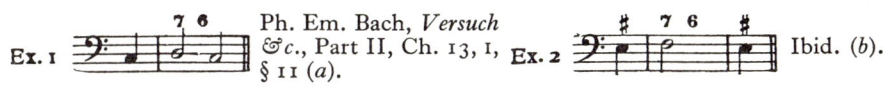

Ex. 1 [musical example] Ph. Em. Bach, *Versuch &c.*, Part II, Ch. 13, I, § 11 (*a*). Ex. 2 [musical example] Ibid. (*b*).

In Ex. 1 either the Bass can be doubled (*a, aa*), or the 3 (*b, bb*).

Of this example Ph. Em. Bach says: "The position in which the Fifth of the first bass note is on the top [1] is the worst, and that in which the Octave is on the top [as (*a*) (*b*)] the best."

In Ex. 2 no position is possible but that with doubled 3:

as otherwise the forbidden progression of an augmented 2nd (♯g ♮f ♯g) would result. Here, too, the position (*c*), with the 5 of the first chord on the top, is the worst, though not so bad as in the case of Ex. 1.

Ex. 3 [musical example] Ibid. (*d*).

In Ex. 3 the augmented Sixth on *c* can only be taken with doubled 3, therefore, to avoid consecutive 8ves (or unisons), the Seventh on *d* must be taken as $^8_7_3$ (*a*) (*b*) (*c*).[2]

---

[1] If one inadvertently finds oneself in this position, the best way to avoid the bad progression of an imperfect 5th rising to a perfect one is to double the 3 (instead of the Bass) of the Seventh on *d* and to take the 6 as $^6_4_3$ [musical example]. Cf. Ch. xxi, II, § 1.

[2] The reason which Ph. Em. Bach gives for not doubling the 3 of the Seventh is the rule that a major 3rd (whether accidental or diatonic) must not be doubled in conjunction with a minor 7th.

He makes no distinction between an essential dominant Seventh, in which the 3 is a leading note, and a case like the present, in which the essential harmony is a Sixth,

570   SEVENTHS   XI IV § 1

Ex. 4 [musical example with (a), (b), (c), and "bad" marked] Ibid. (c).

With regard to Ex. 4 Ph. Em. Bach expresses himself somewhat carelessly. The words supplied in brackets are evidently required to make his meaning clear. He says: "The [perfect] Fifth is contrary to the tonality,[4] and [the imperfect Fifth] cannot subsequently be resolved, a consideration to which one must pay special attention and which in this instance makes the accompaniment with the Fifth dangerous. The other two forms of our chord are therefore alone admissible in this example. The many consecutive Sixths must, if possible, be taken in the top part, as otherwise mistakes, or, at all events, unvocal progressions (*ein schlechter Gesang*) will result."

The way in which the first chord, the Sixth on *c*, is taken $\left(\begin{smallmatrix}6\\3\\8\end{smallmatrix} \text{ or } \begin{smallmatrix}6\\6\\6\end{smallmatrix}\right)$ will determine whether the Seventh which follows is taken with doubled Bass (*a*) or doubled 3 (*b*).

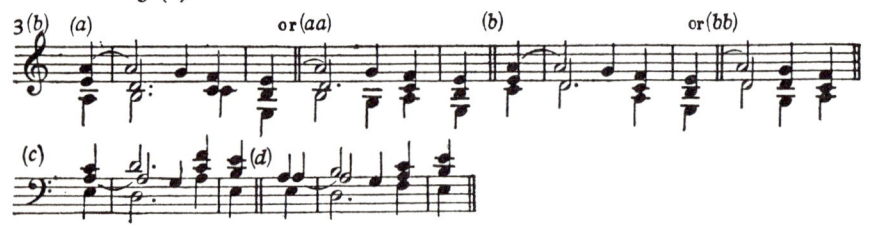

[musical example with labels 3(b), (a), or(aa), (b), or(bb), (c), (d)]

which, apart from the considerations mentioned above, can be correctly taken with doubled 3, as:

[musical example]

[3] The best way out of the difficulty, if the bad position shown at (*c*) is not avoided in time, is to take the 6 on *c* as $\begin{smallmatrix}6\\4\\3\end{smallmatrix}$, as:

[musical example]

N.B.—Ph. Em. Bach condemns the not uncommon practice of figuring an augmented Sixth with a simple 6 where $\begin{smallmatrix}6\\4\\3\end{smallmatrix}$ (a 'French Sixth') is intended (cf. Ch. xxi, 11, § 3).

The case is therefore not parallel with that mentioned in note 1, in which it is universally recognized that the 6 may be interpreted as $\begin{smallmatrix}6\\4\\3\end{smallmatrix}$.

[4] "Nach dem Umfang der Tonart falsch": literally "wrong according to the scope of the scale" or, as it was called in older treatises, the "*ambitus modi*".

SEVENTHS

Examples of the unvocal progressions to which Bach alludes are met with in some of the older treatises,[5] and are occasionally useful at a pinch as a means of gaining a higher or lower position for the right hand.

Ex. 5 [musical notation] Ibid. (*f*).

Of Ex. 5 Ph. Em. Bach says: "Our chord is only good with the Octave,[6] as otherwise unvocal and impure progressions occur."

§ 2. The Seventh in a 7 6 suspension may also include the Fifth, either perfect or augmented.

With regard to the inclusion of the imperfect Fifth in Sevenths of any

---

[5] In the following example from Leonhard Reinhard's *Kurzer und deutlicher Unterricht von dem General-Bass* the full figuring indicates the position in which the chords are to be taken. For the duplication of the ♭♭ in the key-signature, see Ch. xxiv, 'Varieties of Notation', § 1 (*c*).

[musical example]

[6] It will be noticed that it is the passing note *e* (5 in the 7 6 5), falling, as it must, to *d*, which imposes this restriction.

This progression, when the 3 of the Seventh is doubled—

(*a*) [musical example]

produces an impression of collapse, which is least noticeable in the positions (*b*) (*c*) in which the part falling in 3rds with the Bass is not on the top.

(*b*) (*c*) [musical example]

If, on the other hand, the figuring were 7 6 instead of 7 6 5, the doubling of the 3 (*d*) (*e*) (*f*) would give a better progression than the doubled Bass (*g*) (*h*) (*i*).

(*d*) (*e*) (*f*) [musical example]

N.B.—The position shown at (*f*) is less good than (*d*) and (*e*).

(*Note continued on next page.*)

kind, the authorities, as we have seen (II, § 4), differed. Gasparini's 'counsel of perfection' was that the imperfect Fifth was inadmissible *unless it resolved on a 3rd with the Bass*

Ph. Em. Bach demands that the Fifth itself should resolve a degree downwards, irrespective of the progression of the Bass

while Heinichen, after implying that it *ought* so to resolve, admits (in a footnote) that he does not much care whether it does or not.

He would therefore, presumably, not have objected to such a progression as

With regard to 7 6 suspensions Ph. Em. Bach expresses himself as follows:[1] "Generally speaking, single notes [as opposed to sequences] with 7 6 suffer the doubled Third or Octave rather than the Fifth. If the latter is perfect and not inconsistent with the trend of the harmony [2] (*nicht wider die Modula-*

Note 6 continued:

or, as will be seen in § 2, the 5 could be included in the Seventh (*k*) (*l*) (*m*), in which case the 6 is best taken as $\smash{\overset{6}{\underset{3}{4}}}$ (cf. § 3 under Ex. 1).

[1] *Versuch &c.*, Part II, Ch. 13, I, § 10.

[2] Of Ex. 3 in the preceding paragraph Ph. Em. Bach says: "The Fifth [*a*] is contrary to the trend of the harmony on account of the augmented Sixth [♯*a*] over the following bass note, and cannot therefore be taken."

tion) one can upon occasion ³ (*allenfalls*) take it, only one must beware of forbidden progressions of consecutive Fifths.⁴ Sometimes one may even take the augmented Fifth (though not indicated in the figuring) with this 7 6, if it is consistent with the harmony: especially when it comes, as a tied note, from a preceding unresolved augmented Fourth.⁵ The imperfect Fifth also occurs in the case of our 7 6, and one takes it, even though not indicated, if it can be subsequently resolved." ⁶

§ 3. When the perfect Fifth is included it either falls to the 3 (Ex. 1), or rises to the 6 (Ex. 2).¹

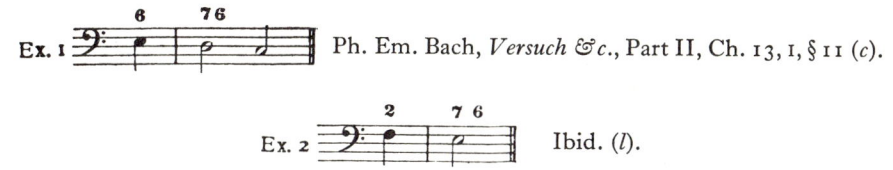

Ex. 1 [music] Ph. Em. Bach, *Versuch &c.*, Part II, Ch. 13, 1, § 11 (*c*).

Ex. 2 [music] Ibid. (*l*).

In Ex. 1 the 5, if included, cannot rise to the 6, because the major 6th

---

³ For the shade of meaning conveyed by *allenfalls* see § 5, note.

⁴ Of Exx. 1 and 2 in the preceding paragraph [music]

Ph. Em. Bach says: "Neither of the two examples will bear the Fifth, because forbidden Fifths would occur on account of the rising first bass notes."

In the first example, as he points out in another connexion (see II, § 4, Ex. 7), the consecutives in question could be avoided by taking the first chord in extended harmony, the only practicable position being the following:

[music]

In the second example this would be even less natural on account of the progression of a diminished 4th which it involves:

[music]

⁵ As § 4, Ex. 1.

⁶ It is evident that this can only be the case when the following Sixth can be taken as $\smash{\genfrac{}{}{0pt}{}{6}{4}}$. Thus the only case in which Ph. Em. Bach would allow the inclusion of the imperfect Fifth in a 7 6 suspension would be on the Supertonic of the minor scale:

[music]

For the cases in which a chord figured 6 may, at pleasure, be taken as $\smash{\genfrac{}{}{0pt}{}{6}{4}}$, see Ch. xxi, 'Incomplete figuring', II, §§ 1, 2.

¹ In 'extended' harmony it may also rise to the 8, as § 6, Ex. 6 (*a*). In 'close' harmony this would be impossible without a crossing of the parts which would obscure the progression of the 7th.

with a minor 3rd (except on the Subdominant of the minor scale) cannot be doubled; it must therefore fall to the 3 (*a*) (*b*).

Of this Ex. Ph. Em. Bach says: "The Fifth, being perfect, can at a pinch be included, but the two other forms of our chord are better."

And, in fact, if the Ex. is treated as above, the Fifth has no real *locus standi* (cf. § 8). If, on the other hand, the 6 on the Supertonic *d* is taken as $^6_4{}_3$ (Ch. xxi, II, § 1), the case is altered, and we have, not a real 7 6 suspension at all, but an essential Seventh on the Supertonic resolving on the 2nd inversion of the dominant Seventh (II, § 5, Ex. 6).

In Ex. 2 the augmented 4th in the first chord must be resolved; it must, therefore, as Ph. Em. Bach points out, remain as the 5 in the following chord, even though not indicated in the figuring, *and must rise*.

In Ex. 3 the inclusion of the 5, as also its progression, depends on the position in which the chords are taken.

The 3 in the Triad on *g* has, as leading note, its fixed upward progression. *When in the top part* (*a*), it must, therefore, remain as the 5 of the following chord, rising to the Tonic when the resolution of the suspended 7 permits it to do so. When *in an inner part*, it may either be treated in the same way (*b*) (*d*), or, on the other hand, it may fall a 3rd, either (1) simultaneously with the resolution of the 7 (*c*) (*e*), or (2) with the entry of the tonic harmony (*f*) (*g*).

N.B.—(*d*) is preferable to either (*e*) or (*g*); (*b*) and (*c*) are, of course, identical in effect on a keyed instrument.

There are certain cases where the inclusion of the perfect 5th in a 7 6 suspension, besides being effective, is convenient, by making it possible to avoid skips, as e.g. in the following stereotyped close:

XI IV § 3   SEVENTHS   575

when the 8ve of the first bass note is taken in the upper part of the accompaniment (a) (b) (c) in order to avoid making the close in unison with the solo part (d) (e).

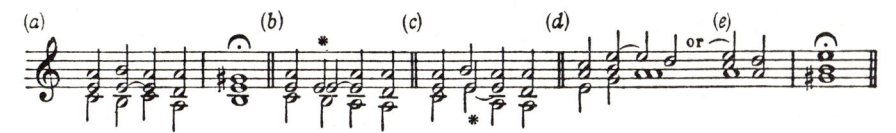

In the position in question, unless the 5th is included in the Seventh (a), consecutive 8ves are only avoided by doubling the 6 on *g* in the unison (b) (c) * *; (b) is preferable to (c), but (a) is better than either.

In every case the 6 on *f* can be taken as $\smash{\overset{6}{\underset{3}{4}}}$ (Ch. xxi, II, § 2):[2]

Ex. 4

[2] Some clue to J. S. Bach's practice in the matter is afforded by the following extract from the accompaniment to a Sonata for Violin and Bass by T. Albinoni (Opera Sesta, 'Trattenimenti armonici per Camera divisi in dodici Sonate', Sonata 6, Adagio *ad fin.*) in which the 7 6 on *f* is treated as $\smash{\overset{7\,6}{\underset{3\,3}{5\,4\,3}}}$.

The accompaniment in question (to the whole of this one Sonata) was set out by way of an exercise in 4-part harmony by Heinrich Nicolaus Gerber, a pupil of Sebastian Bach, and *corrected by Bach himself*. The MS. (now owned by the Brussels *Conservatoire*) passed into the hands of Bach's biographer, P. Spitta, who published it as Supplement VI to his *Life of Bach* (vol. iii of the English translation). He tells us: "I obtained this in the spring of 1876 from the musical collection of Music-director Rühl of Frankfurt a. M., who had died shortly before. The MS. was bequeathed to Rühl by Hofrath André, and to the latter by the younger Gerber. A note by the younger Gerber on the MS. runs as follows: 'Done by Heinrich Nic. Gerber and corrected by Sebastian Bach.' The Solo part and the figures of the Bass are wanting."

Doubts have been thrown upon the authenticity of Bach's corrections by Herr Johann Schreyer of Dresden (*Bach-Jahrbuch*, 1906, pp. 134 sq.), but, as it seems to the present writer, with quite insufficient reason (ibid., 1909, pp. 153 sq.). The absence of the Solo part and of the figures gives a clue to the genesis of the MS. Gerber probably copied the figured Bass (which was all that was necessary for the purpose of an harmony exercise) from a copy of the Sonata in Bach's possession and afterwards took it home and set it out in four parts on another sheet of paper without troubling to copy the figures themselves a second time. He therefore had not got the

Ex. 5 [musical example] Ph. Em. Bach, *Versuch &c.*, Part II, Ch. 13, 1, § 12 (*i*).

Of this example (of which he gives the Bass only) Ph. Em. Bach says: "This example is remarkable: according to the eighth paragraph [which forbids the doubling of the major 3rd in conjunction with a minor 7th] the Third cannot be doubled here; the Octave does not go well with the following bass note ♯*g*; consequently the Fifth is necessary."

(a)   (aa)   (b)   (bb)   (c)   (cc)

Ph. Em. Bach would certainly have preferred (*b*) to (*bb*) on account of the thinly separated 8ves $\begin{smallmatrix}c&b\\c&b\end{smallmatrix}$ in the latter, though, not being equally accented, they are not on a par with those which he so strongly condemns in § 6, Ex. 2 (*e*).

§ 4. The augmented Fifth, if included in a 7 6 suspension, must in all cases rise to the 6.

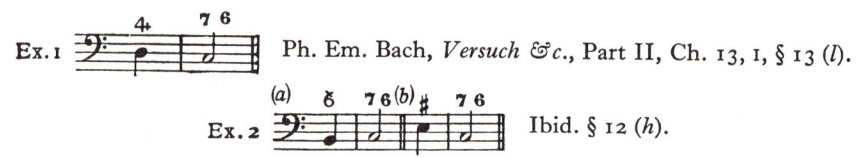

Ex. 1 [musical example] Ph. Em. Bach, *Versuch &c.*, Part II, Ch. 13, 1, § 13 (*l*).

Ex. 2 [musical example] Ibid. § 12 (*h*).

In Ex. 1, which is exactly parallel with Ex. 2 in § 3, the augmented 5th must be included:

(a)   (b)   (c)

Solo part before him when he set out the accompaniment, *neither had Bach when he looked it over.*

This assumption fully accounts for the few cases in which Gerber's harmony clashes with the Solo part, due, in all probability, to his having miscopied or misplaced the figures in the first instance. It also accounts for one instance in which there are consecutive 5ths between passing semiquavers in the Solo part and the accompaniment, which would not otherwise have passed unnoticed. Whether Bach would have altered them or not is open to argument.

In the example given above the Solo part has been supplied, and it will be observed that an appoggiatura [musical example] (performed as [musical example]) is required in the latter, which would otherwise clash with the accompaniment.

Apparent discrepancies between the figuring and the Solo part or parts (especially in cadences) are constantly due to the omission of an appoggiatura, or shake *with the upper note accented*, which to contemporary performers would be a matter of course whether indicated or not. In his *Opinioni de' Cantori antichi e moderni o sieno Osservazioni sopra il Canto figurato*, Bologna, 1723, Pietro Francesco Tosi says: "Now that the pupil has been sufficiently instructed in the subject, the appoggiaturas will by constant practice become so familiar to him that, when he has scarcely left school, he will be able to laugh at the composers who indicate appoggiaturas with notes: either because they want to be regarded as new-fashioned, or because one is to believe that they can sing better than the singers."

XI iv § 4   SEVENTHS   577

Of Ex. 2, of which (as of Ex. 1) he gives the Bass only, Ph. Em. Bach says: "Here the Fifth, if one wishes to take it, must be augmented, and must afterwards proceed to an unison[1] with the Sixth. This Fifth is often as little indicated as the imperfect one, and who can always tell whether the composer wished to have it here? In other cases one certainly does not lightly take, without indication, a dissonant interval which makes a chord, already dissonant, still more unpleasant. It is a different matter when these Fifths are expressly figured. The kind of accompaniment in which four sounding parts were always insisted upon [2] is the cause of these uninvited Fifths having crept in. With the practice of doubling intervals in the unison they are not needed, so here the other two kinds of accompaniment [3] are safer."

[1] As in (a) (b) (1) and (2) below. The term 'Unison', however, is here evidently not meant to exclude the position in which the 7th and augmented 5th resolve on the 8ve (a) (b) (3). Ph. Em. Bach's own definition (ibid., Ch. 1, § 23) makes this clear: "*The Unison, in the strict sense of the term,* is when two or more parts come together on a single key. . . . Very often it is understood to include the Octave, and later on we shall specially treat of the Unison in this sense." There is seldom any difficulty in determining the sense in which the term is used:

[2] See Ch. ii, 'The principal treatises of the 18th century', &c., § 8 (c). Ph. Em. Bach's suggestion throws much light on the cases in which the 5th is included in a 7 6 suspension—whether on a single bass note (§ 3, Ex. 1) or in a sequence (§ 6, Exx. 5 and 6)—without having any real *locus standi* in the chord.

[3] If the Seventh be taken as $\genfrac{}{}{0pt}{}{8}{7}{3}$, the first chord in (b) must have the 5 doubled * to avoid consecutive 8ves with the Bass.

In either case (whether it be taken as $\genfrac{}{}{0pt}{}{7}{3}{3}$ or $\genfrac{}{}{0pt}{}{8}{7}{3}$) the position with the 7 in the upper part (a) (b) (1) and (3) is the more natural.

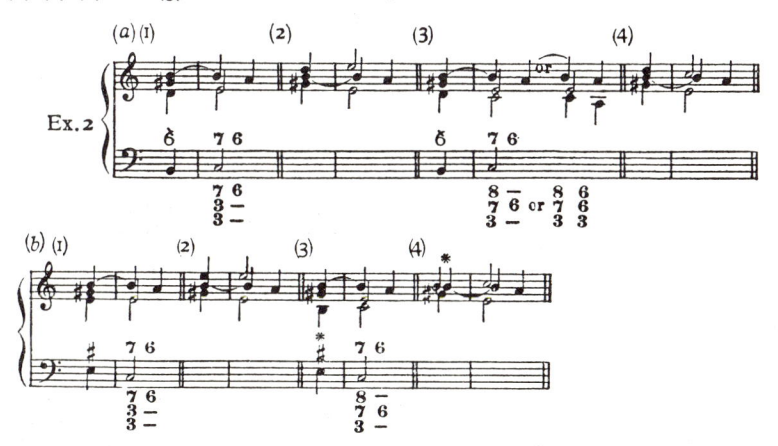

The position with the leading note ♯g in the top part is, of course, impossible unless it remains as 5⁺ in the following chord (cf. note 1, Ex. 2 (a) (b) (3)).

Schröter (*Deutliche Anweisung zum General-Bass*, 1772, § 246, *a*) gives the following example, in which the 7, as well as the 5⊢, is treated as the retardation of an upward progression, as is clearly indicated by the figuring $\begin{smallmatrix}7&8\\5&6\end{smallmatrix}$.

Ex. 3

Schröter adds: "Here the player of a figured Bass must not always take the doubled 6 instead of the retarded 8: for a careful composer expressly indicates by this 8 that it is necessary for it to be in the hand as the preparation of another suspension [4] to follow."

§ 5. As was pointed out in § 2, the imperfect 5th cannot, according to strict usage, be included in any Seventh unless it has its proper resolution.

Strictly, therefore, it is excluded in a progression figured 7 6, except in a case in which the 6 can be taken as $\begin{smallmatrix}6\\4\\3\end{smallmatrix}$ (Ch. xxi, II, § 1); and the only such case (as far as the imperfect 5th is concerned) is that of the Supertonic of the minor scale, as:

Ex. 4   Ph. Em. Bach, *Versuch &c.*, Part II, Ch. 13, I, § 12 (*g*).

Of this example, of which the Bass only is given, Ph. Em. Bach says: "All three forms of the Seventh can be used. The imperfect Fifth may be allowed here,[†] because it can proceed to the Fourth in the major Sixth which follows." All three forms are given below (*a*, *b*, *c*).

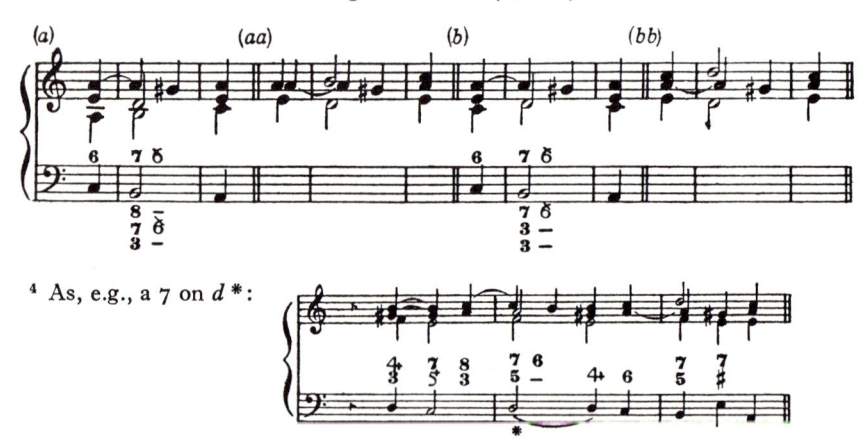

[4] As, e.g., a 7 on *d* ∗:

[†] The original is "wird hier allenfalls erlaubt". 'Allenfalls' is a most difficult word to translate. It may perhaps be paraphrased: "taking into consideration every possible case". In the present instance it conveys the idea that the permission to use the imperfect 5th (though, for the reason given, it cannot be withheld) is given somewhat grudgingly.

It is evident that the progression (c) is not a 7 6 suspension at all, but an essential Seventh on the Supertonic resolving on the 2nd inversion of the dominant Seventh (II, § 5, Ex. 6). Ex. 1 in § 3 is exactly parallel.

§ 6. Sequences of 7 6 suspensions occur both on a falling and a rising Bass. In the former case, which is by far the commoner, a 3-part accompaniment is the simplest, and, according to the principal authorities, the best, except when the occasion calls for fuller harmony. The following example from Schröter's *Deutliche Anweisung zum General-Bass*, 1772, § 238, is a 'Bassetto', in which, in a composition of several vocal or instrumental parts, the use of the tenor clef in the figured Organ or Harpsichord part indicated that the Bass was temporarily silent. In such a case the left-hand part (the temporary Bass) was *never played in Octaves* (Ch. iii, 'General character of a figured Bass Accompaniment', § 6; also § 7, note 6, in the present chapter and section).

When the accompaniment is in four parts there are many opportunities for mistakes which are fully explained by Ph. Em. Bach in the following extract (*Versuch &c.*, Part II, Ch. 13, 1, §§ 14-15):

"The four-part accompaniment preserves its purity by means of duplication, all forms of the chords of the Sixth and Seventh occurring *in alternation* with and without duplication.[1] . . .

"The example below can be accompanied in various ways. Those ways are best in which there is most variety in the matter of duplication (*a, b, c*)."

---

[1] It must be remembered that Bach generally used the term 'duplication' only of

"But where there is too much uniformity owing to the Bass, or the Third, or the Sixth being doubled *too often in succession in the same way*, mistakes are easily made, and sometimes the Fifths and Octaves are too prominent; for instance, the execution of our example with the following figures, $\begin{smallmatrix}5&6&7&6\\3&3&5&3\\8&8&3&8\end{smallmatrix}$, &c., is disagreeable on account of the many Fifths, besides they are not all perfect, and the imperfect ones are not resolved.

"The accompaniment with $\begin{smallmatrix}8&-&3&8&3\\5&6&7&6&7\\3&3&3&3&3\end{smallmatrix}$, &c., is disgusting on account of the Octaves and dangerous on account of the Thirds, as one may easily offend against the eighth paragraph of our chapter [which forbids the doubling of the major 3rd in conjunction with a minor 7th].

"The execution with $\begin{smallmatrix}3&3&3&3&3\\8&6&7&6&7\\5&3&5&3&5\end{smallmatrix}$, &c., is subject to mistakes on account at once of the Thirds and Fifths.

"The accompaniment with $\begin{smallmatrix}3&-&5&3&5\\8&-&3&3&3\\5&6&7&6&7\end{smallmatrix}$, &c., is no good on account of the unresolved imperfect Fifth, and, in fact, of the Fifths lying in the upper part; if there are wrong duplications into the bargain, then there is an accumulation of everything that is bad. The execution with $\begin{smallmatrix}5&6&7&6&7\\3&3&3&3&3\\8&6&8&6&8\end{smallmatrix}$, &c., will pass, as long as no major Sixths with a minor Third are included. The accompaniment with $\begin{smallmatrix}8&-&3&8&3\\5&6&7&6&7\\3&-&5&3&5\end{smallmatrix}$, &c., is not good on account of the imperfect Fifth and on account of the Octave in the upper part."

It is of the utmost importance thoroughly to understand the above, which will be made clearer by setting out Bach's figures as follows:

Ex. 2 *b*

the upper parts (see Ch. ix, 11, § 3, note 4). In the sequel, however, he speaks of the Bass being 'doubled'. His point is that Fifths and Octaves, not actually consecutive, but recurring too frequently in close proximity, are best avoided by *not taking the same form of either Sixth or Seventh twice in immediate succession.*

It will be observed that, except for the difference of position, (*d*) is identical with (*i*), and (after the first two crotchets) (*f*) with (*g*).

In (*i*) the 8ves with the Bass on alternate *weak* beats are in the top part. Similarly, in (*g*) the 5ths on alternate *strong* beats are between extreme parts, while in (*d*) and (*f*) they are between the Bass and an inner part. In all four cases there is an unresolved imperfect 5th * on the third beat of the first bar.

The 'mistakes on account of Thirds' in (*f*), and the 'wrong duplications' in (*g*) can only refer to the doubled major 3rd in the Sixth on *c* ‡ on the last beat of the second bar. It is remarkable that the rule prohibiting the doubling of a major 3rd with a minor 7th, even when the latter is not essential (cf. § 1, Ex. 3, note 2), should be regarded as holding good even *after the resolution of the suspended 7th*.

It will be noticed that in Ex. 2 (*a*) Ph. Em. Bach doubles the Bass *e*, which is the 3rd of the dominant Triad, though, as in the instance under discussion, *not a leading note*.

But that he did not scruple, in the course of a sequence, to double even a leading note in the Bass is shown by the following example:

Ibid., Ch. 3, 1, § 14 *ad fin.*

His extreme sensitiveness in the matter of the doubled major 3rd is therefore somewhat remarkable.

In (*e*) the 'disgusting' 8ves are on the *strong* beat, but not between extreme parts. (It will be noticed that no objection is raised to the 8ves—also between Treble and Tenor—on the *weak* beat in (*f*) and (*h*).) There is furthermore the doubled major 3rd with a minor 7th * on the third beat of the second bar.

In (*h*), if the sequence be continued so as to include the Supertonic, the mistake to which Bach alludes must be avoided by breaking the pattern of the sequence and doubling the 3 (or the Bass) instead of the 6:

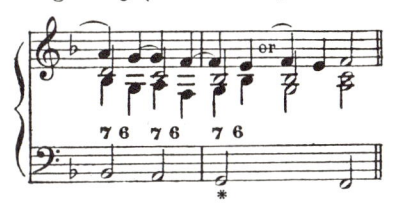

Summarizing the progressions which Ph. Em. Bach condemns, we have, besides the unresolved imperfect 5th:

(1) Octaves between extreme parts on alternate *weak* beats (*i*).
(2) Octaves between Treble and Tenor on alternate *strong* beats (*e*) (but not those on *weak* beats (*f*) (*h*)).
(3) Fifths on alternate *strong* beats between extreme parts (*g*), and also between the Bass and an inner part (*d*) (*f*).
(4) A doubled major 3rd in conjunction, not only with a suspended minor 7th (*e*), but with the 6th on which such a 7th resolves (*f*) (*g*).

Ph. Em. Bach would appear to have been especially sensitive where 5ths and 8ves—even when not immediately consecutive—were concerned.

The form of accompaniment (Ex. 2 e) which he so unequivocally condemns was apparently approved by John Sebastian Bach himself, if the two following examples may be admitted as evidence of his practice.

Ex. 3 is from Gerber's setting out of Albinoni's Bass (§ 3, note 2) and *embodies one of Sebastian Bach's corrections*. Ex. 4 is No. 3 of the examples following Exemplum viii in Cap. X of a short treatise on the treatment of a figured Bass [2] compiled by J. S. Bach for the purposes of tuition, which is printed in Spitta's *Life of Bach* (vol. iii of the English translation), Appendix B, No. 12.

Ex. 3

At * * we have the 8ves which Ph. Em. Bach condemned in Ex. 2 *e*, and which *were not present in Gerber's uncorrected version*:

It will be noticed that Gerber treats the second group of semiquavers as though figured , while Bach adds a 9th:

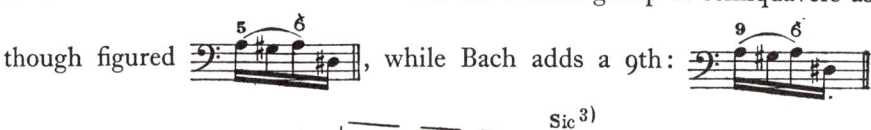

Ex. 4

[1] "Directions and principles for the playing in four parts of the Thorough-bass or Accompaniment by Herr Johann Sebastian Bach of Leipzig, Royal Court-Composer and Chapelmaster, likewise Director of Music, as also Cantor of St. Thomas's School at Leipzig for his scholars in Music", dated 1738.

[2] The genuineness of this work, as well as of Bach's corrections of Gerber's setting out of Albinoni's figured Bass (§ 3, note 2), is disputed by Schreyer. His strongest point is perhaps the fact that Kirnberger, himself a pupil of J. S. Bach, was apparently ignorant of its existence when he stated that that master had never written anything on the theory of music. This statement, however, is not irreconcilable with the existence of manuscript notes which Bach may have dictated to his pupils.

The MS., once owned by Prof. Wagener of Marburg, now in the library of the Brussels *Conservatoire*, abounds in mistakes which are, here and there, corrected by Bach's pupil Johann Peter Kellner. It was evidently the work of a very poor musician, unable to understand or to *hear* the musical examples as he wrote them down, and was presumably copied from a manuscript made by a pupil of Bach—possibly to Bach's own dictation.

Dictation undoubtedly played some part in the history of the manuscript, for a characteristic mistake is the substitution of *d* for *t* ('per Mo*d*um contrarium' instead of Mo*t*um, cf. § 7 preceding Ex. 2), and the incapacity to distinguish between the two sounds, as also between *b* and *p*, is especially marked in Saxony.

The title of the manuscript is in Kellner's handwriting, which seems a strong point in favour of its genuineness. [3] For note 3 see opposite page.

SEVENTHS

The following examples are also interesting:

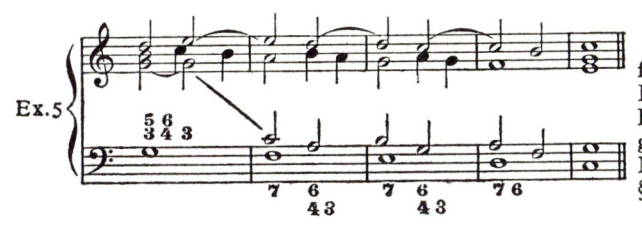

Ex. 5 — Dr. John Blow, 'Rules for playing a Thorough-Bass upon Organ and Harpsicon' [sic], autograph manuscript,[4] Brit. Mus. Add. 34072 (Ch. i, § 22).

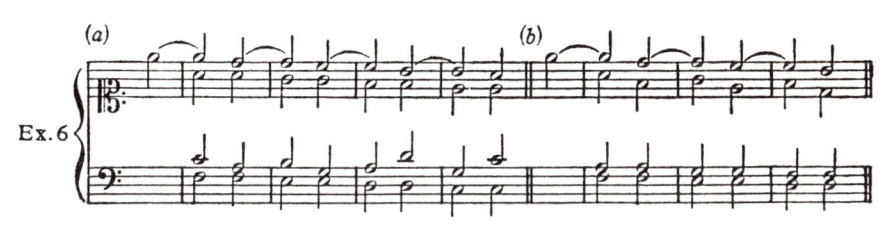

Ex. 6 — Marpurg, *Handbuch beym Generalbass*, Part II, Tab. 4.

Ex. 5 is particularly interesting on account of the appoggiatura (the 4 in the $^6_{4\ 3}$), which by its dissonance with the 3 in the Tenor adds a spice to the progression. Note the extra part in the last chord.

Both Ex. 5 and Ex. 6 *a* exhibit the 'many Fifths' to which Ph. Em. Bach objected in the case of Ex. 2 *d, f, g*.

It will also be noticed that in the last two bars of Ex. 6 *a* the 5 rises to the 8 in a way not possible in close harmony, except by allowing the parts to cross in such a way as to obscure the progression of the 7, and with very ill effect.

In Ex. 6 *b* the progression of the individual parts is the same as in Ex. 2 *e*, which Ph. Em. Bach condemned as 'disgusting on account of the Octaves'.

§ 7. *Sequences of 7 6 on a rising Bass.*

Of a 7 6 sequence on a rising Bass Ph. Em. Bach (*Versuch &c.*, Part I, Ch. 13, 1, § 16) says: "When many rising bass notes in succession are figured 7 6, one cannot well proceed otherwise than in four parts. In this case the right hand moves in the opposite direction to the left. The Octave and Third are taken both with the Seventh and the Sixth; this accompaniment (*a*) is the best; the one given at (*b*) is not so natural."

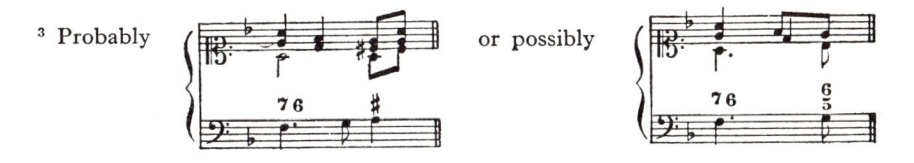

[3] Probably ... or possibly ... was intended. This is a characteristic specimen of the many blunders in the manuscript.

[4] All the examples in the manuscript are on the 6-lined stave which was in common use at the time.

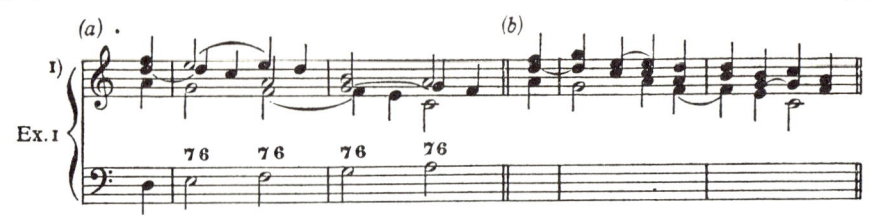

As Ph. Em. Bach points out (whether the Seventh be taken as (*a*) or (*b*)), the Sixth must in all cases be taken with doubled Bass to prepare the following 7.

The disadvantage of this form of accompaniment is that, if the sequence is a long one (which, however, is rarely the case), the hands must start very far apart in order not to meet too soon.

In the above example there is only just room to finish the scale:

J. S. Bach gives the following example [2] in the collection of rules mentioned above (§ 6, note 2):

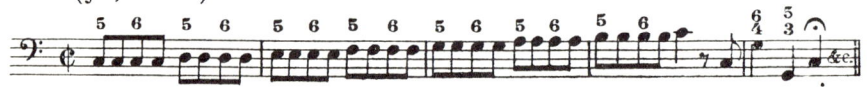

He adds: "The player must begin quite high up with the right hand and proceed *per Motum contrarium*; the Octave is to be taken with the Sixth."

This would be sheer nonsense were the figuring of the example correct, as any one who attempts to follow the above directions will realize.

The ignorance of the person by whom the existing manuscript was written, and possibly the indistinct figuring in the one from which it was copied (combined with the fact that the first two figures 5 6 are correct and that 5 6 on a rising Bass is very common, whereas 7 6 is quite the reverse), are probably responsible for the mistake.

Be that as it may, what Bach beyond any possibility of doubt intended was as follows:

---

[1] Bach gives the example an 8ve lower on a single stave.
[2] Spitta, *Life of Bach*, vol. iii (of the English translation), p. 340.

Schröter (*Deutliche Anweisung zum General-Bass*, 1772, § 238, *e*, *f*, *g*) gives the three following examples which will well repay the trouble of careful consideration. He says: "In *e*, *f*, *g* [Exx. 3, 4, 5] it is shown how, in my humble opinion,[3] one has to proceed when the Bass figured 7 6 rises two or more degrees. It is especially to be noted in such cases that one must always take a good opportunity of effecting the necessary retreat [i.e. gaining a higher position for the right hand] such as the repetition of a Sixth, or a subsequent Triad: otherwise one is caught by one's own hand."

---

[3] 'ohnmassgeblich' (mod. 'unmassgeblich') lit. 'without setting the standard' or (as we should say) 'laying down the law'.

[4] Schröter gives the top part only, with no indication as to whether he means the accompaniment to be taken in four parts (as indicated by the small notes) or as in Ex. 5.

[5] For the figuring $\widehat{5}$, see Ch. xxiii, 'Varieties of figuring', § 19.

[6] The second half of Ex. 4, like the whole of Ex. 5, is a 'Bassetto', cf. § 6, Ex. 1. In compositions of four or more principal parts—especially in fugal entries—the use of the Alto clef in the figured Bass part denotes that the Tenor (as well as the Bass) is silent. Similarly the use of the Soprano clef denotes the silence of the Alto principal part, and there are then no figures, unless two Treble (principal) parts are sounding. This is the strict usage. But in other compositions—Sonatas for one or two Solo instruments with figured Bass, and the like—the choice between the Tenor and Alto clefs, and, indeed, in some cases, even the abandonment of the Bass clef in their favour, is chiefly a matter of convenience. The Soprano clef, on the other hand, is on a somewhat different footing when it occurs in the figured Bass part. In the 'Canzonas' of Purcell's *Sonnatas of Three Parts*, 1683, for 2 Violins and Bass, it is always used to mark the entry of the 1st Violin, and the figures begin with the entry of the 2nd Violin unless the two parts appear together (cf. Ch. iii, § 6, note 2, p. 374).

Ex. 5 *(small notes added)*

In Exx. 3 and 5 we have the 'repetition of the Sixth' (in a higher position) to which Schröter alludes, and in Ex. 4 the change of position on a Triad following the Sixth.

To the latter there can be no objection, and Ph. Em. Bach would probably have prescribed the same form of accompaniment. In the latter half of the example, at all events, that shown in Ex. 1 would be out of place, as the right hand would have to begin too high up with [music] in the top part.

In Ex. 3, in which the Sixth occupies twice the time occupied by the Seventh, the repetition of the Sixth with the 8ve of the Bass in the upper part is better than in Ex. 5, where the effect is almost that of syncopated 8ves:

But the accompaniments prescribed in Ex. 1—

Ex. 3 b

would also be appropriate.

In Ex. 5 the 4-part accompaniment of Ex. 1 would be as inappropriate as in the second half of Ex. 4 and would likewise involve starting very high up:

On the other hand, the effect of thinly disguised consecutives produced by Schröter's accompaniment would almost certainly have been condemned by Ph. Em. Bach, who is our chief authority for the period to which he belonged, though in earlier times it would not have met with disapproval.

Purcell did not hesitate to prepare a 9th with the 8ve of the Bass:[7]

[music], which even in Heinichen's time (1683-1729) was *anathema*.

[7] For note see next page.

In this connexion Ph. Em. Bach (*Versuch &c.*, Part II, Ch. 17, II, § 3) says: "The old people did not scruple to write such examples as:

This syncopated (*nachschlagend*) 8 sounds no better than a 9 prepared by the 8 and resolving on the 8."

But how he would have treated Ex. 5 is another question!

In similar cases the chief vocal or instrumental part is sometimes as the upper part of Schröter's accompaniment, and in such a case the composer could not well have disapproved of the accompaniment in question.

But, much more often, the 7 6 sequence was *divided between two parts which crossed and recrossed as*:

Ex. 5*b*

In the accompaniment, however, any crossing of the parts *which on a keyed instrument produced the effect of a wrong progression* (8ves or 5ths) was expressly vetoed both by Ph. Em. Bach (*Versuch &c.*, Part I, Ch. 24, § 5) and also by Heinichen (*G. B. &c.*, 1728, Part I, Ch. 2, § 32, note *e*), though, as we shall see from Ex. 6, it was, to all intents and purposes, permitted (at all events in the progression under discussion) at an earlier period.

Ph. Em. Bach constantly advocates a delicate accompaniment, even though it involves the omission of one or other of the figures.

He gives the following general direction (ibid., Introduction, § 26): "*An accompaniment in three, or fewer, parts* is used for the sake of delicacy, when the taste, style of performance (*Vortrag*) or feeling (*Affect*) of a piece demands economy (*Menagement*) of the harmony. We shall see in the sequel that, in such cases, often none but a weak accompaniment is possible."

It therefore seems a not unreasonable conjecture that, in such a case as Ex. 5 *b*, he would, in spite of the figuring 7 6, have confined himself to a 2-part accompaniment, in Thirds only: or Thirds and Sixths:

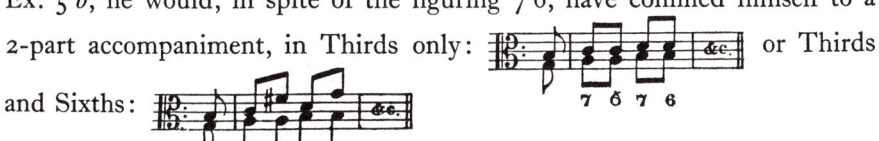

7 *Violins*

Sonatas in Four Parts, 1697, Sonata III, Canzona, antepenultimate bar.

The example might be accompanied (in three parts) as though figured 5 6:

but this would probably not have met with Bach's approval, judging by his comment on the inclusion of the 5 in another case (§ 4, Ex. 2), and Schröter [8] himself expresses his views on the point very emphatically in the following quaint note on the example in question: "If some extra sharp-sighted (*doppeltsehend*) art critic were to raise objections on the score of the example, he would thereby betray himself as having lacked the opportunity to examine passages of the kind by great masters, besides others which we have already had, or which are still to follow. On this point two questions arise: (1) Must not an accompanist (Clavierist) follow the directions of the composer according to the rule *Come sta* ('as written', i.e. 'literally')? (2) Is it not an amusing thing when, in such cases, the accompanist surpasses the composer in judgement by here using § 118, Litera *b*, *c*, at the same time?"

The examples thus alluded to are:

Schröter thus emphatically warns the accompanist against treating 7 6 on a rising Bass as a combination of a 5 6 retardation with a 7 6 suspension:

unless expressly so figured, as in the following remarkable example:

Ex. 6

Dr. John Blow, 'Rules for playing a Thorough-Bass upon Organ and Harpsicon', Brit. Mus. Add. 34072 (cf. § 6, Ex. 5).

---

[8] It seems strange that Schröter should have made no allusion to the form of accompaniment prescribed by Ph. Em. Bach (Ex. 1) and apparently taught by J. S. Bach himself (Ex. 2). Schröter's book, though not published till 1772, was completed in 1754—eight years before the appearance of Part II of Ph. Em. Bach's *Versuch*—

It is evident that a fifth part *d* enters at * and that from that point onwards *the two upper parts cross and recross* as shown below:

As far as the practical question of choosing a particular form of accompaniment is concerned, the golden rule is to adapt the accompaniment so far as possible to the style and taste of the period to which the composition in question belongs. The formula given in Ex. 6 would not have found favour in the eighteenth century by reason of the suggestion (on a keyed instrument) of syncopated 8ves between extreme parts, but, in accompanying a composition of Purcell or Blow it would be charming and appropriate.

The following example differs from the preceding one in that the 5 of the $\frac{7}{5}$ chords, instead of rising to the 6 simultaneously with the resolution of the 7 as in Ex. 6, remains while the 7 resolves, subsequently falling to the 3 of the following chord.

Ex. 7

Leclair, Opera IV, Six Sonatas for two Violins and Bass, Sonata II, Allegro ma non troppo, bar 46.

It will, however, be noticed that the main progression, as indicated by the Violin parts, is:

We, therefore, again have a combination of the progressions 7 6 and 5 6 on a rising Bass 'spiced' by the retention of the 5.

and in the 46th paragraph (p. xix) of the Introduction, which is dated 1769, he tells us that, in spite of all endeavours, he had been unable to procure a copy. But if the form of accompaniment in question had been in common use, he surely would have mentioned it.

§ 8. *The status of the 5 in a 7 6 suspension and the origin of its inclusion.*

As was seen in §§ 2–5, a Seventh resolving on $^6_3$ on the same Bass may include either a perfect or augmented 5th, whereas the imperfect 5th can, according to strict usage, only be included in cases where 7 6 can be treated as $^7_{5\flat}\,^6_4_3$, thus enabling the imperfect 5th to resolve (§ 5, Ex. *c*).

When the 5 is included in a 7 6 sequence on a *rising* Bass, as Ex. 6 in the last section, we clearly have a combination of a 5 6 retardation with a 7 6 suspension; and this is also the case whenever the perfect or augmented 5th, being included, rises to the 6 (§ 3, Exx. 2 and 3 *a*, *b*, *d*, § 4, Exx. 1 and 2).

But what is the status of the 5 which falls to the 3 of the following chord (§ 3, Ex. 1, § 6, Exx. 5 and 6 *a*) or rises to the 8 (§ 6, Ex. 6 *a*)?

Ph. Em. Bach gives an important clue when he says (with regard to the inclusion of the augmented 5th in § 4, Ex. 2): "The kind of accompaniment in which four sounding parts were invariably insisted upon [i.e. to the exclusion of duplication in the unison] is the cause of these uninvited Fifths having crept in."

Accompanists were, no doubt, often hard put to it to get the four sounding parts, and many awkward progressions resulted; and, in the present instance, the 5, being consonant with all the other parts, and therefore harmless, was a convenient addition to the chord.

Moreover, the pattern was set for its inclusion by the resolution of 7 on the Supertonic on $6 = ^6_4_3$ (II § 5, Ex. 6), as well as by the progression shown above (§ 3, Ex. 3), in which the 5 is prepared by the 3 in the preceding dominant Triad.

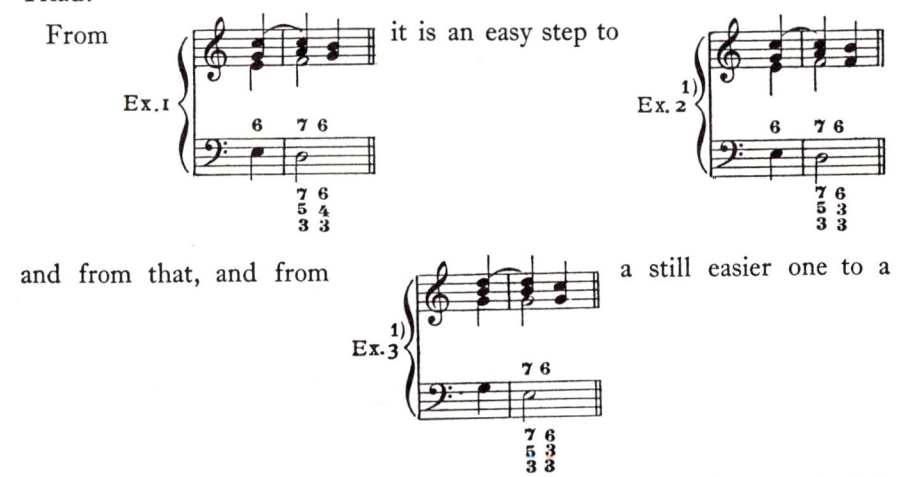

From Ex.1 it is an easy step to Ex. 2[1)]

and from that, and from Ex.3[1)] a still easier one to a

sequential use of the same progression on other degrees of the scale (§ 6, Exx. 5 and 6 *a*).

[1] Or with four sounding parts:

XI iv § 8　　　　　　　　SEVENTHS　　　　　　　　591

Some instances occur of such sequential use of $\smash{\genfrac{}{}{0pt}{}{7}{\genfrac{}{}{0pt}{}{5}{3}}}$, not (as in § 7, Ex. 7) on a rising Bass, but on a falling one, in which the 5, instead of disappearing by rising to the 6 or falling to the 3, is retained, as in the following remarkable example:

Ex 4

Antonio Vivaldi, Opera Prima, *Suonate da Camera a Tre*, Sonata IX, Preludio *ad fin.*

In the above we clearly have a sequence of $\smash{\genfrac{}{}{0pt}{}{7\ 6}{\genfrac{}{}{0pt}{}{5\ -}{3\ -}}}$ upon a falling Bass, in which the resulting consecutive Fifths with the Bass are narrowly avoided by the florid form of the latter

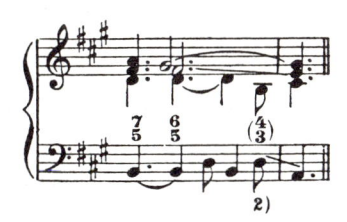

[2]

[2] Though not indicated in the figuring, it is better that the change of the Bass to a different interval of the same harmony (*b* to *d*, *a* to ♯*c*, ♯*g* to *b*) should be accompanied, at the end of each bar, by a corresponding change in the upper part concerned, whereby the latter proceeds to the note vacated by the Bass (Ch. xxii, 'Inversion &c.', § 1), so that the last semiquaver of the Bass, in each of the three groups which con-

while the last $\smash{{}^6_5}$ † of the sequence resolves, not on a Seventh on a Bass falling a degree, but on its first inversion ☰.

With regard to the retention of the 5 after the resolution of the 7: unless it is to be regarded as an entirely irregular enrichment of the harmony (cf. Ch. xii, $\smash{{}^6_5}$ chords, § 8, Ex. 8), it may possibly be explained as an instance of *anticipatio transitus* (Ch. xxii, 'Inversion &c.', § 7), in which case the progression stands for

[musical example]

in which the notes * * * are anticipated passing notes.

It may be objected that the pattern of the above sequence is set by a *wrong progression*, namely, the doubled 6 ♯g on the Supertonic b at the beginning of the first bar.

The only apparent alternative to the above hypothesis is to assume that the real progression is [musical example] and that

the 4 of the $\smash{{}^4_3}$ is delayed by a suspension, which remains *unresolved in the accompaniment* till the entry of the following harmony, but which is resolved in one of the solo parts (the 2nd Violin):

[musical example]

If this explanation is correct, the basis of the sequence is, not a 7 6 suspension, but the root progression:

[musical example]

stitute the sequence, should bear a $\smash{{}^4_3}$ (instead of being treated as a mere ornamental note), as in the suggested accompaniment given with the example. In this way the Fifths between the *accented* notes of the Bass and the accompaniment are somewhat less thinly veiled.

Ph. Em. Bach (*Versuch &c.*, Part II, Ch. 32, § 8, *b*) gives the following examples in which such unfigured inversions of the harmony are necessary, in the case of a florid Bass, in order to escape actual consecutive 8ves (1) and (2), or thinly veiled ones (3):

[musical example]

V. *Unresolving or Stationary Sevenths.*

§ 1. The 'stationary' Seventh which has its place between a Triad and its first inversion, was known in the older German text-books as *Septima in transitu* or 'durchgehende Septime' ('passing Seventh'). This, as Marpurg points out, conveys an entirely wrong idea of the nature of the chord; the 7, which owes its dissonance to a passing note in the Bass, though *transient*, is not 'passing' in the usual technical sense of the word. The 3 of the chord is also a passing note and therefore moves by step.

The chord, which never includes the 5,[1] can be taken:

(1) as $\frac{7}{3}$, either in three parts (Ex. 1), or with doubled 3 (Ex. 2 a), or doubled 8 (Ex. 2 b);

(2) as $\frac{7}{4}_{3}$ (Exx. 3, 4, 5), provided the 4 was present in the previous chord; or

(3) the 7, as an essential concord rendered temporarily dissonant, may be doubled (Ex. 6).

It will be seen that the constitution of the chord ($\frac{7}{3}$ or $\frac{7}{4}_{3}$) is mainly a matter of convenience, depending on the position in which the chords are taken.

[1] In Ex. 7 the Seventh is of a special character.

594   SEVENTHS   XI v § 1

[musical examples Ex. 5 and Ex. 6]

Exx. 1 and 5 are from Schröter's *Deutliche Anweisung zum General-Bass*, 1772, § 302; Ex. 2 (given an 8ve lower on a single stave) and Exx. 3, 4 (Bass only) are from Ph. Em. Bach's *Versuch &c.*, Part II, Ch. 13, I, § 19.

In Ex. 4 *b*, *c*, the progression from a 2nd to the unison is unpleasant, especially on the Organ.

In Ex. 5 (in the minor key) (*b*) is obviously preferable to (*a*), and in the major this would be more markedly the case.

Ph. Em. Bach (ibid., § 4) gives the following example (Bass only) of a somewhat different kind of stationary Seventh.

[musical example Ex. 7 showing (a), (b), (c), (d), (e), (f)]

He gives no indication as to whether he intends the 7 to be taken as $\smash{{}^{7}_{5} \atop 3}$ *a*, *b*, *c* or $\smash{{}^{7}_{3}}$ *d*, *e*, *f*; the former is, however, clearly the more natural.

The *d* in the Bass is really an ornamental or auxiliary note,[2] the progression being

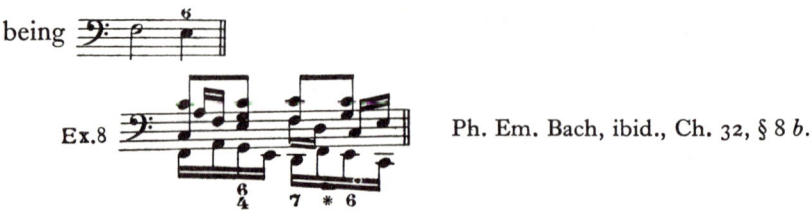

[musical example]

[musical example Ex. 8]   Ph. Em. Bach, ibid., Ch. 32, § 8 *b*.

---

[2] Cf. Ch. xviii, 'Quick notes in the Bass', § 1 (*i*).

SEVENTHS

Ex. 8 is remarkable in that the stationary Seventh on *d* falls on *a stronger beat* than the preceding concord, as in § 4, Ex. 5. Moreover, at * we find an *inversion* of the chord, $^6_5$ without the 3. This inversion is not indicated in the figuring, but (as Ph. Em. Bach points out) is necessary in order to avoid mistakes. The 3 of the 7 (*f*) is a passing note (see beginning of this §), and cannot therefore leap to *c* in the chord of resolution. The alternatives would be either consecutive unisons, *ff gg*, or 8ves with the Bass, *f e*.

The whole progression is a florid modification of

and therefore differs only in rhythm from Ex. 3.

§ 2. A modification of the progression described in the preceding section arises when the transient discord in question leads from a Triad, not to its 1st inversion, but to a $^6_5$.

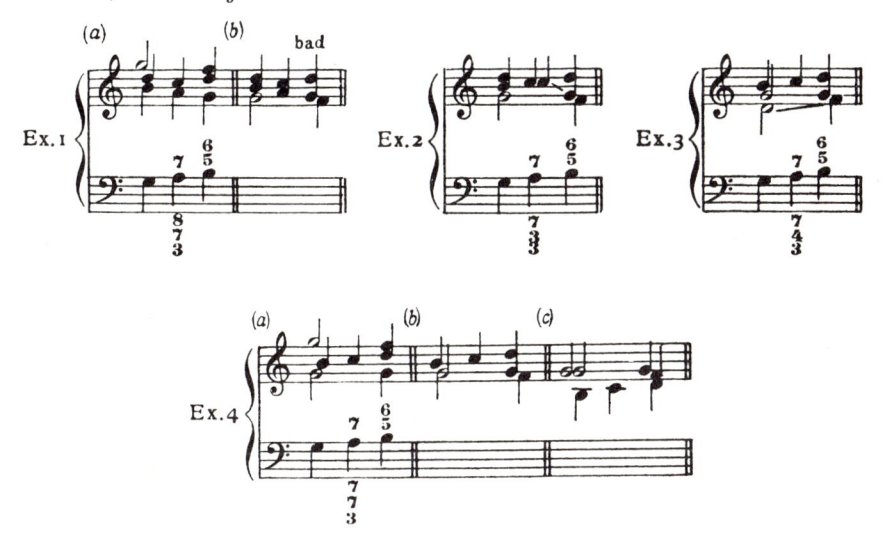

In all the above examples the root progression of the Bass is *g c* with a passing 7th *f* :

or, with the 1st inversion of a passing 7th:

The position shown in Ex. 1 *b* and Ex. 2 is the worst. Ex. 1 *b* is bad, especially on the Organ, on account of the consecutive 2nds. In Exx. 2 and 3 the progression is freest: in Ex. 2, the 3 on *a* being doubled, only one of the intervals in question moves by step; in Ex. 3, too, the 5 of the $^6_5$ on *b* is taken by leap, the preceding 7 remaining stationary. Ex. 4 *c* is sometimes useful when the hands are close together (as in the example), as the right hand is thereby precluded from executing the form of accompaniment shown in Ex. 1 *a*.

It may be noted that the progression under discussion is capable of a different explanation from the one given above.

It may also be regarded as originating in [music] with a suspended 7: [music], the resolution of the suspension then being delayed till the following bass note. This corresponds to the explanation given by Marpurg of No. 1 of the examples in the extract quoted from his *Handbuch &c.* in I, § 2 *ad init.* (see also Ch. xxii, 'Inversion of discord, &c.', § 8).

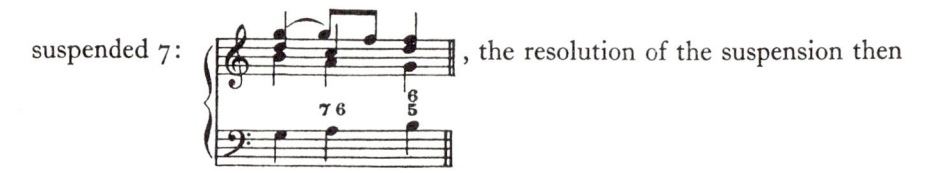

As was pointed out earlier in the present chapter (III, § 3, in connexion with Ex. 1, and § 4 in connexion with Exx. 1, 2, 6), it is quite possible for a progression to have a complex origin; the one explanation does not, therefore, necessarily exclude the other. The second one is obviously the more applicable when the 7 is on a strong beat as in Ex. 5, and vice versâ.

The commonest form of the progression is from Dominant (actual or temporary) to Tonic (Ex. 5); but it may also occur on other degrees of the scale (Ex. 6).

Ex. 5 [music]

Ex. 6 [music]

§ 3. A stationary Seventh, figured $\begin{smallmatrix}7\\6\\3\end{smallmatrix}$ if indicated at all, arises when a Seventh, which includes the 8ve of the Bass instead of the 5, is connected with its first inversion by passing notes in the Bass and the 3, as in the subjoined example:

§ 4. *Irregular unresolving Sevenths.*

Ex. 1

Handel, 7 Trios, Op. 5, Sonata III, Andante Larghetto, bars 15-16.

Ex. 2

Corelli, Opera Terza, Sonata VI, Allegro $\tfrac{6}{8}$, bars 8-10.

† The figuring of the Bass (7 6 on *a*) shows that an appoggiatura was intended in the 1st violin part.

Leclair, *Sonatas for Violin and Bass*, Bk. 3, Sonata X, Allegro assai, bars 9-10.

J. Loellet, Opera Secunda, Sonata II, Allegro, bars 28-9.

Exx. 1, 2, 3 are parallel cases. In all three the 7 *ultimately* resolves—not on 6 on the same bass note, but on the corresponding Triad—*the resolution being delayed by an intervening harmony in which the 7 stays on as a concordant note* (cf. II, § 2, Ex. 1). Thus, in all three cases, we have a disguised form of suspended Seventh. From this point of view, the main progression is:

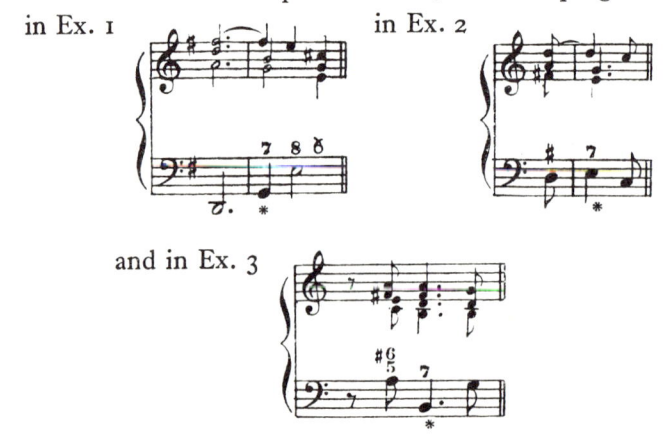

in Ex. 1   in Ex. 2

and in Ex. 3

In Ex. 4 alone the 7 remains unresolved.

All four examples may, however, be regarded—*and would probably have been regarded by most theorists of the eighteenth century*—as instances of ellipse of the resolution, or *catachresis* (Ch. xxii, 'Inversion &c.', § 8), in which case the normal progressions for which they respectively stand are:

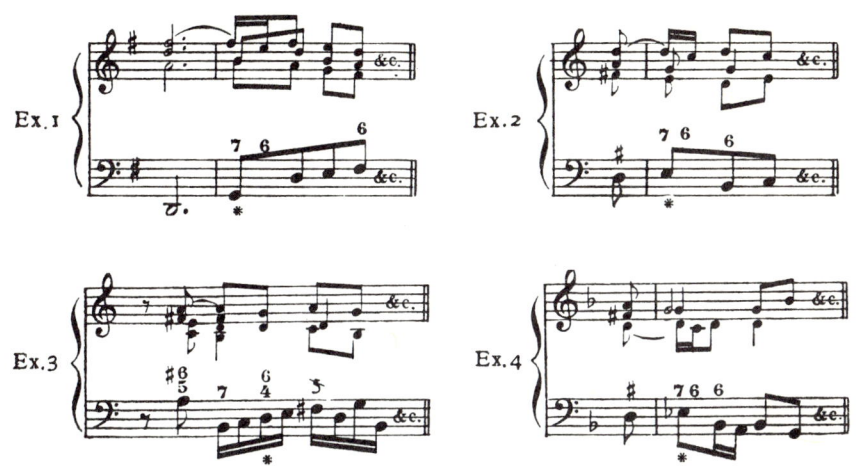

The following example is remarkable on account of the unresolved (stationary) Seventh * on the strong beat (*in thesi*).

Note also the 5 of the $^6_5$ on ♯c taken unprepared †.

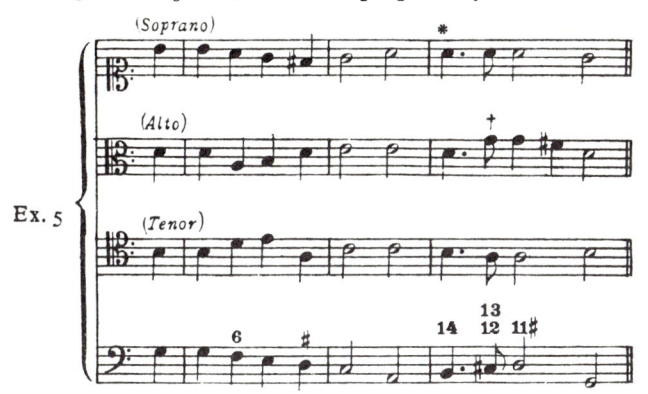

Emilio de' Cavalieri, *Rappresentatione di Anima e di Corpo Riproduzione dell' unica edizione romana dell 1600 a cura di Francesco Mantica preceduta da un Saggio di Domenico Alaleona*, Casa editrice Claudio Monteverdi, Roma, p. 3, last line.

The Bass voice part, being identical with the figured Bass, is omitted, as are also the words.

For the use of the figures 14 13 12 11 (instead of 7 6 5 4) see Ch. xxiii, 'Varieties of figuring', § 15.

CHAPTER XII
$^6_5$ CHORDS

N.B.—In chapters xii–xiv the numbering of the examples and footnotes recommences in each subsection (*a, b* &c.); i.e. the first example or footnote of each subsection is numbered 1 (cf. §2 of these chapters, and §3 of Ch. xiii).

XII
$^6_5$ CHORDS

§ 1. A $^6_5$ chord being the first inversion of a Seventh $\left(^7_3^5\right)$, its resolutions will be best understood by reference to those of the latter chord given in the previous chapter.

Figuring. The chord consists of the Sixth, Fifth, and Third, and is figured $^6_5$, unless the Third is accidentally altered, or a previous accidental contradicted, in which case it is figured $^{6\ 6\ 6}_{5\ 5\ 5}$, the figure 3 itself being usually omitted (Ch. xxiii, 'Varieties of figuring', § 3).

In figuring a $^6_5$ chord on the leading note the 6 is very commonly omitted, in which case the imperfect (diminished) Fifth, even though in accordance with the key-signature, is usually indicated by a ♭ (before or after the 5), or a stroke through the body (*not* the tail) of the figure: ♭5, 5♭, 5♭, 5 (ibid., § 5). In three-part harmony the Third is omitted.

Preparation. The rule for the preparation of the 5 is given, as follows, by Marpurg (*Handbuch &c.*, 2nd ed. 1762, *Abschnitt* (section) I, *Absatz* (subsection) IV, § 42 (1), p. 60): "The Fifth in this chord represents the Seventh in the primary chord, and is dissonant. It must therefore be prepared and resolved. When imperfect [diminished], however (in which case the $^6_5$ is derived either from the dominant Seventh or the diminished * Seventh), it can, in the free style (*in der galanten Schreibart*), be taken unprepared. But just as, in the case of the chords of the Seventh which can be struck unprepared, it is advisable that the Bass should be retained from the previous chord: so, too, in the case of $^6_5$ chords, it is advisable that the Sixth should be there beforehand."

§ 2. $^6_5$ as the first inversion of a Seventh resolving on a Bass rising a 4th (or falling a 5th).

If we take as our basis the progressions

in which a Seventh on the Dominant resolves on a Triad and a Seventh on the Tonic (in their second inversions), respectively, it is evident that, by lowering any one of the upper parts an 8ve, we shall get successively

---

* According to the above rule the taking of a $^6_5$ chord without the preparation of the 5 is therefore more restricted than in the case of the parent chord, inasmuch as the Seventh on the leading note may, in the free style, according to Marpurg's rule (Ch. xi, 'Sevenths', I, § 2), be taken unprepared in the *major as well as the minor key*.

XII § 2 $^6_5$ CHORDS   603

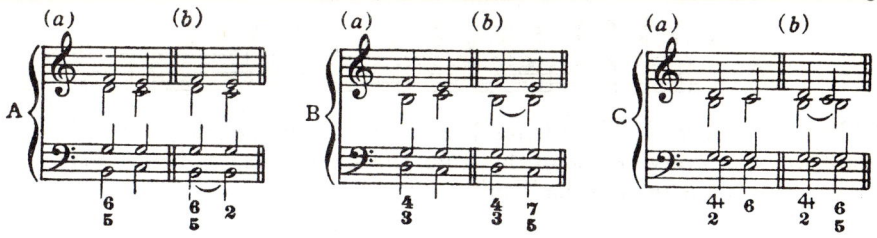

[musical examples A, B, C, each with (a) and (b)]

(*a*) $^6_5$ as the inversion of a Seventh resolving
(1) on a Triad,   (2) on another Seventh:

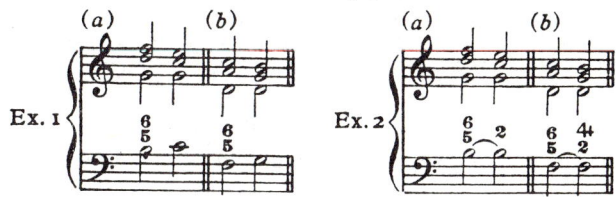

Ex. 1 [musical example with (a) and (b)]   Ex. 2 [musical example with (a) and (b)]

Individually, such $^6_5$ chords may occur on any degree of the major scale except the Supertonic, and—unless modulation follows—the Submediant.

Except in the course of a sequence, a $^6_5$ on the Supertonic, as the inversion of a Seventh on the leading note (Ch. xi, 'Sevenths', III, § 2) naturally resolves on a 6 on the Mediant [musical example], whereas a $^6_5$ on the Sub-mediant, resolving on the diminished Triad on the leading note (or a $^6_4_2$ on the same Bass), is not likely to occur unless modulation to the relative minor follows:

[musical example]

Cf. Ch. xi, 'Sevenths', II, § 5, Ex. 1 *d, dd,* note.

In the repetition of a sequence, however, a $^6_5$, resolving as in Ex. 1 or Ex. 2, may occur on every degree of the scale, Exx. 3 and 4:

Ex. 3 [musical example]

---

[1] For the use of the sign ⌒ see Ch. xxiii, 'Varieties of figuring', § 5, 1 (*b*) *ad fin.*

Ex. 4 [musical example]

In the minor mode $^6_5$ chords resolving on a Bass rising a degree to a Triad [2] may occur on every degree of the scale, the seventh degree being sharpened (Ex. 5 *) when it rises to the Tonic.

Ex. 5 [musical example]

In Ex. 6 we have a $^6_5$ with major 3rd on the 5th degree of the minor scale. In this chord the major 3rd, as the inversion of the augmented 5th in the Seventh [musical example], requires preparation, as seen in the example:

Ex. 6 [musical example]

Schröter, *Deutliche Anweisung zum General-Bass*, 1772, § 177.

[2] It is obvious that, in the minor mode, a sequence on the pattern of Ex. 4 must, in one particular, exhibit a different progression from that shown in Ex. 5, whereby it loses much of its minor character. The seventh degree of the scale, instead of rising to the Tonic as leading note in the Bass (as at * in Ex. 5) will be subject to the conditions of the descending melodic minor scale, and therefore not sharpened. The sequence would accordingly be

[musical example]

The only alternative is to break the pattern by a chromatic alteration of the seventh degree of the scale:

[musical example]

In this case ♮*g* * (the dissonant note in the $^6_4_2$ chord) is not to be regarded as prepared by the preceding ♯*g*, but as the anticipation of a passing note (*anticipatio*

XII § 2 (b) $^6_5$ CHORDS   605

(b) In the case of the $^6_5$ on the Subdominant (Ex. 1), and, less frequently, in the case of that on the leading note (Ex. 2), the resolution may be delayed [1] by the 5 remaining as a concordant note of the next harmony.

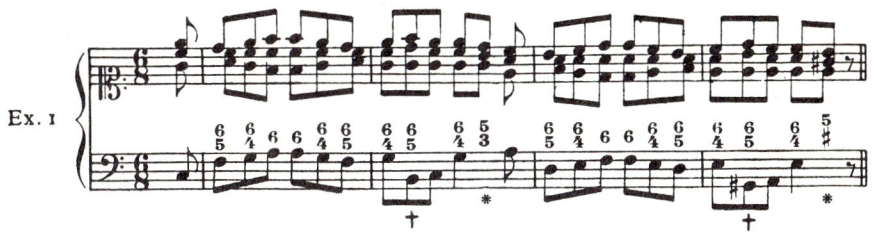

Ex. 1

Schröter, ibid., § 168, c.

Ex. 2

In Ex. 1 the resolution of the $^6_5$ with which each section of the example begins does not take place till the end of the section **, though it is possible to regard the resolution of the 5 as transferred to the Bass at † † (see Ch. xxii, 'Inversion &c.', § 3).

In cadences a $^6_5$ on the Subdominant often resolves on the dominant Seventh:

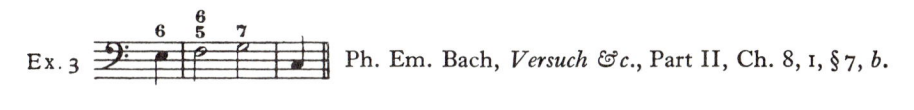

Ex. 3   Ph. Em. Bach, *Versuch &c.*, Part II, Ch. 8, 1, § 7, b.

In this case the rule was to take the chord in five parts to prepare [2] the 7:

(c) A $^6_5$ on the Subdominant, instead of resolving on the dominant Seventh itself as in the preceding example, or on its third inversion (as in § 1, Ex. 2 b), is sometimes found to resolve on its second inversion, as in Ex. overleaf.

(For 6 on the Supertonic * = $^6_4_3$ see Ch. xxi, 'Incomplete figuring', II, § 1.)

transitus per ellipsin, Ch. xxii, 'Inversion &c.', § 7), the progression standing for

(cf. Ch. xi, 1, § 2 *ad fin.*, Figs. 34 and 35 in the extract from Marpurg.

---

[1] See § 8 for cases in which the 5 remains unresolved.
[2] Even in the free style it was not, in this instance, considered good to take the dominant Seventh unprepared, the Dominant itself *not being present in the preceding chord* (see Ch. xi, 'Sevenths', I, § 2, note 4).

Ex. to § 2 c

Leclair, *Sonatas for Violin and Bass*, Bk. III, Sonata XI, Andante, 2nd sect., bar 2.

(*d*) In the minor key a cadential $^6_5$ chord *with flattened Sixth* on the Subdominant (the first inversion of a Seventh on the flattened Supertonic), analogous to the so-called Neapolitan Sixth, is sometimes found.

If the latter be taken with the ♭6 doubled, and a passing 5 * interposed between the ♭6 and the 3 of the following dominant chord, we have our $^{♭6}_5$ with its resolution.[1]

Except when thus taken *in transitu*, as in Ex. 2, the 5 must, of course, be prepared.

As in the case of the 'Neapolitan Sixth', the cadence is often delayed by the interposition of one or other inversion of the tonic chord.

For a fine example of a protracted cadence (in which both the inversions in question occur) see Ex. 3.

Ex. 1

[1] The corresponding progression, with a Seventh on the flattened Supertonic, and the Supertonic itself rising a semitone as the Seventh resolves, has not been included in the previous chapter in the absence of an instance of its use:

XII § 2 (d) $^6_5$ CHORDS   607

Leclair, *Sonatas for Violin and Bass*, Bk. II, Sonata IX, Allegro ma poco, bars 21-8.

(Note.—For Leclair's notation of accidentals, see Ch. xxiv, 'Variety of notation', § 2.)

Or the accompaniment may be taken (perhaps better) as follows:

In Ex. 2 the $^6_5$ is preceded by an ordinary 'Neapolitan' Sixth.

Ex. 2

M. C. Festing, Opera Sesta, *Six Sonatas for two Violins and Bass*, Sonata IV, Poco Allegro, bars 5 and 6 from end.

In Ex. 3 our chord is used twice ** to lead up to the cadence, being followed in each case by an inversion of the tonic chord, while in the cadence itself an ordinary $^6_5$ on the Subdominant † is used with very beautiful effect.

Ex. 3

Leclair, *Sonatas for Violin and Bass*, Bk. II, Sonata VII, Largo, 2nd section, bars 4 and 5.

608 CHORDS XII § 2 (d)

In Ex. 4 our chord * is followed by the second inversion of the tonic *major* Triad †.

Ex. 4

Leclair, Opera IV, *Six Sonatas for two Violins and Bass*, Sonata II, Largo cantabile, bars 3 and 4 from end.

The progression from the ♭$^6_5$ on *c* to the ♮$^6_4$ on *d* presents a difficulty. Taken in four parts, the choice lies between the forbidden interval of an augmented 2nd and the awkward skip of a diminished 4th which latter is best covered up by the temporary inclusion of *d* as a fifth part [2] in the ♮$^6_4$ chord as seen at †.

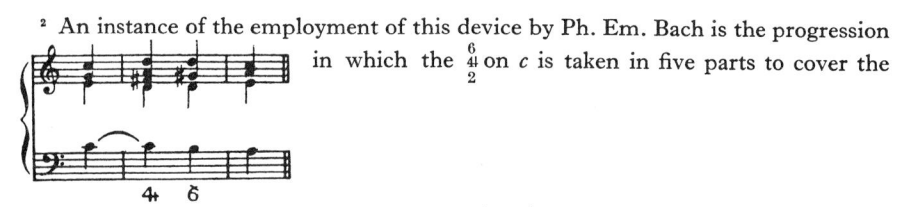

[2] An instance of the employment of this device by Ph. Em. Bach is the progression in which the $^6_{4\atop 2}$ on *c* is taken in five parts to cover the downward skip of the augmented 4th (*Versuch &c.*, Part II, Ch. 9, 1, § 10).

N.B.—The consecutive 5ths arising through the entry of a new part (as at † in Ex. 4) are not forbidden.

Marpurg (*Handbuch bey dem Generalbasse*, 2nd ed. 1762, Abschnitt [Section] II, § 2, II, note 11, pp. 96–7) says: "Fifths may also arise through the entry or disappearance of a part. They are on the same footing as Octaves of the same sort. Some examples may be seen in Fig. 17. It would be just as ridiculous to regard these

XII § 2 (d) $^6_5$ CHORDS   609

Ex. 5

Leclair, Opera IV, *Six Sonatas for two Violins with a Through Bass for the Harpiscord or Violoncello*, Sonata V, Aria, 2nd sect. (major), bars 42-50.

In the above Ex. the flattened Sixth is sharpened †, and inversion takes place ‡, before the final resolution.

(*e*) Cases in which the real resolution is disguised.

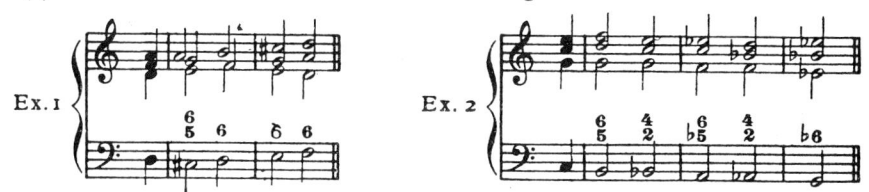

Ex. 1   Ex. 2

Ph. Em. Bach, *Versuch &c.*, Part II, Cap. 8, 1, § 5, *c*.

Fifths as faulty, as the progressions in Fig. 18 where the first Fifth originates with the middle, and the next with the upper part."

Fig. 17

Fig. 18

Ex. 3 { Türk, *Kurze Anweisung zum Generalbassspielen* ('Short Guide to Thoroughbass'), 1791, Cap. 2, I, § 56, Ex. p, p. 67.

Ex. 1 is an instance of *anticipatio transitus*, or the taking of a passing note before its time (Ch. xxii, 'Inversion &c.', § 7), the real progression being

In Exx. 2 and 3 we have instances of *ellipsis* or *catachresis* [1] ('elliptic' or 'catachrestic' resolution), i.e. the passing over or suppression of one or more notes necessary to complete the resolution (Ch. xxii, 'Inversion &c.', § 8).

In Ex. 2 a single note required for the resolution of each discord, and in Ex. 3 an entire chord is thus suppressed, as shown below:

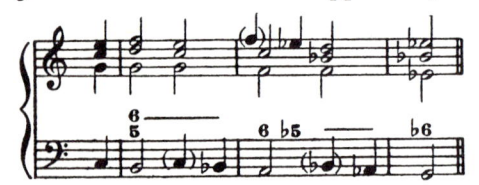

Corelli, Opera Sesta, *Concerti Grossi*, 1712, Concerto XII, Adagio, bar 10.

Ex. 4

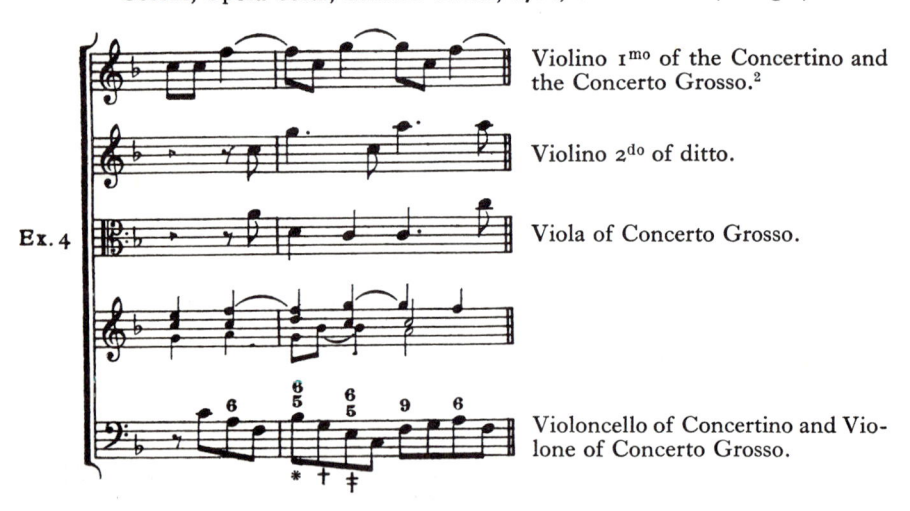

Violino 1mo of the Concertino and the Concerto Grosso.[2]

Violino 2do of ditto.

Viola of Concerto Grosso.

Violoncello of Concertino and Violone of Concerto Grosso.

In the above Ex. the root progression is

---

[1] κατάχρησις = misuse.
[2] In Corelli's Concerti the 'Concertino' took the place of a solo instrument. It

XII § 2 (e) ⁶₅ CHORDS 611

The ⁶₅ on ♭b* proceeds to its root position, ⁷₅ on g†, *not indicated in the figuring* (Ch. xxii, 'Inversion &c.', § 2); the latter resolves, not on a Seventh on c, but on its first inversion, ⁶₅ on e‡, and the 7 rises, its resolution being transferred to the Bass (Ch. xi, 'Sevenths', II, § 2, Ex. 5).

(*f*) The following example: [musical example with figures ⁶₅ 6], given without explanation by Ph. Em. Bach (*Versuch &c.*, Part II, Cap. 8, 1, § 5, *c*), is an instance of transferred resolution, the resolution of the imperfect 5th being transferred to the Bass (whereby its own progression becomes free), and that of the Bass to an upper part.

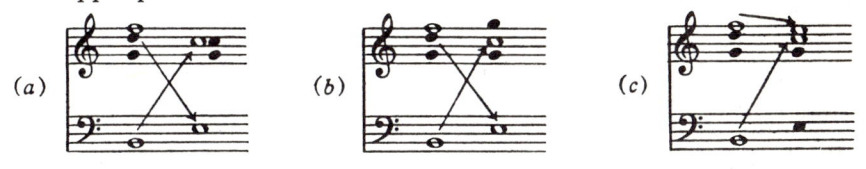

(*a*) [musical example]   (*b*) [musical example]   (*c*) [musical example]

Note.—The discords and their resolutions are printed in white notes and the remaining parts in black.

In (*a*) the Treble and Bass exchange resolutions; in (*b*) the resolution of the Treble is transferred to the Bass and that of the Bass to the Alto; and in (*c*) that of the Bass is alone transferred to the Alto (see Ch. xxii, 'Inversion &c.', § 3).

§ 3. ⁶₅ as the inversion of a minor Seventh, with major 3rd and perfect 5th resolving on a Bass rising a degree, (*a*) a whole tone, (*b*) a semitone, to a major Triad (Ch. xi, 'Sevenths', III, § 1).

(*a*) (*b*) [musical example with figures ⁶₅ 6 ⁶₅ ♭6]

§ 4. ⁶₅ as the inversion of a minor or diminished Seventh, with minor 3rd and imperfect 5th, resolving as shown in the previous chapter (III, § 2, Ex. 1). With reference to the preparation of the 5, see § 1 above.

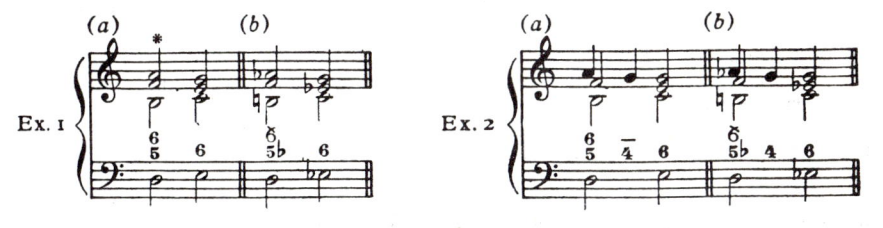

Ex. 1 { (*a*)* (*b*) [musical example with figures ⁶₅ 6 8̸5♭ 6] }   Ex. 2 { (*a*) (*b*) [musical example with figures ⁶₅ ‾4 6 8̸5♭ 4 6] }

consisted of two *obbligato* Violins and a figured Bass for Violoncello and Cembalo (Harpsichord). In the *tuttis* the Concertino was reinforced by the Concerto Grosso which consisted of two *ripieno* Violins, a Viola, and a figured Bass for the Violone, with which was associated an Organ or Cembalo, according as the composition was 'da chiesa' or 'da camera'. The *ripieno* strings could be doubled at pleasure.

* As an indication of the position in which the chord is to be taken, Schröter

§ 5. $^6_5$ resolving on a Bass rising a degree to a 6 (or $^6_5$):

I. As the first inversion of a Seventh on the Subdominant of a major or minor key resolving upon the Triad or Seventh of the Dominant (Ch. xi, 'Sevenths', III, § 3, Ex. 1 *d, e, ee*).

This $^6_5$ chord resolves either:

(1) directly upon the first inversion of the dominant harmony,

or (2) with an intervening $^6_4$ chord, upon the dominant Triad or Seventh (in which latter case the 7 is of course unprepared).

To facilitate comparison the corresponding root progression is appended to each Ex.—Exx. (*a*) are major, and Exx. (*b*) minor. Except where the contrary is stated they can be taken in any position.

It will be observed that in Ex. 1 *b* the Bass of the $^6_5$ chord is ♮*a*, as against ♭*a* in the corresponding chord in (*bb*), in accordance with the conditions of the melodic minor scale.[2]

(*Deutliche Anweisung zum General-Bass*, 1772, § 174) advocates the figuring $^5_6$ instead of the usual $^6_5$. No instances of its being taken in any other position are to hand; but in the case of the Seventh from which it is derived it was seen in the previous chapter (III, § 2) that the authorities were far from unanimous in prescribing that the 7 should be taken in the top part.

[1] In (*aa*) and (*bb*) the position with the 7 on the top is the least good as consecutive 5ths can be avoided only by the skip of the 3 to the 5 of the following chord

Ph. Em. Bach, our greatest authority where taste is concerned, laid the greatest stress on a vocal progression of all the parts ('guter Gesang') and the avoidance of all skips as far as possible.

[2] No first inversion of a Seventh *with minor 3rd* on the Subdominant, resolving on the first inversion of either a Triad or a Seventh on the Dominant, is possible, as it involves the progression of an augmented 2nd:  , neither can it resolve on the dominant chord (Triad or Seventh) in its root position since consecutive 5ths must result:

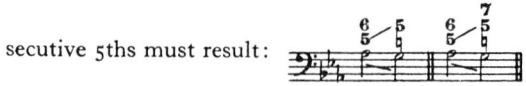

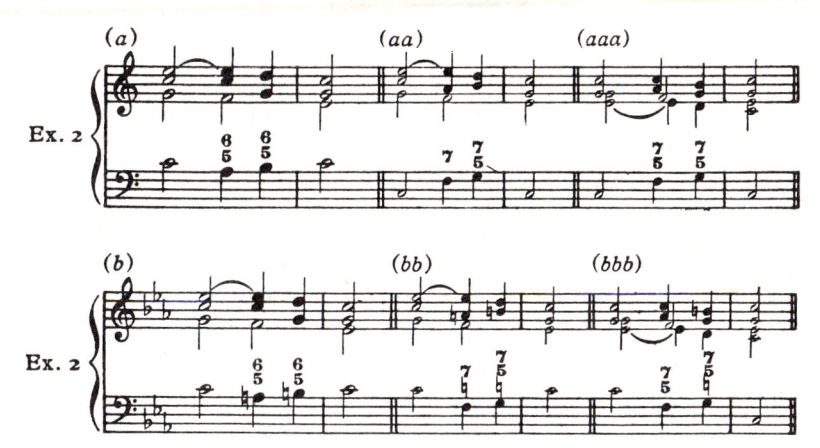

In (*aaa*) and (*bbb*) the 7 on *f* cannot be taken in the top part on account of the resulting consecutive 5ths.

In (*bb*), where the 3 of the Seventh on *f* rises to the leading note, we have ♮*a*, and in (*bbb*), where it falls to the Dominant, ♭*a*.

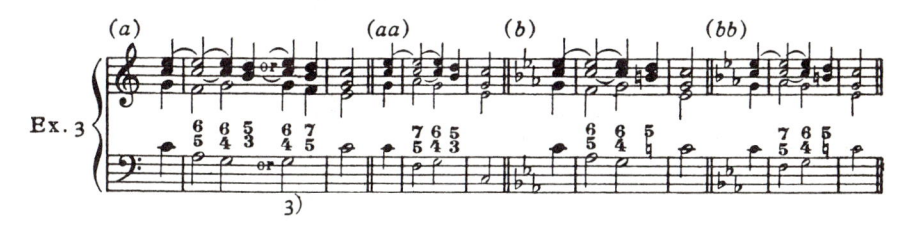

II. As the first inversion of a Seventh on other degrees of the scale resolving on a Bass rising a degree to a Triad.

M. C. Festing, Opera Secunda, *Twelve Sonatas in three Parts*, Sonata VII, Allegro, 15th to 13th bar from end.

[3] The alternative $^6_4{}^7_5$ applies, of course, equally to (*aa*), (*b*), and (*bb*).

The $^6_5$ chords at * * † in the above example represent the following progression:

The nature of the Sevenths * * on *c* and *b* as essentially $^6_5$ chords with unresolved suspended 7 (Ch. xi, 'Sevenths', III, § 3) is here clearly seen; on the following *a* † the 7 resolves. The roots of the chords * * are therefore *a* and *g*, and that of †, #*f*.

From this analysis it will be seen that the last crotchet of the penultimate bar of Ex. 4 should have been figured $^6_5$. The 5 is not present in the Violin parts (except as a passing note), and we have here an instance of 3-part thinking and figuring (Ch. xxi, 'Incomplete figuring', IV, § 1 sq.).

§ 6. $^6_5$ as the inversion of a suspended Seventh (Ch. xi, IV) resolving on $^6_3$.

(1) As the inversion of a Seventh in which the 5 is not included (ibid., § 1). In this case the $^6_5$ is a $^6_4$ chord with the 4 delayed by suspension. The 5 must therefore always be prepared. The chord does not therefore include the Third, the Bass (in 4-part harmony) being doubled instead.

It occurs over a stationary Bass and especially in Pedal points.

The following examples are from Ph. Em. Bach (*Versuch &c.*, Part II, Ch. 8, I, § 8, where they are given an 8ve lower on a single stave).

Ex. 1

Ex. 2

Ex. 3

Ex. 4

Ex. 4 begins in 'extended' harmony and the 6 (instead of the Bass) of the $^6_5$ is doubled.

"As a concession to the tyro" Bach employs Telemann's sign ⌒ (Ch. xxiii, 'Varieties of figuring', § 5, 1 *b ad fin.*) to denote the absence of the 3.

(2) As the inversion of a suspended Seventh, in which the Fifth (perfect or augmented) is included, resolving on $^6_3$ (Ch. xi, 'Sevenths', IV, § 2).

XII § 6 $^6_5$ CHORDS   615

In this case the $^6_5$, of course, includes the 3 which corresponds to the 5 of the suspended Seventh.

Ex. 5 — J. S. Bach, *Sonata in G major for two Flutes and Bass*, Presto, bars 15-16, B-g. ed. IX (K-M. I.), p. 270.

This Ex. clearly represents the progression:

Ex. 6 — Giuseppe Valentini, Opera Quinta, *XII Suonate à Tre*, Sonata VII, La Corelli, Allegro (finale), 2nd section, bars 5-7.

The above Ex. is exactly parallel to Ex. 5 except that the $^6_5$ † on *g* resolves on a Triad instead of a first inversion.

Ex. 7

In Ex. 7 the major 3rd in the $^6_5$ * on *e* corresponds to the augmented 5th in a Seventh on *c* (Ch. xi, 'Sevenths', IV, § 4, Ex. 1).

616        $^6_5$ CHORDS   XII § 6

In Ex. 8 we have the same chord, but with the major 3rd, very exceptionally, taken unprepared.

Ex. 8

J. S. Bach, *Sonata in C major for two Violins and Bass*, Largo, 4th bar from end, B-g. ed. IX (K-M. I.), p. 237.

The following Ex. (Ch. xxi, 'Incomplete figuring', IV, § 2, Ex. 9) is a particularly instructive one:

Ex. 9

M. C. Festing, Opera Sesta, *Six Sonatas for two Violins and Bass*, Sonata IV, Poco Allegro, bar 25.

The Bass is a florid fugue-subject. Cleared of the appoggiaturas and passing notes it is

The $^6_5$ on a ✳ is exactly parallel to that in Ex. 7, except that it resolves, not on $^6_4$ on the same Bass, but on the Triad. This excuses the downward progression of the 3[1] (the leading note) in the accompaniment given above (cf. Ch. xi, 'Sevenths', IV, § 3). The sequential character of the passage accounts for the imperfect Triad on the leading note ♯c †.

---

[1] If the interval in question were taken in the *upper part*, it would, of course, have to rise:

XII § 6 $^6_5$ CHORDS   617

Note also the irregular resolution of the $^6_5$ on the leading note * (cf. Ex. in § 2 *f*).

The Ex. is a characteristic instance of the way in which the unalterable character of a fugue subject is liable to modify a simple progression. If Festing had written the movement after the manner of the Canzonas in Purcell's Sonatas,[2] in which, in addition to the figured Bass of the harpsichord, the Violoncello has a florid Bass, the passage would probably have been treated as follows (omitting the Violin parts):

The following Ex. is a particularly instructive one:

Ex. 10

Corelli, Opera Prima, *Sonate da Chiesa a Tre. Due Violini, e Violone col Basso per Organo.* Roma, 1681. Sonata I, Grave, bars 6–8.

The $^6_5$ on ♭*b* * resolves as the first inversion of a suspended Seventh (including the 5) on the Supertonic *g*, and is, therefore, on a par with the $^6_5$ chords which occur sequentially in Exx. 5 and 6. The $^6_3$ on which it resolves then becomes the pivot chord in the modulation to D minor, being quitted in that key.

The $^6_5$ on *a* † is a $^6_4$, with the 4 delayed by suspension, as in Exx. 1–4.

The $^6_5$ chords in the foregoing examples have been classified, in exact

---

[2] 'Sonnatas [sic] of three Parts', 1683, and 'Sonatas in four parts' (posthumous), 1697. Both sets are for two Violins and Thoroughbass and Violoncello. Curiously enough, the only bit of real four-part writing (not counting the florid Violoncello parts in the Canzonas) is in the 'Sonnatas in *three* parts', Sonata V, Largo).

[3] Consecutive 8ves arising, as above, between a florid part (which the accompanist had not got before him) and the accompaniment were disregarded. In the accompaniment of Ex. 9 8ves with the Bass have been avoided by an inversion of the harmony ‡ †. Cf. Ch. iv, 'Certain niceties &c.', § 5 (*f*), Ex. 17.

accordance with the progression of their intervals, as the inversions of a suspended Seventh in which the 5 is included. This does not, however, necessarily imply that the latter is the parent progression *in the same sense that an essential Seventh is the parent of an essential* $^6_5$.

It seems not unlikely that the $^6_5$ chords in Exx. 5 and 6 have a different origin, namely, the anticipation of a passing note. In such case the progression in Ex. 5 stands for:

which (except for the passing 5) is exactly parallel, in the progression of the intervals, to [music example] (Ph. Em. Bach, *Versuch &c.*, Part II, Ch. 3, § 10.)

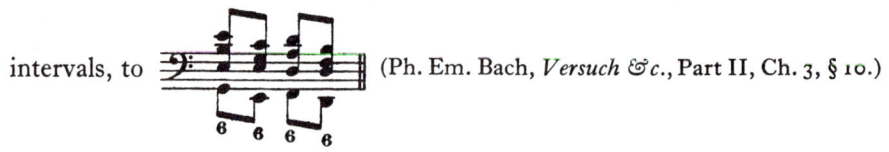

§ 7. $^6_5$ as the inversion of a Seventh resolving on another Seventh on a Bass falling a 3rd, as:

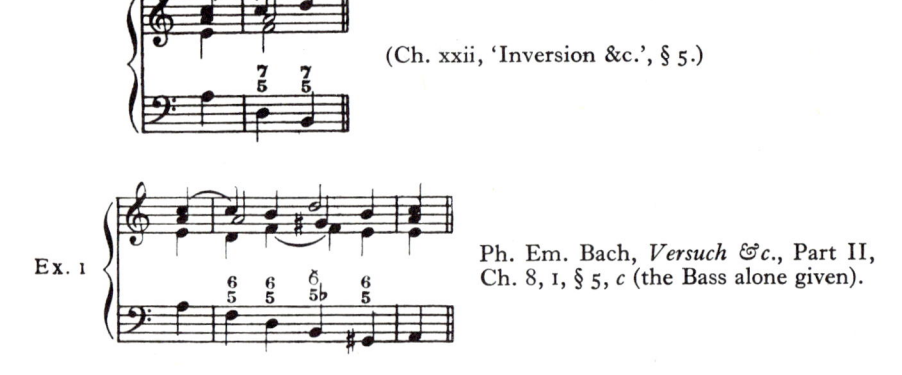

(Ch. xxii, 'Inversion &c.', § 5.)

Ex. 1

Ph. Em. Bach, *Versuch &c.*, Part II, Ch. 8, 1, § 5, *c* (the Bass alone given).

The progression of Sevenths which this represents is

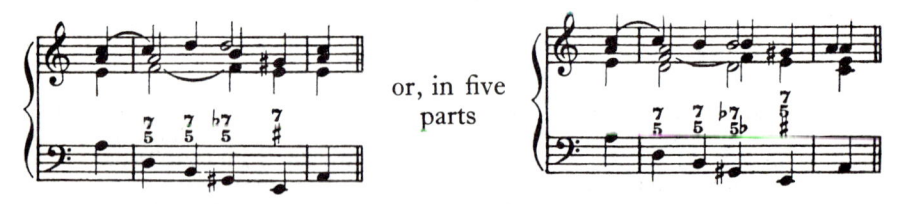

or, in five parts

It will be seen (Ch. xxii, 'Inversion &c.', § 5) that, where one Seventh resolves on another on a Bass falling a 3rd, one or the other *is really a* $^6_5$ *with the* 6

XII § 7 $^6_5$ CHORDS   619

delayed by suspension. In the above progression it is evidently the Sevenths on *d* and ♯*g* which answer this description and the root progression is

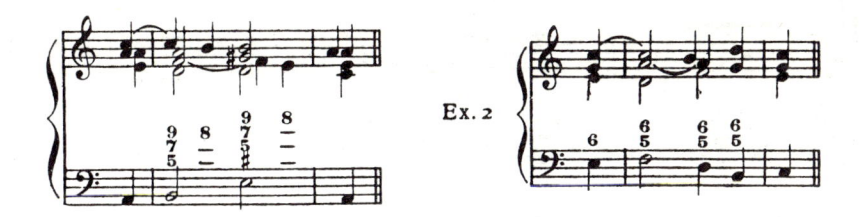

[musical example]   Ex. 2   [musical example]

In Ex. 2 the $^6_5$ on *f* represents an essential Seventh on the Supertonic *d*, and that on *d* a Seventh on the leading note, which, as we saw (Ch. xi, 'Sevenths', III, § 2), is in its origin a $^6_5$ with the 6 delayed by suspension. The progression therefore stands for

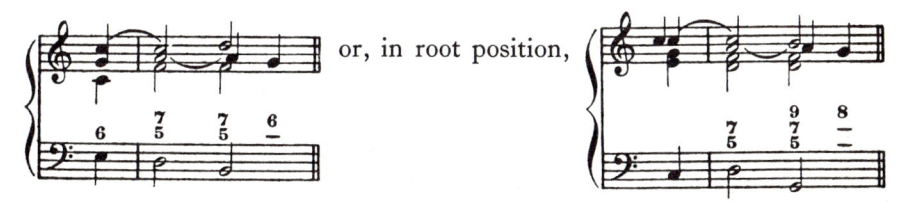

[musical example]   or, in root position,   [musical example]

The analysis of a progression is sometimes complicated by modulation. As was pointed out (Ch. xi, 'Sevenths', I, § 1, note), a chord can be taken as an essential discord and quitted as a suspension, and of course vice versâ.

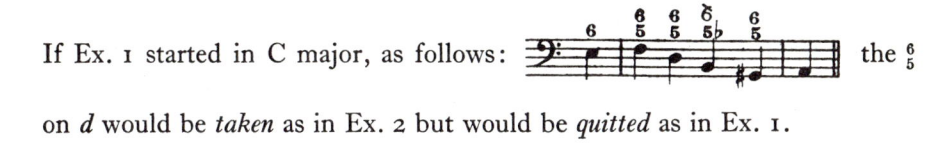

If Ex. 1 started in C major, as follows: [musical example] the $^6_5$

on *d* would be *taken* as in Ex. 2 but would be *quitted* as in Ex. 1.

J. S. Bach, *Sonata for two Violins and Bass in C major*
Alla Breve, B-g. ed. IX (K-M. I.), p. 236, ll. 1 sq.

Ex. 3 [musical example]

[musical example]

Here the root progression (given in five parts, without which every alternate Seventh would lack the 5) is

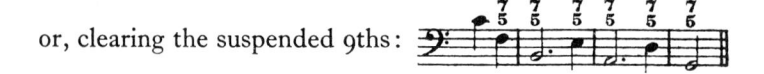

[musical example]

or, clearing the suspended 9ths: [musical example]

This example is particularly interesting from a practical point of view, as an instance in which (at all events on an Harpsichord, on which the chords do not sound so heavy) a 5-part accompaniment is desirable—the fifth part being, of course, dropped as soon as it is no longer required.

The alternatives are:

(1) [musical example]

which entirely spoils the symmetry of the sequence, as the position in which each group of chords is taken is shifted (to a higher one) from bar to bar,

(2)   (a) [musical example]

or, in a higher position (with passing notes † † †, if desired, in the top part),

(b)

in which the 5, expressly prescribed in Bach's figuring, is omitted from the Sevenths * *.

In both (1) and (2) the resolution of the 7 is transferred to the Bass (Ch. xxii, 'Inversion &c.', § 4); in (1) it rises a degree, but in (2) it falls a 4th, a progression of which no instance is to hand except in the case of the dominant Seventh resolving on the first inversion of the tonic Triad (ibid., § 4, Ex. 10).

Of the two alternatives, however, (2) is certainly preferable to (1), and, on a modern Pianoforte, perhaps more suitable than the heavier 5-part accompaniment.

§ 8. $_5^6$ chords in which the 5 does not resolve.

(1) As an inversion of the Stationary Seventh (Ch. xi, 'Sevenths', v, § 1) seen at † in Exx. 1, 2.

Ex. 1

Marpurg, *Handbuch bey dem Generalbasse*, 2nd ed. 1762, *Abschnitt* (Section) I, *Absatz* (Subsection) IV, § 42, 4, p. 62.

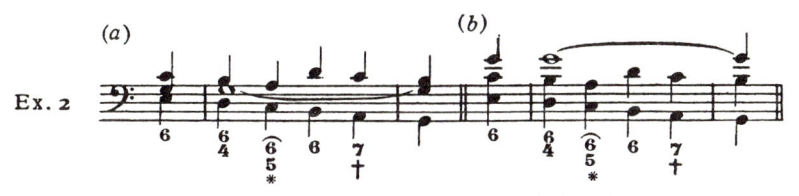

Ex. 2

Ph. Em. Bach, *Versuch &c.*, Part II, Ch. 8, 1, § 10.

The three-part harmony shown in both examples is the most natural. Marpurg gives Ex. 1 (in letters, not in notes) in three parts, and Ph. Em. Bach indicates the absence of the 3 from the $_5^6$ by the use of Telemann's sign ⌒ (Ch. xxiii, 'Varieties of figuring', § 5, (1) *b ad fin.*). He says: "When our chord [i.e. a $_5^6$] occurs as a passing chord (*im Durchgang*) the Fifth is not resolved, but remains stationary; in this case the addition of the Third is not an improvement, so it is better omitted and only the Sixth and Fifth taken." Marpurg condemns the common practice of calling the chord in question a 'passing' chord. He points out that in the stationary 7, $_5^6$, $_3^4$, and $_2^4$ we have a Pedal Point: in the first three instances an inverted one.

For a further Ex. (from Kirnberger) see note 2.

(2) Other instances in which the 5 does not resolve, and in which the Bass does not, as above, move by step.

The most familiar instance is Rameau's 'Grande Sixte' or 'Sixte ajoutée'

622   ⁶₅ CHORDS   XII § 8

('chord of the added Sixth'[1]) on the Subdominant of a major or minor key, Ex. 3:

[Ex. 3: musical notation with (a) and (b)]

The chord probably originated in the 'ornamental' progression [musical notation] as seen in the following example from Leclair:

Leclair, Opera IV, *Six Sonatas for two Violins and Bass*, Sonata III, Allegro, bars 20-23.

[Ex. 4: musical notation]

If this supposition is correct,[2] we again have an instance of *anticipatio transitus* (Ch. xxii, 'Inversion &c.', § 7):

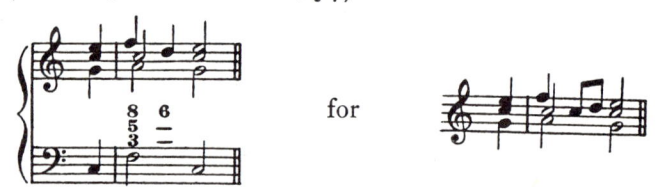

[musical notation] for [musical notation]

---

[1] The term 'Added Sixth' has often been wrongly applied to a cadential ⁶₅ on the Subdominant (§ 2 a, Ex. 1 b) which Rameau himself recognized as the first inversion of a Seventh on the Supertonic, and therefore perfectly distinct from his 'Sixte ajoutée'.

[2] Kirnberger, however, gives a different explanation. In giving the following example of the 'stationary' 5 in a ⁶₅ chord in the free style:

[musical notation]   (Cf. Exx. 1, 2 above.)

he adds, in a note: "It is in this treatment of the ⁶₅ chord that the half close by means

XII § 8 $^6_5$ CHORDS

exactly as Marpurg explains the familiar progression

as originating in   (Ch. xi, 'Sevenths' I, § 1, extract from Marpurg *ad fin*.)

Ex. 5   Leclair, ibid., Sonata II, Adagio, bars 20-22.

In the first bar of the above Ex. there is a temporary modulation to the key of ♭E, but the rest is in ♭B; the $^6_5$* is therefore not, as in Ex. 3, on the Subdominant, but on the Tonic.

Ex. 6   Leclair, ibid., Allegro ma non troppo, bar 55.

of this chord, to which they have given the name of the 'Accord de la Sixte ajoutée', originates." (*Kunst des reinen Satzes*, *Abschnitt* (Section) V, 5, p. 87.) The one explanation does not necessarily exclude the other; as has been pointed out more than once, it is quite possible for a progression to originate in more than one way.

[3] The original edition is not accessible and the Bass part in Walsh's reprint being printed very close it is impossible to determine with certainty whether the figuring was intended as above (in which case it would have been safer to have figured the ♭♭ $^5_3$ $^6_5$) or whether the $^6_5$ was intended to be over the note. In this instance, however, it is not of great moment.

[4] For the use of a fifth part in the first two chords cf. § 2 *b*, Ex. 3.

624 $^6_5$ CHORDS XII § 8

In Ex. 6 the $^6_5$ is again on the Tonic, but is preceded and followed, not by a Triad on the Dominant, but by a *Seventh*.

Leclair had an extraordinary predilection for the $^6_5$ chord (cf. Ch. xi, 'Sevenths', IV, § 7, Ex. 7) and its use here involves the ellipse of the resolution of the leading note in the preceding dominant Seventh (see Ch. xxii, 'Inversion &c.', § 8). The more natural progression would undoubtedly have been:

Leclair, ibid., bar 9.

Ex. 7

N.B.—The accompaniment is given in a low position (below the Bass on the third crotchet of the bar) on the supposition that the Bass is played in 8ves (see Ch. iii, 'The general character of a figured Bass Accompaniment', § 7). The position would be incorrect on account of the diminished Fifth falling to a perfect one, of which Ph. Em. Bach says (*Versuch &c.*, Part II, Ch. 2, I, § 22) that it is 'allowed only in case of need'.

The progression in the above Ex. is exactly parallel to that in the preceding one. The monotony of repeating the same harsh progression twice over in the same position would be avoided by the liberty of taking the $^6_5$ chords as in Exx. 4 and 5, i.e. as Triads with an 'ornamental resolution' (if the term may be applied to a concord) as follows:

XII § 8 $^6_5$ CHORDS   625

Leclair, *Sonatas for Violin and Bass*, Bk. III, Sonata XI, Andante, 2nd section, bar 1.

Ex. 8 [musical notation]

N.B.—The continuation of the passage will be found in the Ex. in § 2 c. The stroke, denoting the continuance of the same harmony, is accidentally omitted in the original after the $^6_5$, but there can be no doubt that it was intended. The figure, as well as the subsequent stroke, is also omitted over the seventh semiquaver *a*.

The above Ex. affords a remarkable instance of Leclair's use of the $^6_5$ with stationary 5.

The main progression is undoubtedly [musical notation]

The suspended Seventh on *g* includes the 5 which, instead of disappearing when the 7 resolves, is retained as a discord (apparently with the sole object of enriching the harmony), again becoming concordant as the Octave of the following Bass *d*.

§ 9. Unessential (passing) $^6_5$ chords.

Just as the resolution of a discord is sometimes to be explained by *anticipatio transitus* (cf. § 2 e, Ex. 1), so the discord itself (as was suggested in connexion with § 8, Ex. 3) sometimes owes its origin to the anticipation, either of a passing note, as in Exx. 1 and 2 below, or of a note *belonging to the following harmony*, as in Ex. 3.

Ex. 1 [musical notation]

Schröter, *Deutliche Anweisung zum General-Bass*, 1772, § 168, *a*.

Ibid., § 176.

Ex. 2 [musical notation]

Ex. 1 originates in

[musical example]

and Ex. 2 in

[musical example]

Ibid., § 168, b.

Ex. 3

[musical example]

N.B.—On the fourth crotchet of each bar Schröter uses Telemann's sign ⌢ (Ch. xxiii, 'Varieties of figuring', § 5, 1 (b) ad fin.), not in its usual signification, but to denote the imperfect (diminished) 5th, as the equivalent of the usual ♭5 or 5̸.

In the above Ex. the $\frac{6}{5}$ * owes its origin to the anticipation of the f in the following chord; thus the progression (no doubt unconsciously conceived on the analogy of that shown in § 5, Ex. 2) stands for

[musical example]

§ 10. $\frac{6}{5}$ as the 1st inversion of a retarded major 7th on the Tonic (Ch. xv, 'Major Sevenths &c', § 5).

(a)   (b)

[musical example]

Schröter, *Deutliche Anweisung zum General-Bass*, 1772, § 178.

In (b) the upward resolution of the 5̸, instead of taking place over the same bass note, is delayed till the following chord.

CHAPTER XIII

$\frac{4}{3}$ CHORDS

N.B.—In chapters xii-xiv the numbering of the examples and footnotes recommences in each subsection (*a*, *b* &c.) i.e. the first example or footnote of each subsection is numbered 1 (cf. § 2 of these chapters, and § 3 of Ch. xiii).

XIII
$\frac{4}{3}$ CHORDS

§ 1. Constitution and figuring of the chord.

As the second inversion of $^7_5_3$ the chord consists of the Sixth, Fourth, and Third.

In three-part harmony the Sixth is omitted in certain cases, and in others, the Fourth.

With regard to the figuring, Ph. Em. Bach (*Versuch &c.*, Part I, Ch. 7, I, § 2) says: "It [i.e. the chord] is indicated by the figuring $^4_3$. The eye is more accustomed to this figuring than to $^3_4$ ‡, which some use. The 6 is only added when it is accompanied by an accidental (*a*); or when it constitutes the resolution of a preceding discord (*b*); or when it is connected by a passing note over the same Bass with an interval of another chord (*c*)."

For special usages in the matter of accidentals and their contradiction see Ch. xxiv, 'Varieties of notation', § 2.

In the case of $^6_4_3$ on the Supertonic (actual or temporary) of either a major or minor key the ambiguous figuring 6 (♯6, 6, ♮6) is commonly found (Ch. xxi, 'Incomplete figuring', II, § 1); so also in the case of $^6_4_3$ on the Submediant of the minor scale. In certain cases, too, 6 on the Submediant of the major scale is to be taken as $^6_4_3$ (as below, § 2*b*, Ex. 1).

For Leclair's use of ♭6 = $^6_4_3$ (irrespective of whether the Sixth be major or minor) see Ch. xxiii, 'Varieties of figuring', §§ 8, 9.

Preparation. With regard to preparation, Marpurg (*Handbuch &c.*, 2nd ed. 1762, *Abschnitt* (section) I, *Absatz* (subsection) IV, § 43, p. 63) says that "the Third in this chord represents the Seventh of the parent chord, and is dissonant. It must therefore be prepared and resolved. In the free style, however, it is perhaps (*allenfalls*) enough if only the Fourth is present beforehand; and the Four-Three chord with the augmented Fourth [and minor Third] on the fourth degree of a minor key frequently occurs, in the free style, with no preparation whatsoever."

It will be remembered that, in the case of the $^6_5$, the latitude above mentioned is accorded only in the case of $^6_5$ *with a diminished Fifth*, as the inversion of either a dominant Seventh or a diminished Seventh.

§ 2. $^6_4_3$ as the second inversion of $^7_5_3$ resolving on a Bass rising a Fourth (or falling a Fifth).

‡ It was only in the case of $^4_3$ on the Subdominant of the major key, resolving on the first inversion of the tonic Triad (§ 3 *a*), that some composers used the figuring $^3_4$ to indicate the position in which the chord sounds best, both in its root position (cf. Ch. xi, 'Sevenths', III, § 2), and in its second and third inversions (cf. Ch. xii, '$^6_5$ Chords', § 4, note).

XIII § 2 $^4_3$ CHORDS   629

In the progression of its Bass this chord has greater freedom than either the corresponding $^6_5$ or $^4_2$. For, whereas the Bass of the two latter has a fixed progression, that of the $^4_3$ can either fall a degree to a root position, Ex. 1 (*a*), or rise a degree to a first inversion (*b*).

Ex. 1

In this latter case the Bass has the note on which the dissonant 3 resolves, and the resolution may be regarded as transferred to the Bass (Ch. xxii, 'Inversion &c.', § 3), thus leaving the 3 free in its progression (*c*).

As a matter of fact, this free progression of the 3 is seldom, if ever, to be met with in the Exx. given by the best authorities of the eighteenth century, except where it is necessary to make the following chord complete, as in the common modulation[1] Ex. 2:

Ex. 2

Ph. Em. Bach, *Versuch &c.*, Part II, Ch. 7, 1, § 6.

(given an 8ve lower on a single stave).

It would also be necessary in order to avoid doubling a leading note, whether accidentally sharpened,[2] as in Ex. 3, or diatonic.

Ex. 3

---

[1] See § 2 *d*, Ex. 1 *a*.
[2] In enumerating the intervals which may not be doubled, the old German treatises on Figured-Bass rarely referred to the leading note (variously known as *Subsemitonium Modi, Semitonium, Character Modi, Chorda VII*, &c.) as such; the rule usually given, e.g. by Ph. Em. Bach, was that an interval *accidentally sharpened* must never be doubled. In his *Versuch* (Part II, Ch. 3, 1, § 14) he gives the following Ex.:

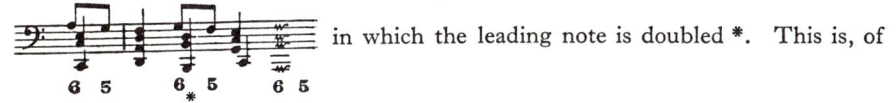

in which the leading note is doubled *. This is, of course, excused by the sequential nature of the passage, but had the Ex. been noted as in the key of F major it is very doubtful whether Ph. Em. Bach would have allowed it.

In the major key, $\frac{4}{3}$ chords, resolving as above, can occur individually on every degree of the scale except the Tonic and Subdominant. Except in the repetition of a sequence, $\frac{4}{3}$ on the Tonic cannot resolve on the imperfect Triad on the leading note (unless modulation follows, and the latter is quitted as Supertonic of the relative minor); the Bass, therefore, can only rise, Ex. 4 *.

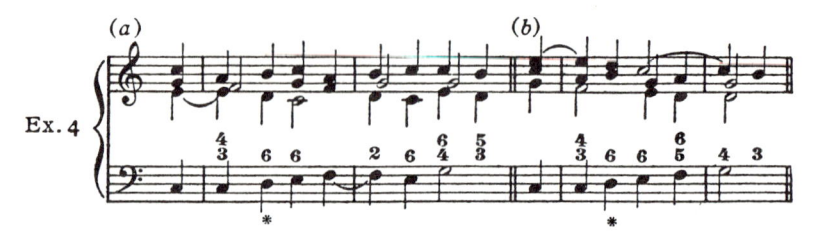

As the inversion of a Seventh on the leading note (Ch. xi, 'Sevenths', III, § 2), $\frac{4}{3}$ on the Subdominant naturally resolves on 6 on the Mediant (§ 3 a).

In the repetition of a sequence, however, $\frac{4}{3}$ on the Tonic and Subdominant resolves as on other degrees of the scale, Ex. 5 * †.

Schröter, *Deutliche Anweisung &c.*, 1772, § 186.

N.B.—The above Ex. is in the free style, as is shown by the change from the first to the second inversion of the same harmony in each bar, while, in the second half of the Ex., the resolution is on a stronger beat than the discord. The root progression is

In the minor key, $\frac{4}{3}$ can occur individually (as opposed to sequentially) on every degree of the descending [3] melodic minor scale. The following points are to be noted:

(1) In $\frac{4}{3}$ on the Tonic the 6 may be either *minor*, in which case the Bass

---

[3] A chord figured $\frac{4}{3}$, and apparently resolving as an essential $\frac{4}{3}$, may occur upon the sharp seventh degree (leading note) of the minor scale, as in the following Ex. *:

It is, however, the inversion, not of an essential Seventh, but of a suspended 7, accompanied by a retarded augmented 5th, on *c* (Ch. xi, 'Sevenths', iv, § 4, Ex. 3). Its

XIII § 2 $\frac{4}{3}$ CHORDS   631

may either fall to a Triad on the flat seventh degree of the scale (Ex. 6 (a) *), or rise to its first inversion (b) *,

Ex. 6

or it may be *major*, in which case (as in Ex. 4) the Bass can only rise to a major Sixth on the Supertonic (Ex. 7 *).

Ex. 7

(2) A $\frac{4}{3}$ chord (with perfect Fourth) on the Subdominant (Ex. 8), as the second inversion of $\frac{7}{5}$ on the flat seventh degree of the scale, is an entirely different chord from $\frac{4}{3}$, the inversion of a diminished Seventh on the leading note, which cannot (like its analogue in the major key) resolve otherwise than on the first inversion of the tonic Triad (§ 3a, Ex. 3), even in a Sequence.

Ex. 8

proper resolution on a Triad on *a* (§ 5, Ex. 2) is disguised by the change of harmony (from $\frac{5}{3}$ to 6) at the moment of resolution.

The progression, therefore, stands for

(cf. Ch. xii, '$\frac{6}{5}$ Chords', § 2a, Ex. 6).

[4] The alternative to the bad progression (c) of a diminished 5th rising to a perfect one would be to leave the following chord minus the 3:

(3) On the Submediant, $\frac{4}{3}$ can only resolve on a Bass falling a degree to the dominant Triad, as in Ex. 8 *a* †.

When $\frac{4}{3}$ occurs sequentially in the minor key, the seventh degree of the scale is sharpened only over the Supertonic (Ex. 9 *).

Ex. 9

§ 2 *a*. $\frac{4}{3}$ as the inversion of a Seventh resolving:

I. *Upon a Triad.*

Schröter, *Deutliche Anweisung &c.*, 1772, 188.

Ex. 1

N.B.—The small notes indicate the parts which Schröter did not trouble to fill in.

The above Ex. presents, in all three positions, $\frac{4}{3}$ on the Dominant of the major scale, which alone was omitted in Schröter's example of a sequence (§ 2, Ex. 5).

In the following Exx. the dissonant 3 appears without preparation, moving by step in Thirds with the Bass, and thus giving the chord the character of a passing chord. In Exx. 2, 3, and 5 the $\frac{4}{3}$ is on a weak beat (*in arsi*); in Ex. 4 it is *in thesi*.

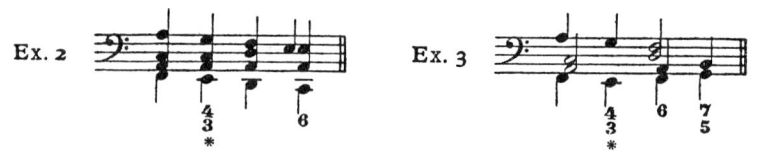

Ex. 2   Ex. 3

Ph. Em. Bach, *Versuch &c.*, Part II, Ch. 7, I, § 8 (=9).[1]

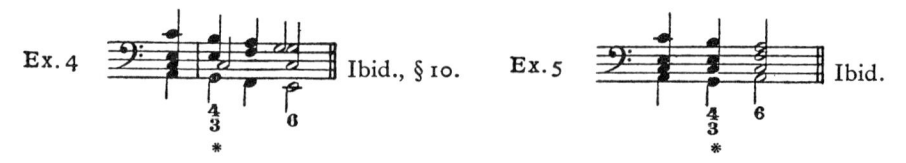

Ex. 4   Ibid., § 10.   Ex. 5   Ibid.

Of Exx. 2 and 3 Ph. Em. Bach says that they "occasionally occur, but are

---

[1] In Ch. 7, I, of the *Versuch*, Part II, by a misprint not rectified in the later ed. of 1797, two consecutive sections are headed '§ 8'.

XIII § 2a $\frac{4}{3}$ CHORDS   633

not particularly good". In the case of Ex. 3 he suggests improving the progression by sharpening the Sixth [2] as follows:

With regard to Exx. 4 and 5 he merely says that they "bear a chord of the Sixth better than $\frac{4}{3}$".

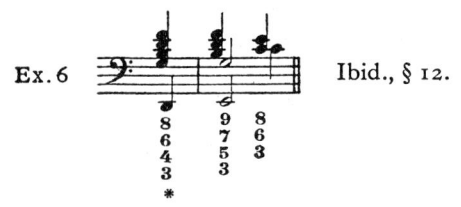

Ex. 6   Ibid., § 12.

In the above Ex. the Bass of the $\frac{4}{3}$ must be doubled, to prepare the following 9. Ph. Em. Bach adds: "It is well that all four figures should be given, that one may not have to guess."

Ex. 7   Ibid., § 6.

In Ex. 7 we have modulation, the $\frac{4}{3}$ on d * being taken as on the Supertonic in c major (§ 2, Ex. 1) and quitted as on the Tonic in d minor (cf. § 2, Ex. 7).

The omission of an interval in three-part harmony.

In three-part harmony the $\frac{4}{3}$ chord is at a disadvantage as compared with either the $\frac{6}{5}$ or the $\frac{4}{2}$, since it is the Bass which corresponds to the interval which can best be spared from the parent $\frac{7}{5}_3$, namely the 5.

If, therefore, an interval is to be omitted, it must be that one of which the absence is least calculated to rob the chord of its character.

The 3, as the dissonant note, can, *primâ facie*, be least well spared.

On the other hand, if the 4 (corresponding to the Bass of the parent chord) be absent, dissonance of the 3 ceases to be real.

The 6 (corresponding to the 3 of the parent chord) can, therefore, best be spared, except when it is the leading note—the *Character Modi*, as it was sometimes called.

Thus, in the case of $\frac{4}{3}$ on the Supertonic (actual or temporary), the 4 must be omitted (Ex. 8), and in the case of $\frac{4}{3}$ on the Submediant (Ex. 9), the 6.

The matter is sometimes complicated, when the interval, naturally to be omitted, is required for the preparation of a subsequent discord as in Ex. 10.

[2] In actual practice this could, of course, only be done if it did not cause a clash with one of the principal parts.

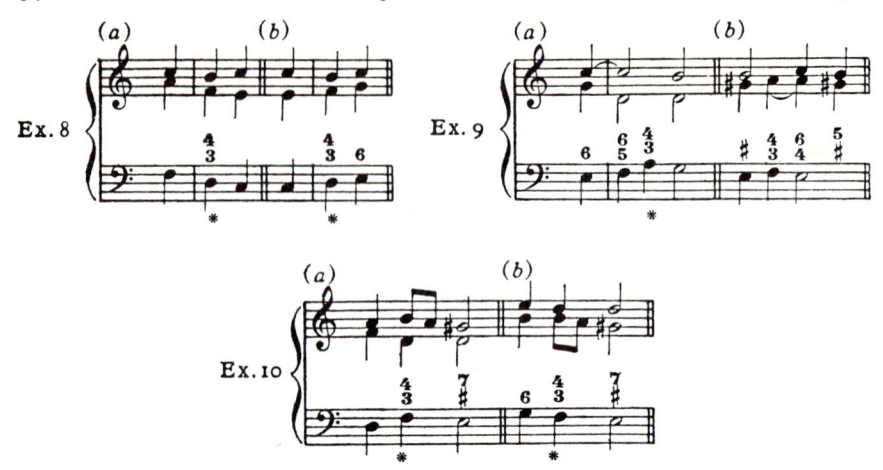

The 4, thus taken as an appoggiatura,[3] though not present simultaneously with the 3, nevertheless serves to suggest the dissonant character of the latter.

Ex. (b) cannot be taken in the alternative position, as consecutive 5ths[4] would not be avoided by the 4 in the second chord: (cf. Ch. v, § 6f, Ex. 29).

II. *Upon another Seventh.*

In Ch. xi, 'Sevenths' (II, § 5, Exx. 6–9), we have seen the same progression, only with the $\frac{7}{5}$ on the strong beat and the $\frac{4}{3}$ on the weak.

§ 2 b. Delayed resolution of $\frac{4}{3}$ on the Submediant.

The resolution of $\frac{4}{3}$ on the Submediant, like that of the corresponding $\frac{6}{5}$ on the Subdominant (Ch. xii, '$\frac{6}{5}$ Chords', § 2b), is often delayed.

---

[3] This is merely a suggestion of the present writer, and must, as such, be taken for what it is worth.

[4] When the example in question is taken in four parts (as the figuring $\frac{4}{3}$ demands) care is needed. Ph. Em. Bach points out (*Versuch &c.*, Part II, Ch. 7, I, § 8) that, if the 3 in the first chord (6 on *g*) be doubled (i.e. in the 8ve), it must remain in the upper part (as the 4 in the next chord) to avoid consecutive 5ths.

It cannot be too carefully borne in mind that one of the most insidious traps in the matter of consecutive 5ths is set for the unwary when the intervals 6 and 3 are present together in two consecutive chords on a Bass moving by step, and when the figuring is such that the presence of these intervals *does not strike the eye* (cf. § 4, Ex. 1).

XIII § 2 b $\frac{4}{3}$ CHORDS   635

Schröter, *Deutliche Anweisung &c.*, 1772, § 187, c.

Ex. 1

Ibid., d.

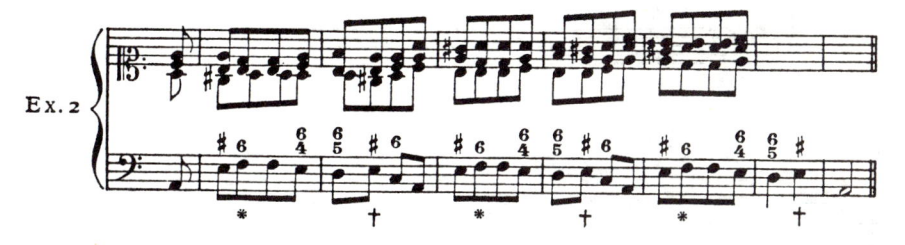

Ex. 2

Ibid., e.

Ex. 3

N.B.—In the above Exx., while giving the upper part as above, Schröter has only partially filled in the inner parts.

In Exx. 1 and 2 the $\frac{4}{3}$ chord resolves at † † † after passing (through an intervening $\frac{6}{4}$ on the Dominant) to the first inversion of the same harmony, $\frac{6}{5}$ on the Subdominant.

In Ex. 3 the $\frac{4}{3}$ * passes in the same way to the corresponding $\frac{6}{5}$ which (with an intervening 6 on the Mediant) resolves at † on the second inversion of the dominant Seventh (cf. Ch. xii, '$\frac{6}{5}$ Chords', § 2 b, Ex. 1).

With regard to the use of the figuring 6 (= $\frac{4}{3}$) in these Exx. Schröter says: "It is clear from the 5 examples that in (a) and (b) [not given here] my attention was directed principally to Chorda II [the Supertonic]; in (c) and (d), on the other hand, to Chorda VI; in (e), moreover, to both the above-mentioned degrees, since, in the music of to-day, they are the ones which most often bear the four-part chord of the Sixth $\begin{bmatrix}6\\4\\3\end{bmatrix}$, even though its proper sign, namely $\frac{4}{3}$, is not expressly put over the Bass, but only 6."

§ 2 c. ♭$\frac{6}{3}$ on the Submediant as the inversion of a Seventh on the flattened Supertonic.

This chord corresponds exactly to the cadential ♭$\frac{6}{5}$ ('Neapolitan $\frac{6}{5}$'),

636     $^4_3$ CHORDS   XIII § 2 c

described in Ch. xii, '$^6_5$ Chords', § 2 d, and generally appears in conjunction with it, as in the two following Exx:

Ex. 1

Leclair, *Sonatas for Violin and Bass*, Bk. II, Sonata IX, Allegro, 3rd section, bars 19-24.

In the above Ex. the $^{\natural 4}_3$ * passes to the first inversion † before the resolution ⟊.

Leclair, ibid., Sonata V, Allegro assai, 2nd section, bars 18-22.

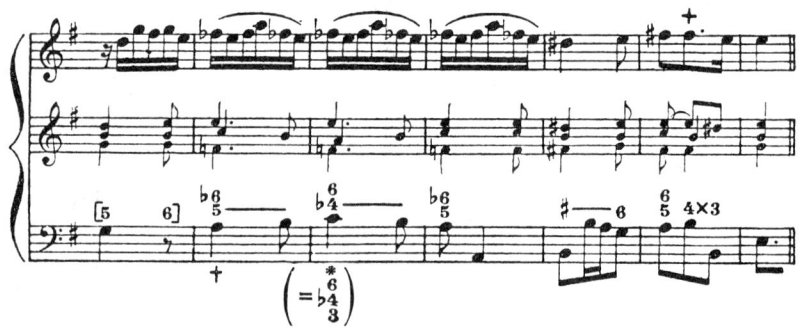

Here the harmony oscillates from the first inversion † to the second *, and back again.

According to Leclair's figuring, the $^{\flat 6}_5$ † is taken without preparation of the 5, but it is highly probable (and the presence of *e* in the Violin part makes it more so) that the figures supplied in brackets in the first bar (and followed in the suggested accompaniment) have been accidentally omitted.

For Leclair's use of ♭ (both in the music and the figuring) to contradict

XIII § 2 c $^4_3$ CHORDS   637

♯f, whereas (as in Ex. 1) he always contradicts ♯d with a ♮, see Ch. xxiv, 'Varieties of notation', § 2 b.

§ 2 d. Cases in which the resolution is disguised.

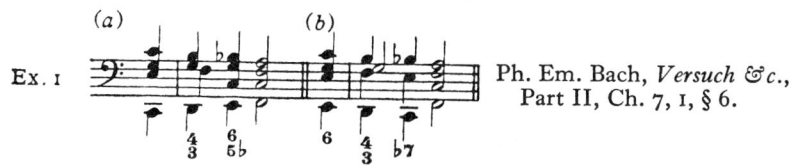

Ex. 1   Ph. Em. Bach, *Versuch &c.*, Part II, Ch. 7, 1, § 6.

Here we have an instance of *anticipatio transitus per ellipsin* (Ch. xxii, 'Inversion &c.', § 7).

The ♭♭, by means of which modulation is effected, is an anticipated passing note, the progression of the upper part in both (a) and (b) standing for

Ex. 2   Ibid.

In Ex. 2 the ♭♭ is to be explained as in Ex. 1.

The real resolution of the $^4_3$ on *d* is, as in § 2, Ex. 1 *b*, on the first inversion of the Triad on *c*, which passes—not, as in Ex. 1 *b* above, to $^6_{5♭}$ on *e* in the key of F—but to the imperfect Triad on the Supertonic of D minor, with the 7 *d* taken *in transitu*.

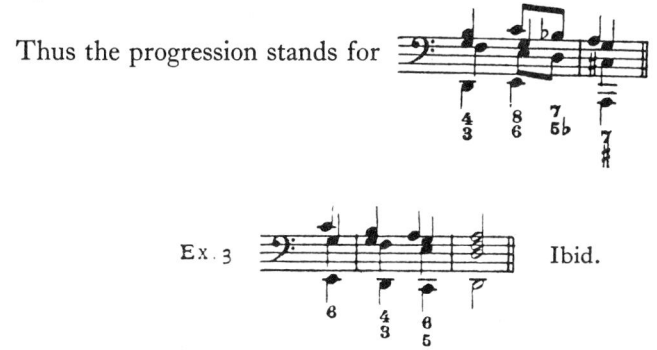

Thus the progression stands for

Ex. 3   Ibid.

Here we have an example of *Catachresis* or ellipse of the resolution (Ch. xxii, 'Inversion &c.', § 8).

The 6 *a* in the $^6_5$ on *c* originates in exactly the same way as that in Rameau's chord of the 'added Sixth'[2] (Ch. xii, '$^6_5$ Chords', § 8, Ex. 3).

---

[1] For the use of the sign ⌒ to indicate, in the present instance, the absence of the 6, see Ch. xxiii, 'Varieties of figuring', § 5 (1) *ad fin*.

[2] It must be noted that, though the two chords originate in the same way, their function is entirely different. For, whereas the 5 in the chord of the 'added Sixth' remains stationary, in the present instance it resolves.

The progression stands for [musical example: $^4_3$, $^8_5_3$, $^6_-_-$ resolving to $^7_3$]

§ 3*a*. $^4_3$ on the Subdominant as the second inversion of $^7_5_3$ on the leading note (Ch. xi, 'Sevenths', III, § 2) resolving on the tonic Triad.

(1) $^4_3$ with augmented 4th and major 3rd.

Of Ex. 1 Schröter says: "A special circumstance frequently arises on the falling IIII *Modi duri* [4th degree of the major scale], inasmuch, namely, as the major Third in the $^4_3$ chord is not pleasant to the ear either below or in the middle [i.e. in the Tenor or Alto], but only in the upper part. Let any one, accordingly, listen to and look at the following three examples (*a*) (*b*) (*c*). Nay! let any one try them in the two other positions, and they will sanction only the position here given, and consequently realize that my inverted figuring: $^3_4$ [1]) instead of $^4_3$, is well grounded. (Here too the first rule of prudence especially applies: Look ahead!)"

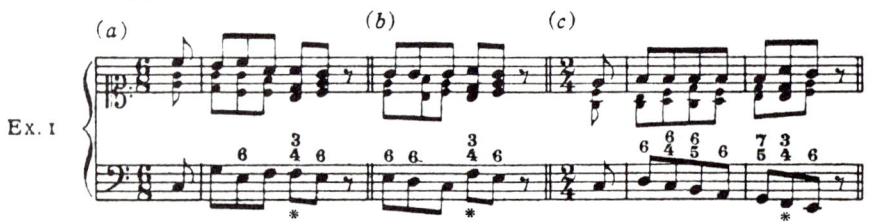

Ex. 1 *(a) (b) (c)* [musical example]

In (*a*) the 3 is prepared, in (*c*) the 4, and in (*b*) *neither*.

With regard to the preparation (cf. § 1), Ph. Em. Bach (*Versuch &c.*, Part II, Ch. 7, I, § 8) says: "Either the Fourth or the Third must lie [i.e. be held from the previous chord]."

With regard to the position, he says: "The position in which the Fourth and Third lie apart always sounds best, but particularly so in the case of this kind of Four-Three chord."

(2) $^{4!}_3$ with augmented 4th and minor 3rd.

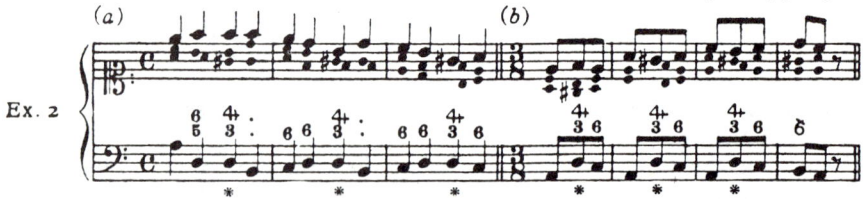

Schröter, ibid., § 189.

Ex. 2 *(a) (b)* [musical example]

N.B.—The inner parts, not filled in by Schröter, are given in small notes. The dots after the $^{4!}_3$ in bars 1 and 2 of (*a*) are Schröter's device (instead of the more usual dash) for indicating that the following bass note *b* is to bear the corresponding inversion of the same harmony (Ch. xxii, 'Inversion &c.', § 2).

---

[1] Cf. § 1, note.

XIII § 3 a $^4_3$ CHORDS   639

In (*a*) the 3 of the chord is prepared, but in (*b*) it is taken without preparation of either the 3 or 4 (cf. the quotation from Marpurg in § 1) as in the following Ex.:

Ex. 3   Ph. Em. Bach, *Versuch &c.*, Part I, Ch. 7, 1, § 9 (Bass only given).

Ph. Em. Bach gives the rule that "*usually* either the Fourth or Third are held [from the previous chord]". He explains Ex. 3 as due to the anticipation of passing notes * *, and as standing for

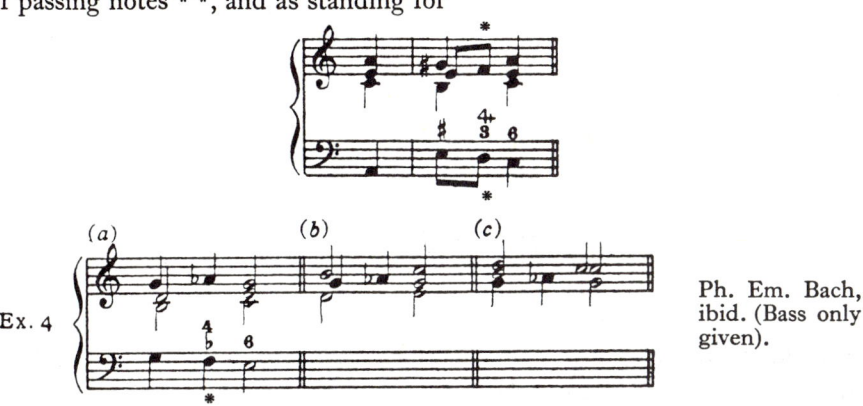

Ex. 4   Ph. Em. Bach, ibid. (Bass only given).

In Ex. 4 we have the same chord in the major key.

In (*a*) and (*b*) the 6 on *e* is taken with doubled Bass to avoid the undesirable progression of an imperfect 5th falling to a perfect one.

In the following Ex., however, this progression is allowable, since the bass note *e* † becomes the leading note of a new key, and must not, therefore, be doubled.

Ex. 5

The position (*c*), in which the progression in question is between the two upper parts, is the worst.

§ 3 *b*. $^{4!}_3$ as the inversion of a diminished Seventh on the leading note resolving on $^6_5$ on the same Bass.

Ex. 1

Ex. 2 [musical example with figures: 6/5, 8/6/4/3, 7/5♯]

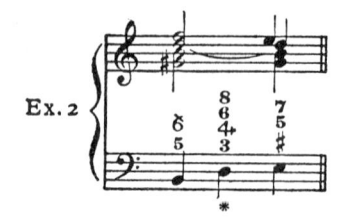

Ph. Em. Bach, *Versuch &c.*, Part II, Ch. 7, 1, § 12 (Bass only given).

Ph. Em. Bach points out that the adoption of a fifth part is necessary for the preparation of the 7 on *e*, and emphasizes the advisability of the full figuring $\smash{\substack{8\\6\\4\\3}}$ as an indication of this.

At first sight the $\smash{\substack{4\!\!\!|\\3}}$ * appears to be the inversion of a diminished Seventh resolving, not on $\smash{\substack{6\\5}}$ on the same Bass, but on the dominant Seventh in its root position, as in the following Ex. from Marpurg (*Handbuch &c.*, Part 2, 1757, *Abschnitt* (section) II, *Absatz* (subsection) II and III, p. 109, Tab. 4, fig. 42).

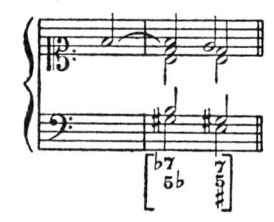

[musical example with figures ♭7/5♭, 7/5♯]

But this is not in reality the case. The progression in Ex. 2 is an irregular one, inasmuch as the Bass of the $\smash{\substack{4\!\!\!|\\3}}$ chord, being the dominant Seventh, cannot rightly be doubled.[1]

[1] A dissonant interval of a chord may be doubled by a Bass passing in arpeggio through the intervals of the harmony in question provided that all is in order at the moment of resolution, as in the following Ex.:

[musical example with figures 7/5/♯ and 7/5/♯ marked * and †]

At * the dominant Seventh *d* is present in the Bass and an upper part, and at † the leading note.

If, however, resolution took place at either of these points, the dissonant interval present in the Bass would disappear from the upper parts in favour of the interval needed to complete that inversion of the harmony represented by the bass note in question, as follows:

[musical example with figures 7/5/♯, 4/2/6, 7/5/♯, 6/5 marked * and †]

It is most important to bear this in mind, as the dashes, so freely used by some

XIII § 3 b $^4_3$ CHORDS   641

The $^4_3$ on *d* cannot legitimately proceed to $^7_5$ on *e* except by first resolving on $^4_2$ over the same Bass, with subsequent transference of discord from the Bass to the upper part (Ch. xxii, 'Inversion &c.', § 2).

Ex. 2 represents, therefore, the catachrestic [2] progression:

the ellipse of the resolution being partially disguised by the five-part harmony, which avoids the progression *f d* in the upper part.

§ 4. $^4_3$ on the Tonic as the inversion of a Seventh on the Subdominant resolving on a Seventh on the Dominant.

It was seen (Ch. xi, 'Sevenths', III, § 3) that $^7_5$, resolving on a Triad or Seventh on a Bass rising a degree, is really a $^6_5$ chord with the 6 delayed by suspension, of which the resolution is delayed till the entry of the following harmony. Consequently $^4_3$, as the inversion of the said $^7_5$, is to be regarded as standing for $^{6\,-}_{4\,-}$ with the same ellipse of the resolution.
$^{3\,2}$

The 3, as a suspended interval, should therefore be prepared; but, since a chord, when once established, comes to be used in a way apparently inconsistent with its origin, the 3 is sometimes found unprepared, as a free appoggiatura, as in Ex. 2, while in other cases the $^4_3$, occurring on a weak beat, has the character of a passing chord, as in Exx. 3 and 5.

Ex. 1

N.B.—In this Ex., as in the two following, the position given is the only one in which consecutive 5ths $^{c\,b}_{f\,e}$ are avoided (cf. § 2 *a*, note 4).

composers, often leave it uncertain whether the chord under the right hand is to be retained bodily, or whether exchange of intervals with the Bass is to take place. Thus the Ex. just given would frequently be figured

(cf. Ch. xxi, 'Incomplete figuring', v, § 3, pp. 834 *sq.*).
  [2] Ch. xxii, 'Inversion &c.', § 8.
  [3] It would also be possible to regard the bass note *d* as a mere passing (arpeggio) note, not bearing an independent inversion of the harmony (cf. note 1), in which case the progression stands for   in which the parts move as in Ph. Em. Bach's example.

It will be seen from the foregoing that Ex. 1 represents the inversion of

Ph. Em. Bach, *Versuch &c.*, Part II, Ch. 7, I,
§ 8 (=9) (see § 2 *a*, note 1) (Bass only given).   Ibid., ditto.

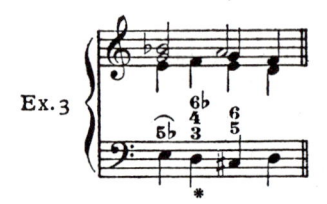

Ex. 2   Ex. 3

In the following Ex. the chord appears in the major key, on a Tonic pedal:

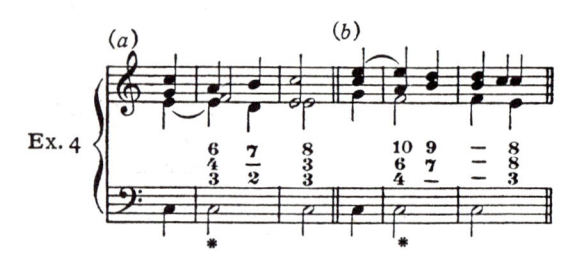

Ex. 4   Ibid., § 10, ditto.

Ph. Em. Bach remarks that $\frac{4}{3}$ with major Sixth and Third, and perfect Fourth, sounds best when the Third and Fourth are separated (as in *b*). In (*a*), however, the chord is not given in this position, as Ph. Em. Bach's figuring $\binom{8}{3}$ expressly indicates the doubling of the 3 in the final tonic chord, which would not sound well in the position in question, unless the 5 were included as a fifth part:

As will shortly be seen (Ch. xv, 'Major Sevenths &c.', § 1), Ph. Em. Bach always made the 2 in a $\frac{7}{4}$ chord on the Tonic rise a degree to the 3, instead of falling to the 8 (or 1), unless the contrary is indicated by the use of 9 $\binom{9}{7}{4}$ instead of 2, as in Ex. 4 *b*, where 10 is also used, instead of 3, to make the progression clearer to the eye.

In Exx. 5 and 6 the $\frac{4}{3}$ resolves, not on $\frac{6}{5}$ on the leading note, but $\flat\frac{7}{5}$, the 6 being delayed by suspension,[1] which, in Ex. 6, remains unresolved.

[1] For the essential character of the Seventh (minor or diminished) on the leading note (or sharpened Subdominant), see Ch. xi, 'Sevenths', III, § 2.

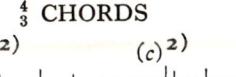

In Ex. 7 (like Ex. 4, in the major key) we have chromatic change to the dominant minor 9th at †; in other respects the progression is to be judged as in Ex. 6.

§ 5. $\frac{4}{3}$ as the inversion of a suspended Seventh which includes either the perfect or the augmented Fifth (Ch. xi, 'Sevenths', IV, §§ 3, 4).

[2] Consecutive Fifths, avoided by suspension, were permitted in progressions of three or more parts, provided that the interval falling from a 4th to a 5th was in an inner part. Marpurg (*Handbuch &c.*, Part I, 2nd ed. 1762, Tab. VI, Fig. 7 [Tab. VIII in the 1st ed. 1755]) gives the following example:

$\frac{4}{3}$ CHORDS

[Ex. 2 musical example with markings (a), (b), (c); figures 6/5, 4/3]

It is evident that in Exx. 1 and 2 we have the inversion of the progressions

[musical example with figures 2, 7/5, 6, 4+/2, 7/5+, 6]

§ 6. $\frac{4}{3}$ with stationary 3.

It is evident that $\frac{4}{3}$ as the inversion of the stationary Seventh (Ch. xi, 'Sevenths', v, § 1 sq.) is an impossibility, since the Bass of the chord corresponds to the very interval which has no place in a stationary Seventh, namely the 5.

Examples, however, occur of $\frac{4}{3}$ chords in which the 3, instead of resolving, remains as a consonance in the following harmony.

Marpurg (*Handbuch &c.*, 2nd ed. 1762, *Abschnitt* (section) I, *Absatz* (subsection) IV, § 43, 6, p. 64, Tab. III, fig. 17) gives the following Ex. (on a single stave with the soprano clef):

[Ex. to § 6 musical example]

The 4 *e* in the chord * is due to *anticipatio transitus* (Ch. xxii, 'Inversion &c.', § 7). Thus the main progression is

[musical example with figures 4+/2, 6, 6/4/3, b, (3 4)]

§ 7. Unessential (passing) $\frac{4}{3}$ chords.
Such chords are due:
(1) To passing notes in the Bass and an upper part.

XIII § 7 $^4_3$ CHORDS   645

Schröter, *Deutliche Anweisung &c.*, 1772, § 188, *a*.

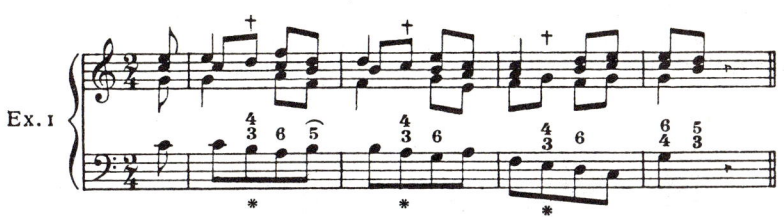

Ex. 1

N.B.—This Ex., of which Schröter gives the upper part (in the soprano clef) with the harmony only partially filled in, is here, for clearness' sake, given in full.

The notes * * * and † † † are passing notes, the main progression being

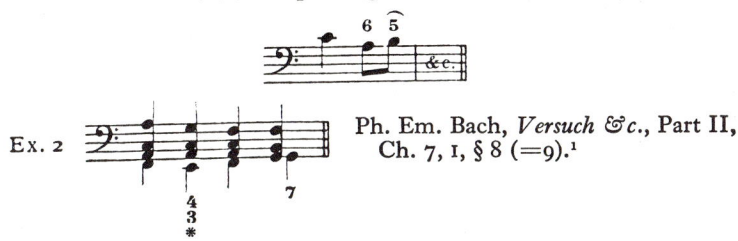

Ex. 2   Ph. Em. Bach, *Versuch &c.*, Part II, Ch. 7, 1, § 8 (=9).[1]

In the above Ex., of which Ph. Em. Bach remarks that it "occurs occasionally, but is not up to much", the $^4_3$ * (which must not be confused with that in § 5, Ex. 1, though the progression to the following chord is the same) is due to the passing notes in the Bass and upper part, the main progression being

(2) To the anticipation of a passing note or notes.

Ex. 3   Ibid., § 8.

The 4♮ ♯f in the $^4_3$ chord * is an anticipated passing note; the progression stands for

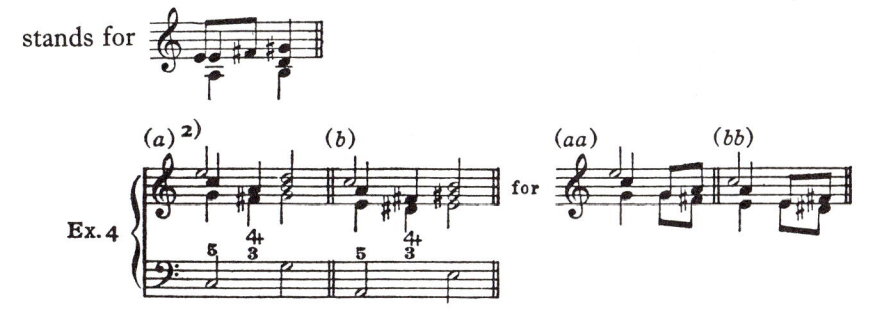

Ex. 4   (*a*)[2]   (*b*)   for   (*aa*)   (*bb*)

---

[1] See § 2 *a*, note 1.
[2] Ex. 4 *a* can of course be taken in such a way that there is no anticipation of the

646 $\frac{4}{3}$ CHORDS XIII §

It is quite clear that the $\frac{4}{3}$ chords in the above Ex. are not to be regarded as comparable with those in § 3 *a*, Exx. 1 and 2, for, were they so, the Bass (as representing the diminished 5th in a Seventh on the sharpened Subdominant) would have to fall a degree.

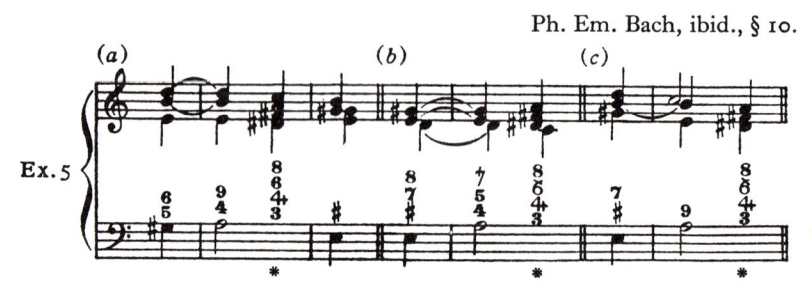

Ph. Em. Bach, ibid., § 10.

Ex. 5

N.B.—The above Exx. are given an 8ve lower in the original, and on a single stave. In (*b*) and (*c*) the Bass only is given. Both (*a*) and (*b*) can be taken in the two other positions. In (*c*) only one other position is good, as the fall from ♯g (in the first chord) to *e* must not be in the upper part. For the doubling (in the unison) of the leading note in the last chord of (*a*), see Ch. xi, 'Sevenths', III, § 2, Ex. 2.

In all three Exx. the resolution of the preceding discord makes it necessary that the $\frac{4\sharp}{3}$ chord * * * should be taken in five parts, with the Bass doubled.

In Ex. 5, in addition to the *anticipatio transitus* (as in Exx. 3 and 4) we have ellipse of the resolution (Ch. xxii, 'Inversion &c.', § 8) of the suspended discords preceding the $\frac{4\sharp}{3}$. The progressions in (*a*) (*b*) (*c*), therefore, stand for

(3) To the anticipation of an interval in the following chord:

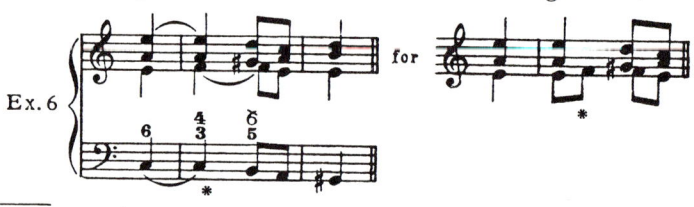

Ex. 6

passing notes , but in the case of (*b*) this is impossible on account of the resulting augmented 2nd *c* ♯*d*.

CHAPTER XIV

$^6_4{}_2$ CHORDS

N.B.—In chapters xii–xiv the numbering of the examples and footnotes recommences in each subsection (*a, b* &c.); i.e. the first example or footnote of each subsection is numbered 1 (cf. § 2 of these chapters, and § 3 of Ch. xiii).

XIV

$^6_4_2$ CHORDS †

1. *Constitution and figuring of the chord.*

As the third inversion of $^7_5_3$, the chord consists of the Sixth, Fourth, and Second.

In three-part harmony the Sixth is omitted.

The full figuring is $^6_4_2$, but the abbreviated figuring $^4_2$, or 2, is more commonly found.

In the case of $^6_4_2$ on the Subdominant (or temporary Subdominant) a common abbreviation is: either 4♯ (whether the augmented Fourth be diatonic or accidental, and, if the latter, whether it be due to the presence of a sharp or the contradiction of a flat), or ♮4 (4♮), if it is due to the contradiction of a flat (cf. Ch. xxiii, 'Varieties of figuring', § 4).

Preparation and resolution. The Bass, as the dissonant note, is in the same position, with regard to the need of preparation, as the corresponding interval in a $^7_5_3$, $^6_5$, or $^4_3$ chord.

On this point Marpurg (*Handbuch &c.*, 2nd ed. 1762, *Abschnitt* (section) I, *Absatz* (subsection) IV, § 44, p. 66) says that "the lower end of it [the $^6_4_2$ chord], and accordingly the Bass, contains the dissonance, since the parent chord is here standing on its head. The Bass must, therefore, be prepared and resolved. The resolution takes place when it falls a degree. In the chord of the Second $\begin{bmatrix}^6_4_2\end{bmatrix}$ on the fourth degree of the scale, in which there is the augmented Fourth, it is perhaps (*allenfalls*) enough, in the free style, if the upper end of the Second [i.e. the Dominant itself] is present beforehand" (cf. Ch. xi, 'Sevenths', I, § 2, note 4).

§ 2. $^6_4_2$ as the third inversion of $^7_5_3$ resolving on a Bass rising a Fourth (or falling a Fifth).

In the course of a sequence such a chord may occur on every degree of the major and (descending) melodic minor scales.

Individually, it may occur on every degree of either, except the Submediant of the major scale, on which, as the 3rd inversion of the Seventh on the leading note (Ch. xi, 'Sevenths', III, § 2), it would, if it occurred, naturally resolve on $^6_4$ on the Dominant.

Thus the $^6_4_2$ has a wider range than the $^6_5$.

For whereas the latter cannot (except in course of a sequence) occur on

---

† Certain cases (treated in §§ 7 and 8) in which the 6 cannot, under any circumstances, find a place in the chord, are included in the present chapter as the inversions of a corresponding chord included in Ch. xi on 'Sevenths'.

the Submediant, since the resolution would be on the imperfect Triad on the leading note, a $^6_4$ on the Mediant can resolve with perfect propriety on the first inversion of the Triad in question (Ex. 3).

Progression of the intervals. The Bass, as the dissonant note, must, as we have seen in § 1, fall a degree.

The progression of the remaining intervals, the 6 and 4, which correspond, respectively, to the 5 and 3 of a Seventh, is governed by the same general considerations as that of the corresponding intervals of the parent chord, when the latter resolves either upon a Triad or another Seventh. A leading note must not, except in following the pattern of a sequence, be doubled; its proper progression must be observed except when, as a licence (either in a sequence, or to secure a fuller harmony), it is allowed to fall a 3rd. Moreover, unvocal progressions in the upper part must be avoided. Thus, in Ex. 1 both the 4 and 6 may rise (*a*) (*aa*) (*aaa*); or the 4 may rise while the 6 falls (*b*) (*bb*) (*bbb*); or they may both fall (*c*) (*cc*), *except when the 4 is in the upper part* (*ccc*).

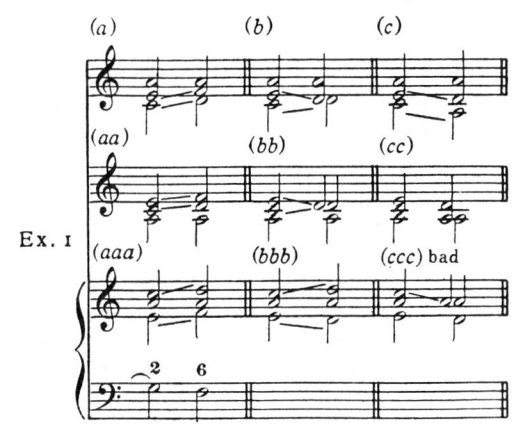

Ex. 1

But, in Ex. 2, whether the 4 rises (*a*) (*b*) (*c*), or falls (*aa*) (*bb*), *the 6 must fall* to avoid doubling the leading note.

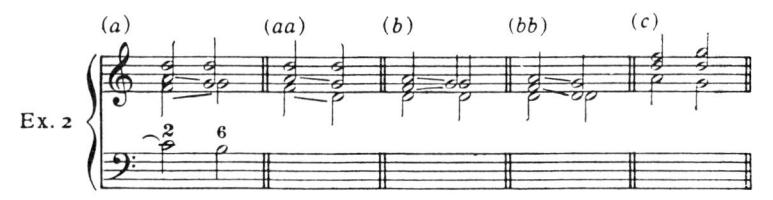

Ex. 2

Similarly, in Ex. 3, either the 4 and 6 must *both rise* (*a*) (*b*) (*c*), or *both fall* (*aa*) (*bb*).

Ex. 3

In Ex. 4 the 4♯, as the leading note, normally rises to the 6 of the following chord.

When, however, the 2 is taken in the upper part, the 4♯ may, as a licence, fall to the 3 of the following chord to secure a fuller harmony (*aaa*).† With the older school of accompanists, who insisted on *four sounding parts*, as opposed to doubling an interval in the unison (Ch. ii, 'The principal treatises of the eighteenth century &c', § 8 c), this progression was, of course, indicated; but Ph. Em. Bach, who constantly emphasizes the advantages of doubling in the unison, preferred to secure fulness of harmony by the expedient of temporarily adopting a fifth part, as the following Ex. shows:

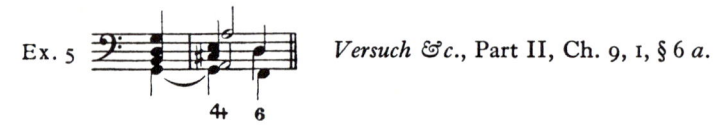

Ex. 5   *Versuch &c.*, Part II, Ch. 9, I, § 6 a.

The upward leap of the 6, Ex. 4 (*ccc*), is not to be commended in the absence of a special reason.

Its downward progression (*a*) (*b*) (*c*) is better than the upward step (*aa*) (*bb*) (*cc*), as it avoids doubling the major Third of the tonic chord; but the latter is necessary, when the chords are taken in the positions (*aa*) (*bb*), if a $\frac{6}{5}$ on the Subdominant (or sharpened Subdominant) follows, as in Ex. 6:

the alternatives being either (1) consecutive 5ths

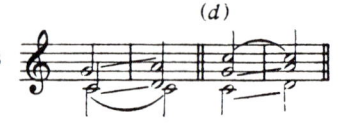

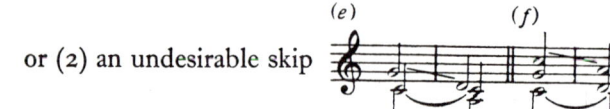

or (2) an undesirable skip

† For the corresponding progression of the 3 of Seventh on the Dominant see Ch. xi, 'Sevenths', II, § 3.

Similarly in such a progression as Ex. 7

it is better, especially in the position (*c*), that the 6 of the $^6_4$ should rise, as a skip is thereby avoided, which in the position (*c*) would be in the upper part.

It will be seen from the above Exx. that, in the case of a $^6_4$ chord, the progression of the upper parts is considerably less restricted than in that of a Seventh or its first and second inversions. This is, of course, due to the fact of the *dissonant note being in the Bass*.

Thus, whereas in a $^6_5$ or $^4_3$ sequence it is impossible, owing to the prepared discord in one of the upper parts, to get away from the position once adopted, in a $^4_2$ sequence the *position can be changed* at the expense of the uniformity of the pattern (Ex. 8):

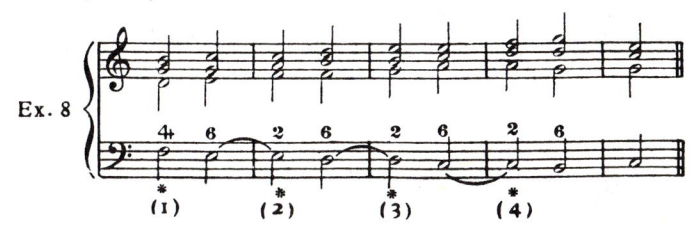

At (1) the 4♯ is in the upper part, at (2) the 6, at (3) the 2, and at (4) again the 4.

This form of accompaniment is, obviously, not to be recommended except as a device, in case of need, for obtaining a higher position for the right hand.

The most natural progression of the upper parts, in a sequence, is for the 4 to rise and the 6 to fall (Ex. 9).

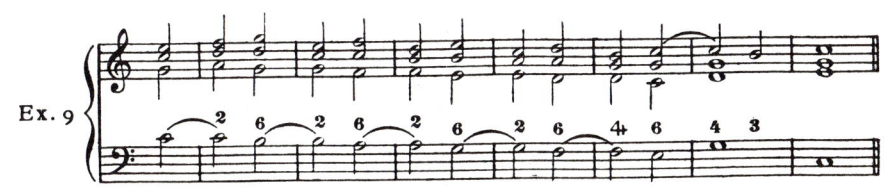

In this way each individual part has the same progression as the corresponding one of a $^7_5_3$ chord resolving on $^6_4$ on the same Bass (Ch. xii, '$^6_5$ Chords', § 2), and a fundamental rule of Thorough-Bass—namely that every interval of a chord should proceed *to the nearest possible interval* of the following one—is observed.

When a $^6_4_2$ chord resolves as the inversion of a Seventh resolving, not on a Triad, but on another Seventh, the 4 remains stationary as the prepared discord in the following $^6_5$ chord, in which case the 6 falls a degree (Ex. 10).

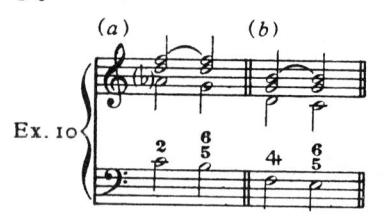

Ex. 10

The 2, in all cases, remains stationary, and corresponds, therefore, to the Bass of a Seventh resolving on the second inversion of a Triad or another Seventh, $^6_4$ or $^4_3$ on the same Bass (Ch. xii, '$^6_5$ Chords', § 2).

§ 2 *a*. $^6_4_2$ as the inversion of a Seventh resolving:

I. *Upon a Triad.*
(1) With the dissonance (the Bass) prepared:
(*a*) Without modulation; for Exx. see § 2.
(β) With modulation:

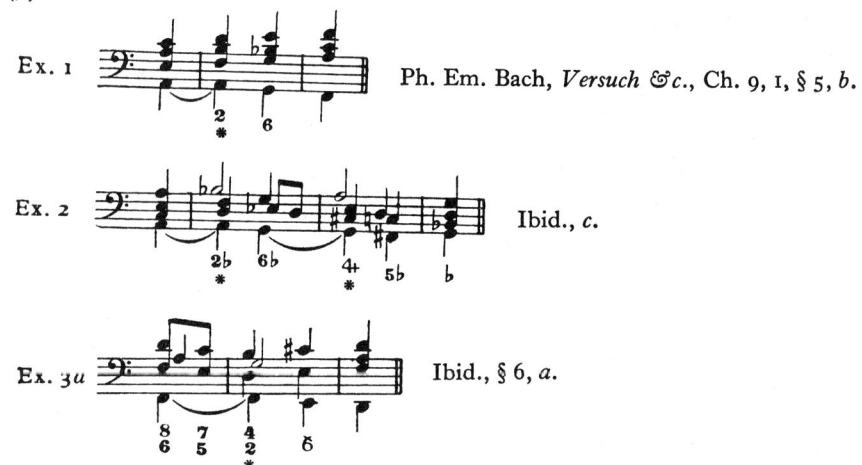

Ex. 1   Ph. Em. Bach, *Versuch &c.*, Ch. 9, 1, § 5, *b*.

Ex. 2   Ibid., *c*.

Ex. 3*a*   Ibid., § 6, *a*.

In Ex. 2 the 4♮ on *g* belongs, in a sense, to II of the present section; but the ♮*c* in the following chord being due to the anticipation of a passing note (Ch. xxii, 'Inversion &c.', § 7) the resolution of the 4♮ is really on the inversion of a Triad, not a Seventh, the progression standing for

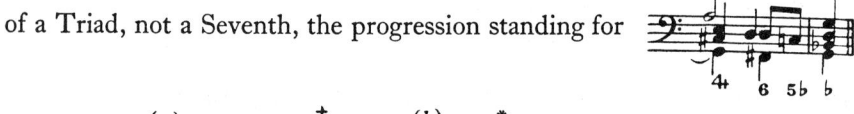

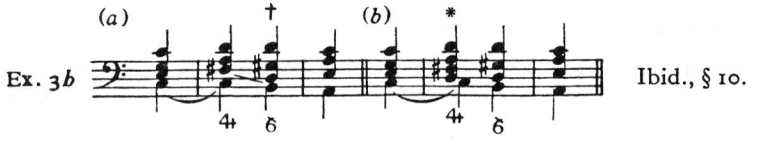

Ex. 3*b*   Ibid., § 10.

In the above example Ph. Em. Bach advises that the $^6_4_2$ chord be taken with

XIV § 2 a $\quad {}^6_4_2$ CHORDS $\quad$ 653

a fifth part (b)*, to cover up the irregular downward progression of the 4 (a)†
(§ 2, Ex. 4 aaa).

This illustrates Ph. Em. Bach's extreme aversion to an avoidable skip in the upper part, as the same end would have been attained, without resorting to a fifth part, by taking the chords as follows:

The progression would then be the same (taken in a different position) as in Ex. 3 a.

(2) With the dissonance (the Bass) unprepared:
(α) Without modulation:

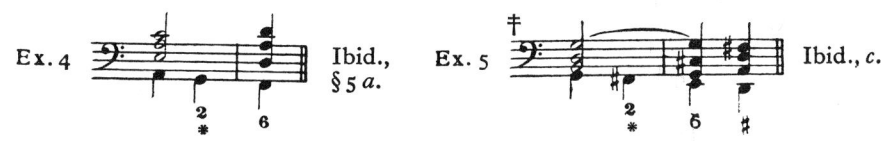

Ex. 4 .... Ibid., § 5 a.   Ex. 5 .... Ibid., c.

(β) With modulation:

Ex. 6 .... Ibid., b.

II. *Upon another Seventh.*
(1) With the dissonance (the Bass) prepared:
(α) Without modulation; see § 2, Ex. 10.
(β) With modulation:

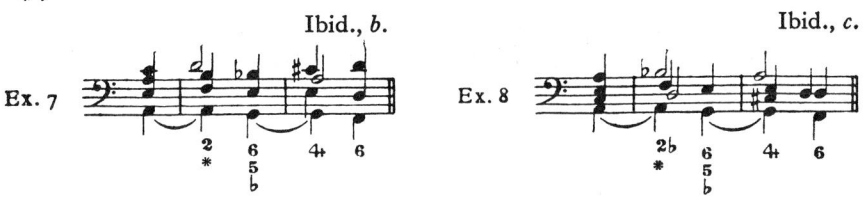

Ex. 7 .... Ibid., b.   Ex. 8 .... Ibid., c.

(2) With the dissonance unprepared:
(α) Without modulation:

Ex. 9 .... Ibid., c.

† Ex. 5 belongs, of course, to either (α) or (β), according as the first chord is regarded as on (1) the Subdominant in D major, or (2) either the Tonic in G major, or the Dominant in C. The same applies *mutatis mutandis* to Ex. 8.

Ph. Em. Bach frequently omits the key-signature from his Exx., using accidentals instead, which often makes the key uncertain.

654    $^6_4{}_2$ CHORDS   XIV § 2 a

The above Ex. differs from Exx. 4, 5 in which the unprepared dissonance is a passing note over which the preceding harmony remains unchanged, and from Ex. 6 in which the root of the chord remains the same. In Ex. 9, either the Bass ♯*f* and the 6 *d* are both passing notes, the main progression being [music] or the main progression is [music], in which case [music] stands for [music] by anticipation of the passing note (Ch. xxii, 'Inversion &c.', § 7).

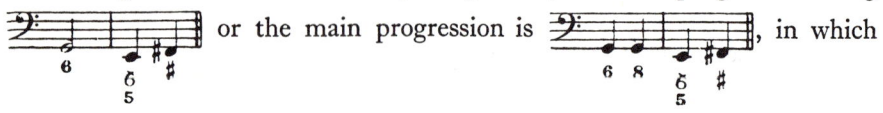

(β) With modulation:

Ex. 10 [music]

§ 2 *b*. Cases in which the real resolution is disguised:
(1) By the suspension of one (or more) of the intervals:
(a) Without modulation:

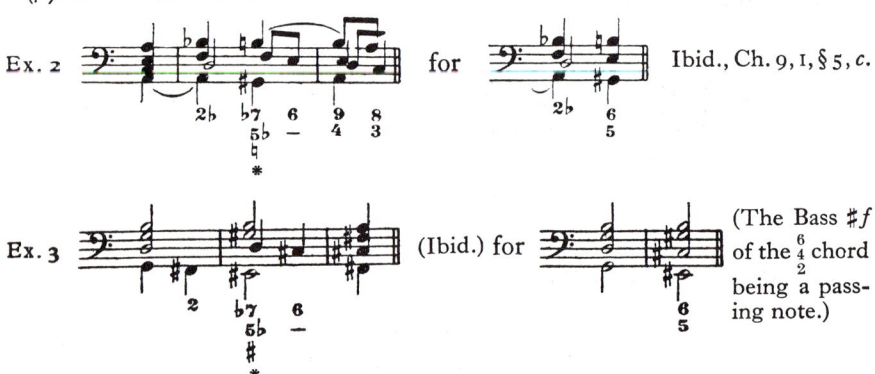

Ex. 1 [music]   Ibid., Ch. 20, § 7.

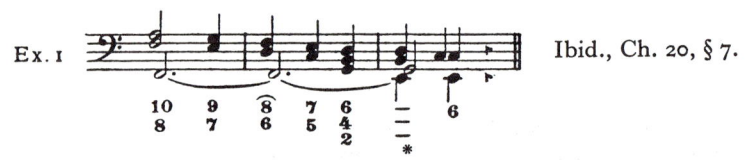

(β) With modulation:

Ex. 2 [music] for [music] Ibid., Ch. 9, I, § 5, *c*.

Ex. 3 [music] (Ibid.) for [music] (The Bass ♯*f* of the $^6_4{}_2$ chord being a passing note.)

(2) By *anticipatio transitus*:

Ex. 4 [music] (*Versuch*, Ch. 9, I, § 5, *a*) for [music]

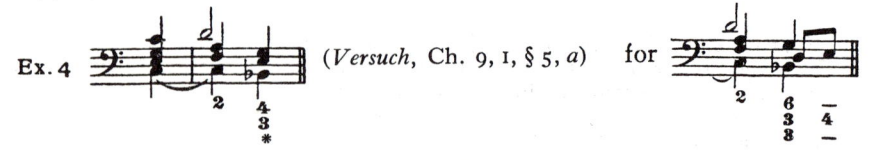

XIV § 2 b $\quad$ $^6_4{}_2$ CHORDS $\quad$ 655

(3) By ellipse of resolution:
(α) Without modulation:

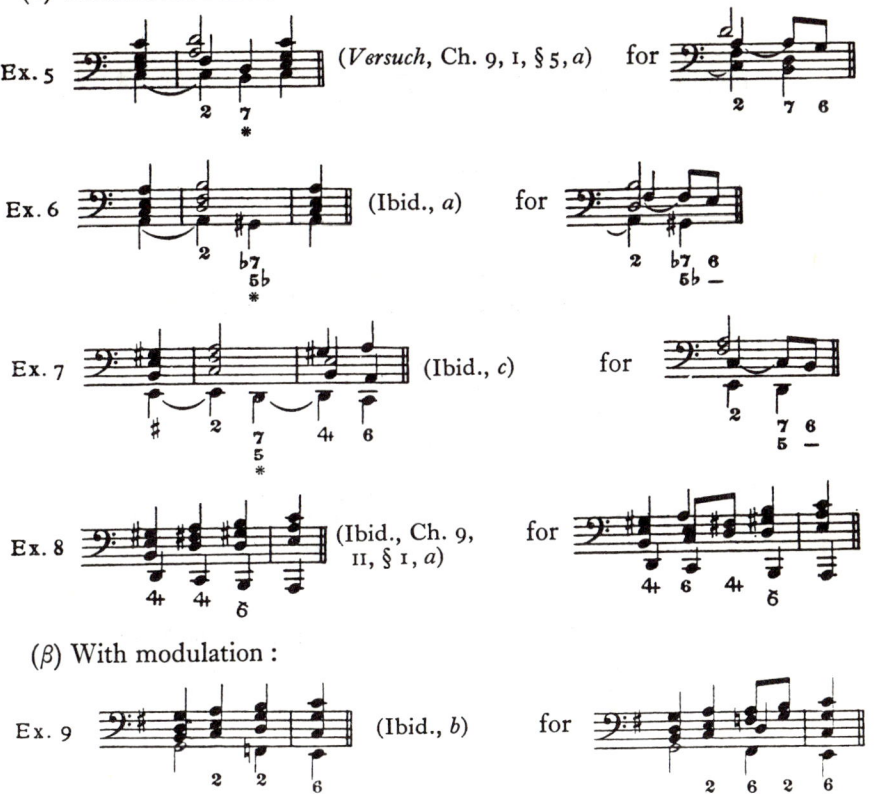

Ex. 5 [music] (*Versuch*, Ch. 9, I, § 5, *a*) for [music]

Ex. 6 [music] (Ibid., *a*) for [music]

Ex. 7 [music] (Ibid., *c*) for [music]

Ex. 8 [music] (Ibid., Ch. 9, II, § 1, *a*) for [music]

(β) With modulation:

Ex. 9 [music] (Ibid., *b*) for [music]

N.B.—The above Ex. can equally well be included in (*a*) by removing the ♯ from the key-signature. In the case of Exx. 8 and 9 Ph. Em. Bach himself explains the progression as due to ellipse.

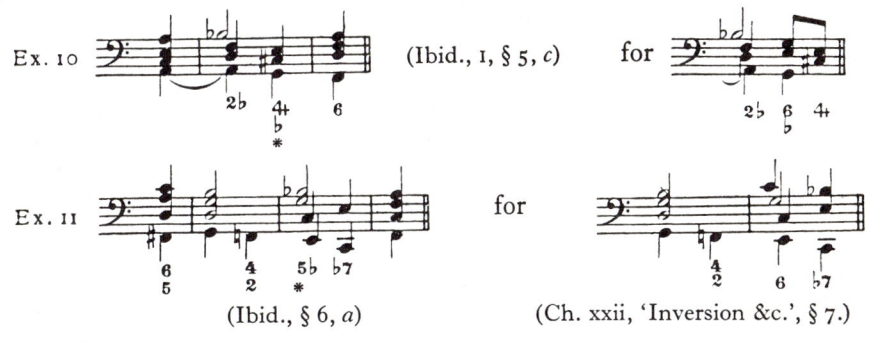

Ex. 10 [music] (Ibid., I, § 5, *c*) for [music]

Ex. 11 [music] for [music]

(Ibid., § 6, *a*) $\qquad$ (Ch. xxii, 'Inversion &c.', § 7.)

§ 3. $^6_4{}_2$ as the inversion[1] of a Seventh on the leading note or sharpened Subdominant (Ch. xi, 'Sevenths', III, § 2).

In the major key no authoritative examples are to hand of $^6_4{}_2$ resolving as

[1] In reality, as we have seen from the extract from Kirnberger there quoted, the

656     $\begin{smallmatrix}6\\4\\2\end{smallmatrix}$ CHORDS   XIV § 3

the inversion of a Seventh on the leading note (Ex. 1), or the sharpened Subdominant (Ex. 2).

[musical examples Ex. A (a) (b) and Ex. B]

But, in the minor key, both cases are of frequent occurrence.

The chord is rarely figured in full; more commonly ♯2, ♮2, or 2, (which serves as the equivalent for either), even when the augmented Fourth is accidental.[2]

The progression is considerably freer than in the case of the diminished Seventh, or its first and second inversions, $\smash{\substack{6\\5\flat}}$ and $\smash{\substack{4\sharp\\3}}$. For whereas the 5♭ in a diminished Seventh and the corresponding interval in the $\smash{\substack{6\\5\flat}}$ and $\smash{\substack{4\sharp\\3}}$ (the 3, and the Bass, respectively) *falls*[3] a degree, in a 2, chord the 6 is free to *rise* as in Exx. 4, 6, 7, 9, 10, 11.

---

root position, *with the root itself retarded*, of a Seventh on the Dominant (or Supertonic with sharpened Third). In its subsequent development,

[musical example]

in the free style, the progression lost its original character inasmuch as the suspended interval was taken unprepared.

[2] With most composers an augmented Second implies an augmented Fourth, just as an augmented Fourth implies a major Sixth, unless the contrary is indicated. Otherwise the chord would contain a diminished Third, which is nearly always specified in the figuring, even though the interval in question be in accordance with the key-signature (Ch. xxi, 'Incomplete Figuring', I, § 1).

[3] In the case of the diminished Seventh an exception might be found in the works of composers or theorists who, like Heinichen, were not strict about the downward resolution of the diminished 5th when included in a Seventh (Ch. xi, 'Sevenths', II, § 4), and who, therefore, would not have objected to such a progression as

[musical example] which Ph. Em. Bach would have condemned.

XIV § 3 $\begin{smallmatrix}6\\4\\2\end{smallmatrix}$ CHORDS 657

Schröter, *Deutliche Anweisung &c.*, 1772, § 200, *e*.

Ex. 1 4)

Ex. 2

Ibid., *f*.

Ph. Em. Bach, *Versuch &c.*,
Part II, Ch. 9, 1, § 6, *b*.

Ex. 3

Ph. Em. Bach, ibid.

Ex. 4

Ph. Em. Bach, ibid.

Ex. 5

Ph. Em. Bach, ibid.

Ex. 6

Ph. Em. Bach, ibid.

Ex. 7

Ph. Em. Bach, ibid.

Ex. 8

Ph. Em. Bach, ibid

Ex. 9

Schröter, ibid., *g*.

Ex. 10

[4] In the Exx. from Schröter given in this section (except in bar 2 of Ex. 11) only the Bass and upper part are given.

Ex. 11

The Bass of the chord appears in Exx. 4, 5, 8, 10, and the penultimate bar of Ex. 11 as a prepared discord, in accordance with the requirements of the strict style. In Ex. 3 it appears as a passing note; in Exx. 1, 2, 6, 7, 9 it is approached from the note immediately below; while in the first bar of Ex. 2 and the third bar of Ex. 11 it is approached by leap.

In Ex. 3 the chord is used to effect modulation. In Ex. 5, though the figuring does not indicate it, the chord passes to another inversion of the same harmony, $\frac{4}{3}$ on *a*. The intervening Triad on *b*, though on a stronger beat, is really a passing chord,[5] the Bass and Alto being 'changing' (i.e. accented passing) notes. The main progression is, therefore,

In Exx. 7, 8 the real resolution of the 2₄ on *f* is the $\frac{6}{4}$ on *e* (which in Ex. 8 is followed by modulation) with an intervening passing chord.

In Ex. 9, which at first sight seems to refute the contention in note 5, *b* and ♯*g* in the 2₄ chord are merely retardations of the doubled Third of the following $\frac{6}{3}$. Thus the main progression is

[5] It may be asked why the Triad on *b* is not regarded as the resolution of the 2₄, and the $\frac{4}{3}$ on *a* as a passing chord. The answer is that the progression

would be as faulty as that given in note 3.

It is true that, when the 2₄ resolves on $\frac{6}{4}$ (on a Bass falling a degree) as in Ex. 4, &c., *the 6 is free to rise*; but the case is very different; for, in Ex. 4, the note *c*, on which the 6 of the 2₄, as the 7 of the root progression (cf. note 1), should resolve, *is present in the* $\frac{6}{4}$: the resolution is simply transferred to another part. The objector may point to Ex. 6 in which 2₄ on *f* resolves on a major Triad on *e*. But here, again, the case is different.

In Ex. 5 the 2₄ is on the strong beat, and both the Bass and the 6 are prepared, though the 6 (being *de facto* concordant and a discord only *de jure*) does not, of course, need preparation, even in the strictest style.

In Ex. 6, on the contrary, the 2₄ is, to all intents and purposes, a passing chord. The progression, which is slightly obscured by the retarded *c* (6 in the $\frac{6}{4}$ on *e*), is

XIV § 3 $^6_4_2$ CHORDS   659

In Ex. 10 the $^6_4_2$ appears as the inversion of a diminished Seventh on the sharpened 3 of the Supertonic *b* in the key of *A* minor. The corresponding progression [6] with ♯*d* as Bass would be

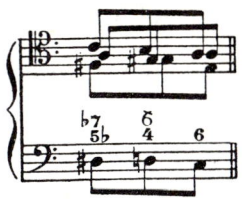

In Ex. 11 the $^6_4_2$ (♮2) in the penultimate bar is exactly the same as that in Ex. 10, while that in bar 3 is the same as in Ex. 4 (cf. note 5).

The $^6_4_2$ (♮2) † in the second bar is of an entirely different nature and is closely parallel to that in Ex. 9. It is simply a retardation, the main progression being

The ♭*b* (6 in the ♮2), being concordant with the Bass, is struck unprepared, exactly like the 4 in the $^{7\ 8}_{4\ 3}_{2}$ in the common progression

(Ch. xv, 'Major Sevenths &c', § 4, Ex. 2.)

§ 4. $^6_4_2$ on the Mediant as the inversion of a Seventh on the Subdominant resolving on a dominant Seventh (Ch. xi, 'Sevenths', III, § 3).

[6] The correspondence is not exact, as the *a*, which, as was explained above, may rise as the 6 of a $^6_4_2$ on *c*, must fall as the 5♭ of $^{♭7}_{5♭}$ on ♯*d*.
(For the doubled leading note ♯*g* see Ch. xi, 'Sevenths', III, § 2, Ex. 2.)
The progression from ♯*d* to ♮*d* is an instance of *anticipatio transitus per ellipsin*
(Ch. xxii, 'Inversion &c.', § 7), the progression standing for

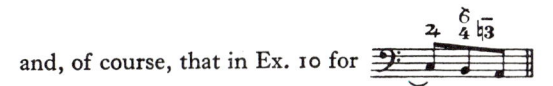

and, of course, that in Ex. 10 for

660 $^6_4{}_2$ CHORDS XIV § 5

§ 5. $^6_4{}_2$ as the inversion of a suspended Seventh which includes the 5 (Ch. xi, 'Sevenths', IV, §§ 2-4 and 8).

Ph. Em. Bach, *Versuch &c.*, Part II, Ch. 9, I, § 5, *a*.

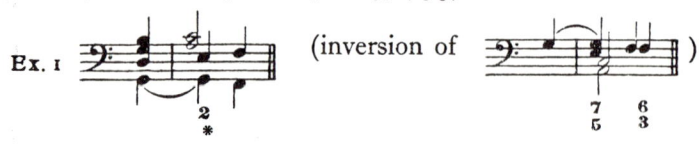

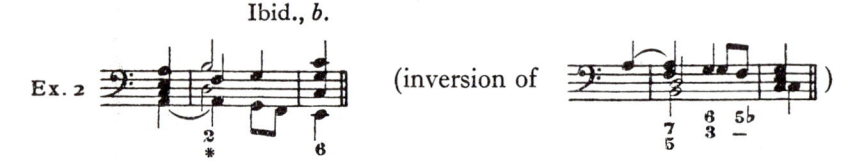

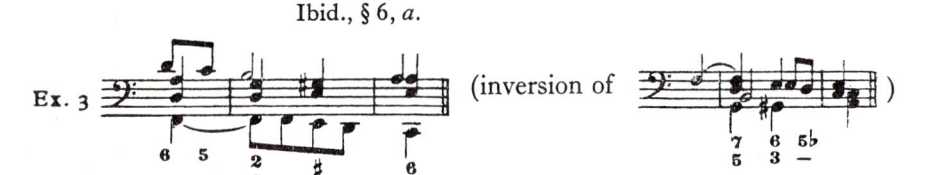

Ex. 1   (inversion of   )

Ibid., *b*.

Ex. 2   (inversion of   )

Ibid., § 6, *a*.

Ex. 3   (inversion of   )

Giuseppe Valentini, Opera Quinta, *XII Suonate à Tre*, Sonata VIII, 'La Fornari', Allegro (before Finale), bars 33-7.

Ex. 4

[1] Note the change of position (and consequent departure from the pattern of the sequence) in the accompaniment at *, in order to gain a higher and better position for the final cadence.

The position taken at the beginning of the sequence is much the best one. The alternatives, [music], and [music], are less good: the first, on account of the 5ths (on the weak beats) between the upper part and the Bass, and the second, on account of the 5ths (on the strong beats) between the upper part and the Tenor.

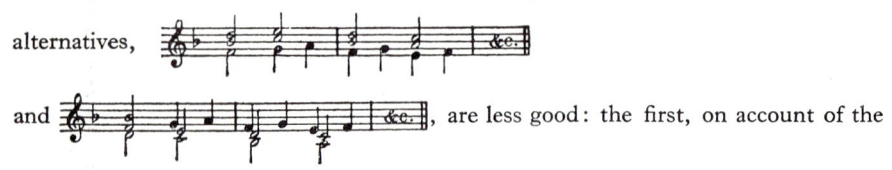

XIV § 5 $^6_4{}_2$ CHORDS   661

The $^4_2{}^5_3$ sequence in Ex. 4 is evidently an inversion of

Ex. 5 — Corelli, Opera Quarta, *Suonate da Camera a Tre.*

Ex. 6 — M. C. Festing, Opera Quarta, *Eight Solos for a Violin and Thoroughbass*, Sonata VII, Gavotta, bars 1-4.

In the above Ex. $^4_2$ * as the inversion of a suspended Seventh including the 5 occurs intermingled with an ordinary $^4_2{}^6_3$ sequence.[2]

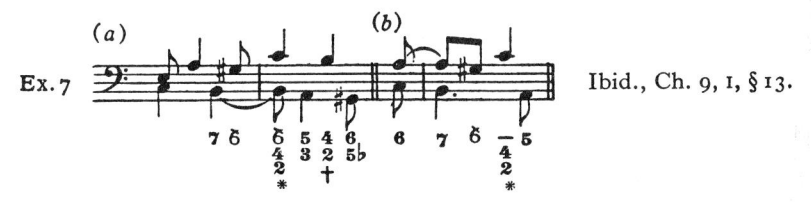

Ex. 7   Ibid., Ch. 9, I, § 13.

[2] It has been shown (Ch. xi, 'Sevenths', I, § 1 *ad fin.*) how a chord, taken (to all appearance) as an essential discord, can be resolved as a suspension. In such cases the dissonant note of the apparently essential discord is due to the anticipation of a passing note. In the above Ex., therefore, the progression stands for

662 $^6_4_2$ CHORDS XIV § 5

The upper part represents the solo part, which we are, of course, at liberty to imagine an 8ve higher, as Ph. Em. Bach gave all his Exx. on a single stave.[3]

The $^6_4_2$ * * in Exx. (*a*) and (*b*) is the third inversion of a suspended Seventh, with augmented Fifth, on *c* (cf. Ch. xii, '$^6_5$ Chords', § 6, Ex. 7), while the $^4_2$ on *a* † in Ex. (*a*) is, of course, the inversion of an essential Seventh on the Supertonic *b* (cf. § 2, Ex. 10 *a*). Taking them as such, the progression in (*a*) and (*b*) would be, respectively:

Ph. Em. Bach appends the following suggested accompaniments, which, for the sake of clearness, are here given over the Bass:

N.B.—In the first chord of (*b* 2) the accompaniment, apparently, goes below the Bass, but the former must be imagined an 8ve higher (see above).

In (*b* 2) it will be observed that the 6 of the $^6_4_2$ chord is omitted in the accompaniment.* Bach remarks: "instead of the Sixth, one can also take the doubled Second, as an anticipation of the Triad which follows."

This is, in the present instance, remarkable, since (1) the interval in question is not present in the solo part,[4] and (2) the upper part of the accompaniment (with a skip, moreover, which Bach generally deprecates) merely duplicates the solo part.[5]

One is almost tempted to imagine that Bach's mind wandered from the single

---

[3] "I have been obliged to give all the examples on a single stave, in order that this work might not become too voluminous and costly; one must, therefore, in these examples, have regard *principally* to the reason for which they are given, and not tie oneself to the pitch [lit. 'height and depth'] prescribed, as, moreover, the necessary information is always given about the positions [in which the chords are to be taken]." —Ph. Em. Bach, *Versuch &c.*, Part II, 1762, Preface, folio 2 *b*.

[4] In accompanying one or more solo instruments (or voices), especially in passages of delicate harmony, it is sometimes better to omit a discord from the accompaniment, even though prescribed by the figures, rather than discount the effect of the solo part by reproducing it in the accompaniment (see quotation from Werckmeister in Ch. i, 'The beginnings &c.', § 24, VII, 1 *b*).

[5] Cf. Ch. iii, 'General character &c.', § 5 B.

solo part given in Ex. 7 (*b*), and that he had in view a case in which the interval which he omits from the accompaniment was present in a second one, as e.g.:

The omission of the ♯*g* (rising to *a*) from the accompaniment would then be exactly in the spirit of Werckmeister's advice referred to in note 4.

In the accompaniment to both Exx., (*a*) and (*b*), Bach takes the 7 (in the 7 6 suspension on *b*) as $\frac{7}{3}$.

As the 6 on the Supertonic may be interpreted as $\frac{6}{4}\atop 3$ (Ch. xxi, 'Incomplete figuring', II, § 1), the 7 can include the imperfect (diminished) 5th, which would then have its proper resolution (Ch. xi, 'Sevenths', IV, § 5).

The accompaniment would then be

or in any other position.

Ph. Em. Bach was, however, evidently not fond of including the 5, unless specially figured, in a suspended Seventh (Ch. xi, 'Sevenths', IV, §§ 2, 5, 8).

Ex. 8   *Versuch &c.*, Ch. 9, I, § 5, *c*.

The above is a very remarkable Ex.

It has already been pointed out (Ch. xi, 'Sevenths', I, § 1 *ad fin.*) that a discord can be taken as an essential discord and resolved as a suspension.

In the present Ex. the $\frac{6}{4}\atop 2\flat$ on *a* is taken as the 3rd inversion of an essential Seventh on ♭B, but resolves as a Seventh on *g* [6] with the Bass delayed by

[6] The essentially dissonant note in the chord is therefore *f*, and the fact that it is taken without preparation is due to the fact that the chord itself was taken in a different capacity from that in which it was quitted.

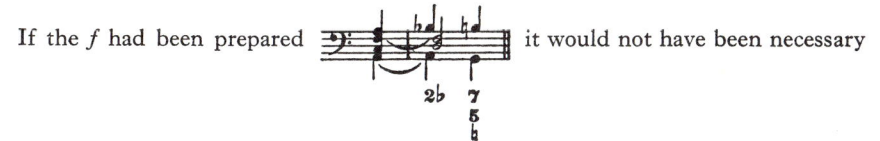

If the *f* had been prepared   it would not have been necessary

to assume this change of character.

suspension, or, in accordance with the method of classification here adopted, as the inversion of a suspended Seventh on ♭♭ resolving on $^6_5$:

Simultaneously with the resolution of the suspension, modulation is effected by the change of ♭♭ to ♮♭.

Ex. 9   *Versuch &c.*, Ch. 9, I, § 5, c.

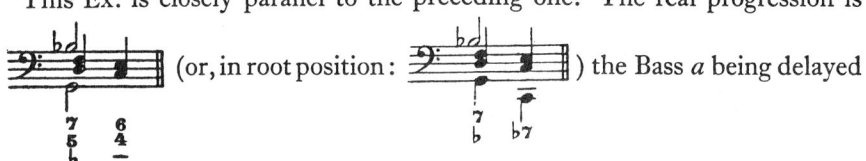

This Ex. is closely parallel to the preceding one. The real progression is (or, in root position:) the Bass *a* being delayed by suspension, of which the resolution is delayed till the entry of the dominant harmony ($^6_4$ on *g*).

The unprepared *f* in the Seventh on *g* ($^6_{4}$ on *a*) is to be explained as in the preceding Ex. (see note 6).

Ex. 10 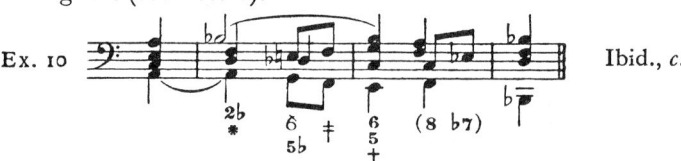   Ibid., c.

The $^6_{4}$ on *a* * in the above Ex. is exactly parallel to that in Ex. 9. The ♭*d* in the following chord is a minor 9th with *c* as its root, resolving on the 6 of the following $^6_5$ on *e* †, the two chords being connected by the passing notes ♯*f* ‡. The essential progression is, therefore, &c.

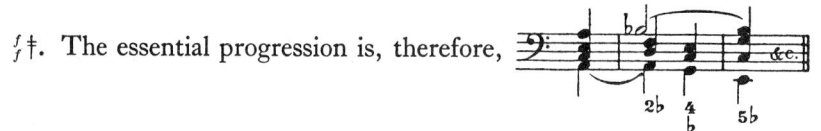

§ 6. $^6_4_2$ chords, of which the Bass is a downward passing note, and falls a degree to a Triad or $^7_5_3$.[1]

---

[1] Where the time is fairly quick, such $^6_4_2$ chords are generally left unfigured unless there are reasons to the contrary. E.g. in Ex. 3 the figure 2 on *b* is necessary to warn the accompanist against taking the chord as $^6_3$. In the sparsely figured Basses of many Italian composers the leading note is constantly left unfigured when 6, or even $^6_5$, is to be understood (Ch. xxi, 'Incomplete figuring', III, § 4).

XIV § 6 $^6_4{}_2$ CHORDS

(a) Without modulation:

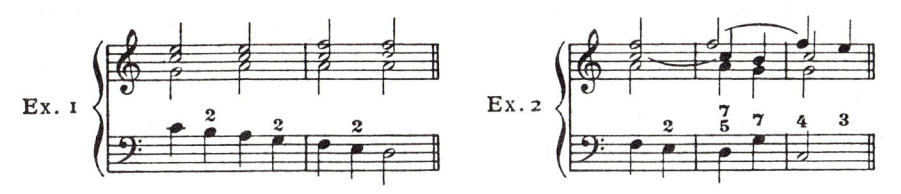

Ex. 1

Ex. 2

A florid Bass sometimes makes caution necessary. In the following Ex. from Ph. Em. Bach, given as usual on a single stave (*Versuch &c.*, Part II, Ch. 9, II, § 4), the last chord must be taken with either the 3 or the 5 doubled to avoid consecutive 8ves.

(a)   (b)   (c)[2]

Ex. 3

(β) With modulation:

Ex. 4   Ex. 5   Ph. Em. Bach, ibid., Ch. 9, I, § 6.

§ 7. $^4_2$, on a stationary Bass, as the inversion of a stationary Seventh (Ch. xi, 'Sevenths', v, § 1).

Of this chord Marpurg (*Handbuch &c.*, 2nd ed. 1762, *Abschnitt* (section) I, *Absatz* (subsection) IV, § 44 (3), p. 67) says: "I will here only remark that in three-part harmony only the Fourth is taken with the so-called[1] Second. If there are to be four parts, the Bass is doubled in the Octave."

He gives the following Exx., without figuring, but adds: "Be it noted at the same time that, in this case, the figure 1 [instead of 8] is generally used to indicate the Octave of the Prime." Cf. Ch. xxiii, 'Variety of figuring', § 1.

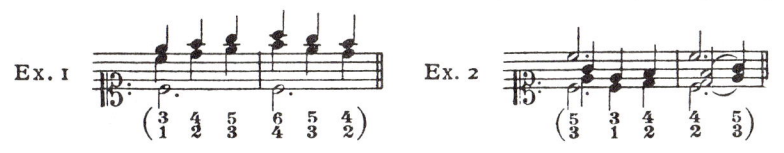

Ex. 1   Ex. 2

Later on (ibid., *Abschnitt* II, *Absatz* II & III, § 7, p. 137 in Part 2, 1757) he says: "We come to Fig. 4 where, in the very first bar, and at the

---

[2] Ph. Em. Bach does not give (c), probably on account of the skip in the upper part.
[1] Marpurg qualifies the term 'Second', on the ground that, in a true Second, the real dissonance lies in the Bass. This objection, however, he subsequently withdraws, as will be seen in the sequel.

666   ⁶⁄₄⁄₂ CHORDS   XIV § 7

beginning of the second, the notes ^f_d occur over the bass note *c* [cf. Ex. 3]; ... the *d*, methinks, does not constitute a Ninth, but a Second, regardless of the fact that we here find the characteristic of a Ninth, namely that the upper part moves. But we must consider whence this *d* takes its origin, and that is from the inversion of a passing [i.e. 'stationary'] Seventh."

Ph. Em. Bach (*Versuch &c.*, Part I, Ch. 9, 1, § 15) gives the two following Exx.:

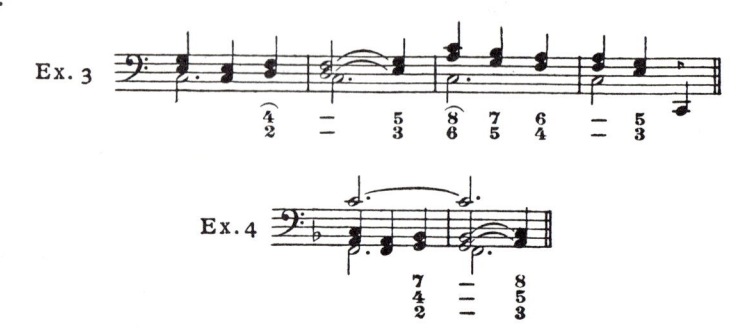

Ex. 3

Ex. 4

of which he says: "With a stationary Bass, or one which keeps to the same note [i.e. changes only to a higher or lower 8ve], the signature $^4_2$ sometimes occurs; this is a three-part chord, and nothing further is taken with it.² The two intervals stand no more in need of resolution than the Bass, because they occur as passing notes, and they can both rise and fall.³ The figures which precede and follow this $^4_2$ are generally also taken in three parts. The parts which one is accompanying generally have the same progression;⁴ now and then one of them sustains the Octave or the Fifth; in the latter case, if the accompaniment has to be in four parts, the major Seventh⁵ can be taken with this chord (*a*) [=Ex. 4]. Here too one can, as a precaution, use Telemann's arc⁶ (*Bogen*)."

---

² This is not, of course, meant to exclude the doubling of the Bass in the 8ve, as in Marpurg's Ex. 2.

³ Bach gives no example of the downward progression, as in the following:

⁴ Presumably, therefore, the upper parts in Ex. 3 are intended to represent both solo parts and accompaniment.

⁵ In this case, if the $^4_2$ is to have an upward progression, as in the Ex., either the 7 or the 2 must be in the upper part (cf. Ch. xv, 'Major Sevenths &c.', § 6). The accompaniment will therefore be

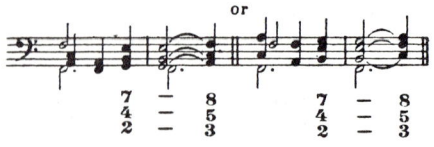

⁶ Cf. Ch. xxiii, 'Varieties of figuring', § 5 (1) *ad fin*.

XIV § 7 $^6_4_2$ CHORDS 667

It will have been observed that the chord treated above, though undoubtedly (as Marpurg points out) an inversion of the 'stationary Seventh', has, in practice, a wider scope than the latter. For whereas the 'stationary Seventh' normally occurs only as a passing chord, and only very exceptionally on a strong beat (Ch. xi, 'Sevenths', v, § 1, Ex. 8), the $^4_2$ under discussion is freely used as a double appoggiatura (cf. Ex. 3, bar 2).

Corelli, Opera Prima, Sonata I, Adagio.

Ex. 5

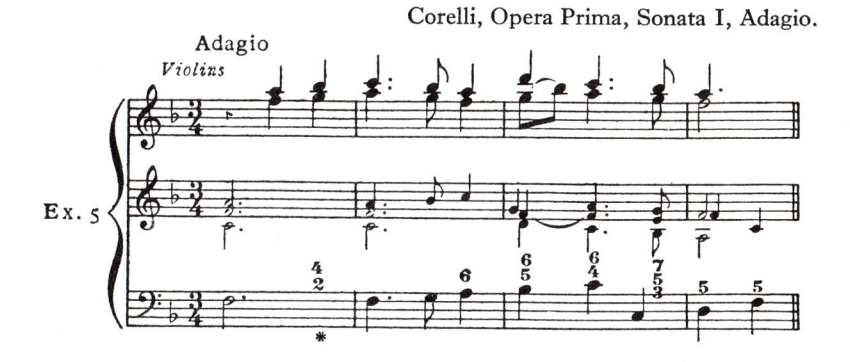

The above Ex. illustrates the advisability of not always including in the accompaniment all the intervals actually figured (Ch. i, 'The beginnings &c.', § 24, VII, 1 b [quotation from Werckmeister]). †

The violin parts are above the compass of the accompaniment (Ch. iii, 'General character &c.', § 5 B), and if the passing notes figured $^4_2$ are played an Octave below the Violins , the effect, especially on a modern Pianoforte, is very unpleasing. It may be asked why Corelli did not omit the figures $^4_2$. In the first place, the effect of playing the same notes as the Violins in a lower Octave would be less unpleasant on a soft stop on the Organ (which was the instrument indicated in Corelli's 'Sonate da Chiesa', but which is not always available), or even on an Harpsichord, which blends with string tone far more than a Pianoforte; and, in the second place, the figuring $^4_2$ is necessary to warn the accompanist, who had *not got the solo parts before him*, against repeating the Triad on the third beat of the bar , which would have had a bad effect.

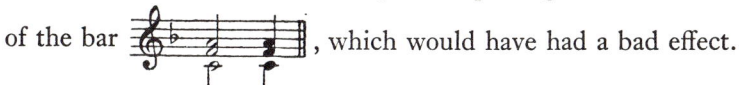

§ 8. The same chord disguised by the progression of the Bass.

In the following example from Schröter (*Deutliche Anweisung &c.*, 1772, § 266, *t*) we have the same chord as that described in § 7, used (as in the Exx. there given) as a double rising appoggiatura, only more freely, i.e. without preparation. It is, moreover, disguised by the downward progression of the Bass, which is due to the anticipation of a passing note (Ch. xxii, 'Inversion &c.', § 7).

† Cf. § 12, quotation from Ph. Em. Bach *ad fin.*

It is evident that the progression in the first bar—slightly modified in the second—is [music] or, with the passing f in the Bass, anticipated in Schröter's Ex. [music]. Schröter's figuring, however, is misleading, and would ordinarily be interpreted (as in § 2 b, Ex. 9) [music]

The progression intended could only be made clear by the use of Telemann's sign ⌒ (never, unfortunately, met with except in theoretical works) as follows: [music]

§ 9. In the two following Exx. the Bass of the $\frac{6}{4}$ chord * appears as the inversion of a retarded 7 on the Tonic, $\begin{smallmatrix}7&8\\5&-\\3&-\end{smallmatrix}$ (Ch. xv, 'Major Sevenths &c.', § 5), and therefore resolves upwards:

Ex. 1.   Ex. 2.

§ 10. $\frac{6}{4}$ as the retardation of $\frac{7}{5}$ on the Dominant resolving on a Triad on

XIV § 10 $^6_4{}_2$ CHORDS 669

the Submediant (Exx. 1-4), or of a diminished Seventh on the leading note (Ex. 5).

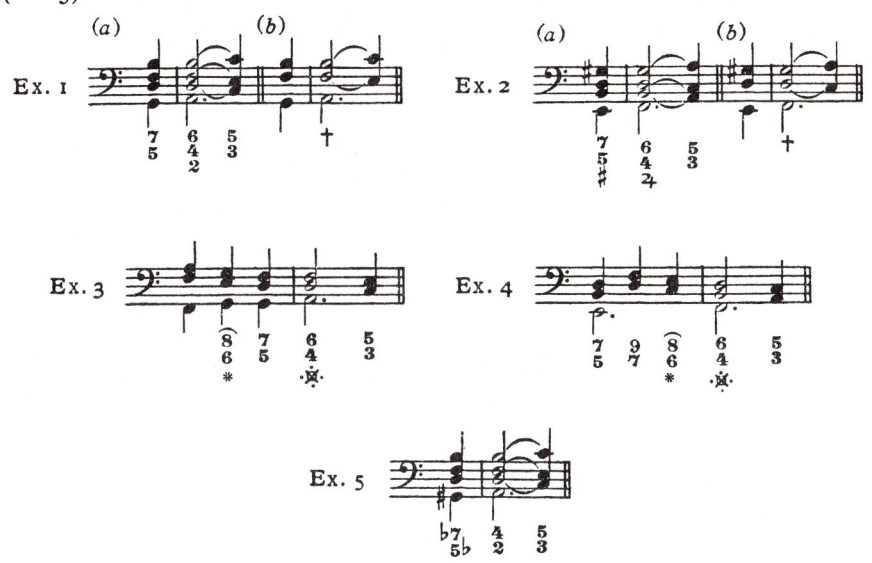

Ex. 1 (a) (b) $\begin{smallmatrix}7\\5\end{smallmatrix}$ $\begin{smallmatrix}6\\4\\2\end{smallmatrix}$ $\begin{smallmatrix}5\\3\end{smallmatrix}$ †

Ex. 2 (a) (b) $\begin{smallmatrix}7\\5\\\sharp\end{smallmatrix}$ $\begin{smallmatrix}6\\4\\2\end{smallmatrix}$ $\begin{smallmatrix}5\\3\end{smallmatrix}$ †

Ex. 3 $\begin{smallmatrix}8\\6\end{smallmatrix}$ * $\begin{smallmatrix}7\\5\end{smallmatrix}$ $\begin{smallmatrix}6\\4\end{smallmatrix}$ ⁑ $\begin{smallmatrix}5\\3\end{smallmatrix}$

Ex. 4 $\begin{smallmatrix}7\\5\end{smallmatrix}$ $\begin{smallmatrix}9\\7\end{smallmatrix}$ $\begin{smallmatrix}8\\6\end{smallmatrix}$ * $\begin{smallmatrix}6\\4\end{smallmatrix}$ ⁑ $\begin{smallmatrix}5\\3\end{smallmatrix}$

Ex. 5 $\begin{smallmatrix}\flat 7\\5\flat\end{smallmatrix}$ $\begin{smallmatrix}4\\2\end{smallmatrix}$ $\begin{smallmatrix}5\\3\end{smallmatrix}$

The above Exx. are from Ph. Em. Bach (*Versuch &c.*, Part II, Ch. 9, I, § 14). He remarks that, in a delicate accompaniment, the 4 may be omitted, as in Exx. 1, 2 (*b*) †, or the 2, as in Exx. 3, 4 ⁑. In Ex. 4 the incomplete $^6_4{}_2$ chord is taken, not as a retardation of intervals in a previous chord, but unprepared.

Türk (*Anweisung &c.*, 1791, § 208) uses the figuring $^9_6{}_4$ (Ex. 6) instead of $^6_4{}_2$, the 9 rising to 10 instead of, as usual, falling to 8. He alludes to Ph. Em. Bach's figuring (Ex. 1 *a*), which he gives below the example.

Ex. 6 $\begin{smallmatrix}9\\6\\4\end{smallmatrix}$ $\begin{smallmatrix}10\\5\\3\end{smallmatrix}$

§ 11. Wrong use of figuring 4♯ ♮4 (4♮).

Ph. Em. Bach (*Versuch &c.*, Part II, Ch. 9, II, § 2) gives the following Exx., of which he says: "If some figurists put the signature of the augmented Fourth alone over the bass note, it is wrong. The chord of the Second $\begin{bmatrix}6\\4\\2\end{bmatrix}$, which is indicated by this 4♯, or 4♮, has no place in the first example, in which ♯g has occurred shortly before, and, in the second, it also cannot be taken, on account of the resolution of the dissonances [the suspended $^9_7$]. It is, therefore, the Six-Four chord which must be taken in both cases."

⁑ ⁑ The ⌒ denotes that the chord is to be taken in three parts, without either 4 or 3. Cf. Ch. xxiii, 'Variety of figuring', § 5 (1) *ad fin*.

Ex. 1 [musical example with figured bass: ♯ 7 $\frac{6}{4♮}$ 6 | 7 4♮ 6 *wrong*]

Ex. 2 [musical example with figured bass: 6 — 7 $\frac{9}{7}$ $\frac{8}{\frac{6}{4♮}}$ 6 | $\frac{9}{7}$ 4♮ 6 *wrong*]

In Ex. 1 it is not the presence of ♯g in the previous bar which, *in itself*, makes a $\frac{6}{4♮}$ chord on *f* wrong. The nature of the progression becomes clearer if the 7 on *f* is allowed to resolve before the apparent change of harmony caused by the *anticipated passing note b* in the upper part. The progression

thus stands for [musical example: ♯ 7 6 3 4♮ 6]

If the modulation had been to C major, $\frac{6}{4♮}$ on *f* would have been quite justifiable, in spite of the previous ♯g.

[musical example: ♯ 7 4♮ 6 $\frac{6}{4}$ $\frac{5}{3}$]

There is ellipse of the resolution of the 7 on *f* (Ch. xxii, 'Inversion &c.', § 8), and the progression stands for [musical example: ♯ 7 6 4♮ &c.]

In Ex. 2 the Seventh on *c* in the first bar resolves, not on a Triad on *d* (Ch. xi, 'Sevenths', III, § 1 *a*), but on its first inversion, 6 on *f*, the resolution being delayed by suspension.† The 6 on *f* becomes the pivot chord in

† But for the suspension the 3 of the 7 on *c* could not, in the position in which the chords are taken in the Ex., fall to 6 on *f* because of the resulting bad progression of a diminished Fifth falling to a perfect one: [musical example: 7 $\frac{6}{3}$ 4♮]

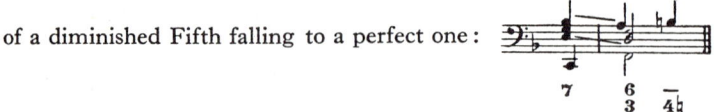

The progression [musical example: 7 $\frac{6}{3}$ 4♮ 6] would have been *possible*, but no more.

If, on the other hand, the 3 of the Seventh on *c* had its proper upward progression (Ch. xi, 'Sevenths', l.c.), the Sixth on *f* would obviously be left minus the 6!

XIV § 11 $\begin{smallmatrix}6\\4\\2\end{smallmatrix}$ CHORDS 671

the modulation to D minor, the ♮b in the upper part being, as in Ex. 1, an anticipated passing note.

In the following Ex. we find the misleading figuring (unfortunately not uncommon) against which Ph. Em. Bach warns us.

The $+4\ (=4\!\!\!\!/)$ on $f*$, as in Ex. 1, is to be taken as $\begin{smallmatrix}8\\6\\4\!\!\!\!/\end{smallmatrix}$.

Leclair, Opera IV, *Six Sonatas for two Violins with a Through Bass for the Harpsicord or Violoncello*, Sonata I, Allegro ma non troppo, bar 30.

Ex. 3

§ 12. Ph. Em. Bach (*Versuch &c.*, Part II, Ch. 9, II, § 3) gives the following Exx. (as usual, on a single stave), to illustrate the way in which long appoggiaturas are to be treated both in the figuring and the accompaniment. In Ex. 1 a $\begin{smallmatrix}6\\5\end{smallmatrix}$ chord (5♭) is retarded by a double appoggiatura $\begin{smallmatrix}4\\2\end{smallmatrix}$, and in Ex. 2 the 6 of a $\begin{smallmatrix}6\\4\\2\end{smallmatrix}$ chord is retarded by a chromatic appoggiatura:

Ex. 1

Ex. 2

Of these Exx. Bach says: "When, in the Six-Five chord with the false [i.e. diminished] Fifth, the latter and the Third are retarded by a slow double Appoggiatura, and if *this somewhat unpleasant Appoggiatura is to be played* [in the accompaniment], one must put $^4_2\,^{5\flat}_3$ over the notes and omit the 6 from this $^4_2$.

"When, in the case of the chord of the Second $\begin{bmatrix}6\\4\\2\end{bmatrix}$, the Second is retarded by a slow appoggiatura of the augmented Octave, one takes—especially if the [musical] idea is expressed softly—only the Fourth, and does not add the Second and Sixth until the former enters in the principal part [Ex. 2 *a*]. However, as this augmented Octave is more alarming to the eye than to the ear, and as the ear is not unpleasantly deceived when it resolves, if the tempo be slow, and only the Fourth be taken with this Octave, one can both figure it and play it (*b*).

"The treatment shown at (*c*), where the Third proceeds to the Fourth by an appoggiatura, does not sound bad either. Any one whose ear is quite too delicate is at liberty, in both cases [Exx. 1 and 2], to let these appoggiaturas pass without accompaniment in the right hand.

"When the accompaniment is to be very delicate, *these refinements are, in any case, left to the principal parts.*

"The augmented Octave is a dissonance which rises, and which only occurs as an appoggiatura."

N.B.—The italics in the above are not Bach's.

CHAPTER XV
MAJOR SEVENTHS RESOLVING UPWARDS OVER THE SAME BASS

XV

MAJOR SEVENTHS RESOLVING UPWARDS OVER THE SAME BASS

§ 1. A Dominant Seventh $\frac{7}{\frac{5}{3}}$, instead of resolving directly, may be retarded, in which case we get $\frac{7}{4}\frac{8}{3}$ over the Tonic (Exx. 1, 2, 3).

This retardation does not affect the progression of the intervals: the 7, as the leading note, must rise; the 4, as the 7 in the Dominant harmony, must fall; while the 2 may either rise (Exx. 1, 3) or fall (Ex. 2).

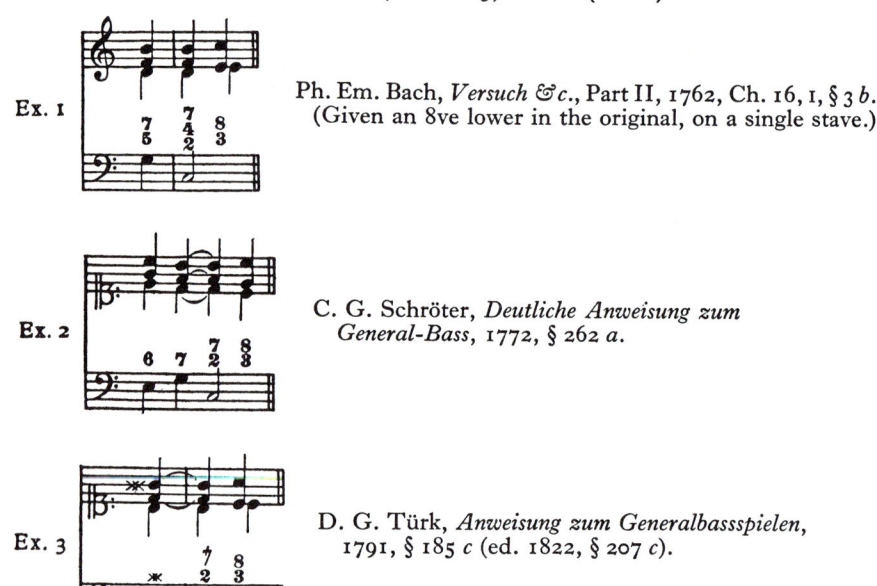

Ex. 1

Ph. Em. Bach, *Versuch &c.*, Part II, 1762, Ch. 16, 1, § 3 b. (Given an 8ve lower in the original, on a single stave.)

Ex. 2

C. G. Schröter, *Deutliche Anweisung zum General-Bass*, 1772, § 262 a.

Ex. 3

D. G. Türk, *Anweisung zum Generalbassspielen*, 1791, § 185 c (ed. 1822, § 207 c).

The proper figuring is seen in Ex. 1. For the inadequate figuring shown in Exx. 2 and 3 see Ch. xxi, 'Incomplete figuring', IV, § 3 ($\frac{7}{4}\frac{7}{2}=\frac{7}{4}$).

Many composers use the figuring $\frac{9}{7}$ instead of $\frac{7}{4}$. Ph. Em. Bach (ibid., Ch. 16, 1, § 4) remarks that certain cases bear either figuring (cf. § 3, Exx. 6, 7). He adheres to the distinction that 2 rises a degree, as in Ex. 1 above, while 9 falls, as in Ex. 2. He evidently preferred the former progression of the interval in question. He writes: "As it occurs over a tied Bass note [by which he here means a stationary Bass, as in § 6, Exx. 1, 2], and, therefore, only as a passing note, or as a retardation [as in Exx. 1–3 above] it has the same right here as in other cases, namely to rise." Apropos of the following example (in which the upper parts represent the principal parts, and not the accompaniment)

Ex. 4

Ibid., Ch. 16, II, § 5 c. (Given on a single stave in the original.)

he writes: "The example clearly shows the difference between the resolution of $\frac{9}{7}$ and $\frac{7}{2}$. Whoever, in the last bar, plays $\begin{smallmatrix}9&8\\7&8\\&4&3\end{smallmatrix}$ [as in Ex. 2 above] will, it is true, make no mistake in the resolution; but he will also hardly be able to deny that the accompaniment with the progression prescribed [$\begin{smallmatrix}7&8\\4&3\\2&3\end{smallmatrix}$, as in Ex. 1] comes nearest to the sense of the composer."

§ 2. In the following example $\frac{7}{4}\atop{2}$ on the Tonic is prepared by 6 ($=\frac{8}{6}\atop{3}$) on the Supertonic. In this case *the 4 is free to rise*:

C. G. Schröter, ibid., § 262.

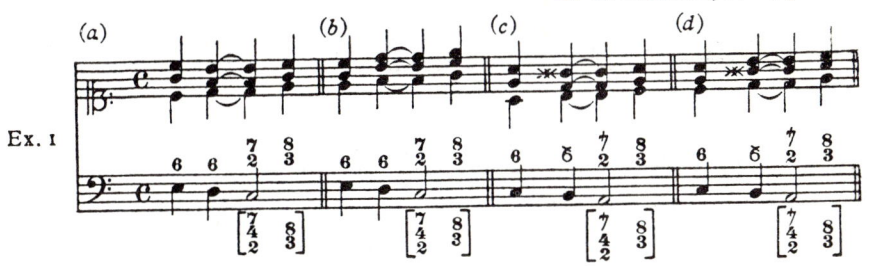

Ex. 1

The full figuring is added in brackets below the Bass.

The 7 must never be prepared by the 8ve of the Bass of the preceding chord, as in the following example:

Ex. 5

Ph. Em. Bach, ibid., Ch. 16, II, § 10. (Given, in the original, on a single stave, an 8ve lower (cf. Ch. III, § 3, notes 29 and 30) and with the Bass unfigured.)

'wrong'

The consecutive 8ves in the above progression, avoided only by the retarded resolution, are similar to those which arise when a 9, resolving on 8, is prepared by the 8ve of the Bass.

§ 3. The same retardation occurs in the resolution of $\frac{8}{7}\atop{3}$ on the Dominant (Ex. 1), and of $\frac{4}{3}$ on the Supertonic (Exx. 2, 3); also in that of $\overset{6}{\underset{3}{4}}$, with augmented Sixth and major Third on a Bass note falling a semitone (Ex. 4).

The resulting chord $\begin{smallmatrix}7\\5\\4\end{smallmatrix}\left(\begin{smallmatrix}\sharp7\\5\\4\end{smallmatrix}\begin{smallmatrix}\natural7\\5\\4\end{smallmatrix}\right)$ is often figured $\frac{7}{4}$ (as in Ex. 3), and often, quite incorrectly, $\frac{7}{2}$ (as in Exx. 1 and 2).

676   MAJOR SEVENTHS RESOLVING UPWARDS   XV § 3

The 5, being consonant with the Bass, does not require preparation; $\smash{\genfrac{}{}{0pt}{}{7}{\genfrac{}{}{0pt}{}{5}{4}}}$ may therefore be prepared by 6 = $\smash{\genfrac{}{}{0pt}{}{6}{\genfrac{}{}{0pt}{}{3}{3}}}$, with major Sixth and minor Third, on a Bass note falling a tone (Ex. 5 a), or by $\overset{6}{\flat}$ = $\smash{\genfrac{}{}{0pt}{}{6}{\genfrac{}{}{0pt}{}{3}{3}}}$, with augmented Sixth and major Third on one falling a semitone (Ex. 5 b and c).

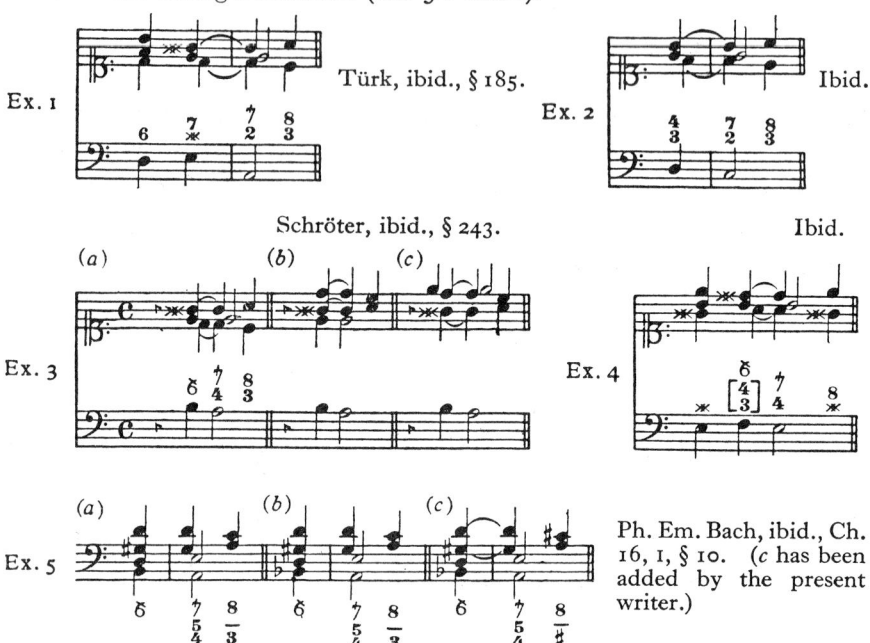

Ex. 1   Türk, ibid., § 185.   Ex. 2   Ibid.

Ex. 3   Schröter, ibid., § 243.   Ex. 4   Ibid.

Ex. 5   Ph. Em. Bach, ibid., Ch. 16, 1, § 10. (c has been added by the present writer.)

In Exx. 6, 7 we have the chord in five parts. In Ex. 6 it is prepared by a Dominant Seventh, and in Ex. 7 by the second inversion of a diminished Seventh on *d* sharp:

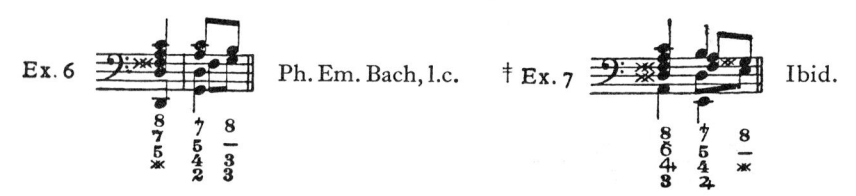

Ex. 6   Ph. Em. Bach, l.c.   † Ex. 7   Ibid.

Ph. Em. Bach mentions that in such cases the figuring $\smash{\genfrac{}{}{0pt}{}{9}{\genfrac{}{}{0pt}{}{7}{\genfrac{}{}{0pt}{}{5}{4}}}}$ is sometimes used instead of $\smash{\genfrac{}{}{0pt}{}{7}{\genfrac{}{}{0pt}{}{5}{4}}}$. This use of 9 instead of 2 (cf. Ch. xxiii, 'Varieties of figuring', § 14) suggests that the interval in question should fall to the 8 instead of rising to the 3 as in Bach's examples.

† For the origin of the progression on which this example is based see Ch. xiii, '$\smash{\genfrac{}{}{0pt}{}{4}{3}}$ Chords', § 7, Ex. 4.

§ 4. A Triad on the Dominant, in either three or four parts, may be retarded over the Tonic, as in Ex. 1:

Ex. 1

N.B.—In (*b*) the more correct figuring would undoubtedly be $^{7\,8}_{5\,-}_{2\,3}$, but it is rarely found. Türk gives the example in three parts only (ibid., § 185 *f*, ed. 1822, § 207 *f*).

Such a Triad may also be followed by $^7_4_2$ over the Tonic, the 4 being taken unprepared, as Ex. 2:

Ex. 2   Ph. Em. Bach, ibid., Ch. 16, I, § 3 *c*.

In this case the 4 is under the same obligation to *fall*, as if it had been present in the preceding chord, as in § 1, Exx. 1–3.

§ 5. In the following examples the leading note alone is retarded:

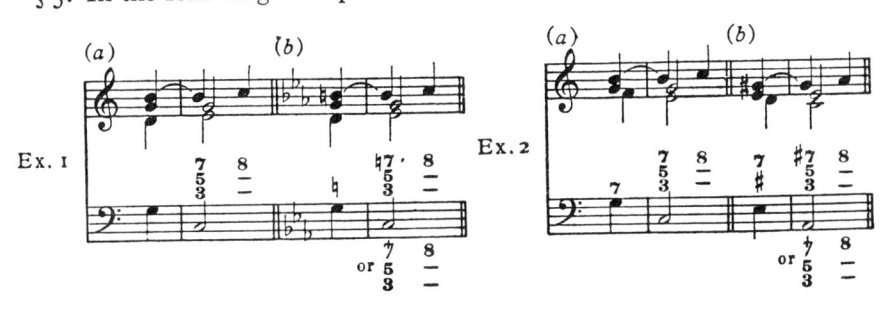

Ex. 1

Ex. 2

Ex. 3

In this case the full figuring $^{7\,8}_{5\,-}_{3\,-}$ is necessary, as 7 8 is constantly to be found as an abbreviation of $^{7\,8}_{4\,3}_{2}$ (cf. Ch. xxi, 'Incomplete figuring', IV, § 3).

§ 6. The chord ($^7_4_2$ over the Tonic) which, in § 1, appeared as a retardation, can also occur without preparation as a passing chord over a stationary Bass, in which case the 4 *is free to rise*:

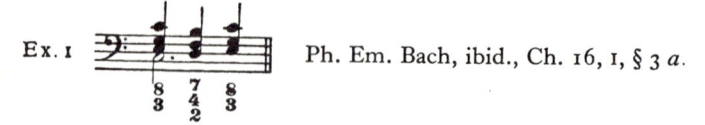

Ex. 1 [musical example] Ph. Em. Bach, ibid., Ch. 16, 1, § 3 *a*.

In the following examples the chord is taken in five parts, the full figuring being $\begin{smallmatrix}7\\5\\4\\2\end{smallmatrix}$:

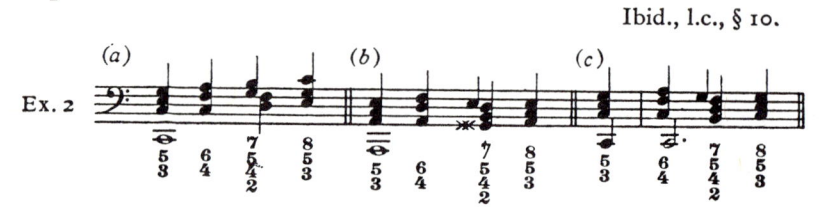

Ibid., l.c., § 10.

Ex. 2 [musical example with (a), (b), (c)]

Sometimes the 7, instead of rising to the 8, will be found to fall a degree; this progression, like so many others, originates in the ellipse of the true resolution. Ph. Em. Bach writes (l.c. II, § 5): "If, in the following examples (*a*), the Seventh appears to fall, an Ellipsis is to blame. The complete progression is given at (*b*):

Ex. 3 [musical example with (a), (b)]

Ex. 4 [musical example with (a), (b)]

§ 7. The full chord of the Dominant Ninth $\begin{smallmatrix}9\\7\\5\\3\end{smallmatrix}$, suspended over the Tonic, is figured $\begin{smallmatrix}7\\6\\4\\2\end{smallmatrix}$, Exx. 1, 2:

Ex. 1 [musical example with (a), (b)]

Türk, ibid., ed. 1722, § 207 *h*.
(Example not given in 1st ed. 1791.)

Ex. 2 [music] Ph. Em. Bach, ibid., l.c., I, § 9 b.

In the minor key the same chord may also appear over the Tonic *with the 6 taken unprepared*, the 9 not being present in the preceding chord, Ex. 3:

Ex. 3 [music] Ph. Em. Bach, ibid. c.

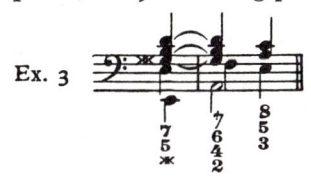

In four parts the chord appears as $^7_6$, lacking the 2. As such, it may be prepared by $^6_{5\flat}$ on the Supertonic, the first inversion of a diminished Seventh on the leading note (Ch. xi, 'Sevenths', III, § 2), Ex. 4, or by an augmented Sixth ($^6_5$, $^6_3$, or $^6_{4\atop 3}$) on the Submediant, Ex. 5:

Ex. 4 [music] Ph. Em. Bach, ibid. (3).

Ex. 5 [music] (a) (b) (c)

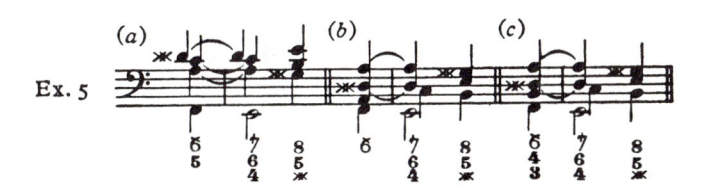

In Ex. 5 (b) (c), as in Ex. 3, the 6 is not present in the previous chord. Ph. Em. Bach remarks that in Ex. 4 the inclusion of the 2 is optional.

Besides the cases mentioned above, a $^7_{6\atop 4\atop 2}$ chord on the Dominant of a minor key can be prepared by $^6_{4\atop 3}$ on the Tonic, the second inversion of a diminished Seventh on the sharpened Subdominant,[1] Ex. 6:

Ex. 6 [2)] [music] Ph. Em. Bach, ibid. b.

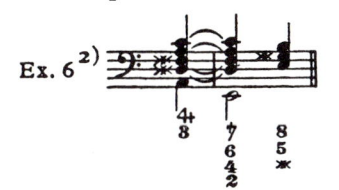

---

[1] Cf. § 3, Ex. 7, note.
[2] Bach's notation of the example does not indicate whether the 2 is intended to rise, thus doubling the leading note in the unison, or to fall. In the position in which

In the case of an ornamental resolution, as Bach points out, the 2 must be omitted, Ex. 7:

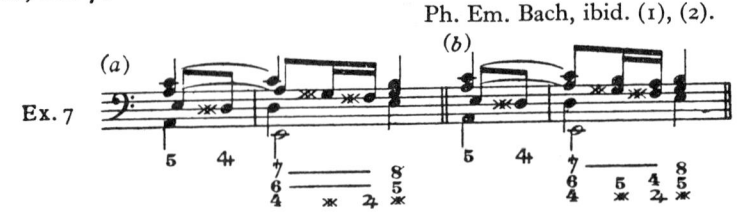

Ex. 7 [musical example] Ph. Em. Bach, ibid. (1), (2).

§ 8. The chord which appeared in § 7, Exx. 1, 2, composed of retarded discords (and, with the exception of the 6, in § 7, Ex. 3), occurs without preparation over a stationary Bass (cf. § 6):

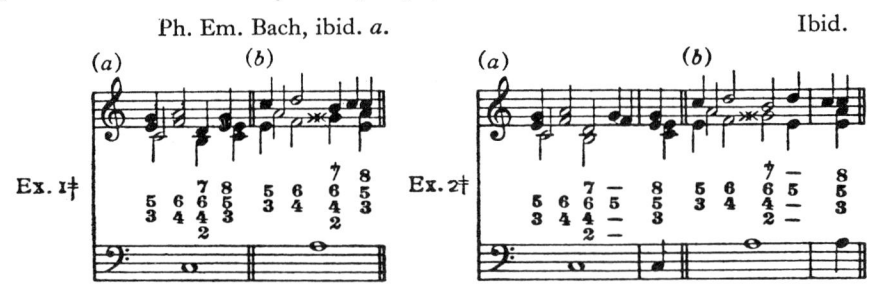

Ex. 1† [musical example] Ph. Em. Bach, ibid. *a.*   Ex. 2† [musical example] Ibid.

§ 9. When $\begin{smallmatrix}7\\4\\2\end{smallmatrix}$ and $\begin{smallmatrix}7\\6\\4\\2\end{smallmatrix}$ chords occur over a stationary Bass (§§ 6, 8), one or more of the intervals may be retarded:

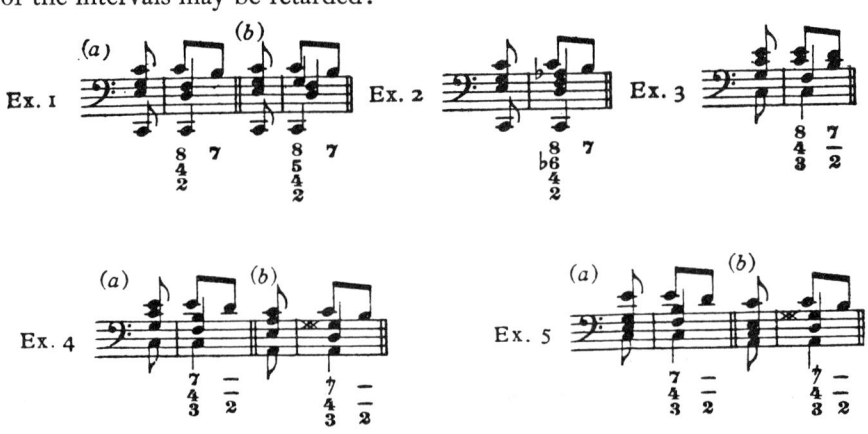

Ex. 1 [musical example]   Ex. 2 [musical example]   Ex. 3 [musical example]

Ex. 4 [musical example]   Ex. 5 [musical example]

the example is given the difference, so far as a keyed instrument is concerned, exists only on paper. If, however, the first chord were taken with the 6 (*f* sharp) in the upper part, the upward progression of the 2 in the following chord would result in the doubling of the leading note in the Octave. In this case, therefore, it would be necessary to treat the example as though figured: [musical example]

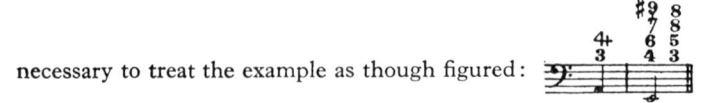

† Given in the original on a single stave and an 8ve lower.

Ph. Em. Bach, from whom the above examples are taken (ibid., Ch. 16, II, § 2), writes: "When the Seventh in our chord $\begin{bmatrix} 7 & 7 & 7 \\ 5 & 5 & 6 \\ 4 & 4 & 4 \\ 2 & 2 & 2 \end{bmatrix}$ is retarded by the Octave the other parts are not affected, but enter simultaneously with the Bass. This Octave is here in the position of a dissonance: it is suspended over the Second and resolves downwards on the major Seventh. In the figuring of this progression the 8 and 7 are side by side; the other figures, which are taken together with the Octave, must stand below it. In example (*a*) [=Ex. 3 above], besides the Seventh, the Second is also retarded by the Third. The latter then, like the Octave, assumes the character of a dissonance. In (*b*) [=Ex. 4] only the 2 is retarded by the 3; the latter can be doubled in the preceding Triad, (*c*) [=Ex. 5]. The position prescribed in all these examples is the most serviceable one."

§ 10. All Ph. Em. Bach's hints on the adjustment of the accompaniment (sometimes at the expense of a literal interpretation of the figures) to the requirements of the principal part, or parts, deserve to be recorded. Of Ex. 1, which, as usual, he gives on a single stave, he writes (l.c. II, § 3): "When, in the principal part, the Fourth is retarded by an appoggiatura,[1] one takes $\begin{smallmatrix}7\\5\\4\\2\end{smallmatrix}$, $\begin{smallmatrix}7\\4\\2\end{smallmatrix}$, or only $\begin{smallmatrix}7\\2\end{smallmatrix}$, according as a strong or a light accompaniment is required, immediately upon the entry of the Bass."

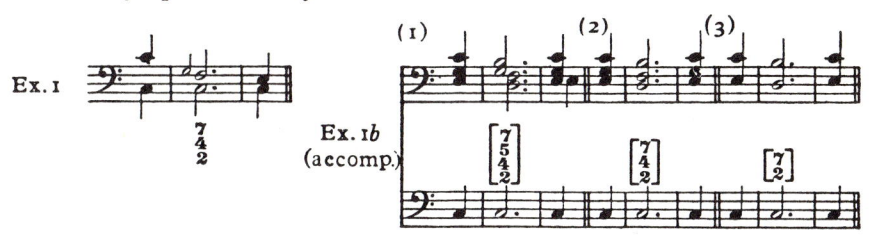

Of Ex. 2 Bach writes (l.c. § 4): "In the following example it is *best* to play in three parts only; but if a fourth part is, at all costs, to be included, one takes the Fifth instead of the Fourth:[2] partly in order that the number of appoggiaturas, of which, owing to their repetition [they occur in the 1st and 2nd bars], there is anyhow an accumulation, may not be further increased by the Fourth,[3] and distaste be excited; partly in order that the appoggiatura heard in the principal part may stand out (*vorzüglich gehört werden*), and partly in order that the Triad may be complete when resolution takes place.[4]

---

[1] A long appoggiatura before a dotted note, as in the present case, occupies *two-thirds* of the value of the note. This important rule is often overlooked at the present day.

[2] Bach is evidently presupposing that the composer of a passage similar to the example in question has used the figuring $\begin{smallmatrix}7\\4\\2\end{smallmatrix}$, as might easily be the case.

[3] i.e. in order that the double appoggiaturas already present may not become triple ones. The appoggiaturas in the example are not noted as such, but the notation might equally well have been:

[4] In Ex. 1 b (2) the 4 rises to the 5 of the Tonic Triad (cf. § 6), but in the present instance it would have to fall, thus leaving the Triad incomplete (cf. § 4, Ex. 2).

This completeness cannot here be brought about by a fifth part, for this example does not well bear an accompaniment in four parts, let alone in five."

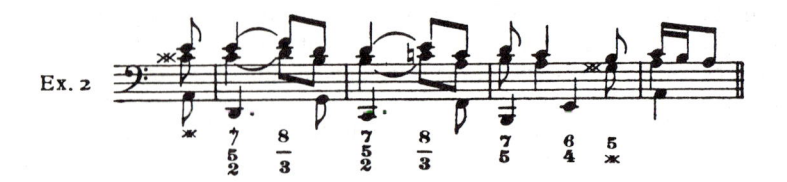

The accompaniment which Bach has in mind is, therefore, as follows:

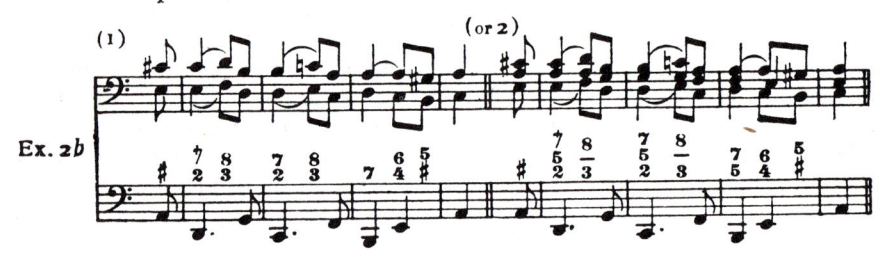

CHAPTER XVI
CHORDS WITH AN AUGMENTED SIXTH

XVI

CHORDS WITH AN AUGMENTED SIXTH

§ 1. There are three chords which contain an augmented Sixth, all having their natural seat on the sixth degree (Submediant) of the minor scale. They consist, respectively, besides the Bass, of (1) the major Third and augmented Sixth (sometimes known as the "Italian Sixth"), (2) the major Third, augmented Fourth, and augmented Sixth (or "French Sixth"), and (3) the major Third, perfect Fifth, and augmented Sixth (or "German Sixth").

The explanation of the augmented Sixth has always been a problem to theorists. To preserve the uniformity of his system, Marpurg[1] classifies all three chords as inversions of (admittedly) non-existent Triads, which he calls "mixed", inasmuch as they contain intervals characteristic of two different keys. Thus, the "Italian Sixth", $\substack{\sharp d \\ a \\ f}$, hypothetically based on the "mixed" Triad $\substack{a \\ \sharp f \\ \sharp d}$, belongs (he tells us) to the key of *A* minor in virtue of the $\natural f$, and to *E* minor in virtue of the $\sharp d$, though, as far as its actual employment is concerned, it belongs to the former key alone.

There seems, however, little difficulty in the way of supposing that the augmented Sixth owes its origin to the anticipation of a passing note (*anticipatio transitus*),[2] a process responsible for many harmonic irregularities.

The passing note might be introduced at either end of the chord, as in the following examples. In Ex. 1 (*b*) it will be observed that there is a transitory modulation to the key of *E* major.

If the passing notes ** in both examples are anticipated (*c*), we get the augmented Sixth as an apparent constituent of the harmony:

Ex. 1

The same explanation would, of course, apply equally when the augmented Sixth is associated with the augmented Fourth, or the perfect Fifth, in addition to the major Third.

§ 2. The augmented Sixth with major Third ("Italian Sixth").

In this, as in the other two chords of the augmented Sixth, that interval is independent of preparation. The chord may occur on either a weak or a strong beat, and the only interval which, in four-part harmony, can be doubled is the Third, as:

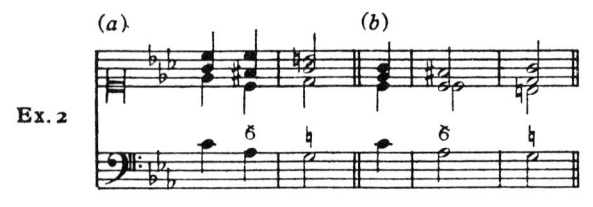

Ex. 2

---

[1] *Handbuch &c.*, 2nd ed. 1762, pp. 44 sq.   [2] Cf. Ch. xxii, "Inversion", &c., § 7.

The augmented Sixth must always rise, and the Bass fall, a semitone. Any other progression of the Bass is possible only when the augmented Sixth occurs as a mere passing note, as in the following example from Ph. Em. Bach:[3]

Ex. 3

The essential progression is seen at (*b*) (not given by Bach).

§ 3. Augmented Sixth with major Third and *augmented Fourth* ("French Sixth").

This chord, like the one just described, occurs alike on a weak and on a strong beat. The 6 resolves a semitone upwards, and the Bass and the 3 a semitone downwards, though the resolution may be delayed, as in all but the first of the following series of examples from Ph. Em. Bach.[4] Either the 3 or the 4, Bach tells us, must be present in the preceding chord. The latter condition is fulfilled in Ex. 4 *a*, the former in the remaining examples:

Ex. 4

§ 4. The augmented Sixth with major Third and *perfect Fifth* ("German Sixth").

The 5 is more commonly present in the preceding chord (Ex. 5 *a*), but

---

[3] *Versuch &c.*, Part II, 1762, Ch. 3, I, § 21, where it is given on a single stave, an 8ve lower than here.
[4] o.c., Ch. 7, I, § 11. Bach gives the figured Bass only. The chords which have here been added in small notes can be taken in any other position; the one in which the 4 and 3 are separated is always considered the best.

may be taken without such preparation when another harmony on the *same Bass* precedes [5] (Ex. 5 b, c):

Ex. 5

The resolution of the chord upon the major Triad of a bass note falling a semitone is usually retarded (as in the above examples) by an intervening $^6_4$, to avoid the consecutive Fifths which must otherwise arise between the Bass and an upper part. Marpurg, however, held that the Fifths involved by a direct resolution (as in the following example) are justifiable by a supposed crossing of the parts: [6]

Ex. 6

The other two positions, in which the Fifths would appear either between extreme parts or between Tenor and Bass, are, of course, impossible.

Ph. Em. Bach gives the following remarkable example of a delayed resolution, in which the Bass, instead of falling a semitone to $^6_4$ on the Dominant, falls a Fourth to the first inversion of the Tonic chord: [7]

Ex. 7

[5] This rule is given, in substance, by Ph. Em. Bach (o.c., Ch. 8, I, § 9), illustrated by an example, to be given presently (Ex. 7), on which Ex. 5 c above is based. He adds, however, that the Sixth "should properly speaking enter a quaver later", as:

presumably on the ground that it is *better*, if possible, to avoid taking the 5 without preparation.

[6] Cf. Ch. iii, § 9, 1 *ad fin*.

[7] o.c., Ch. 8, I, § 9, where the example is given, as usual, on a single stave, an 8ve lower than here. Bach makes no mention of the irregular resolution; the example is given to illustrate the way in which the 5 in a $^6_5$ chord (with augmented Sixth) may be taken unprepared (cf. note 5).

§ 5. Instances of the "inversion" of either of the three chords described above are rarely to be met with. The following two examples from Leclair exhibit a remarkable chord, composed of the minor Third, augmented Fourth, and minor Sixth, on the Subdominant of the minor mode. In accordance with its figuring it should, perhaps, have been included in the chapter dealing with $\frac{6}{4}$ chords, but since the diminished Third (between the augmented Fourth and the minor Sixth) may be regarded as the inversion of an augmented Sixth, it seemed more appropriate to include it here. The entire chord, indeed, may be regarded, if one so pleases (simply as a means of classification), as the first inversion of a "German Sixth" on, not the sixth degree of the minor scale (as in the text-book example quoted in note 10), but its *flattened Supertonic*; it is, thus, closely akin to the "Neapolitan Sixth":

Ex. 8[8)]

It will be seen that the position in which the chord at *, in Exx. 8 and 9, is taken in the suggested accompaniment is the only one in which consecutive Fifths, which must arise if the 3 is above the 6, can be avoided. It is, however, for the individual to decide whether academic correctness need, in this instance, outweigh other considerations. In all discords the position in which the two intervals between which the dissonance lies (6 and 5 in a $\frac{6}{5}$ chord, 4 and 3 in a $\frac{6}{4}$, &c.) are *not in adjacent parts* is, generally

[8] Jean-Marie Leclair, *Sonatas for two Violins and Bass*, Op. 4 (Walsh), Sonata III, Aria, 2nd section, bars 23 sqq.

speaking, always the best and most effective; and this principle applies very forcibly to the augmented Fourth and minor Sixth in the chord now under discussion. The consecutive Fifths involved by employing the position in

Ex. 9 [9)]

question would undoubtedly have been condemned by Ph. Em. Bach, and perhaps by others, but they would also have had defenders whose high authority cannot be gainsaid.[10]

If we are prepared to accept the view of the latter, the two examples above may be accompanied as follows:

Ex. 10 [11)]

[9] Jean-Marie Leclair, *Sonatas for Violin Solo and Bass*, Book II, Sonata X, Vivace, 1st section *ad fin.*

[10] Marpurg would probably have included them in the category of special cases of which he said that "the dissonance here stifles the annoyance to the ear" (cf. Ch. iii, § 10 *e*, Ex. 13). Schröter gives the following example, which exhibits Fifths similar to those now in question, the chord at * being, indeed, the first inversion of a "German Sixth" on the sixth degree of the minor scale:

Deutliche Anweisung &c., 1772, § 215 *f*, p. 112.

Of this he writes: "In the example at (*f*) various persons of defective intellect will see consecutive Fifths, which are not, however, noticed by musical ears." He reminds the reader of a previous example concerning which he expressed a similar opinion (see Ch. iii, § 10 *e*, Ex. 14).

[11] It will be observed that, in this example, owing to the accompaniment being in five parts, the Consecutive Fifths at * are even less noticeable than they would otherwise be.

CHORDS WITH AN AUGMENTED SIXTH

Ex. 11

[12] It often happens, in choosing the position in which to take a series of chords, that one fault can be avoided only at the expense of incurring another. Thus, the form of accompaniment shown in Ex. 11 (though better in, at least, one respect than that in Ex. 9) is open to criticism on the following grounds: (1) it is higher in pitch than the rules allow, though this is partly excused by the fact that the Bass is rather high; (2) the upper part is too nearly identical with the Violin part; and (3) a considerable skip, such as that at the beginning of the penultimate bar, is always to be avoided in the absence of some good reason to the contrary; in this instance the alternative would be to close an Octave above the Violin.

CHAPTER XVII
HARMONIES DUE TO THE RETARDATION OR ANTICIPATION OF ONE OR MORE INTERVALS

XVII

HARMONIES DUE TO THE RETARDATION OR ANTICIPATION OF ONE OR MORE INTERVALS

§ 1. *Introductory.*

A good many discords due to retardation [1] have already been dealt with in the course of Chapters XI–XV, as it seemed more convenient to include in one chapter all chords bearing the same figuring, irrespective of their different origin. Of the many that remain it is proposed to treat only those which are more generally recognized in the text-books, and which are likely to be met with in actual practice.[2] The student who has thoroughly mastered the fundamental chords (Triads and Sevenths, and their several inversions) and their possible progressions should be in a position to solve most problems arising out of an unfamiliar figuring, and, in particular, to determine the progression of the harmony indicated thereby.

The examples given in the present chapter are taken largely from Ph. Em. Bach, and in their notation the practice adopted in previous chapters will be adhered to.[3]

---

[1] The term *retardation* is convenient inasmuch as it applies equally to an upward and to a downward progression, whereas the term *suspension* always suggests the latter, unless the contrary is expressly indicated.

[2] Illustrations of almost every imaginable harmony arising through retardation, or anticipation, are to be found in the respective works of Schröter (*Deutliche Anweisung &c.*, 1772, Ch. XIX, §§ 218–80, pp. 114–62) and of Türk (*Kurze Anweisung &c.*, 1791, Chs. VI–VIII, §§ 144–90, pp. 198–244).

Türk's exposition is much the clearer of the two, while that of Schröter contains occasional quaint touches not to be found in the pages of the younger writer; his distribution of all the harmonies in question into forty-three "harmonic parcels" (*harmonische Pakete*) is very characteristic. With both Schröter and Türk the basis of classification is the *number of intervals* retarded in the essential harmonies: $\frac{5}{3}$, $\frac{6}{3}$, $\frac{6}{4}$, $\frac{7}{5}$ $\left(\frac{8}{7}\right)$, $\frac{6}{5}$, $\frac{6}{4}$, $\frac{6}{2}$. First come the chords with only one retardation, then those with two, and last those with three or more. The retardation of four intervals is, of course, only possible when the chord of preparation is taken in five parts, as in the following example from Türk (o.c. § 187 c, p. 241) of a retarded chord of the Sixth on the third degree of the minor scale:

Chords in which the retardation is in the Bass alone, as [music example], are styled by both writers *anticipations* (i.e. of the upper parts), and are treated by Türk in a separate chapter.

[3] Where Bach gives an example in full, on a single stave, it is here given on two staves, generally an 8ve higher than in the original; where he gives the figured Bass

XVII § 2   HARMONIES DUE TO RETARDATION, ETC.

§ 2. $\begin{smallmatrix}9\\5\\3\end{smallmatrix}$.

When the Octave of the Bass of a Triad is retarded by a suspended Ninth, the latter may resolve either on the same Bass (Ex. 1 *a*, *b*), in which case the figuring is 9 8 (the 9 being, if necessary, qualified by an accidental), or on the first inversion of the same harmony (*c*), or on another harmony (*d, e, f*):

When it is over a diminished Triad that this suspension occurs, it is better, Ph. Em. Bach tells us, though not necessary, that the diminished Fifth should be prepared, as in the last of the three following examples:

When 9 is associated with an augmented Fifth, the latter usually rises to 6 at the same time that the 9 resolves:

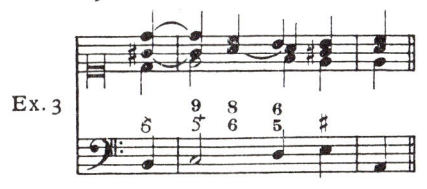

only, it is here given as in the original, with the addition (wherever it seemed advisable) of an upper stave on which the realization of the figures is supplied in small notes. In the latter case it will be understood that Bach is not responsible for the position in which the chords are taken, unless it is stated that the latter was selected in obedience to directions given by himself.

⁴ *Versuch &c.*, Part II, 1762, Ch. 17, I, § 7. In the original the Bass of Ex. 2 *b* appears as follows: (cf. note 3).

None of the earlier authorities, so far as the writer is aware, mention the possibility of a Ninth resolving upwards. Türk, however, gives the following examples (possible only in the free style) in which that interval appears as the retardation, not of an Octave, but of a Tenth.[5] This progression is best taken in three parts only; in the first example, however, Türk has added a fourth part in small notes, doubtless as a warning that, when the 9 rises to 10, the 3 of the Triad must not be present at the same time, since the Seventh arising between the 9 and the 3 would call for a downward resolution of the former. In the second example the Ninth is augmented.

Türk gives a further example, which may as well be included here, in which there is a triple retardation, the augmented Ninth being associated, not with 5, but with $^6_4$:

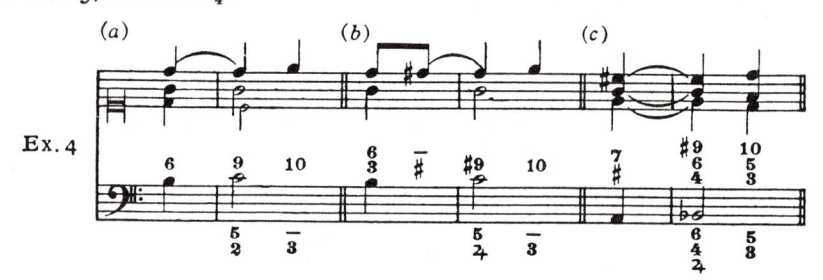

Ex. 4

He adds a note to the effect that the figuring given below the Bass, though more usual, is less correct than that given above, because the figure 2 is associated with a discord in the Bass itself, and suggests a downward resolution of the latter.

§ 3. $^8_5_4$.

When the 3 of a Triad is retarded by 4, the resolution generally takes place over the same Bass. The figuring is then 4 3 or $^5_4$ $^-_3$. If the 3 is accidentally sharpened or flattened, the figure is accompanied, or, more often, replaced,[1] by the appropriate accidental (4 ♯3, 4 ♮3, 4 ♭3 or 4 ♯, 4 ♮, 4 ♭). The Fifth may be either perfect (Ex. 1 *a–d*), or diminished (as in the second chord of Ex. 1 *e*), but the Fourth, except when taken as a free appoggiatura (cf. Ex. 4 *c*), is always perfect. In the following examples the chord is seen in all three positions:

Ex. 1

---

[5] *Kurze Anweisung &c.*, 1791, § 145 *e, f, g*, p. 201.
[1] When the figure is omitted [and, indeed, in any case] it is extremely desirable, as Ph. Em. Bach points out (o.c. Ch. 21, § 2), that the accidental should be placed far enough to the right of the 4, in order that it may not seem to apply to the latter, a confusion which might very easily arise owing to the absence of any definite rule as to whether the accidental should be placed before or after the figure which it qualifies. Thus 4♭3 might stand for either ♭4 3 or 4 ♭3.

XVII § 3   ANTICIPATION OF ONE OR MORE INTERVALS   695

[musical example (e)]

If the resolution of the 4 takes place over a different Bass (Ex. 2 *a*, *b*), or if the resolution over the same Bass coincides with a change of harmony (*c*, *d*), the figuring will be 4 or $\frac{5}{4}$:

Ex. 2 [musical examples (a), (b), (c), (d)]

Ph. Em. Bach gives the following examples (l.c. § 6) in which special care is required in order to avoid consecutives. In Ex. 3 (*a*) Fifths are avoided by doubling the 5 of the $\frac{5}{4\,3}$ and omitting the Octave of the Bass. In (*b*) and (*c*) Octaves would result if the chord of preparation included the Octave of the Bass; instead of which the 3 is doubled. In (*d*) and (*e*) the 4 3 is taken in extended harmony; otherwise there would be consecutive Octaves, and the harmony would be incomplete $\left(\begin{smallmatrix}8&-\\4&3\\8&-\end{smallmatrix}\right.$ instead of $\left.\begin{smallmatrix}8&-\\4&3\\5&-\end{smallmatrix}\right)$:

Ex. 3 [musical examples (a), (b), (c), (d), (e)]

[2] Ex. 2 (*c*) is from Ph. Em. Bach (l.c. § 4).

696 HARMONIES DUE TO THE RETARDATION OR   XVII § 3

In the free style, Ph. Em. Bach tells us (l.c. § 7), an appoggiatura in the principal part is sometimes responsible for the appearance in the figured Bass of a $\frac{5}{4}$ chord with the Fourth, sometimes even an augmented Fourth, *unprepared*. He gives the following examples: the perfect Fourth may be taken either by step (Ex. 4 *a*), or by leap (*b*), whereas the augmented Fourth can only be taken by step (*c*).[3] The position given, Bach tells us, is the "most tolerable"; he adds, however, that "one may well pass over this appoggiatura in the right hand WITHOUT ACCOMPANIMENT (*d*). Special caution is needed when the 4 3 is preceded by 6 on a bass note a degree below (*e, f, g*): when the 3 of the $\frac{6}{3}$ chord is in the upper part, it must be doubled[4] (*g*); if the 6 were doubled, or the Octave of the Bass included, consecutive Fifths would result (*h, i*):

Ex. 4

It will be remarked that Bach has given all the above examples in $\frac{3}{4}$ time, and that the appoggiatura, unlike the prepared 4, falls on a beat weaker than the preceding one.

When 4 3 occurs sequentially on a Bass alternately falling a Fourth and rising a Fifth, means must be taken to prevent the hands from getting too close together. Kirnberger gives the two following examples,[5] between which the difference, except in notation, is very small indeed: in Ex. 5 (*a*) a new part (indicated as such by the crotchet rest before it) is taken at the top (* *), the lowest middle part being dropped immediately afterwards (as indicated by the crotchet rest after it);[6] in Ex. 5 (*b*) the 5 of every alternate $\frac{5}{4}$ 3 rises to 8,

---

[3] Bach mentions that when the Fourth is augmented the full figuring $\frac{5}{4\ 3}$ (rather than 4 3) must be used, in order, no doubt, that the composer's intentions may be the more unmistakable, and, in particular, to prevent the possibility of confusion with 4♯ $\left(=\genfrac{}{}{0pt}{}{6}{\genfrac{}{}{0pt}{}{4}{2}}\right)$ so commonly found on the Subdominant.

[4] The duplication may be either in the 8ve (as in Bach's example) or in the unison:

[5] *Grundsätze des Generalbasses &c.*, 1781, Third Part of the volume of examples, Fig. xxiii, pp. 5 sq.

[6] Cf. Ch. iii, § 4, 1.

thus keeping the right hand at the same distance from the Bass, and so preserving the pattern of the sequence:

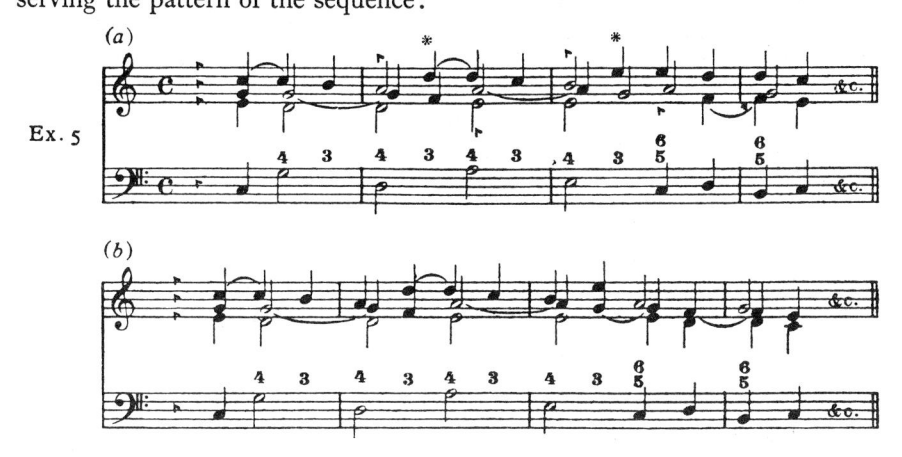

Ex. 5

§ 4. $\begin{smallmatrix}9\\5\\4\end{smallmatrix}$.

When the 3 of a Triad and the Octave of its Bass are retarded simultaneously by 9 and 4, and resolve over the same Bass, the figuring is $\begin{smallmatrix}9&8\\4&3\end{smallmatrix}$, with any necessary accidentals attached to the figures. The Ninth may be major or minor, and the Fifth, perfect, diminished, or augmented; but the Fourth, except when taken as a free appoggiatura (cf. Ex. 3 b), is always perfect. When the Fifth is perfect, the Ninth may be either major (Ex. 1 a) or minor (b); when it is diminished, the Ninth is always minor (c); when it is augmented, the Ninth is always major, and the augmented Fifth (5♯, 5♮, 5+) usually rises to 6 at the same time that the 9 and 4 resolve (d):

Ex. 1

The above examples can all be taken in either of the two remaining positions (or in extended harmony), but the positions in which either the 9 or the 4 is in the upper part (Ex. 1 a, b, c) are usually much to be preferred, save when the Fifth is augmented (d).

Sometimes the 9 and the 4 do not resolve simultaneously. Ph. Em. Bach gives the following examples (o.c. Ch. 19, § 3):

Ex. 2

In the later part of the eighteenth century, in the free style, the 4 came not infrequently to be taken unprepared as a free appoggiatura, as in the following examples given by Türk.[1] In the second example (Ex. 3 b), in three parts, of which Türk says that "the treatment is especially free and not worthy of imitation",[2] the 4 is augmented, and the 9, as well as the 4, is taken unprepared:

Ex. 3

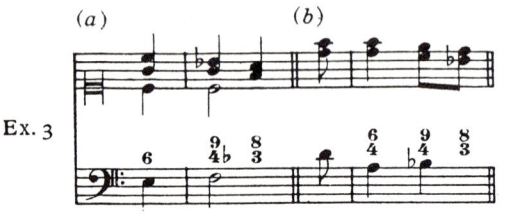

§ 5. $\begin{smallmatrix}9\\6\\3\end{smallmatrix}$.

When the Octave of the Bass of a chord of the Sixth is retarded by 9, and the resolution takes place over the same Bass, the figuring is $\begin{smallmatrix}9\\6\end{smallmatrix}$ 8 with any accidentals that may be necessary. The position with the Ninth in the upper part, Ph. Em. Bach tells us (o.c. Ch. 18, § 3), is, generally speaking, the best. He gives the following examples:

Ex. 1

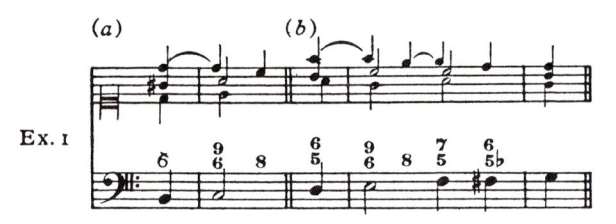

In the following example the 9 resolves, not on the Octave of the Bass of the chord of the Sixth, but on the 3 of the corresponding Triad:

Ex. 2

---

[1] *Kurze Anweisung &c.*, 1791, § 174, p. 228.
[2] The $\begin{smallmatrix}6\\4\end{smallmatrix}$ on *A* is itself a double appoggiatura, of which the resolution is delayed; the progression, as Türk explains, stands for:

or, without appoggiatura:

XVII § 5   ANTICIPATION OF ONE OR MORE INTERVALS

Schröter gives the following curious example, in which the resolution of the 9 takes place over a different Bass (*Deutliche Anweisung &c.*, 1772, § 239 *c*, p. 130):

Ex. 3

§ 6. $\begin{smallmatrix}9\\7\\3\end{smallmatrix}$.

When, in addition to the retardation of the Octave of the Bass of a chord of the Sixth by the 9 (just described) the Sixth itself is retarded by 7, and when both the suspended intervals resolve over the same Bass, the figuring is $\begin{smallmatrix}9&8\\7&6\end{smallmatrix}$ with any accidentals that may be necessary.

It will readily be seen from the following example that this progression corresponds exactly, *so far as the three upper parts are concerned*, with the $\begin{smallmatrix}9&8\\4&3\end{smallmatrix}$ described above (cf. § 4),[1] and that the latter stands to it in a relation analogous to that of a Triad to its first inversion:

Ex. 1

All three intervals, Ninth, Seventh, and Third, may be either major or minor, as may be seen in the following example from Schröter (o.c. § 248, p. 137):

Ex. 2

[1] It may also be noted incidentally that the progression of the upper parts is the same as with a $\begin{smallmatrix}6\\5\end{smallmatrix}$ chord on a Bass rising to a Triad:

In the next two examples, also from Schröter (l.c. p. 137), the resolution of the $\frac{9}{7}$ takes place over a different Bass:

Ex. 3

Ex. 4

The 9 and the 7 sometimes resolve separately, as in the following examples from Ph. Em. Bach (o.c. Ch. 20, § 3). In (*a*) the 9 resolves first, and in (*b*) the 7:

Ex. 5

It not infrequently happens that a chord figured $\frac{9}{7}$ has to be taken in five parts, the Fifth (which may be either diminished, perfect, or augmented) being included, even though not indicated in the figuring. In the following examples from Ph. Em. Bach (l.c. § 5) it will be observed that the chord of preparation is itself in five parts, the Octave of the Bass being included in order to prepare the 7. In all three examples it is evident that the 6 in the chord of preparation cannot do otherwise than remain as the 5 of the harmony which follows:[3]

[2] It will be noticed that, in (*b*), the progression of the leading note, ♯g in the Bass is irregular. Not only is its "resolution" transferred to the Alto, but, being delayed by suspension, it arrives a crotchet late.

[3] In such cases the inclusion of the 5 is often indicated in the figuring, and many composers would figure the Bass of Bach's examples as follows:

XVII § 6   ANTICIPATION OF ONE OR MORE INTERVALS   701

Ex. 6

The inclusion of the 5 (even though not figured) is also necessary when $\frac{9}{7}$ is followed by $\frac{6}{5}$ on the same Bass as in the following example:

Ex. 7

This is of particularly frequent occurrence in the works of Jean-Marie Leclair.

§ 7. $\frac{7}{6}$ and $\frac{7}{6}$.
      $\frac{3}{}$ $\frac{4}{}$

(a) When the 5 of a $\frac{7}{5}$ chord is retarded by 6, the figuring is $\frac{7}{6}$ 5, accompanied
                        $\frac{3}{}$ $\frac{}{}$
by any accidentals that may be necessary. The Third is not indicated unless accidentally altered: $\frac{7}{6}$5, $\frac{7}{6}$5. The 6, which must be present in the preceding
                                                  ♯   ♮
chord, becomes dissonant in relation to the 7, which is itself taken unprepared; from this latter circumstance it follows that this retardation is almost entirely confined to the chord of the Dominant Seventh. The Seventh will then be minor, and the Third major, while the Sixth is major or minor according to the key. The best position, Ph. Em. Bach tells us, is with the 6 in the upper part. He gives the following examples:[1]

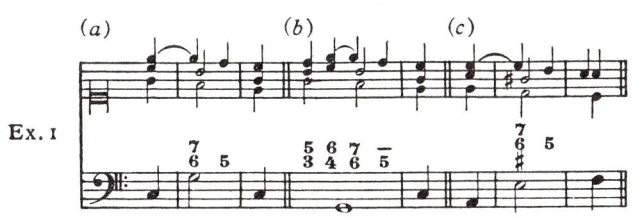

Ex. 1

In the next example, from the same source, the Seventh is not on the Dominant but on the leading note; the Third is therefore minor:

Ex. 2

[1] N.B.—*All the examples in the present section are from the same source* (*Versuch &c.*, Part II, 1762, Ch. 14).

Ph. Em. Bach also gives the following very remarkable examples of a diminished Seventh (on the sharpened Subdominant) with the 5 retarded by 6. In Ex. 3 the Sixth is minor, and in Ex. 4 diminished:

(b) When not only the 5 of a $\smash{\genfrac{}{}{0pt}{}{7}{\genfrac{}{}{0pt}{}{5}{3}}}$ chord is retarded by 6, but the 3 is also retarded by 4 (which, like the 6, must be prepared, while the Seventh itself is unpreparared), the figuring is $\smash{\genfrac{}{}{0pt}{}{7\,-}{\genfrac{}{}{0pt}{}{6\,5}{4\,3}}}$, with any accidentals that may be necessary:

Besides the above, Ph. Em. Bach gives the following very interesting example of $\smash{\genfrac{}{}{0pt}{}{7}{\genfrac{}{}{0pt}{}{6}{4}}}$ in the course of a Pedal point. Here the 6 and 4 resolve, not simultaneously, but successively:

---

[2] Of Ex. 3 Bach writes: "This chord [i.e. the diminished Seventh with the minor Sixth and minor Third] sounds unpleasant (*widrig*) in all positions; even the one in which the Sixth is uppermost does not sound much better; I should therefore prefer the treatment shown at (d) [=Ex. 3 b]. It is a remarkable thing that the diminished Octave, once so violently decried, is here undoubtedly better than those quite ordinary intervals in (b) [=Ex. 3 a] to which nobody has ever made any objection at all."

[3] Of Ex. 4 Bach writes: "Here, again, the Fifth is retarded by the Sixth. When the latter is uppermost, the treatment shown at (e) [=Ex. 4 a] does not sound so very bad; otherwise, however, there is need for ears as extraordinary as the example itself. The three-part accompaniment at (g) [=Ex. 4 b] is more tolerable."

Here, again, it will be seen (though Bach does not trouble to figure the Bass) that a diminished Octave is substituted for a diminished Seventh on the first half of the ♯D in the Bass.

XVII § 7   ANTICIPATION OF ONE OR MORE INTERVALS   703

Ex. 6

§ 8. $\frac{8}{7}$ and $\frac{7}{5}$.
$\quad\;\,^{4}\qquad\quad\;\,^{4}$

(a) The figuring $\frac{7}{4}$ is used to indicate two distinct harmonies:

I, a $\frac{6}{4}$ chord $\left(\frac{8}{6}\atop 4\right)$, with the 6 retarded by 7, $= \frac{8}{7}$;

II, a chord of the Seventh taken either (1) as $\frac{7}{5}\atop 3$, with the 3 retarded by 4, $= \frac{7}{5}\atop 4$, or (2) as $\frac{8}{7}\atop 3$, with the 3 retarded by 4, $= \frac{8}{7}\atop 4$.

(b) When the 6 of a $\frac{6}{4}$ chord is retarded by 7, the latter interval must, normally, have been present in the preceding chord, as in the following example:

Ex. 1

In the free style, however, the 7 is liable to be taken without preparation, either by step or by leap, as a free appoggiatura. Ph. Em. Bach gives the following examples:[1]

Ex. 2

[It will be observed that the progression $\frac{7\;6}{4\;-}$ on G corresponds exactly to $\frac{9\;8}{6\;-}$ on E (cf. § 5) and to 4 3 on C (cf. § 3), the upper parts being, in all three cases, identical.]

(c) When the 3 of a chord of the Seventh is retarded by 4, it depends upon

---

[4] Bach writes as follows: "The last example belongs to the category of Pedal points. Of these we shall treat specially further on, and merely mention in advance, for the comfort of those to whom the figuring appears too terrible, that, in these Pedal points, the right hand generally rests, and that one therefore does not figure them, but simply writes *tasto solo* over them [cf. Ch. xx, § 2]. Here it was necessary to give the figures, to show the progressions of the parts and the changes in the harmony."
[1] o.c. Ch. 15, § 15.

circumstances whether the $\frac{7}{4}$ is taken as $\frac{7}{5}_{4}$ or $\frac{8}{7}_{4}$. As Ph. Em. Bach points out,[2] it is *when the Seventh itself is unprepared* that the player has most liberty to choose between the Fifth and the Octave as the fourth part; and, when there is this liberty, it is better, he tells us, to choose the Fifth (Ex. 3 *a* and *aa*) as giving fuller harmony than the Octave (*b* and *bb*):

Bach expressly tells us that, when the 5 is included, the best position is that in which the 4 appears in the upper part (as in Ex. 3 *aa*), though he does not choose this position in the example which he actually gives (cf. note 3).

In the next two examples[4] the inclusion of the Octave is necessary in order to provide one of the intervals in the following chord.

In Ex. 4 it prepares the 7 on *A*, and in Ex. 5 it provides the 4 of the $\frac{4}{3}$ on *G*. In the latter example it will be observed that the 4 of the $\frac{7}{4}$ on *C* resolves, not on 3 over the same Bass, but on the 6 of the $\frac{4}{3}$ on *G*, the second inversion of the same harmony:

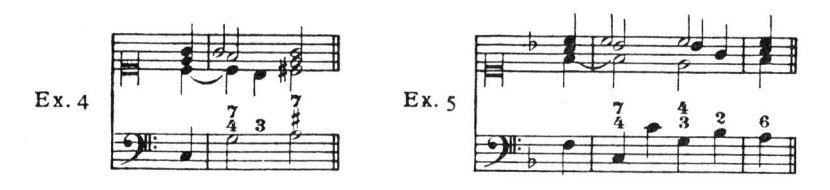

Bach adds a series of examples which illustrate a small, but not altogether unimportant, point. It is best described in his own words:

"In the example (*c*) [=Ex. 6] one doubles the Third or the Fifth in the preceding Triad (1) (2); otherwise, it is better to abandon the preparation of the Fourth (3) than to hold the latter (4). The reason of this is as follows: If we examine the progression of the Bass from *A* to $\sharp G$, and of the middle part from *A* to *F*, and if, in the latter, we supply the intermediate interval [$\natural G$], we find a FALSE RELATION (*unharmonischen Querstand*), which is not, it is true, of the same consequence nowadays as formerly, but which can, nevertheless, easily be avoided. Nobody will deny that the execution of this example, seen in its simple form [i.e. without the retardation], in contrary motion (5) is better than that in similar motion (6). Except in the free style (*Ausser dem galanten Styl*) we adhere to (1) and (2):

---

[2] l.c. §§ 10, 11.
[3] Ex. 3 (*aa*) and (*b*) have been added to the two examples (*a* and *bb*) given by Bach in order that the two harmonies ($\frac{7}{5}_{4\,3}$ and $\frac{8}{7}_{4\,3}$) might be seen in pairs of examples starting in the same position.   [4] From Ph. Em. Bach; l.c. § 10.

XVII § 8 (c)   ANTICIPATION OF ONE OR MORE INTERVALS   705

Ex. 6 [musical example]

(d) In the following examples [5] *the Seventh is prepared*, and it will be seen that, in most of them, the constitution of the preceding chord leaves no choice as to whether $\frac{7}{4}$ should be taken as $\frac{7}{5}$ or $\frac{8}{7}$. In (b) and (bb) the chords of preparation are the same, and it is the fact of the 4 being unprepared (and capable of being taken either by step or by leap) that makes the alternative treatment of the $\frac{7}{4}$ possible:

Ex. 7 [musical example]

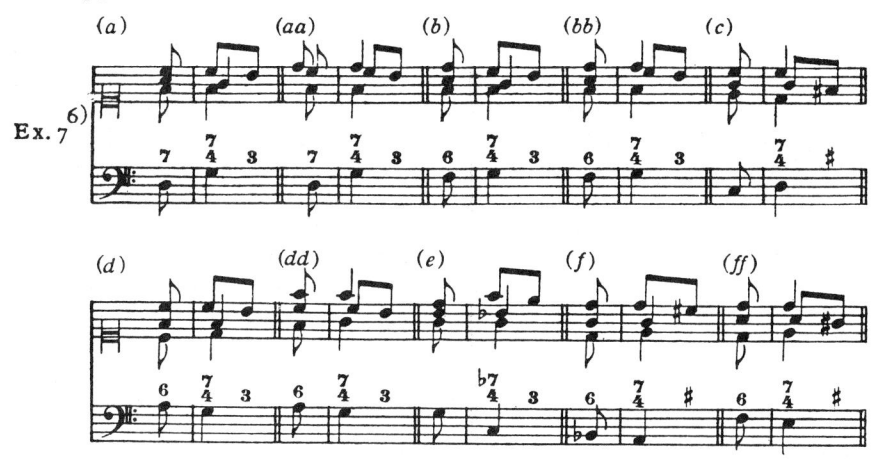

Ph. Em. Bach [7] gives the following examples of a sequence of Sevenths on a Bass alternately rising a Fourth and falling a Fifth, in which 4 3 is associated with every alternate Seventh:

Ex. 8 [musical example]

[5] From Ph. Em. Bach, l.c. § 11.

[6] Ph. Em. Bach remarks that, in (e), the way of treating the $\frac{7}{4}$ is the one which "sounds best in the prescribed position [i.e. of the preceding chord]".

Not only is this the case, but the only possible alternative, *in the prescribed position*, would involve consecutive 5ths: [musical example]

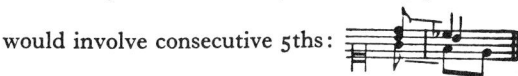

[7] l.c. § 12.

"But, should 4 3 occur with all the Sevenths," he tells us, "one can, with a good conscience, adhere to a three-part accompaniment. This case arises in the free style only; at (b) [=Ex. 9 a] the passage [i.e. principal parts and Bass] is indicated in detail, and at (bb) [=Ex. 9 b] its accompaniment."

Ex. 9

[It will be observed that, in the principal parts (Ex. 9 a), the Sevenths have an "ornamental" progression, first rising to the Octave and then falling to the appoggiatura (4) on the following bass note.]

(e) "When the Seventh resolves on the Sixth over the same Bass", Ph. Em. Bach writes,[8] "our chord is of rare occurrence, and rarest of all, in such a case, is the simultaneous resolution of the Seventh and the Fourth, because the progression in Fourths of a DOUBLE appoggiatura sounds bad, and also involves the risk of mistakes, according to the position taken. I deliberately say: DOUBLE appoggiatura, because dissonances, especially such as resolve over the same Bass, are in reality nothing but appoggiaturas."

Bach gives the following examples of the simultaneous resolution of the 7 and the 4, from which it will be seen that the position in which the 4 is *above* the 7 is impossible when it involves the progression of one perfect Fifth to another:

Ex. 10

In these examples Bach notes the following points:

(1) The $\frac{7}{4}$ in (b) is best interpreted [without indication in the figuring] as $\frac{7}{4}$, as shown in (bb).[9]
$\phantom{\frac{7}{4}}_{3}$

---

[8] l.c. § 7.

[9] It will be remembered that 6 on the Supertonic may always be treated as $\frac{6}{4}$ (cf. Ch. xxi, "Incomplete figuring", II, § 1), and this liberty is naturally not affected_{3} by the retardation of the 6 [see, however, A. Scarlatti's rule, ibid., Ex. 6].

XVII § 8 (e)   ANTICIPATION OF ONE OR MORE INTERVALS   707

(2) The diminished Fifth in (c) and the augmented Fifth in (d) must be expressly indicated in the figuring.[10]

(3) At (e) a three-part accompaniment is best.

(4) The progression indicated by the figures at (f) is not particularly good, because the best position (shown in the example), in which the Third and augmented Fourth on the first bass note, F, are separated, is not available because of the consecutive Fifths involved.[11]

Bach adds the two following examples in three parts,[12] in which the resolution of 7 and 4 over the same Bass (or the same Bass chromatically altered) is *not* simultaneous. In Ex. 11 the 4 resolves first, and in Ex. 12 the 7.

Ex. 11

Ex. 12

[10] N.B.—This applies *chiefly* to the diminished Fifth (5♭) in (c), as the augmented Fifth (♯g) in (d) is present in the preceding chord. When an accidentally altered interval is "prepared", many figurists, especially of the older school, did not trouble to mark the accidental in the figuring; thus, in such a progression as: the ♯ before the 9 was frequently omitted.

The case of an augmented or diminished interval (Fifth or Fourth), however, is somewhat different, and it is always preferable that the interval in question, even though "prepared", or indicated by the key-signature, should be characterized in the figuring.

[11] The only position in which Fifths are avoided is the following:

Apart from the retardation, however, the natural progression of the 6 on F, in the position shown in Bach's example, would be *upwards*:

It will be remembered that Türk gave examples of a rising Ninth (§ 2, Ex. 4), and there seems no logical reason why the same liberty should not, in the present instance, be extended to the Seventh:

[12] l.c. § 9.

708 HARMONIES DUE TO THE RETARDATION OR XVII § 9 (a)

§ 9. *Retardations of the Bass.*

(a) $\begin{smallmatrix}7\\4\\2\end{smallmatrix}$.

The harmonies which arise when the Bass is retarded by the suspension of the note a degree above it are classified in some of the treatises of the eighteenth century as *anticipations*, because the upper parts appear to anticipate the harmony of the bass note which follows. The figuring of such suspensions in the Bass is the same as that of changing (i.e. accented passing) notes with a downward progression,[1] and the same alternative method of figuring is sometimes employed,[2] and will be given below the Bass in the examples which are to follow, wherever it seems advisable.

Apart from the latter, certain small variations are possible, as may be seen from the following example of a Triad with retarded Bass, in which the different ways of figuring are given:

Ex. 1

Instead of $\begin{smallmatrix}7\\4\\2\end{smallmatrix}$ the incomplete figuring $\begin{smallmatrix}7\\2\end{smallmatrix}$ is used by some figurists to indicate the same retardation, as in the following example from Schröter:[3]

Ex. 2

(b) $\begin{smallmatrix}5\\2\end{smallmatrix}$.

When the Bass of a chord of the Sixth is retarded, the figuring varies according to whether (1) either $\begin{smallmatrix}6\\3\\6\end{smallmatrix}$ or $\begin{smallmatrix}3\\6\\3\end{smallmatrix}$, or (2) $\begin{smallmatrix}8\\6\\3\end{smallmatrix}$ represents the harmony following the resolution of the suspension in the Bass.

In the former case the figuring is $\begin{smallmatrix}5\\2\end{smallmatrix}$. The duplication of the one or the other interval may be in the 8ve or the unison, exactly in the same way as when there is no retardation of the Bass. In (a), (b), (c) of the following series the 5 is doubled, and in (d), (e), (f) the 2:

---
[1] *Vide* Ch. xix, "The figuring of transitional notes", § 6, examples (b).
[2] *Vide* ibid. § 5.
[3] *Deutliche Anweisung &c.*, 1772, § 230 f, p. 121.
Where Schröter omits the inner parts, they are here indicated by small tailless notes, as in future examples from the same source. The alternative figuring, below the Bass, has also been added.

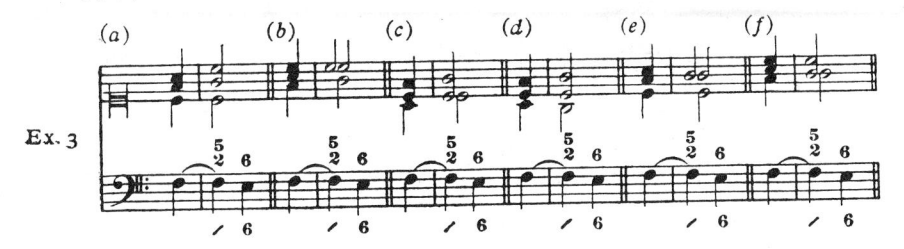

XVII § 9 (b)   ANTICIPATION OF ONE OR MORE INTERVALS   709

Ex. 3

Sometimes the resolution of the suspension in the Bass coincides with a change of harmony in the upper parts, as:

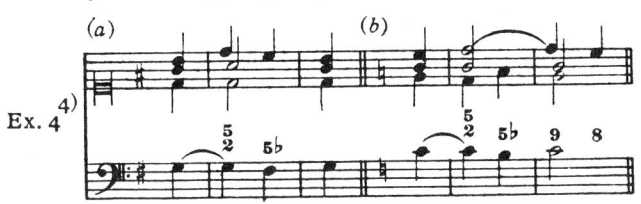

Ex. 4 [4)]

Schröter gives the following extended example: [5]

Ex. 5

(c) $\begin{smallmatrix}7\\5\\2\end{smallmatrix}$.

When a chord of the Sixth is definitely intended to contain the Octave of the retarded Bass (instead of being taken with the Sixth or Third doubled), the suspended note by which the Bass is retarded is figured $\begin{smallmatrix}7\\5\\2\end{smallmatrix}$, as in the following example (in which the same harmony is shown in two different positions) from Schröter: [6]

[4] Ex. 4 *a* is from Ph. Em. Bach (*Versuch &c.*, Part II, 1762, Ch. 10, § 3).
[5] He gives only the extreme parts (o.c. § 236 *i*, p. 127). The inner parts have here been added throughout.
[6] o.c. § 239 *d*, p. 131.

[Ex. 6 musical example]

(d) The alternative method of figuring (with an oblique dash over the suspended note pointing to the figure, or figures, over its resolution) alluded to above (cf. Ex. 1 d, also Exx. 2 and 3 below the Bass) gives no indication as to whether $\smash{{}^5_2}$ or $\smash{{}^7_5 \atop {}_2}$ is intended. Therefore, where chords of the Sixth (with retarded Bass) are concerned, this method is satisfactory only when (1) the composer attaches no importance to the distinction, or (2) when the rules of harmony leave no choice. Thus, in the following example from Schröter [7] (in which the alternative figuring has been added below the Bass), the chord on the first crotchet of bars 1-3 can only be taken as $\smash{{}^5_2}$ (with either the 5 or the 2 doubled), because a chord of the Sixth on a leading note cannot, normally, include the Octave of the Bass, whereas the chord at the beginning of the fourth bar, *if figured as shown below the Bass*, can equally well be taken as $\smash{{}^7_5 \atop {}_2}$:

[Ex. 7 musical example]

(e) $\smash{{}^5_3}$ or 5, $\smash{{}^7_5 \atop {}_3}$ or $\smash{{}^7_5}$.

When the Bass of a $\smash{{}^6_4}$ chord is retarded from above, the latter can be taken with the 4 doubled, omitting the Octave of the Bass. In this way a certain harshness, arising from the anticipation in an upper part of the resolution of a suspension in the Bass,[8] is avoided.

Ex. 8 (a) is from Schröter,[9] and (b) is from Türk:[10]

[Ex. 8 musical example]

---

[7] o.c. § 236 h, p. 127.

[8] This anticipation is seen in Ex. 6, where the 2 in the $\smash{{}^7_5 \atop {}_2}$ chords anticipates the retarded Bass.

[9] o.c. § 237 c, p. 127.

[10] *Kurze Anweisung &c.*, 1791, § 192 c, p. 246.

XVII § 9 (e) ANTICIPATION OF ONE OR MORE INTERVALS 711

If it is expressly intended that the $^6_4$ chord should appear as $^8_6_4$ on the resolution of the suspension in the Bass, the latter would have to be figured $^7_5_3$ (or $^7_5$) as in the following example: [11]

Ex. 9

(f) $^5_4_2$.

When the Bass of a $^6_5$ chord is retarded from above, the suspended note is figured $^5_4_2$.

When the $^6_5$ chord is one of which the 5 can be taken without preparation, the same liberty attaches to the 4 of the corresponding $^5_4_2$.

In the two following examples [12] the $^6_5$ chord is the first inversion of the Dominant Seventh, in the major and minor mode, respectively:

Ex. 10

Ex. 11

In the two next examples [13] the $^6_5$ is the first inversion of the diminished Seventh on the leading note of the minor key, and of the minor Seventh on the leading note of the major key, respectively:

---

[11] It must here be stated that the writer has hitherto failed to find an example of this progression in any of the text-books, or figured Basses, of the seventeenth or eighteenth century.
[12] From Schröter, o.c. § 266 *b* and *f*, pp. 149 sq.
[13] From Schröter, l.c. *k* and *r*, pp. 150 sq.

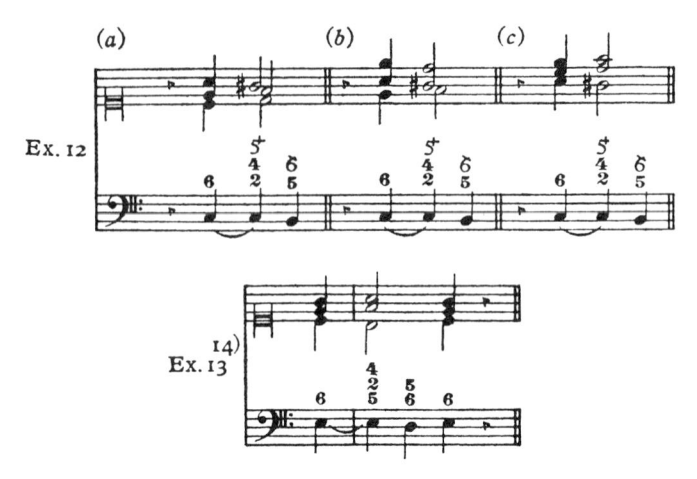

In the next example [15] the $\substack{6\\5}$ is on the Subdominant of the minor scale; the 4 of the $\substack{5\\4\\2}$, it will be observed, is prepared:

In Ex. 15 (a) and (b) the $\substack{6\\5}$ *would have been* on the Subdominant of the major and minor scales, respectively, but for the change of harmony in the upper part, which coincides with the resolution of the suspension in the Bass:[16]

---

[14] The exceptional arrangement of the figures in this example $\left(\substack{4\ 5\\2\ 5\\5\ 6}\text{ instead of }\substack{5\ 6\\4\ 6\\2\ 5}\right)$ is intended by Schröter to indicate the position (which he regards as the only suitable one) in which this harmony is to be taken (cf. Ch. xii, "$\substack{6\\5}$ chords", § 4, note).

[15] This example and Ex. 15 are both from Schröter, l.c. *o, p, q*, p. 150.

[16] Without the suspension in the Bass the progression in Ex. 15 *a* (and the same applies *mutatis mutandis* to *b*) is: The fundamental progression is, therefore, a Seventh (unprepared) on the Supertonic, in its first inversion, resolving on the third inversion of a Seventh on the Dominant (cf. Ch. xii, § 2, Ex. 2 *b*).

XVII § 9 (g) ANTICIPATION OF ONE OR MORE INTERVALS 713

(g) $\begin{smallmatrix}5\\3\\2\end{smallmatrix}$.

When the Bass of a $\frac{4}{3}$ chord is retarded from above, the suspended note is figured $\begin{smallmatrix}5\\3\\2\end{smallmatrix}$, or, *more commonly*, $\begin{smallmatrix}5\\2\end{smallmatrix}$. If the 5 is accidentally sharpened, it must, of course, be included in the figuring $\left(\begin{smallmatrix}5\sharp\\3\\2\end{smallmatrix},\begin{smallmatrix}5\natural\\3\\2\end{smallmatrix}\right)$. The following examples are taken, except where the contrary is stated, from Schröter.[17]

In Ex. 16 (a) and (b) the $\frac{4}{3}$ chord is on the Supertonic of the major and minor scales, respectively, and is, therefore, the second inversion of the Dominant Seventh:

Ex. 16 [18)]

In Ex. 17 (a) and (b) the $\begin{smallmatrix}4\sharp\\3\end{smallmatrix}$ ($\frac{4}{3}$) chord is the second inversion of the diminished Seventh on the leading note of the minor key, and of the minor Seventh on the leading note of the major key, respectively. In (b) it will be observed that Schröter has adopted an arrangement of the figures corresponding to that in Ex. 13 (cf. note 14), in order to ensure the harmony being taken in no other position than the one given (cf. Ch. xiii, "$\frac{4}{3}$ chords", § 3 a):

Ex. 17

Ph. Em. Bach gives three examples of a $\begin{smallmatrix}5\\3\\2\end{smallmatrix}$ chord with major Third and minor Second (as in Ex. 17 a);[19] though the latter is in accordance with the key-signature, he is careful to append a $\flat$ (2$\flat$). This is a good instance of how the same chord may be so figured by different composers that their respective figurings present a totally different appearance; here Schröter uses $\begin{smallmatrix}5\\\sharp3\\2\end{smallmatrix}$, and Ph. Em. Bach $\begin{smallmatrix}\sharp\\2\flat\end{smallmatrix}$.

---

[17] o.c. § 267 (c, g, l, n), p. 152.

[18] It will be noticed that, in Ex. 16 a, Schröter uses the (less customary) full figuring $\begin{smallmatrix}5\\3\\2\end{smallmatrix}$; also that he is (like so many of the old figurists) inconsistent in his figuring: in (a) he figures D with a simple 6; in (b) he figures the corresponding note (B) $\begin{smallmatrix}6\\4\\3\end{smallmatrix}$, though 6 (or $\bar{6}$) on the Supertonic may always be taken as $\begin{smallmatrix}6\\4\\3\end{smallmatrix}$ $\left(\begin{smallmatrix}\bar{6}\\4\\3\end{smallmatrix}\right)$, and *must* be so taken after a preceding $\begin{smallmatrix}5\\3\\2\end{smallmatrix}$ $\left(\begin{smallmatrix}5\sharp\\3\\2\end{smallmatrix}\right)$.

[19] *Versuch &c.*, Part II, 1762, Ch. 12, § 3. The examples are here given an 8ve higher than the original, where they appear, as usual, on a single stave.

Two of the examples are somewhat remarkable. Ex. 18 (b) exactly corresponds, in all essentials, with Ex. 17 (a), but in Ex. 18 (a) and (c), instead of the Bass being retarded, the 2♭ (f) is a genuine anticipation of the following harmony: [20]

Ex. 18

[20] The progression in Ex. 18 (a) and (c), apart from the anticipation in the Alto of (a) and the Treble of (c), is:

CHAPTER XVIII
QUICK NOTES IN THE BASS

XVIII

QUICK NOTES IN THE BASS

§ 1. *Different forms of passing note.*

(*a*) One of the greatest difficulties in playing from a Thorough-Bass (especially in the case of the older Basses, in which dashes, denoting the continuance of the preceding harmony, were not employed) arises in connexion with the notes which, in their relation to the unit of the measure in which they occur (a minim in *Allabreve* and $\frac{3}{2}$, a crotchet in $\frac{4}{4}$, &c.), are quick enough to be treated as passing notes, but which might also, without violating any rule of harmony, bear a chord of their own. How are we to distinguish?

(*b*) It must be clearly understood at the outset that (in connexion with a Thorough-Bass) the term 'passing', used in its widest sense, is applied to *all bass notes not bearing an harmony of their own*, irrespective of whether the note in question is approached and quitted by step or by leap, and also, in the former case, of whether it is approached and quitted *in the same direction* (upward or downward), or whether it, so to speak, doubles back.

(*c*) In its strictest (and original) sense, the term is applied primarily to an unaccented (or *virtualiter* [1] short) note bridging the interval of a (rising or falling) Third between two accented (or *virtualiter* long) notes essential to the harmony, as:

[Ex. 1.]

Abridged from Heinichen, *General Bass &c.* 1728, Part I, Ch. IV, § 3, p. 258.

This was known as *transitus regularis*.

N.B.—The leap of a Seventh following a *virtualiter* long note is to be treated as equivalent to a progression by step; this applies equally to a leap of a Ninth. Therefore such figures as (*a*) (*b*) (*c*) experience the same treatment as (*aa*) (*bb*) (*cc*):

(*a*)   (*aa*)   (*b*)   (*bb*)   (*c*)   (*cc*)

(Cf. Heinichen, l.c. Appendix, p. 366.)

This must be remembered in connexion with a form of passing note to be described presently (*f*).

[1] i.e. in accordance with its *virtus* or *real* (as opposed to *nominal*) value. It is

XVIII § 1 (d) QUICK NOTES IN THE BASS 717

(d) Contrasted with this was *transitus irregularis*. Here, too, the interval of a (rising or falling) Third is bridged by a note foreign to the harmony; but, in this instance, it is the *bridge-note that is accented* (*virtualiter* long). Though not written as such, it is, in fact, an appoggiatura, over which a chord is struck *in anticipation of its true Bass*.

Its proper designation is a *changing note* (Ital. *nota cambiata*, Germ. *Wechselnote*), though, since this term has, unfortunately, come to be used in another sense (cf. note 12), it is more commonly known as an accented passing note:

Heinichen, ibid., l.c. § 4, p. 259.

[Ex. 2]

Ibid., l.c. § 15 *ad fin.*, p. 270.

In the absence of special device,[2] the occurrence of the *transitus irregularis* is indicated when the last of a group of short notes [3] is either (1) *followed by a leap* (as in Ex. 2 a), or (2) *figured* (as the 4th semiquaver of Ex. 2 e).

sometimes convenient to revive this term as being quite free from ambiguity, whereas 'accented', when applied to notes of very small value, is liable to be misleading and to convey the impression of referring to the *first* note of a group. On the other hand, in a group of (say) eight demisemiquavers, the term *virtualiter longa* applies equally to the first, third, fifth, and seventh.

[2] The safest method, which Heinichen mentions with qualified approval (cf. note 10 *ad fin.*), whereas J. S. Bach himself not only employed it, but, as we learn from Kirnberger (*Grundsätze des General-Basses, ad fin.* note) inculcated it into his pupils (in spite of the extra figurings that had to be learnt), is to figure the *changing note itself*. Thus Ex. 2 e would appear as follows:

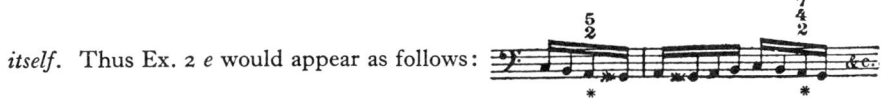

(cf. Ch. xix, 'The figuring of transitional notes', § 6).

The other method (far less satisfactory owing to the displacement liable to arise at the hands of copyists and printers) is to figure the *harmony note* and to connect the changing note with the figuring by means of an oblique dash pointing from the figure to the note. Thus Ex. 2 b would appear as follows: (cf. Ch. xix, 'The figuring of transitional notes', § 5, Ex. 1).

It is doubtful whether this device was employed in Heinichen's time: it is mentioned by Ph. Em. Bach (*Versuch &c.*, Part II, Ch. 39), but it is more at home in text-books than in actual Thorough-Basses.

[3] 'Short (or quick) notes' may be defined, in the present connexion, as those notes

If the harmony to be indicated is a *Triad*, and if no leap follows (as in Ex. 2 *d*), much ambiguity would be avoided by figuring the Triad (5 or $\frac{5}{3}$), as:

[musical example] but the precaution is often omitted, as in Heinichen's example.

In some cases, the necessary preparation of a discord, to be inferred from the figures which follow, is the only indication of the *transitus irregularis* (as in Ex. 2 *b*).[4]

of which, *normally* (i.e. unless the contrary be expressly indicated in the figuring) *not less* than two go to a single harmony. This applies, in $\frac{4}{4}$ time, to all semiquavers, and also to pairs of quavers moving by step and not followed by a leap; in a spurious *Allabreve* (*Semi-allabreve*), or quick $\frac{4}{4}$ time (which can be exemplified by dividing the final bar of Ex. 2 *e* into two, and doubling the note-values, as:

[musical example]

to *all* quavers; and, in the true *Allabreve*, with two minims and *not more than two harmonies* to the bar, to all crotchets; and so on.

[4] This example is a particularly instructive one, as illustrating the difficulties alluded to above (*a*). If the Bass were altered as follows, the *transitus irregularis* would be definitely contra-indicated by the necessity for preparing the 7 on *b*:

Ex. A [musical example]

If, on the other hand, the figuring were such as to leave the door open for either of the two following interpretations, the first would be in accordance with Heinichen's rules (of which an account will be given presently) in ordinary (moderate) $\frac{4}{4}$ time, and the latter in *quick* $\frac{4}{4}$ (i.e. the *Semi-allabreve* alluded to in note 3):

Ex. B [musical example]

But, with a Bass figured as above, it is not always possible to decide offhand between the two, whereas a figure in the one case, and a dash in the other, would remove all doubt: [musical example]

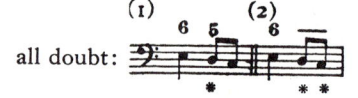

Ex. 2 *c*, too, is not free from ambiguity: in ordinary $\frac{4}{4}$ time it might be intended by the composer as follows:

Ex. C [musical example]

Here, again, a 5 (or $\frac{5}{3}$) on the third quaver would meet the case.

In actual practice (i.e. in accompanying instruments or voices at sight from a figured

XVIII § 1 (e)   QUICK NOTES IN THE BASS   719

(e) Besides the strict *transitus regularis* described above (c), the term *transitus* is also applied *in sensu lato & improprio* (cf. Heinichen, ibid., l.c. § 5, p. 260) to notes bridging an interval of a 4th, a 5th, and even a 6th, 7th, and 8ve, and bearing a single harmony. The following is Heinichen's example:

Ex. 3 [musical example with sections labeled [a] Transitus in 4^tam, [b] in 5^tam, [c] in 6^tam, [d] in 7^mam, [e] in 8^vam]

Bass) it is obviously best, when confronted with a similar difficulty, to avoid a clash by passing as lightly as possible over the dangerous ground. This can be done by either (1) omitting the accompaniment of the doubtful Bass notes altogether, or (2) merely following them in Thirds. In the latter case, Exx. B and C would appear as follows:

Ex. D [musical example with sections (1) and (2)]

[5] In the above series, Exx. c, d, and e demand some notice.

(1) As regards Ex. c: according to Heinichen's rules and examples (ibid., l.c. § 31, pp. 316 sq.), in triple time, when the unit of the measure (a minim, or a crotchet, or a quaver, in $\frac{3}{2}$, $\frac{3}{4}$, $\frac{3}{8}$, and their compounds, respectively) is followed by four notes of half its value, all rising or falling by step (as in Ex. c), the *first two* short notes pass, but *the third bears its own harmony* [or, of course, that of the fourth (*transitus irregularis*), if the latter is figured, or followed by a leap].

Heinichen tells us, however, elsewhere (ibid., l.c. § 34, and note z, pp. 324 sqq.), that in *very quick* triple time ($\frac{6}{4}$, $\frac{6}{8}$, $\frac{9}{8}$, $\frac{12}{8}$), and in *certain Bass figures* (among which are included the rising and falling ones shown in Ex. c), *all four short notes*, following one of double their value (the unit of the measure), may pass (as in Ex. c). Quickness of time is relative, and it is therefore plain that, in such cases, instinct is the only guide, unless dashes, denoting the continuance of the harmony, or figures over the doubtful notes, are employed. The former are preferable, because figures, as:

Ex. A [musical example]

always suggest *repercussion*.

It is noteworthy that, in *all* Heinichen's examples illustrating the exception alluded

(f) Besides the cases exemplified above (c, d, e), in which notes unessential to the harmony bridge the interval between rising or falling harmony notes, there is a further possibility: a bass note, short in relation to the unit of the measure (cf. note 3), but *virtualiter* long (cf. note 1), may move a degree (in either direction) and *back again*, without affecting the harmony.

to above, the chord in the right hand is sustained *only during the first two beats* of the triple measure, and then followed by a rest (exactly as in Ex. 2 d above), though he sometimes follows the Bass in Thirds, with a rest in the other parts. The following quotation illustrates both cases:

Ex. B

(2) Ex. *d* runs counter to Heinichen's own rules, and this time there is no saving clause. We are told (ibid., l.c. § 28. 2, p. 300) that, in triple time (simple or compound), when six short notes (i.e. half the value of the unit of the measure) rise or fall by step, and are not followed by a leap, *the penultimate one bears its own harmony*. (If a leap follows, or if the last short note is figured, *transitus irregularis* is indicated, as already explained.) According to this rule, then (in the absence of dashes, denoting the continuance of the harmony, or of figures), Ex. *d* would be treated as follows:

Ex. C

How is the discrepancy to be explained?

It is worth while to elucidate this question fully, as the explanation will be found to apply *mutatis mutandis* to many similar ones.

In framing his rule, Heinichen *failed to take into account all the possible cases.*

It is evident that six notes bridging the interval of a *falling* or *rising* Seventh, and bearing a single harmony (as in Ex. 3 *d*), represent the same progression as a *single harmony note* (equal in value to the whole six above mentioned) *rising or falling one degree.*

Thus, the essential Bass of Ex. 3 *d* is as follows:

Ex. D

If, on the other hand, *the 5th semiquaver is to bear its own harmony*, we get the following progression of the Bass:

Ex. E

Before framing a rule, therefore, such as that of Heinichen, it would be necessary to test the possibility (and probability) of the two progressions of the Bass shown in the following example, *starting on every degree of the scale, major and minor*. The clef is purposely omitted, in order to show the intervals *independently of their place in the*

XVIII § 1 (f)　　QUICK NOTES IN THE BASS　　721

Ex. 4 (a) (Heinichen, ibid., l.c. § 8, p. 263, concluding bars of example) shows passing notes of this description * * * * (besides the *transitus regularis*); in (b) we see the same Bass reduced to its essential form:

Ex. 4

In Heinichen's time the employment of this form of *quasi*-passing note in the true *Allabreve* (the strictest of all styles) seems to have been regarded as something of an archaism. In giving the following example, he says (ibid., l.c. § 39, p. 335): "In the works of old composers it is often found that an unaccented crotchet, instead of completing the *Transitus in Tertiam*, returns to the preceding note.[6] An accompanist will not let himself be put out by this practice, though not all composers care to imitate it:

Ex. 5

(g) We now come to those short and unaccented (i.e. *virtualiter* short) notes, as defined above (cf. notes 3 and 1), which bear no harmony of their own, and which are either (1) approached and quitted by leap, or (2) approached by leap and quitted by step (in the direction opposite to that of the leap), or (3) (in one particular instance, cf. *m*) vice versâ.

Such notes may conveniently be described (*in sensu lato et improprio*, as

scale, while the letters x denote *any possible figuring* that the notes in question might bear (consistent, of course, with the intervening Triad):

Ex. F

This is, of course, a *reductio ad absurdum*, for it is plain that such a rule, with all its possible exceptions, once elaborated, could never be remembered; it therefore comes to this: that, *in the absence of adequate indication*, the accompanist must rely on his musical instinct, and, when in doubt, be prepared to adjust his accompaniment accordingly (cf. note 4 *ad fin.*).

(3) Heinichen gives no rule to account for the passing of the last four semiquavers of each group in Ex. 3 *e*. (The crotchet rests in the right hand do not, of course, affect the fact that the same harmony holds good, whether actually sustained or not, for the duration of a minim.) The only indications, in the Bass itself, of the composer's intentions are: (a) the time-signature ₵ (which Heinichen does not confine to the true *Allabreve*, but, apparently, always uses simply to denote that the measure is quick); (b) the absence of a sharp *over* the third semiquaver in the second bar of the example: if a major Triad on *d* had been intended, this would have been needed.

[6] Heinichen's German, very freely rendered above, is as follows: "Bey alten *Autoribus* findet man öffters folgende Arthen einer Bewegung wieder den Tact, da das *virtualiter* kurze 4tel, statt eines vorhabenden *Transitus in Tertiam*, wieder in vorigen Ton zurückschläget."

Heinichen would say) as free passing notes, inasmuch as they share the important characteristic of bearing no chord, and thus passing without effect on the harmony.

(*h*) The simplest and most obvious case is when these notes represent an interval in the preceding chord, in which case (unless incomplete harmony is being used) their upper 8ve will usually be present in the right hand, as:

Ex. 6

Ph. Em. Bach, *Versuch &c.*, Part II, 1762, Ch. 36, § 3 (Bass only given).

(*i*) A special case arises when a bass note *bearing a Triad* falls a Third (sometimes with an intermediate passing note), thus giving rise to a passing $\smash{\begin{smallmatrix}7\\5\\3\end{smallmatrix}}$ chord. The 7, thus arising, should find its downward resolution in the following chord, as:

Mattheson, *Organisten-Probe*, 1719, 'Mittel-Classe' [Middle Grade], 'Prob-Stück' [Test-piece], 15, bar 4, ditto 16 *ad fin.* (Bass only given).

Ex. 7 (a) (*Allabreve*)   (b)

Ex. 8 (*Presto*)

Heinichen, ibid., l.c. § 21. 1 *ad fin.*, p. 285.

(*k*) In many instances the passing note can best be regarded as an anticipation of the following harmony:

Handel, *Seven Trios*, Op. 5, Sonata II, Adagio *ad fin.*, and Allegro, bar 20.

Ex. 9 (a)   (b)

XVIII § 1 (k) QUICK NOTES IN THE BASS 723

Leclair, *Sonatas for Violin and Bass*, Book I, Sonata IV, Andante, bars 14–18.

Ex. 10 [7)]

In the above example the anticipation of the following harmony by the passing notes * * * is evidently due to the desire to preserve the sequential figure in the Bass.

In the following one it is determined by the imitation, in the Bass, of the theme:

Ex. 11

Leclair, ibid., Book I, Sonata XI, Giga, bars 7 and 8.

(*l*) A particular form of free passing note, approached by leap but quitted by step, occurs when a bass note leaps, not directly to the following harmony note, but one degree below it. This is particularly common in approaching a full close:

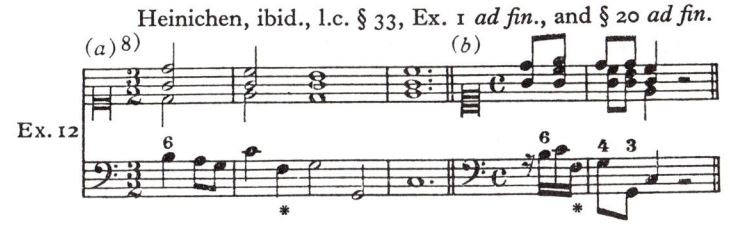

Heinichen, ibid., l.c. § 33, Ex. 1 *ad fin.*, and § 20 *ad fin.*

Ex. 12

[7] For Leclair's use of a crossed 6 to denote $\frac{6}{4}$ (in Book I *only* of his Sonatas) see Ch. xxiii, 'Varieties of figuring', § 8.

[8] It will be noticed that this is one of the cases in which a dash, denoting the continuance of the previous harmony, or a figure, is particularly desirable:

especially if the time inclines to be slow. The very same Bass would, in ordinary (moderate) $\frac{4}{4}$ time, normally be treated as follows:

The notes * * pass, not from the bass note itself, but *as though from another interval of its harmony*, as:

It is a recognized principle in Music (as also in Language) that a particular usage, once firmly established, is liable to extend its sphere, and to be employed independently, sometimes, indeed, in direct negation, of the circumstances *to which, in the first instance, it owed its origin.*

Thus, the passing notes last described, with nothing apparent from which to pass, are analogous to those suspended discords which, in the free style, came to be used without preparation, as appoggiaturas.[9]

The next example (in which the passing note * incidentally anticipates the following harmony, as in Exx. 9–11) illustrates the same principle.

It differs from the two previous examples (Ex. 12 *a* and *b*) in that the passing note * leads, not direct to an harmony note, but to a changing, or accented passing, note † (*transitus irregularis*), which (like the one in the following bar ‡) can only be recognized as such, owing to the fact that the progression of the harmony is determined by the necessary resolution of the preceding discord (7 on *g*), specially indicated, in this instance, by the figuring $\frac{8}{6}$ on *e*, instead of the usual 6:

Heinichen, ibid., l.c. § 53, 2nd example, p. 362.

Ex. 13

[9] Cf. Ch. iii, § 4, IV, note 11, Exx. 5 and 6.
[10] The observation made in note 8 applies equally to the above example. In ordinary (moderate) $\frac{4}{4}$ time (in which each crotchet, or equivalent combination of shorter notes, and, under certain circumstances, each quaver or pair of semiquavers, bears its own harmony, *unless the contrary is expressly indicated*) the first bar would be treated as follows:

Ex. A

Taking the example as it stands, it will be seen that a dash after the 7 over *g* (as used in Leclair's examples, Exx. 10 and 11), and an oblique dash (as described in note 2) over the changing note *d*, would place the intentions of the composer beyond doubt:

Ex. B

Heinichen tells us that some composers figure the changing notes themselves and

XVIII § 1 (m)   QUICK NOTES IN THE BASS   725

(*m*) One form of passing note, approached by step and quitted by leap (cf. *g*), still remains to be noticed.

It is best described in Heinichen's own words (ibid., l.c. § 43, pp. 338 sq.):

"The figure in the first two bars [and also in the 4th and 5th bars] of the following example is privileged in *Allabreve*, and is regarded as a *Transitus in 4^{tam}* although one passing note is lacking.[11] Therefore, in this case, too, two crotchets go, as before, to a single chord, as shown in the following example:

Ex. 14
12)

§ 2. *Repercussion and modification of the harmony over passing notes.*

(*a*) In the course of the preceding section it was said, more than once, that passing notes (of whatever kind) in the Bass in no way affected the harmony already struck. There are, however, certain exceptions, which it seemed better to reserve until now, rather than risk confusion by introducing them piecemeal under the headings to which they respectively belong, or even creating sub-headings for their accommodation.

The examples, presently to be given, are taken from the masterly series with which Ph. Em. Bach concludes his chapter 'On passing notes' (*Versuch &c.*, Part II, 1762, Ch. 36, § 14). They will here be given on two staves, and, in most instances, an 8ve higher than in the original (cf. Ch. iii, § 3, V, note 30).

The cases presented by Bach fall mainly into two groups: (1) one in which the repercussion of the preceding harmony is dictated by considerations of *taste*, and (2) one in which a *modification* of the harmony is necessary in order to *avoid consecutives with the Bass*, or (in one instance) to prepare a subsequent discord.

---

repeats the example with this alternative figuring, at the same time expressing his views on the respective merits of the different methods (cf. Ch. xix, 'The figuring of transitional notes', § 5, Ex. 3 *a* and the text immediately following).

[11] Heinichen here adds the following footnote: "The object of the old composers, in this instance, was to avoid the frequent repetition of interpolated quavers (*der eingeflickten 8^{tel}*), for, otherwise, the above example would have to appear as follows:

It must here be mentioned, in explanation of Heinichen's note, that, in the true *Allabreve*, quavers were rarely admitted, as will be seen later on.

[12] It will readily be seen that, when the figure in question appears in an *upper part*, the note *, though unaccented in its relation to the preceding crotchet, is *accented*, or *virtualiter* long (cf. note 1), *in its relation to the omitted quaver*, and therefore, *when discordant with its Bass*, satisfies the conditions of *transitus irregularis* (cf. *d*), as in the following example:

This is how Fux came to apply to this particular usage the term *nota cambita* (Ital. *cambiata*), which term has come to be used in modern works on Counterpoint almost exclusively in this sense.

Bach also adds some typical examples in which it is especially necessary to indicate the continuance of the preceding harmony by means of a dash, or, vice versâ, to figure a note which would otherwise be allowed to pass.

(*b*) Of the following examples Bach says: "A special expression, to be inferred from the general character (*Inhalt*) of a piece, sometimes, too, from the accompaniment of the *ripieno* parts, occasionally demands the repetition of the harmony in the right hand with each short dotted note, instead of, as would otherwise be the case, always letting the second one pass. This case is of frequent occurrence in accompanied Recitatives."

This is not very clearly worded, and only the Bass is given, but it seems pretty evident that the following was intended:

Ex. 15

Of the next example Bach writes: "If, for the sake of expression, the composer wishes the passing note *e*, in the first bar, to be accompanied,[13] he must expressly put a 6 over it." Only the Bass is given:

14) Ex. 16

[13] In speaking of the passing note *e* being 'accompanied', Bach is here thinking of the repercussion of the chord *as a whole*. Even if the *e* remained unfigured and were treated as a passing note, it would be necessary, *if the chords were taken in the position shown above*, to avoid consecutive 8ves by moving the upper part, either in Thirds with the Bass (*a*), or (by contrary motion) to a Sixth with the Bass (*b*); the only alternative would be the awkward progression (*c*):

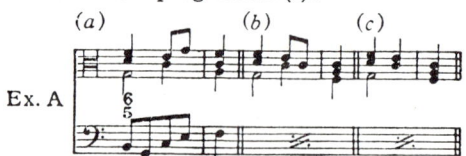

Ex. A

In either of the two remaining positions this necessity could be obviated by doubling the 5 of the Triad on *f*, either in the 8ve (*a*), or in the unison (*b*):

Ex. B

[14] For the (optional) treatment of the 6 on *d* (in the last bar of the example) as $\substack{6\\4\\3}$ see Ch. xxi, 'Incomplete figuring', II, § 1.

XVIII § 2 (c) QUICK NOTES IN THE BASS 727

(c) The following examples afford instances of the necessity (already exemplified in note 13) of avoiding consecutives with the Bass by a modification of the harmony over passing notes, and it will be seen that the passing notes here concerned are those where the Bass leaps to another interval of the same harmony, either directly (as in Ex. 6), or with an intermediate changing, i.e. accented passing, note (*transitus irregularis*).

In Ex. 17 it will be seen that an exchange of intervals is effected between the Bass and an upper part, the latter proceeding to the interval relinquished by the former and vice versâ. The harmony changes, in fact, from one inversion of the same discord to another *without the second one being indicated by figures over the passing note*.

In the examples given, only the part in question moves; Bach tells us, however, that the entire chord may be struck afresh: it is, of course, a question, partly of *pace*, and partly of taste:

Ex. 17 (Given an 8ve lower in the original.)

The next series of examples is of a somewhat different character, inasmuch as the modification of the harmony is determined, not by absolute necessity, but by expediency: the desirability of maintaining the accompaniment at the same level (and not getting into too low a position with the right hand), of avoiding unnecessary and melodically valueless skips, inelegant progressions, and so forth.[15] In these examples we see the (optional) repercussion of the entire chord alluded to above.

[15] Of Ex. 18 *b* Bach writes: "If one does not want to get too far down with the right hand, and at the same time has to avoid Fifths, the preceding harmony must be repeated [with due modification] over the passing notes."
The alternatives in question, to be avoided, are, of course:

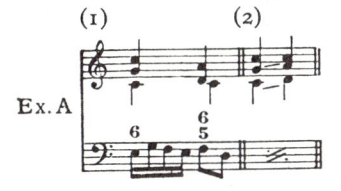

Ex. A

The same applies *mutatis mutandis* to Ex. *a*, in which the modification of the harmony over the passing notes could be avoided as follows:

Ex. B

Of Ex. *c* Bach tells us that, by the repetition of the harmony (in its modified form),

Ex. 18

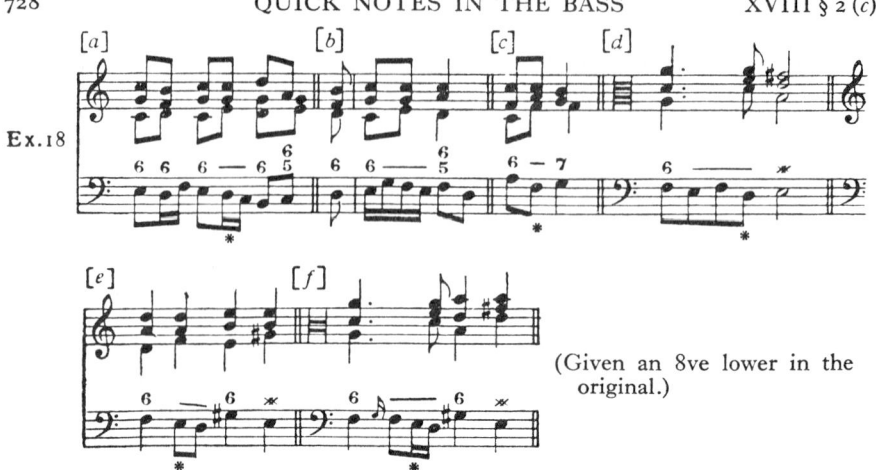

[Ex. C and Ex. D musical examples]

(d) We now come to an instance in which the repetition of the preceding consecutive 5ths (with the Bass) are avoided if the 6 over a is taken as $\smash{\genfrac{}{}{0pt}{}{3}{\genfrac{}{}{0pt}{}{6}{3}}}$ (as in the example), and 8ves if it is taken as $\smash{\genfrac{}{}{0pt}{}{\genfrac{}{}{0pt}{}{6}{3}}{8}}$. (In the former case the 7 would include the 5, and in the latter the 8.) The consecutive 8ves in question would be mitigated by the intervening passing note f in the Bass, and would, therefore (in accordance with Marpurg's *dictum*: that many things which are faults in composition are not so in an accompaniment from a figured Bass), not be of much account unless between extreme or, at least, adjacent parts.

Bach might have added that directly-consecutive 8ves would arise if the 6 were taken as $\smash{\genfrac{}{}{0pt}{}{\genfrac{}{}{0pt}{}{6}{3}}{6}}$, and the 7 as $\smash{\genfrac{}{}{0pt}{}{\genfrac{}{}{0pt}{}{7}{3}}{8}}$, but would be avoided if the latter were taken as $\smash{\genfrac{}{}{0pt}{}{\genfrac{}{}{0pt}{}{5}{3}}{7}}$. The following example will illustrate all these cases:

Of Exx. e and f (which are practically identical as far as the Bass is concerned) Bach tells us that it is *presupposed* that a necessity exists [determined by a preceding harmony (not given in the example), as e.g. a major Triad on e] for the doubling of the 6 or 3 (instead of the 8) in the first chord. This applies also to Ex. d.

Even so, the necessity for the repetition of the chord (in an altered form) over the passing notes could be avoided, in Exx. d and f by an awkward progression (skip), and in Ex. e by the employment of extended harmony, as shown below:

XVIII § 2 (d) QUICK NOTES IN THE BASS 729

harmony in a different shape ($\begin{smallmatrix}8\\7\\\#3\end{smallmatrix}$ instead of $\begin{smallmatrix}7\\5\\\#3\end{smallmatrix}$) is necessary in order to prepare a subsequent discord:

16)
Ex. 19   (Given an 8ve lower in the original.

(e) The next examples illustrate an old vocal tradition. They are only partially relevant to the subject of the present section, but are of considerable interest to any one concerned with eighteenth-century Italian vocal music, and it therefore seemed a pity to separate them from the series in which Bach chose to include them. They are best explained in his own words:

"In accordance with good Italian vocal style, singers are in the habit, at the end of a sustained note, of rising a tone, or a semitone, according to circumstances (*nachdem die Modulation ist*), and dropping again to the previous note, without the slightest indication. . . . Occasionally we find this mode of delivery written out. One accordingly lets this embellishment pass without accompaniment, and strikes the harmony [in the bar in question] only once with the right hand [either omitting or discontinuing the interval which would clash with the voice] in order that the rising and falling of the principal part may not lose in distinctness."

The examples illustrate the method of *performance*:

Ex. 20 (Given an 8ve lower in the original.)

The *notation* of the voice part (except in the rare instances, to which Bach alludes, in which the embellishment is written out) is, in both examples:

---

[16] The alternative to the alteration of the harmony would here be the temporary adoption of a fifth part (cf. Ch. iii, § 4, III), as follows (or in any other position):

730   QUICK NOTES IN THE BASS   XVIII § 2 (e)

The following method of figuring [and, of course, of accompanying], Bach tells us, is *wrong*:

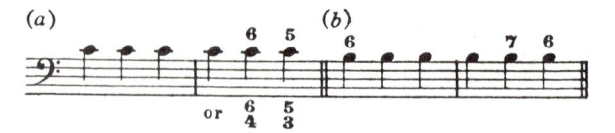

(f) The remaining examples serve admirably to illustrate the kind of ambiguities liable to arise in connexion with passing notes unless adequate indication of the composer's intentions is given. Bach writes as follows:[17]

"If the composer does not figure accurately enough, particularly if he does not indicate the passing notes in passages where one supposes (*vermuthet*) a resolution (Ex. 21 a),[18] likewise if he fails to figure notes which have the appearance of passing, but which, nevertheless, require an harmony of their own (Ex. b),[19] even the most experienced accompanist is liable to mistakes, and is free from blame, unless the principal part is given above the Bass. . . .

"In Ex. *c* we see the good practice of putting [theoretically] superfluous figures over passing notes. A mediocre accompanist is thereby distinctly given

---

[17] The references to examples occurring in the following quotation have necessarily been substituted for those in the original.

[18] In some of the older Basses (seventeenth and earlier eighteenth centuries) 6 *was regularly omitted* on a bass note falling a degree after a $\frac{4}{2}$ chord (cf. Ch. i, § 23 d, note 4, p. 176). It was natural, therefore, in such a case, to 'suppose a resolution' in the absence of the figure denoting it.

In the present instance, however, assuming the Bass to be one in which 6 is *not* omitted after $\frac{4}{2}$, convenient as the horizontal dash used in Bach's example undoubtedly is, it ought, nevertheless, to be possible to dispense with it.

Heinichen's rules for the determination of passing notes, though a splendid attempt, are far from providing for all possible cases (cf. note 5), but they will serve us here, if slightly supplemented, as all such general rules must necessarily sometimes be. In triple time, when three units of the measure (minims, crotchets, or quavers, as the case may be) rise or fall by step, we are told (l.c. § 26. 1, pp. 293 sq.) that, normally (*ordentlicher Weise*), the *second one passes* (unless, of course, it is figured, which, in the present instance, *it is not*), and *the third bears its own harmony*, unless the time is very quick (as sometimes in $\frac{3}{8}$, $\frac{6}{8}$, &c., and *very exceptionally* in $\frac{3}{4}$, $\frac{6}{4}$), in which case *the third one passes also*.

In the present instance there is no need to assume an exceptionally quick time: if the second note passes, *in accordance with the rule*, the third obviously *must* pass also, pending the resolution of the $\frac{4}{2}$ on the first beat of the next bar. We have already seen how a changing (i.e. accented passing) note may be recognized as such by the necessity for preparing or resolving a discord (cf. Ex. 2 b, note 4, and Ex. 13). The same applies *mutatis mutandis* in the present instance. The above rule (for the third note) might, therefore, be modified as follows: "Except in very quick time, the third note bears its own harmony [i.e. a Triad, as the note is, of course, presumed to be unfigured] *unless a predetermined progression of the harmony* [i.e. the necessary preparation or resolution of a discord, &c.] *forbids*."

[19] Ex. *b* illustrates admirably what Heinichen impresses upon his readers at the commencement of his rules (l.c. § 8, note a, p. 263):

"It is a matter of course that a composer can always depart from the regular rules and intimate the same by the appropriate figures. . . ."

XVIII § 2 (f)   QUICK NOTES IN THE BASS

to understand the need for duplication,[20] in order that mistakes may be avoided. In Exx. *d* and *e* the horizontal dash is necessary, in order that, instead of repeating the preceding harmony, one may not strike the Triad of the following note, over the rest." [21]

Ex. 21

§ 3. *Heinichen's rules.*

(*a*) It has been made abundantly clear, in the two preceding sections, how very difficult it may sometimes be, in the absence of special device, to determine whether a particular note in the Bass should bear an independent harmony or not.

Ph. Em. Bach writes as follows (l.c. §§ 1, 2):

"The indication of passing notes is, in the majority of cases, just as necessary as the indication of the figures [i.e. the intervals thereby denoted]. Since, now, figurists are, in this matter too, not sufficiently precise, one must learn little by little, by diligent practice in accompanying and by an attentive ear, to learn to distinguish the passing notes (*a*). *Occasionally* they are to be guessed from the preceding harmony, which fits the notes which follow (*b*), and from the necessary preparation and resolution [of a discord] (*a*) and (*c*):

---

[20] The duplication referred to is that of the 3 or 6 (1), to avoid the 8ves with the Bass which would arise if contrary motion were employed without it (2).
Without contrary motion, the progression would still not be good (3):

[21] In Exx. *d* and *e* the only alternative to the horizontal dash is a *figure*, as:

Ex. A

This precaution, however, is too frequently omitted, even where no dashes are employed, in which case another danger frequently arises in passages such as Ex. *d*. If the printing is close, and the figures carelessly placed (as is too often the case), it is sometimes impossible to tell (unless the principal part appears over the Bass) which of the two following is intended:

Ex. B

[Ex. 22] (Bass only given.)

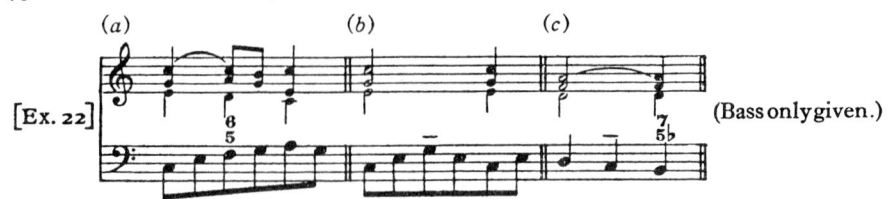

"We have, it is true, certain rules for the recognition of passing notes; but they are not always reliable. Since, therefore, we cannot always build securely on these rules, as passing notes cannot always be guessed with certainty, and since we know that there are disproportionately more bad accompanists than good ones, the safest course is a precise indication, and it is better to do too much than too little. A good accompanist is not to be confused by an horizontal dash or two too many, and to a beginner they are a great help...."

There can be little doubt that it is to Heinichen's rules that Bach is alluding. What he says about the necessity for precise indication is very true, but it is a counsel for composers rather than accompanists, and does not help us to deal with existing Basses in which such indication is lacking.

Heinichen's rules, though admittedly inadequate, contain much that is very helpful, especially so, perhaps, his descriptions and illustrations of the characteristic habits (if such an expression may be used) of the different measures, particularly the true *Allabreve* and its counterfeits, 'Overture time' (*Ouverteur-Tact*), &c.

The rules, and the necessary examples, take up a great deal of space; it will, therefore, be necessary to condense them as much as possible.

(b) *Crotchets in common time*.

Heinichen begins (l.c. §§ 7–22, pp. 263–90) with common time, with the signature C, which, he says, will serve as a model [or rather, perhaps, as a standard of comparison] in all other measures.

In this, the quavers and semiquavers ordinarily count as quick (or short) notes (cf. note 3), while each crotchet (though Heinichen does not expressly mention this) bears its own harmony.[22] There is, however, as we shall

[22] It must, however, be continually borne in mind, in applying these rules, that the signature C, or $\frac{4}{4}$, is often used to denote a spurious *Allabreve* (cf. note 3), often referred to by Heinichen as *Semi-allabreve* (though this term, as we shall see, does not always denote the same thing), in which the crotchets and quavers are respectively treated as the quavers and semiquavers in true common time. When dealing, therefore, with Basses in which the passing notes are not indicated by dashes (and it is of these that we are now treating), it is of the greatest importance to realize the true nature of the measure: by reference to the principal part or parts in cases where the time-signature gives no guidance.

The following example shows the two different treatments of the same Bass in true common time (*a*), and quick $\frac{4}{4}$ (or *Semi-allabreve*) (*b*), respectively:

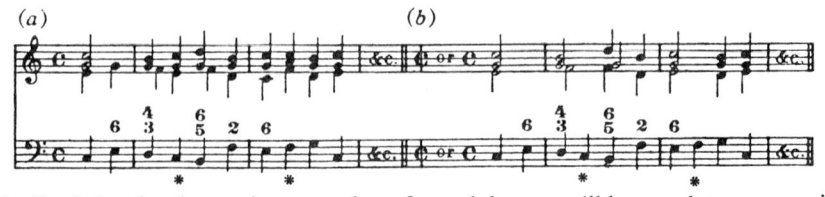

In Ex. *b* the chords are given exactly as figured, but, as will be seen later on, passing

presently see, this important distinction to be made, that whereas, under particular conditions, each quaver may bear an harmony of its own, a single semiquaver (except after a dotted quaver, *d* 7, Rule 4) never does,[23] though, as will be seen, an unaccented (*virtualiter* short) semiquaver, if figured, or followed by a leap, may have its harmony struck *by anticipation* over the preceding semiquaver (*transitus irregularis*).

Heinichen tells us nothing of the treatment of dotted crotchets followed by quavers, but he tells us (l.c. § 21. 4, p. 288) that semiquavers, following dotted quavers, are subject to the same treatment as quavers; we may, therefore, apply the same principle to the case mentioned above. If an example is needed, it is only necessary to imagine the rhythm in question applied to Ex. *a* in note 22.

(*c*) *Quavers in common time.*

(1) When quavers (with or without crotchets interspersed) move *entirely by step*, each accented (*virtualiter* long) one bears its own harmony, and each unaccented (*virtualiter* short) one passes, *unless figured* (as the last quaver in the third and fourth bars of the example to be given). It will be noticed that the passing notes are of the kind described in § 1, *c* and *f*.

[Ex. 23]

Heinichen uses the above example to illustrate the different treatment of passing notes on the Organ and on the Harpsichord.

"It is to be observed generally," he writes (l.c. § 8, p. 264), "that a great difference is to be made in the accompaniment of all quick notes according to whether one is accompanying on an instrument with pipes or one with strings. On the former, the right hand may remain motionless till the passing notes are over; on the Organ, therefore, the accompaniment in the above chords (not indicated in the figuring) may be introduced, whenever it can be done without discounting the effect of the principal part or parts, by following the passing note in the Bass with a consonant interval in the right hand. The latter may bridge the interval of a Third in an upper part with a passing note (cf. Ch. iv, § 3, II *b*), or may move in Thirds with the Bass, as we shall see presently. Ex. *c*, compared with Ex. *b*, will show what is meant:

[23] It must always be remembered that we are considering what normally happens, or does not happen, *in the absence of an indication to the contrary* (cf. note 19). If a composer chooses to figure every semiquaver in a bar, he is perfectly at liberty to do so.

example would not be amiss. But on the Harpsichord (*Clavecin*) it would sound far too empty (especially if the time were slow), and therefore, on instruments of this class, the usual tendency is to double the harmony, i.e. to repeat the preceding chord when the passing note is struck."

The previous example is then repeated (now marked *Larghetto*), with quaver chords and unbroken quavers in the Bass (except in the case of the penultimate chord).

Heinichen then continues (l.c. § 10): "But this reiterated form of accompaniment has a far more workmanlike (*geschickt*) and harmonious effect if the right hand seizes every opportunity of moving in 3rds with the quavers that move by step (retaining [i.e. striking again], however, the other parts which have already been struck once, over the accented note); in what manner, now a stationary 7th (*7ma in transitu*),[24] now a 6th, and now a common chord, comes into being, as it were by chance (*gleichsam von ohngefehr*), on the unaccented (*virtualiter* short) notes, the following example will show...."

The passing harmonies above mentioned, *generated by the progression of an upper part in Thirds with the Bass*, will be found as follows:

1. *Stationary Seventh* ∗, on the 2nd quaver of bar 1, the 4th and 6th quavers of bar 4, the 2nd and 6th quavers of bar 5, the 6th quaver of bars 6 and 7.
2. *Sixth* †, on the 4th quaver of bar 2, the 2nd quaver of bar 4, the 4th and 8th quavers of bar 5, and the 4th quaver of bar 7.
3. *Triad* ⌧, on the 4th quaver of bar 1, the 8th quaver of bar 2, the 6th quaver of bar 3, and the 8th quaver of bar 7.

It will be noticed that the example is an extension of Ex. 23.

25) Ex. 24

---

[24] The term *septima in transitu* (Germ. *durchgehende Septime*) properly designates a *true passing Seventh*, i.e. a 7th which is *itself* a passing note, but it was also used indiscriminately to denote a *stationary Seventh*, which owes its existence to passing notes in *other* parts. Marpurg called attention to this misuse of the term.

[25] This example demands close attention, as illustrating the *actual practice* of a man like Heinichen.

It is obvious that any harmonies arising, "as it were by chance", through the progression of an upper part in Thirds with a passing note in the Bass, are (theoretically)

XVIII § 3 (c) QUICK NOTES IN THE BASS 735

(2) An unaccented (*virtualiter* short) quaver *followed* by a leap,[26] bears its own harmony, whether approached by step (Ex. 25), or by leap (Ex. 26):

on an entirely different footing from an harmony (on the same note) *intended and figured* by the composer.

It is essential to the nature of a 'passing chord' that any interval in it *extraneous to the preceding and following main harmony* should move *by step*, both from the preceding, and to the following chord.

Let us examine the four instances in which a Triad occurs on a passing note ⊠, and it will be seen that these conditions are disregarded.

In bar 1 they could have been maintained, either by taking the passing chord as $\frac{7}{5}$ instead of $\frac{8}{5}$ (Ex. A 1), or by dropping a part and not resuming it till the 5th quaver of the bar (Ex. A 2), or by employing a progression involving consecutive 5ths (Ex. A 3), to which, however, Heinichen himself would certainly not have objected (though Ph. Em. Bach would), unless between adjacent parts (Ex. A 4):

The same applies *mutatis mutandis* to the cases in bars 2 and 7.
In bar 3 the conditions of a passing chord can easily be satisfied as follows:

In all these cases, then, Heinichen treats the Triad ⊠ *as though the Bass note were figured* $(8, 5, \frac{5}{3})$, not as a passing harmony that "comes into being, as it were by chance".

This applies equally to the two Sixths † in bar 5 (between which and bar 6 it will be noticed that consecutive 5ths $\substack{g\ e\\c\ a}$, between Tenor and Bass, are saved only by the passing note *b* in the Bass).

The reader will understand that all this is said, not by way of finding fault, but simply in order to call attention as emphatically as possible to the kind of licence actually employed at the time by a musician of acknowledged eminence.

Finally, it is important to note the (perfectly legitimate) alternation between three- and four-part harmony. In some of the chords with only three sounding parts it is evident that two parts are regarded as *coinciding in the unison* (as on the 4th and 7th quavers of bar 2, the 7th quaver of bar 3, &c.), while in other cases (as on the 5th, 6th, and 7th quavers of bar 7) the fourth part is dropped, thereby facilitating the progression in Thirds with the Bass, and the passing harmonies discussed above.

It need hardly be said that the kind of accompaniment described and illustrated by Heinichen is only admissible when it can be employed without discounting the effect of the principal part or parts, either by the meaningless duplication (in the unison or 8ve) of passing notes occurring in them, or by disagreeable clashes.

It is obvious that, *under some circumstances*, the mere repercussion of the harmony (with or without modification) over each passing quaver in the Bass might have an extremely bad effect.

[26] Heinichen gives no rule for a *virtualiter* short quaver, *preceded*, but *not* followed,

[Ex. 25]

27) [Ex. 26]

Before proceeding to describe the treatment of semiquavers in common time, Heinichen states an important rule, of which the substance has been given in note 22, but which it is better to give here in his own words (l.c. § 13, p. 268):

"When, however, the measure (*Mensur*) of this common time goes very quick, e.g. in *Semi-allabreve*, in Overture Time, or where, in addition to the signature C or ₵, the word *allegro* or *presto* occurs, &c., the quavers, by reason of their quickness, are regarded no longer as quavers, but as semiquavers, and so treated."

To illustrate this, we are told that all the examples of semiquavers (subsequently to be given) can be translated [by making two bars out of one, and] by changing the semiquavers into quavers, the quavers into crotchets, &c. (cf. § 1 *d*, note 3 *ad fin.*).

(*d*) *Semiquavers in common time*.

Heinichen distinguishes five cases upon which to base his rules:

(1) a group of four semiquavers all moving by step,[28]
(2) a group of four semiquavers broken by a single leap,
(3) broken by either two or three leaps,
(4) consisting of notes all of which represent intervals of the same chord,
(5) one or more (consecutive) groups of semiquavers in which all the accented (*virtualiter* long) notes move by step.

by a leap. It may, however, be inferred from a subsequent example (cf. *d* 7, Rule 4, Ex. 39 *a*) that it bears its own harmony, as:

[27] When a quaver bearing a Triad rises a Third, as at the end of bar 1, the 6 is very often omitted, especially in the older Italian Basses (cf. note 30).

[28] This does not refer to the further progression of the final semiquaver of the group, which may or may not be followed by a leap.

XVIII § 3 (d)   QUICK NOTES IN THE BASS   737

(1) "As regards the first case," Heinichen writes (l.c. § 15, p. 268), "when the 4 semiquavers of a group (4 *zusammengezogene* 16 *theil*) rise or fall continuously, and are not followed by a leap, all four have but a single chord; [29] but if the upward or downward movement is not continuous, and the 4th note moves in the reverse direction, each pair has a chord.[30] But if 4 semiquavers rise or fall continuously and are followed by a leap, or if the last *virtualiter* short note [i.e. the 4th semiquaver] is figured, it is, in either case, a sign of *transitus irregularis*, and the chord appertaining to the 4th semiquaver is struck by anticipation (*anticipando*) over the 3rd one; all of which cases are made clear by the following example:

[31)]
[Ex. 27]

N.B.—The instances in which the 3rd semiquaver bears its own harmony have been marked with an asterisk *, and those of *transitus irregularis* (which it is *most* important to note) with an *obelus* † under the harmony note.

To illustrate the treatment of quavers in quick $\frac{4}{4}$ time (*Semi-allabreve*), the above example, Heinichen tells us in a footnote, can be altered as follows, and all future examples of semiquavers in true $\frac{4}{4}$ time can be treated in the same way. By inadvertence Heinichen prefixes the signature C, but (judging by his other examples) ₵ is evidently meant:

[Ex. 27a]

[29] Heinichen appends the following footnote: "Struck only once, or repeated, in accordance with the measure [i.e. pace] and with the different character of Organ or Harpsichord (*nach dem Unterscheide der Mensur und des Pfeiff- oder Saiten-Werckes*)."
[30] An important footnote is here appended: "On the 11th note of bar 3 a 6 appears; but since, in actual practice (*in praxi*), it is not always added in a similar case, as it certainly ought to be, a beginner may note the following exception to the above rule: namely that when the first semiquaver of the figure (*Clausul*) in question bears a common chord, the remaining three semiquavers pass, because they can be regarded as a mere variation of a single crotchet."
[31] Heinichen's rule for four semiquavers (not followed by a leap) of which the upward or downward movement is not continuous, is incomplete. It should be added

(2) The examples in which a group of four semiquavers is broken by a single leap demand very careful attention.

They fall into two classes: (1) that in which the whole group bears a single chord, and (2) that in which a fresh chord is struck over the third semiquaver, though it may be the *fourth* that is the harmony note (*transitus irregularis*). It is in this latter case that the insight of the accompanist is liable to be specially taxed by the inadequate figuring which renders such rules as Heinichen's necessary, as there are certain semiquaver figures in which the *transitus irregularis* occurs *unannounced by the usual signal* in the shape of a figure on the last semiquaver, or a leap after it [cf. note 34 (2) (4) (7)]. The employment of the figure 5 ($^5_3$, 8), where no leap follows, would obviate the difficulty, but we have to deal with Basses as we find them.

Heinichen writes as follows (l.c. § 16, p. 270 sq.): "Regarding the second case, that in which a single leap occurs between the 4 semiquavers of a group, everything turns upon whether the fundamental note from which these 4 semiquavers are derived [32] was a single crotchet or two successive quavers. In the latter case the 4 semiquavers bear two separate chords, but in the former case, only a single chord. But, since a beginner is not capable of estimating this difference, we will here append the commonest figures (*Clausuln*) of such-like varied crotchets and quavers (those, namely, in which there is a single leap between the 4 semiquavers of a group), and, above them, indicate the appropriate accompaniment:

'Common variations of crotchets, with a single chord to 4 semiquavers.'

33) [Ex. 28]

───────────────────────

that, when it is the *third* (and not the fourth) semiquaver that *begins the movement in the reverse direction*, all four bear a single chord (as the last group in bar 1 of the example and the first group in bar 4).

[32] "For all quick notes are nothing else but *variationes* or breakings-up of those slow notes which might have stood in their stead," says Heinichen in a footnote. The old English term for such variations was *divisions*, and the process of thus converting a fundamental Bass (illustrated by Christopher Sympson in his *Division Violist*) was known as *breaking the ground*. The Italian term *diminuire* (and the Latin *diminutio*) was most frequently applied to the extemporaneous embellishment of a principal part, but also to the Bass.

[33] There are several points to be noted in the above series of examples:

(1) In Exx. 1–3, in which the fourth semiquaver of each group is, in every case, *identical with the first*, it is obvious that the number of harmonies in the bar would not be affected by the intervention of a leap between two groups, as:

In Ex. 4, on the other hand (as Heinichen points out in connexion with Ex. 6 of the following series, in which *the same figure occurs*), the absence of a leap is the determining factor.

(2) The figure shown in Ex. 3, in the second half of the bar (where the harmony notes *fall*), may also (as Heinichen points out in connexion with Ex. 4 in the next series of examples) require a chord to each pair of semiquavers. As will be seen, the determining factors in this case are (1) the preparation, and (2) the resolution of a discord. With ordinary attention, therefore, no serious difficulty need arise.

(3) On the fourth beat (the 13th semiquaver) of Ex. 2 it will be noticed that Heinichen carefully avoids 8ves ($^{e\ d}_{e\ d}$) between Tenor and Bass by taking the chord in three parts (or allowing two parts to coincide in the unison), whereas, in the second bar of Ex. 4, he disregards the 8ves ($^{b\ c}_{b\ c}$) arising between the Alto and the fourth and fifth semiquavers of the Bass. Other 8ves ($^{a\ g}_{a\ g}$) occur in Ex. 6.

These cases differ in two very important particulars: in Ex. 2 the semiquaver *e* in the Bass (though, in the present sense, a passing note) *is identical with the harmony note* (the first semiquaver of the group), the memory of which lingers in the ear; in the second place, the 8ves would be between *adjacent parts*, whereas in Ex. 4, as also in Ex. 6, they are covered by an intervening part.

In the examples which follow (and in many others, not quoted here) Heinichen (unlike Ph. Em. Bach) *consistently disregards 8ves arising between an upper part and a quick passing note in the Bass, when another part intervenes*, but rarely, if ever (so far as the present writer has observed), *between adjacent parts*.

Instances, as they occur, will be marked in the usual way.

(4) In Exx. 6 and 7 the two semiquavers, an Octave apart, with which each group begins, are, for present purposes, obviously on a par with a single quaver, rising or falling to a semiquaver which, in its turn, falls or rises to the original note, as:

Of these latter figures, however, we are told later (l.c. § 21. 2, pp. 285 sq.) that, in *moderate time* [i.e. the true common time, with which Heinichen's rules are at present dealing (cf. note 22)], *a fresh chord is struck on the first of the two semiquavers* (cf. Ex. 36), but that, in *quick time* (*Semi-allabreve*), all three notes bear a single chord, *like the four semiquavers in the example now under discussion*. It is, therefore, difficult to avoid the conclusion that, in the present case, Heinichen's illustration is incomplete, and that the treatment of the semiquaver figures shown in Exx. 6 and 7 differs in accordance with the measure. (This does not, of course, mean that the *same series* of sixteen semiquavers in a bar would bear eight harmonies in slow time, and four in quick. On the contrary, if the composer designed his Bass to bear eight harmonies, it would only be by chance if it could be made to bear only four with satisfactory results, and vice versâ).

In any case it is evident (as was pointed out above, in connexion with Ex. 3) that

QUICK NOTES IN THE BASS — XVIII § 3 (d)

'Common variations of quavers, with two chords to 4 semiquavers.'

34)
[Ex. 29]

the exigencies of the harmony (the preparation and resolution of discords) are liable to necessitate a fresh chord * on the third semiquaver of a group, as will be seen by changing the figuring of the Bass in the second half of Ex. 6:

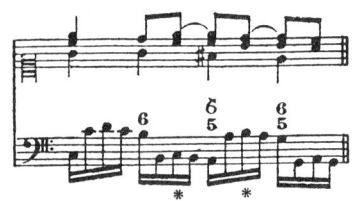

It is also evident that similar cases are more likely to arise when the trend of the Bass is *downward* (as in Ex. 6) than when it is upward (as in Ex. 7).

[34] Heinichen appends the following footnote. Some passages are here given in italics, and the whole has been divided into numbered paragraphs to facilitate reference:

"Concerning these Variations we will make the following remarks:

(1) In the first and second examples the fundamental notes are always to be found in the first and 3rd semiquaver.

(2) But, in the third example, the first and 4th semiquavers are always the fundamental notes, *whether a leap follows or not*. For, in this Variation, the second semiquaver is regarded as an *anticipation of the following harmony*, and the 3rd semiquaver as a *transitus irregularis*.

(3) The 4th example shows that, in a figured Thorough-Bass, identical figures (*Clausuln*) can sometimes occur with a totally different accompaniment. For, further

XVIII § 3 (d)   QUICK NOTES IN THE BASS   741

(3) Heinichen continues:

"Regarding the third case: when, in a group of 4 semiquavers, either 2 or 3 leaps occur, and the third and 4th semiquavers do not, *both together*, fit into the chord of the first semiquaver, a fresh chord is struck on the 3rd semiquaver. The following example shows many varieties of these leaping semiquavers, all of which have the same treatment.

"Thus, in the first bar, two leaps always occur between the first 3 semiquavers, but, in the second bar, between the first two and the last two.

"In the 3rd bar there are always three leaps in a group of 4 semiquavers, i.e. they move entirely by leap, but in such a way that, as in the case of the preceding varieties, neither the 3rd nor the 4th semiquaver is included in the chord of the first one [except, inadvertently, the fourth semiquaver of the bar], whereas, on the other hand, in the 4th bar, with the same number of leaps, the 3rd semiquaver is, it is true, included in the chord of the first, but the 4th one never harmonizes with it, and, consequently, here too, only 2 semiquavers go to a chord:

back, we found this very figure, with a single chord, among the varied crotchets [Ex. 28. 3, second half-bar (cf. note 33. 2)], but here the figures above the Bass show that they call for resolution as early as the 3rd semiquaver, and that, consequently, two quavers are, in this instance, the fundamental notes. [It will be noticed, in this example, that Heinichen entirely disregards the consecutive 8ves which, in similar cases, Ph. Em. Bach was so careful to avoid (cf. § 2 c, Ex. 17).]

(4) In the 5th example the second semiquaver again counts as an *anticipation of the following harmony*, and the first and last semiquavers in every case furnish the fundamental notes, *whether a leap follows or not*. The one exceptional case, in which they [i.e. the group of 4 semiquavers] are regarded as a variation of a single crotchet, is when the first semiquaver bears a common chord and the second semiquaver leaps upwards no more than a 3rd, as the first half of the second bar and the last 4 semiquavers of the example show.

(5) In the 6th and last example the 2 fundamental notes are to be found in the first and 4th semiquavers. Here, it is the leap which follows that is the determining factor, for we saw this very same figure further back, among the varied crotchets, with only a single chord [Ex. 28. 4 (cf. note 33. 1 *ad fin.*)].

Therefore, instead of numerous examples, which might still be added, of varied quavers of this kind, the following general rule may be noted: that, as often as 4 semiquavers between which there is a single leap, N.B. immediately after the *first* semiquaver, are in their turn followed by a leap, just so often the 4th semiquaver, as a fundamental note, bears its own chord."

(6) [This rule, though perfectly correct as regards the particular semiquaver figure shown in Ex. 6, is somewhat misleading, inasmuch as the leap after the first semiquaver has nothing whatever to do with the *transitus irregularis* that follows, as a glance at the first half of bar 3 in Ex. 27 will show. A simpler, and more general, statement would be: that, whenever the last three semiquavers of a group move by step in the same direction (irrespective of what precedes them), and are followed by a leap, the first and fourth are the harmony notes.]

(7) [It may also be pointed out, in this connexion, that the two cases in bar 1 of Ex. 5, in which the fourth semiquaver of a group (though not followed by a leap) is the harmony note, differ from the *true transitus irregularis* as defined above (§ 1 *d*), inasmuch as the changing (i.e. accented passing) note does not bridge the interval of a Third, but separates two notes of the same denomination.

In this instance, as also on the eighth semiquaver of Ex. 3, a figure (5, $\frac{5}{3}$, or 8) would have removed all difficulty. But, most unfortunately, the figurists of Heinichen's school did not realize that, *as a danger signal* (i.e. an indication of *transitus irregularis*) it was just as necessary to figure a Triad as a Sixth (cf. Ex. 27, bar 3, last semiquaver) or any other harmony.]

[Ex. 30]

(4) "Regarding the 4th case, on the other hand, when all the four semiquavers of a group fit in with the chord of the first one and, so to speak, represent an Arpeggio of it, they bear only a single chord (struck only once, or repeated, according to the nature of the instrument employed). . . ."

An example follows (showing various kinds of broken harmony, from a true Arpeggio to an 'Alberti Bass'), of which it will be enough to quote an extract (bars 5-7):

35) [Ex. 31]

[35] The repercussion (and *modification*) of the harmony on the 7th semiquaver of bar 1 of the above extract, and on the 7th and 15th semiquavers of bar 2, must not be confused with the repercussion of each chord to which Heinichen alludes as "dependent on the nature of the instrument employed"—i.e. Harpsichord as opposed to Organ. In the present instances, the first semiquaver of the group is a *leading note* (omitted, as such, from the chord struck over it), and the *quite arbitrary* addition of this same leading note to the harmony on the 3rd semiquaver of the group (with the incidental repercussion of the entire chord) is practically on a par with the following

XVIII § 3 (d) QUICK NOTES IN THE BASS 743

(5) Heinichen continues:

"Regarding the 5th, and last, case: when, in a succession of 4, 8, or more consecutive semiquavers, the *virtualiter* long [i.e. accented] notes move continually by step [i.e. in relation to each other], while the *virtualiter* short [i.e. unaccented] notes move by leap [i.e. in relation to the accented notes], 4 semiquavers, it is true, go, here also, to one chord, but, in this instance, there is a special tendency habitually to follow the *virtualiter* long notes in 3rds [36] (*doch pfleget man hier sonderlich gern die* virtualiter *langen Noten mit einhergehenden 3en zu begleiten*):

37)
[Ex. 32]

(6) Besides the five cases described above, in which a group of four semiquavers is to be regarded as a variation of either (1) a single crotchet, or

of the Bass in Thirds ($^{o\ e}_{e\ c}$) at the end of the last bar. If bar 2 be modified as follows, the matter will be clear:

---

[36] Cf. *c* (1), Ex. 24, and the quotation from Heinichen which precedes it.

[37] It will be observed that the second example of the series does not, strictly speaking, come under Heinichen's rule, inasmuch as the 5th and 9th semiquavers, respectively, do not move by step to the next accented (*virtualiter* long) semiquaver; but, as they are both figured 6, and fall a Third, it is obvious that the harmony remains unchanged. Also, the 13th semiquaver (*a*), since it does not bear a Triad, requires the figure 7 (as supplied above in square brackets); though, here again, the harmony is obvious. The second half of the bar could be figured in either of the two following ways:

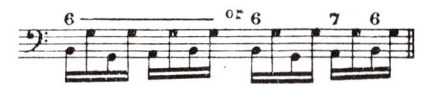

(2) two quavers, there are the two further cases, of a group of three semiquavers preceded by a semiquaver rest, and of two semiquavers following a quaver (♪♬), or a dotted crotchet (♩. ♬), or a crotchet preceded by a quaver (♪ ♩ ♬).

Regarding the first of these Heinichen writes (l.c. § 20, pp. 280 sq.):

"When, instead of the first semiquaver, there is a rest, the chord belonging to the note which follows may be struck first [i.e. over the rest], and the note itself afterwards, and here the rules for semiquavers hitherto given are to be applied *mutatis mutandis*, as follows:

[Rule] (1) "When all 3 semiquavers move by step, and no leap follows, a single chord is struck with them (once only, or repeated); but if a leap follows [or if the last semiquaver is figured], the chord belonging to the last note is struck by anticipation over the second, as distinguished in the following example:

38)
[Ex. 33]

[Rule] (2) "If, however, there is a leap between the second and third notes, or between all three, and if the last two are not included in the chord of the first one, a fresh chord is struck with the second semiquaver. On the other hand, if all three leaping notes are included in the chord of the first one, they have only a single chord (struck once only, or repeated); the following example illustrates every case." [39]

(7) Regarding the second of the two cases mentioned above, Heinichen writes (l.c. § 21, pp. 282 sq.):

"Quavers and semiquavers are combined together in various ways, concerning which we will make the following remarks:

[Rule] (1) "After a crotchet, quaver, or dotted crotchet, two semiquavers,

---

[38] At the beginning of the first and second bars it will be noticed that the right hand follows the Bass in Thirds in the manner already described. In both cases the lowest note in the right-hand part is assumed to be a crotchet, and is here given (for the sake of clearness) with a downward tail. In the original the whole chord is apparently intended to have a single (upward) tail, though (as in many other cases) the clumsiness of the music-type employed in Heinichen's work makes it difficult to determine.

[39] It is unnecessary to quote this example here, as Exx. 30 and 31 provide sufficient illustration.

XVIII § 3 (d)   QUICK NOTES IN THE BASS   745

rising or falling continuously, ordinarily pass (*passiren ... frei aus*), if no leap follows. If, however, there is one [or if the second semiquaver is figured], it is a sign of *transitus irregularis*, and the chord belonging to the last semiquaver is struck with the first one, as shown in the first of the following examples. But the second example shows that, in a quick measure (e.g. in *Semi-allabreve*), two such semiquavers may pass *ascendendo*, even though a leap follows.[40] Although this is almost the only case. For, if such a case is found *descendendo*, the accidental result (if the quaver bears a Triad) will be a Seventh on the last semiquaver, which Seventh must certainly be resolved over the following note,[41] as shown in the accompaniment of the 4th and 5th bars of the example:

[Ex 34]

[Ex. 35]

Presto

[40] Heinichen here appends the following footnote: "Because, in such a case, they are mere variations of a crotchet, which requires only a single chord. Thus the fundamental notes of this example [Ex. 35] would present the following aspect:

[41] This is an exceedingly important point. It is obvious that, under the circumstances described, the two falling semiquavers cannot pass under the harmony of the preceding quaver *except when the leap which follows is one of a Fourth upwards or a Fifth downwards*.

[Rule] (2) "When, after a quaver, the first semiquaver moves [rises or falls] by step, and the second one, reversing the movement, returns to the previous note, a fresh chord is, in moderate time, struck with the first semiquaver. But in quick time (as in *Semi-allabreve*) all three notes have a single chord. The distinction will be seen from the two following examples:

[Ex. 36] *Larghetto*

[Ex. 37] *Allegro*

[Rule] (3) "When, between 3 such notes (namely a quaver and 2 semi-quavers following it), there is a leap, whether it be after the quaver or the first semiquaver, a fresh chord will in both cases be struck with the said first semiquaver, unless all three notes are included in the chord of the first one, in which case they only have one chord, as distinguished in the following example:

42)
[Ex. 38]

[Rule] (4) "When, after the quaver, a dot and a semiquaver follow, this semiquaver, both *in saltu* and *in transitu*, is treated, according to the difference

[42] Attention is called (1) to the type of passing note exemplified in the fourth and sixth semiquavers (c) in bar 1 (cf. § 1 *l*, Ex. 12), and (2) to the fourth semiquaver (a) in bar 2, on which we see that 'accidental' Seventh, resolving over the following Bass note, to which Heinichen called attention in connexion with Ex. 35 (cf. note 41).

XVIII § 3 (d)   QUICK NOTES IN THE BASS   747

of the measure (*Mensur*), exactly as though it were a real quaver.[43] The 2 following examples must, therefore, suffice as a brief recapitulation of the rules given above for slow and quick quavers. If any one desires more examples, let him, in all the examples of quavers already given, as well as in those still to follow in connexion with other measures, add dots to the *virtualiter* long [i.e. accented] notes and change all the *virtualiter* short notes into semiquavers (e.g. for ♫♫ substitute ♩.♫ ♫), and he will have what he wants."

It is unnecessary to give Heinichen's examples in full, since Exx. 23-6 will serve to illustrate the point in true $\frac{4}{4}$ time, if a dotted rhythm is mentally substituted for the even quavers as directed above. The only example of quavers in quick $\frac{4}{4}$ time (*Semi-allabreve*), hitherto given, is Ex. 27 a; but further examples can be derived from Exx. 28-32 (in the same way as Ex. 27 a from Ex. 27) and will serve in the present instance, if the necessary change of rhythm be imagined.[44]

We will quote only the last bar of each of Heinichen's two examples, in order to draw special attention to the different treatment (in slow and quick time, respectively) of the note marked * (cf. § 1 *l*, note 8):

[Ex. 39]

(8) In an Appendix (l.c. *Zusatz*, VI, pp. 373 sq.) Heinichen gives an example (designed to follow immediately after Exx. 34 and 35, but which it seemed better to keep separate) which is particularly instructive as illustrating two different possible treatments of the syncopated figure which arises in the Bass when two semiquavers follow a crotchet (itself preceded by an accented quaver).

The point illustrated by the first eight bars of the example is a different and by no means unimportant one; it is, however, the bars which follow that mainly concern us.

Heinichen's description of the example is as follows:

N.B.—The italics have been added by the present writer.

"The following example may be added, concerning which it is to be remarked that the first 8 bars (unless any one chooses, for the sake of

---

[43] That is to say, in *true* $\frac{4}{4}$ time a semiquaver following a dotted quaver is subject to the same rules as quavers in the same time, but in *quick* $\frac{4}{4}$ time (spurious *Allabreve* or *Semi-allabreve*, cf. § 1 *d*, note 3) it is subject to the rules which govern semiquavers in true $\frac{4}{4}$ time.

[44] Thus, Ex. 28 will appear as follows:

beginners, specially to figure the crotchets occurring therein) are mere variations of minims moving by step, and are consequently treated with a single chord. As soon, however, as this precise variation is overstepped, i.e. as soon as the note following the first quaver no longer leaps a 3rd upwards, or the remaining notes are altered [i.e. figured, as in bar 10], just so soon is the second quaver (or the first half of the crotchet) in every bar regarded as an *anticipation* of the chord appertaining to the 3rd quaver [or the second half of the crotchet], *and it is at the discretion of the accompanist*, either, in every case throughout (especially in quick time), *to let it pass* ('frei aus passiren lassen'), *and not to strike the proper chord till the third quaver* [or the second half of the crotchet], as shown in the 10th, 11th, 12th, and 13th bars of the following example, *or, upon the entry of the second quaver, at once to strike the chord appertaining to it*, as shown in the 9th, 14th, 15th, and 16th bars. *The latter course is the more regularly taken in moderate time:*

[Ex. 40]

"If one were to give this example a very quick measure, and to allow the second quaver to pass [under the preceding harmony] as an anticipation of the following chord throughout, the fundamental notes would appear as follows, and the accompaniment would be treated accordingly:

[Ex. 40a] 45)

(e) *Triple Time (e–m).*

Before proceeding to the *Allabreve* and 'Overture Time', Heinichen treats of the triple rhythms, $\frac{3}{2}, \frac{3}{4}, \frac{3}{8}, \frac{6}{4}, \frac{6}{8}, \frac{9}{8}, \frac{12}{8}$, as next in order of importance. Concerning these he gives us (l.c. § 24, pp. 292 sq.) the following general rule: "All those notes from which each triple measure takes its name [i.e. the units

---

[45] In bar 12 the last quaver *f* is a passing note; the bar should, therefore, appear as follows:

XVIII § 3 (e) QUICK NOTES IN THE BASS 749

of the measure: minims in $\frac{3}{2}$, crotchets in $\frac{6}{4}$, &c.] are treated like the slow quavers in common time with the signature ₵; on the other hand, the half-notes, or the halves of those notes from which each triple measure takes its name, are treated like the semiquavers in common time."

According to this, then, one unit of the measure may pass under the harmony of the preceding one, or each may bear its own harmony (as in the case of the quavers in true $\frac{4}{4}$ time, Exx. 23–6), while the half-unit cannot (unless the figuring specially demands it) bear a chord of its own.

With regard to this latter condition, however, Heinichen cites an important exception in his Appendix to the chapter under discussion (l.c. *Zusatz*, VII, pp. 376 sq.): "In $\frac{3}{2}$ time," he writes, "the crotchets, and, in $\frac{3}{4}$, the quavers, can in two instances be treated as slow notes (i.e. such as, when not moving *per transitum*, have each their own chord), namely: (1) in the case of a very slow measure (*Mensur*), (2) in the case of an Allegro in which still quicker notes prevail (*dominiren*), as:

[Ex. 41]

Adagio

Allegro

[Ex. 41a]

Adagio

(*f*) Heinichen's rules for the units of triple time (minims, crotchets, or quavers, as the case may be) are as follows (l.c. § 26, pp. 293 sq.):

"We begin with those notes from which each triple measure takes its name and say that when:

(1) "3 such notes rise or fall by step, the middle (*virtualiter* short)[46] note

---

[46] Heinichen here appends the following footnote:

"The notes from which each triple measure takes its name [i.e. the units of the measure] have *ratione quantitatis intrinsecae* the following peculiarity, namely that the first is always *virtualiter* long, while both the second and third are *virtualiter* short, so that sometimes the second, and sometimes the third, passes *in transitu*, and sometimes [as we shall see presently], both together. . . ."

passes, while, in moderate [i.e. not very quick] time, the 3rd note has a fresh chord, as may be seen in No. 1 of the following examples."[47]

(2) "But, if the first such note be followed by a leap, a fresh chord is struck on the second note, and the 3rd note passes, if it moves by step and is not followed by a leap, as may be seen in No. 2 of the following examples."

(3) "But if the second or third note is followed by a leap, or if they are all followed by leaps, then each note has its own chord, as shown in No. 3 of the following examples."

(4) "If the 3rd such note is preceded by a note of double its time-value, the said 3rd note may pass if it is not followed [or preceded] by a leap. But if a leap follows, or if it is preceded and followed by a leap, a fresh chord is struck, as shown in No. 4 of the following examples."

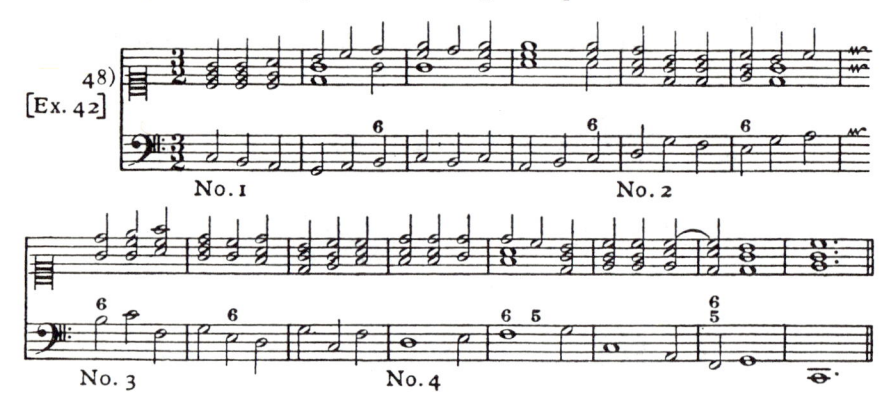

48) [Ex. 42]

49) [Ex. 42a]

[Ex. 42b]

---

[47] Heinichen here explains in a footnote that henceforth *the same example*, repeated with due alteration of the time-values, $\frac{3}{2}$, $\frac{6}{4}$, $\frac{6}{8}$, &c. (cf. Exx. 41 and 41 a), will be made to serve for *all triple measures*.

[48] Bar 3 of No. 1 (Ex. 42) does not fit in with the rule given, inasmuch as the three notes do not all rise or fall by step. The Sixth on the passing note *b* (the second beat of the bar) is due to the following of the Bass in Thirds in the upper part, as is also the Seventh on *e* at the end of bar 1 of No. 4 (cf. the text immediately preceding Ex. 24).

[49] In the original, Exx. 42 *a* and *b* are given in full.

XVIII § 3 (f)   QUICK NOTES IN THE BASS   751

Heinichen continues (l.c. § 27):

"If, however, the triple rhythms which are more inclined to speed, $\frac{3}{8}$ $\frac{6}{8}$ $\frac{9}{8}$ $\frac{12}{8}$, have a very quick measure,[50] their quavers are treated like the quick quavers in common time [Heinichen means the quavers in quick $\frac{4}{4}$ time (*Semi-allabreve*), cf. note 3], or, to speak more plainly, like semiquavers [i.e. in true $\frac{4}{4}$ time].[51] Consequently, when:

(1) "3 such quavers move by step, they ordinarily have but a single chord, as shown in No. 1 of the following examples."

(2) "If only the first and the 3rd move continuously by step, while the middle one leaps to some interval of the chord struck (*die mittlere aber hält sich in andern Sprüngen des angeschlagenen Accordes auf*), all 3, it is true, again have but a single chord, but, in this case, there is a tendency to move in Thirds with the first and 3rd notes, as shown in No. 2."

(3) "If, apart from this case [i.e. when the 1st and 3rd quavers move by step], the second note leaps [i.e. to an interval of the chord struck], and the 3rd is not included in the chord of the first, then the said 3rd note has a fresh chord, as shown in No. 3."

(4) "But, if all three notes leap in such a way that they are all included in the chord of the first one, they have but one chord, struck once only or repeated, as shown in No. 4."

[Ex. 43]

No. 1   No. 2

No. 3   No. 4

[50] Heinichen here appends the following footnote: "This quick measure does not commonly occur in $\frac{3}{4}$ and $\frac{6}{4}$ time, but, should such an exceptional case arise, the crotchets would necessarily have the same treatment as, in the present instance, the quavers."

[51] The following footnote is here appended: "That is to say, what was said above concerning groups of 4 semiquavers is here applied *mutatis mutandis* to groups of 3 quavers."

(g) We now come to the more complicated subject of the half-units (crotchets, quavers, or semiquavers) of which Heinichen tells us that they are "treated throughout like the semiquavers in slow common time" (i.e. true $\frac{4}{4}$ time, as opposed to quick $\frac{4}{4}$ or *Semi-allabreve*), *subject, however, to the very important exception exemplified in Ex. 41.*

He begins by distinguishing five cases, of which all *except the second* correspond closely to his classification of the different cases arising in connexion with semiquavers in common time (§ 3 *d ad init.*).[52]

"We come", he writes (l.c. § 28), "to the half-notes, or the halves of those notes from which every triple measure takes its name, which are treated throughout like the semiquavers in slow common time; therefore,

(1) "when 4 such notes (the first or the last 4) rise or fall continuously, and are not followed by a leap, all 4 have but a single chord. But if the upward or downward movement is not continuous, and the 4th note reverses the movement, each pair bears a chord.[53] And if 4 such notes rise or fall continuously, and are followed by a leap, or if there is a figure over the last, *virtualiter* short note, it is, in either case, a sign of *Transitus irregularis*, and the chord appertaining to the last note is struck by anticipation over the *penultima* (the last note but one), all of which cases are shown in No. 1 of the following examples."

(2) "When 6 such notes rise or fall by step, and are not followed by a leap, a fresh chord is struck over the 5th; but if a leap follows, or if there is a figure over the 6th, *virtualiter* short, note, in either case there will again be *Transitus irregularis*, and the chord appertaining to the 6th note will be struck by anticipation over the 5th, as shown in No. 2."

(3) "As long as every 2 such notes have a leap between them, and the two following ones do not both together fit in with the preceding chord, a fresh chord is struck with every pair, as is clearly illustrated in No. 3."

(4) "But if 4 or 6 such leaping notes all fit in with the chord of the first note, which chord they, as it were, represent in Arpeggio form, then all together have but a single chord (struck twice or three times),[54] as may be seen in No. 4."

---

[52] The case in which a single leap occurs in a group of 4 semiquavers in common time occupied the second place in Heinichen's classification. In the present instance (triple time), the case in which a single leap occurs in a group of 4 (or 6) half-units is treated separately, no doubt because the examples required to illustrate it could not conveniently be included in the continuous series with which Heinichen illustrates the other cases.

[53] The following footnote is here appended: "Except that the Sixth which occurs in bar 6 of the following example may, in actual practice, not be figured; as, after all, 4 such notes are all struck with the Triad over the first note; a similar exception was made in a note [cf. note 30] in the case of the semiquavers. Furthermore, it may be remarked here that, in slow time, the effect is more harmonious if such notes, moving by step, more particularly *descendendo*, are struck with only a pair to each chord, as:

Largo

[54] i.e. according as 4 or 6 notes go to a single harmony; this optional repercussion is not shown in the example.

XVIII § 3 (g)   QUICK NOTES IN THE BASS   753

(5) "But when, in a succession of 4, 6, 12 or more such notes, the *virtualiter* long notes proceed continuously by step, while the intervening *virtualiter* short notes move by leap, then 4 of them (the first or last 4) go to a single chord; at the same time, there is a tendency to follow the *virtualiter* long notes continuously in 3rds in the accompaniment, as is shown in No. 5."

[55) [Ex. 44]]

[55] Two points are to be noted in connexion with the above series of examples:

(1) In No. 2 it will be seen that the principle is the same as when three units of the measure rise or fall by step (Ex. 42, No. 1), namely that the fresh harmony is struck on the third, rather than on the second, beat of the bar (or, in compound time, section of a bar), always subject to the exception mentioned in note 53, in virtue of which, in *slow time*, and especially in the case of a *falling Bass* (as bar 1 of Ex. 44, No. 2), *each* pair of half-units (moving continuously by step) bears an harmony.

(2) In No. 5 it would seem that the third crotchet (*e*) of the second and fourth bars should bear the figure 6, and that the figure 7 on the fifth crotchet of the fourth bar should be omitted. It is plain that, in both bars, the harmony changes on the *second* beat (the third crotchet), and that the $\frac{7}{3}$ on the third beat (the fifth crotchet) is one of those passing harmonies which, as Heinichen tells us, arise 'as it were by chance' when an upper part follows the Bass in Thirds (cf. Ex. 24 and the text immediately preceding), and which *he never figures*. The Bass of the two bars in question should therefore appear as follows:

[Musical notation: examples with figured bass, labeled No. 4 and No. 5]

N.B.—In the original the following examples (Exx. 44 *a* and *b*) are given in full.

[Ex. 44*a*] [Musical notation labeled No. 1]

[Ex. 44*b*] [Musical notation labeled No. 1]

(*h*) Heinichen next proceeds to describe and illustrate the case parallel to that which occupied the second place in the five categories into which he divided groups of semiquavers in common time (cf. *d ad init.*).

"But if", he writes (l.c. § 29, p. 308), "there is only a single leap between 4 (the first 4 or the last 4), or 6 of the above-mentioned notes [i.e. half-units], then it depends whether the figures (*Clausuln*) in question are derived from one or from 2 fundamental notes. In the latter case, the 4 or 6 notes have

XVIII § 3 (h)   QUICK NOTES IN THE BASS   755

2 chords; in the former, only a single chord. But, as a beginner is not capable of estimating this difference, we will here append (as in § 16 above, in connexion with semiquavers [cf. Exx. 28, 29]) the figures of commonest occurrence in such variations [i.e. of one or two fundamental notes, as the case may be], and indicate above them their distinctive accompaniments:

"Common *Variationes* with a single chord [56] to 4 or 6 such notes."

[Ex. 45]

'Common *Variationes* with 2 chords to 4 or 6 such notes.' [57]

[Ex. 46]   58)

---

[56] A footnote is here appended: "Struck twice or three times in accordance with the difference of the pace (*Mensur*) and of the instrument."

[57] A footnote is here appended: "The remarks made above, § 16 in a note [note 34], concerning the semiquaver variations, can be applied in the present case also, for the figures are *mutatis mutandis* identical."

[58] In Ex. 46. 2, in the first half of the second bar, it will be seen that the Bass does

"N.B. All these *Variationes* ought now to follow here in the remaining triple measures. To save space, however, beginners can themselves change them into the measures in question, note by note, in the following manner, e.g.:

[Ex. 45a]

not conform to the pattern set in Ex. 29. 2. It is just possible that the following was intended, though we see that Heinichen avoided consecutive 8ves arising between a passing note in the Bass and the *adjacent* upper part [cf. note 33 (3)]:

In the fifth example of the same series, too, there is apparently a misprint in the second half of the second, and also the last bar, as the six quavers in both cases contain *two* leaps instead of the single one for which the rule provides. The following may have been what was intended:

XVIII § 3 (h)   QUICK NOTES IN THE BASS   757

[Ex. 45b]

It is significant that, in the above examples, Heinichen starts by taking the crotchet, rather than the minim, as the unit of the measure, thus indicating that the figures which the examples illustrate are less likely to occur in slow than in quick time.

(*i*) Heinichen next proceeds (l.c. § 30, p. 313) to the case in which the first half-unit of a series is replaced by an equivalent rest, for which he refers his readers to the rules relating to semiquaver-groups in common time under similar circumstances (cf. *d*, 6). These must of course be supplemented by the five general rules for the half-units of triple time given above (*g*). The following general example is given, to which is added a translation (omitted here) of the opening 1½ bars into $\frac{3}{8}$ ($\frac{6}{8}$ $\frac{9}{8}$ $\frac{12}{8}$) and $\frac{3}{2}$ time:

59)
[Ex. 47]

[59] No instance occurs in the above example of five half-units (preceded by a rest) rising or falling continuously by step. We may, however, safely assume that the rule, quoted above (*g*, Rule 2), for *six* half-units (so rising or falling) applies *mutatis mutandis* to the case above mentioned, and that, in default of any indication to the contrary, a fresh harmony is to be struck over the penultimate note:

Ex. A

If a leap follows there will, of course, be *transitus irregularis*:

Ex. B

(k) Heinichen next gives rules (l.c. §§ 31 and 32, pp. 316 sqq.) for the cases in which one unit of the measure is followed by two half-units, corresponding closely to those already given for combinations of quavers and semiquavers in common time (cf. d, 7).

In the present, as in the former case, where certain combinations are concerned, there is one rule for slow (moderate) time, and another for quick.

The rules are, in substance, as follows:

(1) When, after a unit of the measure, two half-units either rise or fall by step, and are not followed by a leap, they pass under the preceding harmony;[60] but if a leap follows, or if the last of the two notes is figured, there will, *in moderate time*, be *transitus irregularis*, and the first of the two notes will bear the harmony appertaining to the second (cf. Ex. 48, No. 1).

In *quick time*, however, two such notes pass, *even though followed by a leap* (cf. Ex. 49).

This will also be the case, as Heinichen points out (l.c. § 33, p. 323), when a half-unit is followed by two quarter-units, as a crotchet by two quavers in $\frac{3}{2}$ time, or a quaver by two semiquavers in $\frac{3}{4}$ $\frac{6}{4}$ (cf. Exx. 50, 50 a).

(2) Similarly, if the second note of a group of three (1 unit and 2 half-units) either rises or falls by step, and the third *reverses the movement* (thus returning to the previous note), *in moderate time* a fresh chord is struck on the second note of the group (cf. Ex. 48, No. 2), but *in quick time* both half-units pass (cf. Ex. 49). So, too, in the cases exemplified in Exx. 50 and 50 a, in which a half- is followed by two quarter-units.

(3) If there is a leap between the first and second note of the group (consisting of a unit and two half-units), or between the second and third, or both, a fresh chord is struck on the second note, *unless both it and the third*

---

[60] It will be seen that this does not tally with a rule previously given (cf. g, rule 1) to the effect that "when 4 such notes [i.e. half-units] (the first or the last) rise or fall continuously, and are not followed by a leap, all 4 have but a single chord."

The following example shows: (a) the treatment prescribed by this previous rule, and (b) that in accordance with the present one:

It might be possible to amend the rules in question up to a certain point, but the fact is that this is one of the cases where, as Ph. Em. Bach says, rules "are not always reliable" (cf. a, text immediately following Ex. 22). In many cases, in default of adequate indication of a composer's intentions (in the shape of dashes to indicate the continuance of an harmony, figuring of Triads, &c.) the accompanist will have to rely on his instinct and ear rather than on the most carefully formulated rules.

XVIII § 3 (k) QUICK NOTES IN THE BASS 759

note belong to the harmony of the first, in which latter case they both pass (cf. Ex. 48, No. 3):

[Ex. 48]

N.B.—Heinichen repeats the entire example in $\frac{3}{4}\frac{6}{4}$ and $\frac{3}{8}\frac{6}{8}$, &c. time; it will be enough to give the beginning here. This applies also to Exx. 49 a and 50 a.

[Ex. 48a]

[Ex. 48b]

[Ex. 49]

[Ex. 49a]

[Ex. 50]

[Ex. 50a]

(*l*) Heinichen finally tells us (l.c. § 34, p. 324) that, *in very quick time*, there are cases in which, after a crotchet or a quaver (as unit of the measure), four half-units may all pass under the harmony of the preceding unit. He calls attention in a footnote (l.c., pp. 327 sq.) to five characteristic figures (*Clausuln*) as being especially liable to this treatment; the fundamental progression is, in each case, given underneath. They are as follows:

[Ex. 51] 61)

I   II   III   IV   V

[61] The figures 6 added in square brackets are in accordance with the examples now

XVIII § 3 (*l*) QUICK NOTES IN THE BASS 761

It will be seen that, in I, the quavers are simply a turn (∽) connecting the two fundamental notes, while in II they are little else.

In III the quaver figure is the same as in II, but instead of leading to a note a semitone below the first fundamental note (and bearing a Sixth), the downward movement is continued.

In IV and V we have passing notes (i.e. in the wider sense, as defined by Heinichen earlier in the chapter under discussion, cf. § 1 *e*) bridging the interval of a Sixth.

Besides these figures, as shown above, Heinichen's examples (now to follow) show others, identical in the rise or fall of the notes, but *differing in the relative position of the semitones*: [62]

[Ex. 52]

to follow. In an earlier example, however, the Bass figure shown at V occurs with a *Triad* on the second fundamental note (cf. § 1 *e*, Ex. 3 *c*), and there is no reason why this should not be the case with I, or even, possibly, with IV.

[62] The figures shown in Ex. 51 (or ones identical as far as the relative position of tones and semitones is concerned) appear in Exx. 52 and 53 as follows:

Ex. 51 I appears in Ex. 53, 1st quarter of bar 3.
  ,, II   ,,   Ex. 52, 1st half of bar 7, and Ex. 53, 1st quarter of bar 5.
  ,, III   ,,   Ex. 53, 1st quarter of bar 4.
  ,, IV   ,,   Ex. 52, 1st half of bar 2.
  ,, V   ,,   Ex. 52, 1st half of bars 1 and 6, and Ex. 53, 1st quarter of bar 1.

Besides these, Exx. 52 and 53 exhibit, in the following instances, a figure differing as above mentioned from one shown in Ex. 51:

With Ex. 51 I compare Ex. 52, 2nd half of bar 4, and Ex. 53, 2nd quarter of bars 3 and 5.
  ,, IV   ,,   Ex. 52, 1st half of bar 9, and Ex. 53, 1st and 3rd quarters of bar 2.
  ,, V   ,,   Ex. 52, 1st half of bar 5.

[Ex. 53]

Note—It will be observed that, in the 2nd quarter of bar 3, the 1st quarter of bar 4, and the 2nd quarter of bar 5, an upper part moves in Thirds with the Bass, *but that the harmony remains unchanged.*

(*m*) Heinichen concludes his rules for triple time with a brief mention of quavers as *quarter*-units in $\frac{3}{2}$ time. These, he tells us (l.c. § 35), are treated *exactly like semiquavers in common time*, and he gives a general example which constitutes a *résumé* of those already given in connexion with the latter. The example deals solely with groups of four quavers, except where the first quaver of the group is replaced by a rest. It will suffice to quote the end of the example, omitting the first ten bars:

[Ex. 54]

In the above, unlike any of the previous examples in triple time, we see *two harmonies falling to a single unit of the measure.*

We saw at the outset (cf. Ex. 42) that, in triple time, the unit of the measure may occupy a position *intermediate between that of a crotchet and of a quaver*

XVIII § 3 (m)   QUICK NOTES IN THE BASS   763

in true common time, inasmuch as, when three units move by step, the *second passes under the harmony of the first* (like an unaccented quaver in common time), while the *third bears its own harmony* (like a crotchet in common time).

Heinichen tells us, too, that the treatment of *half*-units in triple time corresponds with that of semiquavers in common time (cf. *g ad init.*), but the above example shows that this is only true to a limited extent, inasmuch as we now see two quarter-units (or the equivalent of one half-unit) bearing their own harmony, which *a single semiquaver in common time* (except after a dot, or unless specially figured) *never does*.

It is evident, then, that with the introduction of *quarter*-units as the quickest note in the measure (i.e. in the Bass), different conditions are introduced from those which prevail when the *half*-unit is the quickest note. The unit, the half-unit, and the quarter-unit now become exactly on a par with the crotchet, the quaver, and the semiquaver, respectively, in common time.

This becomes clear from the following example, of which Heinichen gives the Bass only:

63)
[Ex. 55]

Note especially the two half-units (quavers) at the end of bar 2, each bearing its own harmony.[64]

[63] Heinichen had made no previous mention of semiquavers in triple time, but we are doubtless intended to assume that his example of quavers in $\frac{3}{2}$ time (cf. Ex. 54) may be translated into $\frac{3}{4}$ ($\frac{6}{4}$) time. Regarding the possible occurrence, in the Bass, of demisemiquavers in $\frac{3}{8}$ time and its compounds, he tells us (l.c. § 36) that they are not likely to occur in a musical composition ('in einem zur Grund-Stimme gesetzten General-Basse'), but that, should they be presented to the student *by way of an exercise*, either by themselves or intermingled with semiquavers, he is simply to imagine that all the notes have one stroke the less, and treat them accordingly. He then gives the above example (Ex. 55), both in the notation of $\frac{3}{8}$ time and also in that of $\frac{3}{4}$ (as here). He also adds the following duplicate passage in common time, in which, as he tells us, the treatment of demisemiquavers (should they occur) and of semiquavers is identical:

[64] Of course, any of Heinichen's examples of triple time, in which half-units occur as the quickest notes, could easily have been so framed that the half-unit would, in some cases, have borne its own harmony. To provide an instance, we need only take the Bass of the bar under discussion, translating it freely into $\frac{3}{2}$ time, *with half-units as the quickest notes*:

It is clear that the last two crotchets * * will bear each its own harmony. We must,

(n) Heinichen next proceeds to describe the true *Allabreve* (characterized by a *maximum* of two harmonies to the semibreve bar), and also its variants (l.c. §§ 38–47, pp. 333–47).

Of the former he remarks in a footnote: "This antique, pathetic style is surely the most beautiful and the most convenient, the one in which a composer can best display his fundamental science and accuracy in composition. For the harmonies (*Sätze*) in this style must always be pure, their *progressiones* and *resolutiones* strict (*legal*) and far removed from all liberties, the *cantabile* sustained, without many leaps, in all the parts, the latter laden with syncopations (*Rückungen*) and beautiful bindings (*Syncopationes*) of consonances and dissonances,[65] and filled, through and through, in all the parts, with pathetic ideas, themes, and imitations, to the exclusion of anything fanciful in character (*ohne fantasirendes Wesen*). It is here that we must look for a strict (*legal*) composer."

Heinichen's rules are, in substance, as follows:

(1) In the *Allabreve* the only recognized *quick notes* of the measure (cf. § 1 *d*, note 3) are *crotchets*: quavers are either not admitted at all, or else very sparingly, and *not more than two at a time*, in certain syncopated figures (cf. Ex. 56, bar 14). The signature may be either C or ₵.

The said crotchets may move either by step or (though sparingly) by leap, and, normally, two crotchets in the Bass (*never* less) go to a chord, though, in certain cases, all four may go to a single harmony, namely:

(*a*) When four crotchets, of which the first bears a Triad, rise by step and are followed by a note a Fifth above the first (cf. Ex. 56, bars 8 and 19), or when the fourth crotchet falls a Third back to the original note (cf. ibid., bar 20).

[In both cases it will be noticed that the third crotchet, though unfigured, bears a Sixth.]

(*b*) In two figures in both of which the first crotchet is followed by a leap of a Third, in the one case *upwards*, and in the other, *downwards*, after which a progression by step in the *reverse direction* leads back to the original note. In the former case the first crotchet bears a Triad, and in the latter a first inversion [66] (cf. ibid., bars 12 and 4). The result in either case is *transitus irregularis* on the third crotchet, and (as Heinichen tells us) the stationary Seventh (*7ma in transitu*) thus arising is sometimes indicated by a figure. The movement of an upper part in Thirds with the Bass is at the discretion of the accompanist.

---

therefore, understand that, in framing his examples as he did, Heinichen was presenting the harmonic scheme which he regarded as *normal to the measure in question*, i.e. triple time *with half-units as its quickest notes*. Heinichen himself reminded us that a composer is at all times at liberty to *depart from the ordinary rules*, and to signify the same [if necessary] by figures (cf. note 19). In the 'translated' bar given above no figures are necessary, as the last crotchet *g* cannot possibly pass under the harmony of the preceding one.

[65] The term *Syncopatio* (which in some German treatises of the eighteenth century, e.g. Mattheson's *Organisten-Probe*, 1719, is applied to a broken harmony, Germ. *Brechung*) is here used by Heinichen as the Latin equivalent of the Germ. *Bindung*. The difference between the latter and a *Rückung* (a difference, however, which is often ignored) has already been explained (Ch. i, § 18, note 2). The *bound consonance* of which Heinichen speaks is a *discord* prepared by a *concord* (as 9 by 3), while the *bound dissonance* is one prepared by a *discord* (as 4 by 7).

[66] In the example given (Ex. 56) the first inversion is that of a *Triad*, but in a

[Ex. 56]

(2) If four crotchets moving by step are followed by a leap, or if the last one is figured, there is *transitus irregularis*, and the harmony appertaining to the last one is struck, by anticipation, over the third:

[Ex. 57]

N.B.—Note Heinichen's alternative use of the barred semicircle as time-signature in the above, and of the unbarred in Ex. 56.

---

subsequent general example (reluctantly omitted here) we find $^6_5$ on the leading note:

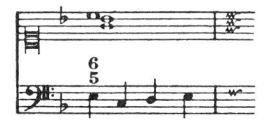

It would probably not be difficult to find cases (though an example is not to hand) in which the first crotchet (when followed by the *downward* leap of a Third) bears a Triad, when the further progression is such that the passing $^7_{5}$, thus arising on the second crotchet, finds its resolution (cf. *d*, note 41) as:

(3) When two (unfigured) crotchets following a minim, or a semibreve [representing two syncopated minims (cf. Ex. 58, bars 4 and 5)],[67] rise or fall by step, and are not followed by a leap, they pass under the preceding harmony; but if a leap follows, there is *transitus irregularis*, and the first of the two crotchets bears the harmony of the last:

[Ex. 58]

(4) In certain rare cases *transitus irregularis* may arise apart from the conditions mentioned in the two preceding rules, being conditioned solely by the necessary preparation of a subsequent discord, as:

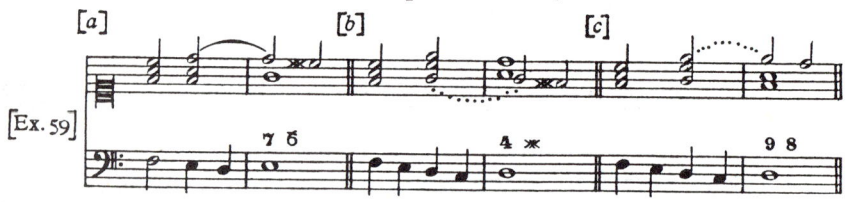

[Ex. 59]

(5) Heinichen's explanation and illustration (l.c. §§ 39 and 43) of two special forms of *transitus* have already been given (§ 1 *f*, Ex. 5 with the text immediately preceding, and § 1 *m*, Ex. 14) and need not be repeated here.

(*o*) Besides the true *Allabreve* Heinichen describes three varieties, which, though differing in other respects, share the important characteristic that the harmony of each semibreve bar, instead of being divided into (at most) two

---

[67] Heinichen should have added: the alternative of a *semibreve's value* in the shape of a crotchet following a dotted minim of the same denomination 𝅗𝅥 | . 𝅘𝅥. . The following instance occurs in a subsequent general example (omitted here):

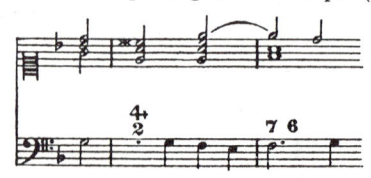

It differs from those in Ex. 58 (bars 2, 5, 10, 13, 16) only in the repercussion of the harmony on the penultimate crotchet, together with the addition of a fifth part in order to gain the desired position in the following bar.

XVIII § 3 (o)   QUICK NOTES IN THE BASS   767

parts, is divided into four, so that a crotchet is capable of bearing an independent harmony, while quavers are freely used. They therefore correspond, to that extent, with what has hitherto been frequently alluded to as *Semi-allabreve*.[68]

Of these three varieties two differ from each other only in the extent to which they respectively diverge, in detail and in general character, from the parent style: in the one case a semblance remains, in the other, none.

They are best described in Heinichen's own words. He writes (l.c. § 45):

"Now there are other kinds of *Allabreve*. For, whereas the *Allabreve* hitherto described divides the harmony of each bar into 2 parts only, so that not less than 2 crotchets can go to a chord, some [composers], on the contrary, divide the harmony of each bar into 4 parts, giving each crotchet a chord of its own, and also take the liberty of indulging in a number of *variationes* and bizarre leaps with the said crotchets,[69] contrary to the nature of the Antique *Allabreve*, although, at the same time, they seek to imitate the latter by introducing the usual syncopations (*Rückungen*) and bindings (*Syncopationes*) of the consonances and dissonances.[70]

"Others go further still, and, over and above the fact that their *Allabreve* makes no sort of profession of syncopations and bindings ('Rückungen, Bindungen und *Syncopationibus*'), they also indulge in a number of fanciful passages and leaps with the quavers,[71] just as slow common time does with the semiquavers. Hence this *Allabreve* is justly styled an *Allabreve spurium*, because it exhibits no characteristic of the true *Allabreve* beyond its outward dress, I mean the notes [72] and the borrowed *Allabreve* time, and is, in itself, nothing else but translated common time." [73]

Heinichen continues (l.c. § 46): "These two varieties have the same accompaniment as what we have hitherto known as *Semi-Allabreve*: [74] the crotchets are treated like the quavers in slow common time, that is to say, each crotchet has its own chord (except where they move *per transitum*),[75] and the quavers are treated as semiquavers ordinarily are, and that is all. We will illustrate

[68] Heinichen explains (l.c. § 47) that the term *Semi-allabreve* has hitherto been used, for the sake of brevity, to designate *any* quick $\frac{4}{4}$ time in which the quavers are treated like the semiquavers in true common time (cf. § 1 *d*, note 3).

He further explains (ibid., *Supplementa*, p. 945) that the term is generally used in Germany, in place of the grammatically more correct *Alla Semibreve*, to indicate that the notes are of half value as compared with the *Allabreve*, the quavers in the former corresponding to the crotchets in the latter. The term *Allabreve*, he reminds us, has itself become a misnomer, being a survival of the time when a *breve* (instead of, as later, a semibreve) went to the bar.

[69] As in bars 6–8 and 13–15 of Ex. 60. The *variationes* are seen in bars 13–15, in which the crotchet figure may be said to constitute a mere variation of the funda-

mental Bass (cf. *d*, note 32).

[70] As in bars 5, 20–2, 25, 26 of Ex. 60 (cf. note 65).
[71] As in bars 11, 12, 23, 24 of Ex. 60.
[72] i.e. the note-*values* employed: minims, crotchets, quavers (which last occur, though extremely rarely, in the true *Allabreve*), and the absence of semiquavers.
[73] Cf. § 1 *d*, note 3.
[74] Cf. note 68.
[75] i.e. *transitus regularis* (cf. § 1 *c*, Ex. 1), as in bars 17 and 19 of Ex. 60. There seems, also, to be no reason why the form of *transitus* described in § 1 *f* (Exx. 4, 5) should not occur.

768　　　　　　　QUICK NOTES IN THE BASS　　　　XVIII § 3 (o)

both varieties by the following mixed example. Such *Inventiones* may pass for a not unpleasing *Bizarrerie* in borrowed *Allabreve* time:

(*p*) The variety still remaining to be described uniformly exhibits the essential characteristics of the true *Allabreve*, from which, we are told (l.c. § 47), "it hardly differs [77] except in the [quicker] measure (*Mensur*) and the

---

[76] The above example will repay careful examination.
　Bars 1–5, 9, 10, 20–2, and 25–8 would, with one possible exception, pass muster in the 'true *Semi-Allabreve*' presently to be described. The exception in question is in the four *descending* quavers bearing a *single harmony* (struck twice) in bars 2 and 4. In the true *Semi-Allabreve* the quavers, we gather, are subject to the same rules as the crotchets in the true *Allabreve*, in which, as we learned, four crotchets *rising* by step may bear a single harmony (cf. Ex. 56, bars 8 and 19), but not (as far as can be gathered from Heinichen's rules and examples) four *falling* ones.
　Bars 16–19 would pass, except for the fresh harmony struck on the second crotchet of bar 18, in the true *Allabreve*.
　(N.B.—Three obvious misprints have been corrected in the example besides one mentioned in Heinichen's long list of *Errata*.)
　[77] Such difference as exists (which Heinichen, unfortunately, does not specify) would appear to lie chiefly in the frequent occurrence of syncopation in the Bass and upper parts simultaneously (as in bars 1, 2, 3, 6, and also between bars 4 and 5 of

XVIII § 3 (*p*)   QUICK NOTES IN THE BASS

face value of the notes". Heinichen speaks of it as the 'true *Semi-Allabreve*' or the 'pathetic Antique *Semi-Allabreve*', and, in giving the following example, he tells us that more can be provided, if desired, by translating the examples of the true *Allabreve* hitherto given (Exx. 5, 14, 56–9, as well as a general example omitted here): that is to say, by changing semibreves into minims, minims into crotchets, and crotchets into quavers [and, of course, throwing two bars into one].

"In the following example", he adds, "take note of the form (*Clausul*) of *Transitus in 4tam*, occurring in the 3rd, 4th, and 5th bars [* * *], which this style has in common with the Antique *Allabreve* [cf. § 1 *m*, Ex. 14]; from this, too, the close kinship of the two styles becomes apparent:

[Ex. 61]

(*q*) Heinichen concludes his account of the different measures by describing and illustrating (l.c. §§ 48–51, pp. 348 sq.) what he calls Overture Time (*Ouverteur-Tact*), i.e. the measure employed in a form of French Overture consisting of a slow Introduction followed by one or more movements of a lively character. The second of the two examples which Heinichen gives of the latter is, in fact (though not so entitled), a Gavotte.

Heinichen tells us that the proper time-signature of the slow Introduction is 2, and that of the quick movements 2 or ₵, but that, in actual practice,

the example). In bars 5 and 9, too, the penultimate quaver is treated as a passing note, whereas, in the true *Allabreve*, a fresh chord (a Triad) would be struck on the corresponding crotchet (cf. Ex. 56, bar 23). This latter slight difference is naturally accounted for by the (presumably) quicker measure of the *Semi-Allabreve*.

[78] Note the augmented interval (♯*g f*) in bar 10.

The *transitus irregularis* on the second quaver of the penultimate bar is indicated by the necessity for preparing the subsequent discord (cf. *n*, Rule 4, Ex. 59).

the signatures 2 ₂ C ₵ are used quite indiscriminately, so that it is quite common to find the barred semicircle ₵ prefixed to the slow Introduction.

In every case, as is made clear by the examples,[79] the crotchets are subject to the same rules as the quavers in slow common time (cf. *c*), while, similarly, groups of four quavers are treated like semiquavers in slow common time (cf. *d*), or (what amounts to the same thing) as quavers in $\frac{3}{2}$ time (cf. *m*).

In the following example, illustrating the style of the slow introductory movement, the dotted rhythm is a noticeable feature, and in connexion with this the following rule is to be noted: *if a dotted crotchet and the following quaver move by step, and are not followed by a leap, the quaver passes under the preceding harmony; in any other case the quaver bears a chord of its own* (cf. note 79).

The reader will observe throughout the example that, even where a quaver passes under the harmony of the preceding dotted crotchet, there is *repercussion* of that harmony (as in the first half of bars 4 and 12, and the second half of bar 7), *modified*, wherever it is convenient, *by the movement of an upper part in Thirds with the Bass* (as in the first half of bars 1, 3, 5, 11).

The Sevenths ($\frac{7}{4}$ or $\frac{7}{3}$) thus arising at the discretion of the accompanist (cf. *c*, 1, Ex. 24 and the text immediately preceding) must on no account be confused with the cases in which a fresh essential harmony is demanded (as e.g. in bar 6).

Quick passages in the Bass (containing notes of smaller value than quavers), like those in bars 7 and 9, always pass, we are told, under a single harmony.

[Ex. 62]

---

[79] Heinichen's *rules* are somewhat misleading on this point. In describing the slow introductory movement he tells us that "not only crotchets but single quavers following a dotted crotchet (unless they move by step) have their own chord". This is in exact accordance with the rules for dotted quavers followed by a semiquaver (which, as we know, *are the same as those for even quavers*) in slow common time (cf. *d* 7, Rule 4). All is clear so far, but later on, in speaking of the unreliability of the time-signatures (mentioned above), Heinichen goes on to say that "a beginner need only keep to the rule that, in Overture Time, *whenever the measure is quick*, he is to *treat the crotchets just like the quavers in slow common time*". [The italics are not Heinichen's.] He does not appear to remember that, on his own showing, there is, in this respect, no difference between the slow and the quick measure.

XVIII § 3 (q)   QUICK NOTES IN THE BASS   771

(r) In proceeding to give examples of the quicker measure which follows the slow introductory movement, Heinichen first gives rules for the crotchets. As has been said, these are identical, *mutatis mutandis*, with those which have already been given for the quavers in true common time (cf. c), and need not be reproduced here.

There is, however, one point which must be specially noted. It is, as Heinichen points out (l.c. § 50, note h), in accordance with the crisp and lively character of this style that every crotchet beat (or rather half-beat) should [except, of course, in the case of a *caesura*] be marked in the right hand, even where, so far as the rules are concerned, no fresh harmony is demanded.

For this reason the passing harmonies which arise "as it were by chance" when an upper part moves in Thirds with the Bass (cf. c, 1, Ex. 24) are to be regularly employed, and Heinichen tells us that "they are indicated [by figures] [80] over the *virtualiter* short notes much more diligently than is generally the case, in order that the accompanist may not allow the latter to pass under the preceding harmony without a fresh percussion [81] (*ohne neuen Anschlag*)".

[80] Heinichen only mentions 7ths and 6ths, but a figure is of course no less necessary in the case of a passing Triad (as on the 4th crotchet of bar 1 of Ex. 63) if its employment is not to be left to the discretion of the accompanist. At this rate the opening bars of Ex. 63 would be figured as follows:

[81] It will be noticed that in Ex. 63 (except on the second crotchet of bar 3) *only*

In conclusion, an important point is mentioned concerning the combination of a *crotchet with two following quavers*.

It might have been expected that the treatment would be exactly the same as in the case of a quaver followed by two semiquavers in true common time, but such is only partially the case.

It will be best to give the rules in Heinichen's own words:

"The quavers [i.e. groups of 4 quavers], again, are here treated like the semiquavers in slow [common], or the quavers in $\frac{3}{2}$ time; there is therefore nothing to note with regard to them. But when a crotchet is combined with 2 following quavers, and the 3 notes in question move

"(1) straight up- or downwards, and are not followed by a leap, they have only a single chord (inclining to be struck twice).[82] But if they are followed by a leap, the harmony appertaining to the third note is anticipated over the second [*transitus irregularis*], a distinction which is illustrated here and there in the following example.

"(2) But if only the first two notes move up- or downwards, and the 3rd one reverses the movement, then, properly speaking (*ordentlicher Weise*), it is true, all three notes go to a single chord; but the first section (*reprise*) of the following example shows that, in this measure, there is a tendency to strike independently the common chord which follows a 6th when the Bass rises a degree (*dass der nach der 6te auffwerts folgende ordinaire Accord gerne besonders angeschlagen wird*)[83] as is shown by the melody which has here been purposely introduced:

---

a single interval (in every case the 3 of the passing chord) is struck, the remainder being retained from the previous harmony. In Ex. 62, on the other hand, the entire chord is struck, as the ponderous dotted rhythm demands.

[82] Heinichen here appends the following footnote: "In accordance with the general tendency of the right hand, in this lively (*aufgeweckt*) style, not often to rest for the length of a minim, much less a semibreve, especially as Overtures are ordinarily accompanied on quilled instruments ('auff denen *Clavecins*') and not with the sustained tone of the Organ (*auff nachklingenden* [sic] *Pfeiffwercke*)."

In the present example, however, there is no such repercussion. The figure in question occurs *descendendo* in the 3rd and 9th bars of the first section and the 1st bar of the second section, and, *ascendendo*, in the 3rd bar of the second section. In the former case a passing note in the upper part leads to the next chord (in Sixths with the Bass), and, in the latter, the right hand sustains the harmony.

[83] A footnote is here appended: "Because here again, as mentioned above [see the text immediately preceding Ex. 63], the *virtualiter* short crotchets look for a harmony of their own."

It seems clear, from the example, that when Heinichen speaks of a Triad being struck 'independently' (*besonders*), he means to indicate a chord of simple percussion (to use the old-fashioned term) as distinguished from the passing chord which would, in any case, arise if a single upper part moved in Thirds with the Bass, as:

Such passing Triads may be seen in a previous example (*d* 7, Ex. 37, bar 1, 1st semiquaver, and bar 2, 3rd semiquaver) in which each group consisting of a quaver and two semiquavers (in *quick* $\frac{4}{4}$ or *Semi-allabreve* time) is supposed to bear a single harmony.

QUICK NOTES IN THE BASS

[Ex. 64]

If we compare the above two rules with those given for a quaver followed by two semiquavers in true (i.e. slow) common time (*d* 7, Rules 1 and 2, Exx. 34 and 36), it will be seen that the only divergence is in the second one, in which we are told that "properly speaking [subject, however, to the important exception mentioned] *all three notes go to a single chord*".[84] This is in accordance with the rule given for a quaver followed by two semiquavers in *quick* 4/4 or *Semi-allabreve* time (in which, as a general rule, the quickest notes are quavers), as may be seen by comparing Ex. 64 (2nd section, 2nd half of bar 3 sq.) with Ex. 37 (part of penultimate bar); and this is, so far as we can

---

[84] Heinichen does not mention that the necessary resolution of a discord might make it imperative for the first quaver to bear a chord of its own, as will be seen if we alter the harmony in bar 4 of the 2nd section of Ex. 64 (and the sequel), as may be done without detriment to the character of the example, as follows:

gather, the only case in which the rules for true common time cannot be applied, *mutatis mutandis*, to the measure now under discussion.

(*s*) It is hoped that no apology is needed for the full presentation of Heinichen's rules, now brought to a conclusion.

Whatever may be their deficiencies, they represent the result of a vast amount of painstaking research on the part of one whose qualifications for such a task were unsurpassed among his contemporaries.

In an Appendix (l.c. p. 366) our author speaks of "this rich material, which has to gather its rules from the whole wide field of composition ('aus der ganzen *Massa* der weitläufftigen Composition'), and which, so far as I am aware, no one has as yet minutely investigated", and the fact that his attempt thus stands alone gives it the greater claim, after the lapse of over two centuries, to be freshly placed on record.

In estimating its success it must be remembered that any such rules can only be based on the relation between the Bass and the upper parts which is found *most generally to prevail* in the measure in question, but which is always subject, as we were reminded (cf. *b*, note 19), to perfect liberty on the part of the composer to introduce (and indicate in the figuring) any exception that he pleases. It is the failure to indicate such exceptions that so often causes trouble.

It must further be remembered that it is, in many instances, impossible to take into account all possible cases and combinations of circumstances without framing rules so complex as entirely to defeat their own object, so far as any possibility of remembering them is concerned (cf. § 1 *e*, note 5).

As we have already seen, the use of an horizontal dash (or dashes), to indicate the continuance of the preceding harmony, removes a large proportion of the difficulties and ambiguities which Heinichen's rules were designed to meet, but no one who has even approximately mastered the latter can fail, when dealing with Basses in which the above-mentioned device is not employed, to recognize their value.

§ 4. *Repeated notes*.

(*a*) When the Bass consists of quick reiterated notes, a great deal depends on whether a keyed instrument is alone responsible for the accompaniment, or whether one or more string Basses are associated with it.

In the former case it may be expedient for the accompanist to substitute some other figure for the reiterated notes (cf. Exx. 2, 3, 5 *a*); in the latter, he is absolved from the necessity of participating in the quick movement of the Bass. It may be remembered that Michel de Saint Lambert gave a rule to this effect with regard to quick Basses generally (cf. Ch. i, § 23 *i*, 1 *a*).

(*b*) Heinichen concludes the chapter which formed the subject of the preceding section (l.c. *Zusatz* [Appendix] VIII, pp. 377 sq.) with the following example, concerning which he writes:

"Finally, one must not allow oneself to be disconcerted by a number of quick repeated notes, but, as long as no fresh figure appears over the notes, the previous chord is repeated in slower notes, once or several times (according to the measure), and the execution of the quick notes left to the other accompanying Basses. For instance, the following 3 bars:

[Ex. 1]

XVIII § 4 (b) QUICK NOTES IN THE BASS

"might be accompanied somewhat as follows:

[Ex. 1a]

"There are various ways of accompanying such notes, which we will reserve for a future occasion."

Accordingly, in a later chapter (ibid., Part I, Ch. vi, § 39, pp. 576 sq.), he gives the following examples in which the quick (semiquaver) movement of the Bass, shown on the lowest stave, is reproduced on the Harpsichord, though not as written. We must therefore suppose, though Heinichen does not say so, that these examples are intended to illustrate the methods to be employed *when no string Basses are associated with the Harpsichord*.

In the first example, broken Octaves and Sixths are substituted for the reiterated notes in the Bass, while, in the second, the semiquaver movement is transferred to the right hand in the figure familiar to all in the 'Alberti' Bass:

[Ex. 2]

[Ex. 3]

[1] Note the progression in the left hand in bar 3, where the 4 of the $\frac{5}{4}$ chord (*g*), resolved correctly in the right hand, rises to *a* (cf. Ch. iii, § 3, Ex. 9 a, p. 338).

(c) Ph. Em. Bach gives the following instructions (*Versuch &c.*, Part II, 1762, Ch. 29, § 17):

"When, in a slow *tempo*, a number of *slurred* notes of the same pitch occur in succession, and it is desired to double them in the lower Octave, this is done only in the case of the first and third, or, with triplets, only in that of the first. The lower, duplicated notes are then held to their full value (*werden alsdenn ausgehalten*) (a) [= Ex. 4]. But if such notes are to be executed *quickly* and *detached* ('abgestossen'), in order that they may make a great noise (b) [= Ex. 5], the procedure shown in (c) [= Ex. 5 a] may be followed:

[Ex. 4]

[Ex. 5]

[Ex. 5a]

"Such passages must not last too long, or the hands will get stiff and tired. In such a case, it is better to play them like other Drum-Basses (*Trommelbässe*) and to follow the instructions given in the Introduction to the first part of this Essay (*Versuch*), in a note." [2]

The note in question, though of great interest, is too long to quote *in extenso*; the passages bearing most directly upon the point under discussion are as follows:

"For the benefit of those who are entrusted with the office of playing the Thorough-Bass I have deemed it necessary to take this opportunity of making known my views on the manner of disposing of quick repeated notes with the left hand. These afford the surest means whereby the best of hands may be spoiled and become stiff, as such notes are very frequent in our present style of composition. . . .

"The quick repeated notes of the injuriousness of which I am speaking are quavers in quick, and semiquavers in moderate time. I am further presupposing that, besides the *Clavier*, some other instrument is playing the Bass as well. If the *Clavier* is alone, such notes, resembling crackers (*Schwärmer*), are played by changing fingers. In this way, owing to the omission of the [lower] Octave, the Bass will not always be penetrating enough; but this little imperfection must be preferred to other and greater evils. Of such notes, then, it is best [i.e. when one or more string Basses are associated with the

[2] l.c. § 9, note.

XVIII § 4 (c)   QUICK NOTES IN THE BASS   777

Clavier] to let one, three, or five, according to the *tempo* and the measure (*nach Beschaffenheit der Zeit-Maasse und Tact-Art*), pass without being struck, and those which are struck are played with the [lower] Octave, or even, in a *fortissimo*, with full chords in both hands, with a weighty touch, somewhat sustained, so that the strings may vibrate sufficiently, and one tone be joined with the next. One might, perhaps, in order not to confuse one's fellow accompanists, play the first bar as it stands, and afterwards let the notes pass. Or, if every note is at all costs to be heard on the Harpsichord (*wenn ja jede Note auf dem Flügel sollte und müsste gehöret werden*), there still remains the following device, namely to produce the movement indicated by striking the notes with alternate hands; [3] but I have learnt by experience that this manner of accompanying is somewhat misleading for the other players, as the right hand always comes too late, and this has confirmed me in my opinion that it is the *Clavier* that always is and will be looked to to set the time (*dass das Clavier allezeit das Augenmerk des Tactes seyn und bleiben wird*). . . ."

[3] In this way the quick movement would be maintained, and, in so far, "every note" would be "heard on the Harpsichord", though the repeated notes in the Bass would not be played *as written*. Thus, Ex. 5 would be treated somewhat as follows:

CHAPTER XIX
THE FIGURING OF TRANSITIONAL NOTES

XIX
THE FIGURING OF TRANSITIONAL NOTES

§ 1. The nature of passing notes, both unaccented (*transitus regularis*) and accented (*transitus irregularis*), has already been explained (Ch. xviii, 'On quick notes in the Bass', § 1 c, d), as also that of those notes which are 'passing' only in the more general sense of bearing no harmony of their own.

In this latter category are included notes which bridge an interval exceeding that of a Third between two harmony notes (l.c. *e*) and also those which (without corresponding to an interval in the preceding harmony) are not approached and quitted by step (l.c. *i, k, l, m*).

As regards *transitus regularis*, it is obvious that the need for figuring arises only when the time-value of the note in question is higher than that of the notes which, in the particular measure in which they occur (C, ₵, ¾, &c.), would, as a matter of course, pass under the preceding harmony.

Thus, in quick ⁴⁄₄ time (spurious *Allabreve*), the notes marked * in the following example pass *as a matter of course*:

Ex. 1

But in true ⁴⁄₄ time, the same Bass would, *in default of indication to the contrary*, be treated as follows:

Ex. 2

The most convenient method of indicating the continuance of the preceding harmony is by means of a (more or less) horizontal dash:

Ex. 3

Kirnberger, *Grundsätze des Generalbasses*, Vol. of examples, Abtheilung [Section] II, Fig. LVI.

This device, which according to Fétis (*Traité complet &c.*, 2nd ed. 1844, Livre Second 239 (Ch. xii), p. 148) was first introduced by Rameau, is to be found in French Basses at an early period, but, where it was not adopted,

XIX § 1   THE FIGURING OF TRANSITIONAL NOTES   781

the only alternative was to figure the individual notes, as in the two following examples from Corelli:

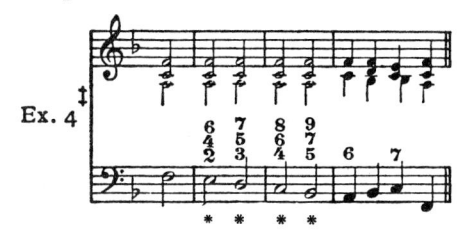

Ex. 4‡

Corelli, Opera Sesta, Concerto II, Allegro (finale), 2nd section, bars 25–7.

Ex. 5

Ibid., Concerto VIII, Adagio, 4 bars from end.

Sometimes, in the case of a running Bass, several notes may intervene between the original chord and the figures indicating its repercussion (or sustention), in which case extremely unfamiliar combinations of figures are liable to occur, as in the following example from Vivaldi, in which an horizontal dash, extending from the figures $^6_5$ to the end of the run, would have obviated all difficulty:

Ex. 6

Antonio Vivaldi, Opera Prima, *Suonate da Camera a tre*, Sonata XII, Folia, Variation 17, bar 6.

§ 2. If we figure a complete ascending and descending scale with sustained Tonic harmony (Exx. 1, 2), it is obvious that the passing notes * * * in the ascending scale will be changing (i.e. accented passing) notes † † † in the descending scale, and vice versâ.

It is also obvious that the figures of both passing and changing notes are to be calculated from those of the fundamental note, which, in the former case, is the *preceding*, and in the latter case, the *following* one.

Therefore, in the case of passing notes, each figure of the fundamental note is *diminished* by 1 as the scale *ascends* ($^8_5_3$ becoming $^7_4_2$, &c.), while, in the

‡ The last minim in Ex. 4 might also be figured $^7_5_2$ (cf. Ch. xxiii, 'Varieties of figuring', § 14, 1).

782   THE FIGURING OF TRANSITIONAL NOTES   XIX § 2

case of changing notes, exactly the opposite takes place. (It must, of course, be remembered that 8 and 1 are interchangeable.)

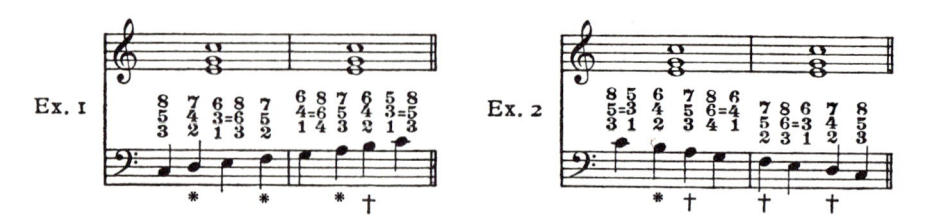

Such calculations, however, have no further practical value when once the principle has been grasped: *the figures, as such, must be impressed on the memory.* The matter is, unfortunately, somewhat complicated by the alternative use of 9 and 2 in certain figurings (cf. § 3 *ad fin.*), but when once it has become a matter of instinct that an accented bass note figured $\frac{7}{4}$ (or $\frac{9}{7}$) falls to a Triad (Ex. 3 *a*) and rises to its first inversion $\frac{8}{6}$ (Ex. 3 *b*), and that a similar note figured $\frac{7}{5}$ falls to a first inversion $\frac{8}{6}$ (Ex. 3 *c*) and rises to a second inversion $\frac{8}{6}$ (Ex. 3 *d*), a great part of the difficulty will have been overcome.

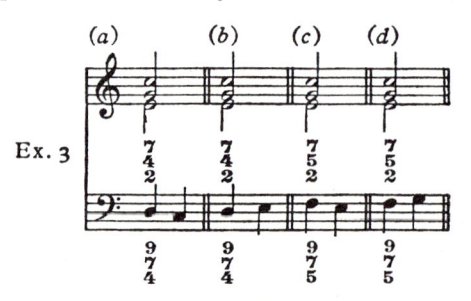

§ 3. When the student is familiar with these latter figurings in connexion with the first inversion of a perfect Triad, no difficulty will be experienced in recognizing them in connexion with a Sixth $\frac{8}{6}$ on the Supertonic (actual or temporary).‡ In this connexion $\frac{7}{5}$ ($\frac{9}{5}$) is by far the commoner of the two, as the Supertonic is more often approached by a changing (i.e. accented passing) note from above (Ex. 1) than from below (Ex. 2).

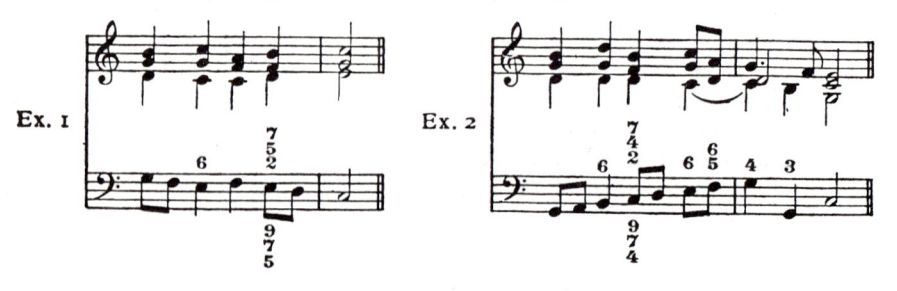

‡ It is important to note the intervals to which an accidental will be prefixed when

XIX § 3   THE FIGURING OF TRANSITIONAL NOTES   783

The use of 9 as an alternative to 2 in the figuring of accented passing notes is fully dealt with elsewhere (Ch. xxiii, 'Varieties of figuring', § 14, 1).

§ 4. When a descending accented passing note is figured $\frac{5}{2}$, and an ascending one $\frac{7}{4}$, it indicates a chord of the Sixth, not taken as $\frac{8}{6}$ (as in previous examples), but *without the Octave of the Bass*: either (1) in three parts, or (2) with either the 3 or the 6 doubled:

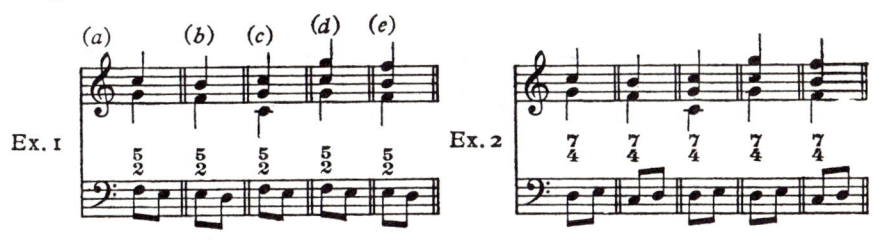

§ 5. *Different methods of indicating 'transitus irregularis' in the Bass.*

It has already been mentioned (cf. § 1) that the retention of the foregoing harmony came to be indicated by an horizontal dash, whereby the employment of unusual figurings was avoided.

In the case of *transitus irregularis* the difficulty of the figuring was sometimes evaded by figuring the (unaccented) harmony note and either (1) leaving the accented passing note (on which the chord is to be struck) without indication (Ex. 1 *a*), or (2) connecting it with the figure above the following harmony note by means of an oblique dash (Ex. 1 *b*), or some other mark (Ex. 1 *c*, *d*, *e*):

Ph. Em. Bach, from whom the above examples are taken (*Versuch &c.*, the above figurings, $\frac{7}{5}$ $\left(\text{or } \frac{9}{7}\right)$ and $\frac{7}{4}$ $\left(\text{or } \frac{9}{7}\right)$, occur in connexion with a *temporary* Supertonic.

If the modulation is from a sharper key (e.g. from G to C major), the interval affected will, in the case of the former, be 2 (or 9); in the case of the latter it will be 4.

If it is from a flatter key (e.g. from F to C major), the intervals affected in the two figurings will be, respectively, 5 and 7. Thus, with the key-signatures of (1) G and (2) F, the Basses of Exx. 1 and 2 will appear, respectively (subject to variety of notation, e.g. ♭ and ✕ in the older Basses for ♮, &c.), as follows:

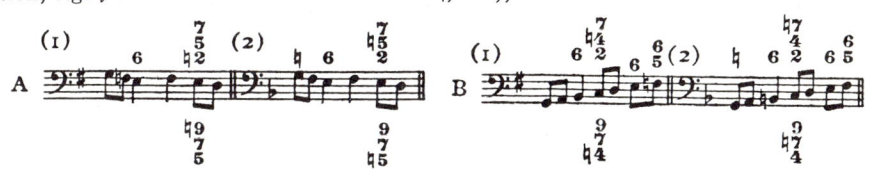

Similarly, when the key is minor, the 5 of $\frac{7}{5}$ $\left(\text{or } \frac{9}{7}\right)$ on the note above the Supertonic, and the 7 of $\frac{7}{4}$ $\left(\text{or } \frac{9}{7}\right)$ on the note below the Supertonic, will require a ♯ or ♮.

Part II 1762, Ch. 1, § 76), pronounces (*b*) to be the best. It is, however, seldom met with, and (*c*) (*d*) (*e*) are of still rarer occurrence.

In spite of its obvious disadvantages the method exemplified by (*a*) was commonly employed in the earlier part of the eighteenth century, and was championed by no less a person than Heinichen, from whom the following examples, afterwards given with alternative figuring, are taken (*General-Bass &c.*, 1728, Part I, Ch. iv, § 53, pp. 362 sq.):

Ex. 2

Ex. 3

Of these Heinichen writes (l.c. § 55) as follows: "In these examples ... the *resolutiones* are to be found, throughout, indicated over the fundamental note to which they apply, just as we have been accustomed to indicate the consonances, too, in cases of *transitus irregularis*. Some composers,[1] however, are in the habit of indicating such *resolutiones dissonantiarum* (and *transitus irregularis* generally) in a different way, namely immediately above the changing [i.e. accented passing] note itself ('*praecise* über der in gedachten *Transitu* vorfallenden Note'), sometimes with, and sometimes without the remaining intervals belonging to the harmony.[2] Accordingly, the two pre-

---

[1] In speaking of 'some composers' it is quite possible that Heinichen may have had no less a person than J. S. Bach in mind. Bach's general practice was to figure changing notes, and we learn from Kirnberger that he expected his pupils to master the unfamiliar combinations of figures thus arising (cf. § 7, note 3).

[2] In bar 2 of Ex. 2 *a*, and bar 4 of Ex. 3 *a* it will be noticed that the third note is figured with a 7 only instead of the full figuring $\frac{7}{4}$ (cf. § 4, Ex. 2). On the penultimate semiquaver of the second bar of Ex. 2 *a*, too, $\frac{7}{4}$ is used instead of the full figuring $\frac{7}{4}_{2}$ $\left(\text{or } \frac{9}{7}_{4}\right)$. It will also

XIX § 5   THE FIGURING OF TRANSITIONAL NOTES   785

ceding examples, figured in this way, would present the following appearance, while the accompaniment would remain as before:

Ex. 2a
[musical notation]

Ex. 3a
[musical notation]

"Now the question is," Heinichen continues (l.c. § 55), "which of these two methods of figuring is the better? Answer: The first is the more fundamental, and doubtless demands a practised accompanist. But the second method is the easier, especially for beginners; but it has this drawback, that the figures 9. 7. 4. $\frac{5}{2}$ &c. over the notes often strike the eye as genuine resolving discords ('*religiöse* zur *resolution* geneigte *dissonantien*') and cause a fundamental accompanist more annoyance and confusion than anything else. It seems, however, as though, in a few particular cases,[3] this method of indication could not be entirely rejected, and one must therefore leave every composer free to use, now the one, and now the other method of indication, as

be noticed that 9 and 2 are used quite indiscriminately (cf. Ch. xxiii, 'Varieties of figuring', § 14, 1): e.g. on the 5th semiquaver of bar 3 of Ex. 2 a $\begin{smallmatrix}9\\7\\4\end{smallmatrix}$ is used under exactly the same conditions as $\begin{smallmatrix}7\\4\\2\end{smallmatrix}$ on the 7th semiquaver of the last bar; so, too, on the 3rd crotchet of bars 1 and 2, respectively, of Ex. 3 a. This variety was, no doubt, intentional, in order to familiarize the student with the different methods of figuring which he would be likely to encounter.

[3] Heinichen here appends the following footnote: "For instance, I should not care to figure the two following progressions (always supposing that they may be allowed to pass muster) in accordance with the first method, thus:

[musical notation: 9 8 7 8]

because the suspicion of faulty (*vitiös*) Octaves is here expressed too plainly, especially if an unpractised accompanist carefully delayed the resolution of the 9 and 7 till the entry of the last note. On the other hand, suspicious *progressiones* are more concealed if the passages (*Sätze*) are figured in accordance with the second method, as follows below. For the rest, the fact remains that, as has been remarked before, a too frequent

786   THE FIGURING OF TRANSITIONAL NOTES   XIX § 5

the difference between the cases demands. But it is better to lead a beginner straight to the first and fundamental method, because, apart from other considerations, the other method involves not the slightest difficulty, and no art is needed in order simply to strike the intervals indicated, just as one finds them over a changing note thus figured ('die Ziffern platterdings so anzuschlagen, wie man sie über dergleichen bezeichneten *Transitu irregulari* findet')."

§ 6. *Summary of the figurings of changing notes in the Bass.*

The following summary of the figurings thus arising in connexion with (1) the Triad and its inversions, and (2) the Seventh and its inversions, is taken mainly from Kirnberger (*Grundsätze des Generalbasses*, volume of examples, Section (*Abtheilung*) III, Fig. L); additions by the present writer are marked with an asterisk. The essential harmony is prefixed to each example:

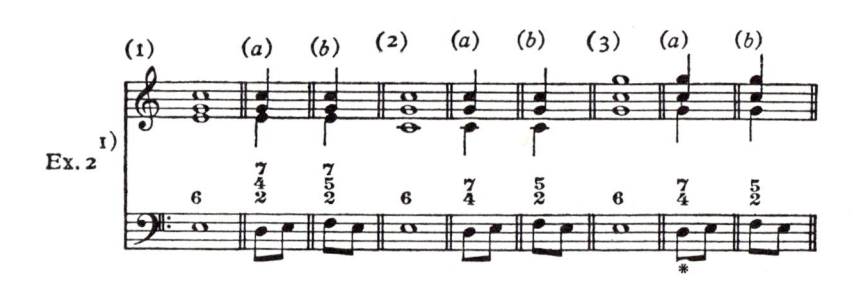

use of *transitus irregularis*, especially in the fundamental part of the whole harmony [i.e. the Bass], is not entirely to be approved:

[1] The figuring $^7_4$ as used in Ex. 2, 3 *a*, though omitted by Kirnberger in his summary, will be found in the example from J. S. Bach to be given presently (cf. § 7, Ex. 4, bars 26, 27).

XIX § 6   THE FIGURING OF TRANSITIONAL NOTES   787

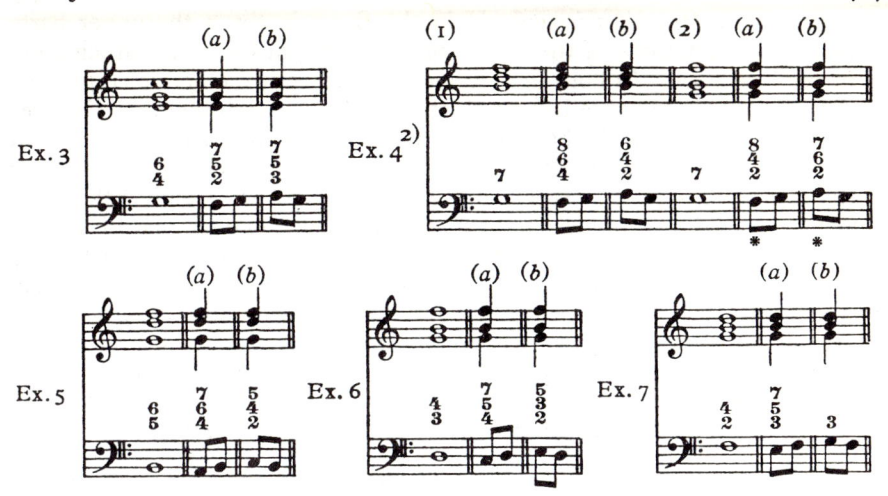

N.B.—In Ex. 6 (b) the figuring regularly used in actual practice is $\frac{3}{2}$, the 5 being omitted except when it requires an accidental: $\sharp^5_3, {}^5_3, {}^{5\natural}_3$, &c.

For less regular abbreviations of the figuring the reader is referred to Ch. xxi, 'Incomplete figuring', IV, § 2, and, for the alternative employment of 9 and 2, to Ch. xxiii, 'Varieties of figuring', § 14, 1.

All the examples in Kirnberger's summary are given by him in duplicate: (1) figured as shown above (Exx. 1–7), and (2) with an oblique dash over the changing note, connecting it with the figure or figures over the harmony note, as shown in § 5, Ex. 1 b.

Of this latter method he tells us that "it is to be preferred on account of its greater intelligibility". He, very rightly, does not share Heinichen's opinion that these unaccustomed combinations of figures "involve not the slightest difficulty" (cf. § 5 *ad fin.*), though, on the other hand, he emphasizes the importance of familiarity with both methods: "The necessity", he writes, "of knowing these different methods of figuring will be evident to any one who makes a practical use of Thorough-Bass."

§ 7. *Further illustrations.*

In order, therefore, to assist the student in this difficult matter, Kirnberger gives the following excellent examples which cannot be studied too carefully.

In Ex. 1 we have plain, straightforward four-part harmony. In Exx. 2 and 3 a dislocation of *the same harmony* is effected, akin to that produced by

[2] The figuring $\frac{8}{4}$, in Ex. 4, 2 *a*, is given by Kirnberger in the following supplementary example:

changing notes (*transitus irregularis*) in the Bass: in Ex. 2 the upper parts anticipate the harmony of the following bass note; in Ex. 3 the anticipation is in the Bass itself. In both these examples the easier method is employed: in Ex. 2 the harmony note is figured, and an oblique dash points to the preceding note, on which the harmony in question is to be struck; in Ex. 3 an horizontal dash denotes the continuance of the preceding chord. In Exx. 2 *a* and 3 *a* (which, in other respects, are identical with Exx. 2 and 3) the more difficult method is employed: the unaccustomed combinations of figures shown above (§ 6, Exx. 1–7) are placed above the note on which the harmony is struck, and in Ex. 2 *a* they are followed by horizontal dashes indicating the continuance of the said harmony over the following note (its true Bass). Of these two latter examples Kirnberger remarks that they "exhibit the most difficult figurings, in the shape of $\frac{7}{4}$ &c., that one can imagine: these ought [one would think] to resolve,[1] and it is only after a careful examination of the chords that one grasps the difficulty, and so finds it at once removed".

[1] It will be remembered that it was this very fact that constituted Heinichen's main objection to the figuring of changing notes (cf. § 5, the text following Exx. 2 *a*, 3 *a*).

XIX § 7 THE FIGURING OF TRANSITIONAL NOTES

Kirnberger concludes his examples with the *Andante* from J. S. Bach's Sonata in C minor for Flute, Violin, and Bass which forms part of the *Musicalisches Opfer* (ed. Peters, No. 219, pp. 34 sqq.), with the accompaniment fully set out from the figured Bass. As it is probably the only example of the accompaniment of an entire movement set out by a contemporary master[2] (a pupil, moreover, of the composer) that has come down to us, no apology should be needed for presenting it here.

[2] Gerber's accompaniment to a Violin Sonata of Albinoni with corrections purporting to be by J. S. Bach, given in Spitta's Life of that composer, is the work of a beginner, and is of inferior interest (cf. Ch. xi, IV § 3, note 2, p. 575).

790   THE FIGURING OF TRANSITIONAL NOTES   XIX § 7

Kirnberger writes as follows: "In order, finally, to have a convincing proof of the necessity for a knowledge of the different figurings, I have appended an example by John Sebastian Bach,³ out of a Trio, which, though it be only a Trio, must, nevertheless, be accompanied in four parts; and this may serve as a refutation of the common idea that Trios, Sonatas for a Solo and Bass, and likewise Cantatas that are accompanied only by an Harpsichord, are not accompanied in four parts."

Ex. 4⁴⁾

I   II   III

³ A note is here appended: "It was a maxim of the late Bach (John Sebastian) that people must learn to read figurings correctly. . . ."

⁴ Some obvious misprints have been corrected, and omissions rectified. Especial attention is called to the figuring $_2^6$ (occurring in bars 15, 16, 26, 27) in which the 2 is an anticipation of the following harmony, as:

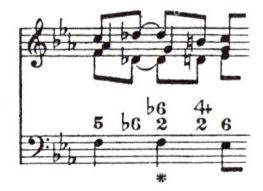

In bar 21 it seems probable that the first two quavers in the Treble and Tenor were meant to be semiquavers (and the crotchet in the Alto a quaver):

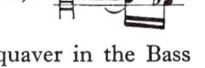

The Flute and Violin resolve the $_4^9$ suspension over the first quaver in the Bass (b flat), as follows:

The reading given in Kirnberger's text is, however, retained in an undated reprint of his work (Hamburg, Böhme), and the *figuring is altered to suit it*, as follows:

It seemed better, therefore, to give the reading of the original.

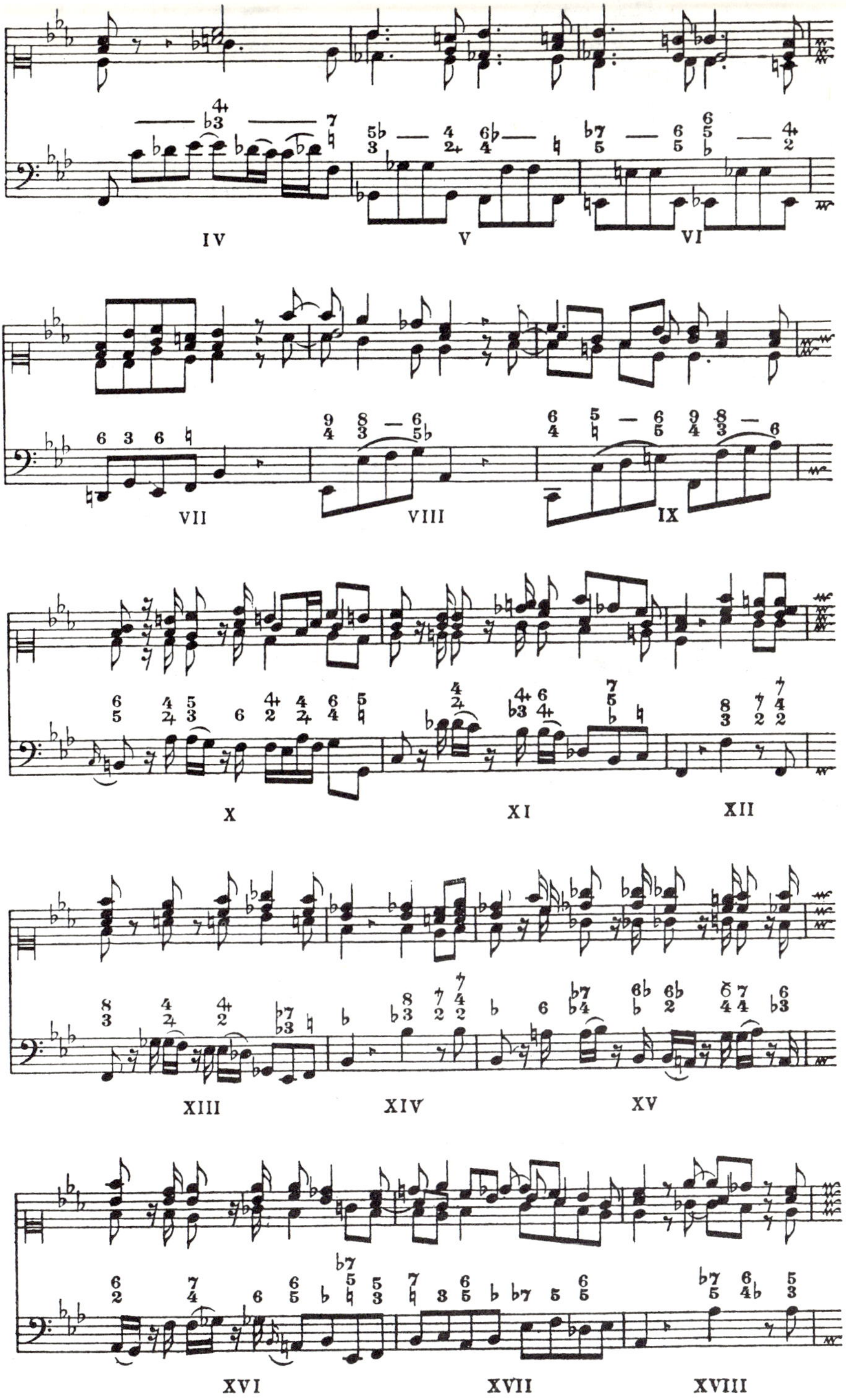
IV
V
VI
VII
VIII
IX
X
XI
XII
XIII
XIV
XV
XVI
XVII
XVIII

§ 8. Figurings arising through the combination of a transitional note in the Bass with one in an upper part.

In passing from an essential discord to its first inversion and vice versâ, and from one inversion to another, an intervening passing note often occurs in the Bass, and a corresponding one may be introduced in the upper parts.

XIX § 8   THE FIGURING OF TRANSITIONAL NOTES   793

This is often left to the discretion of the accompanist, but such passing chords are not infrequently indicated, and it is therefore important to be familiar with the figurings so arising. The following examples will make the matter clear:

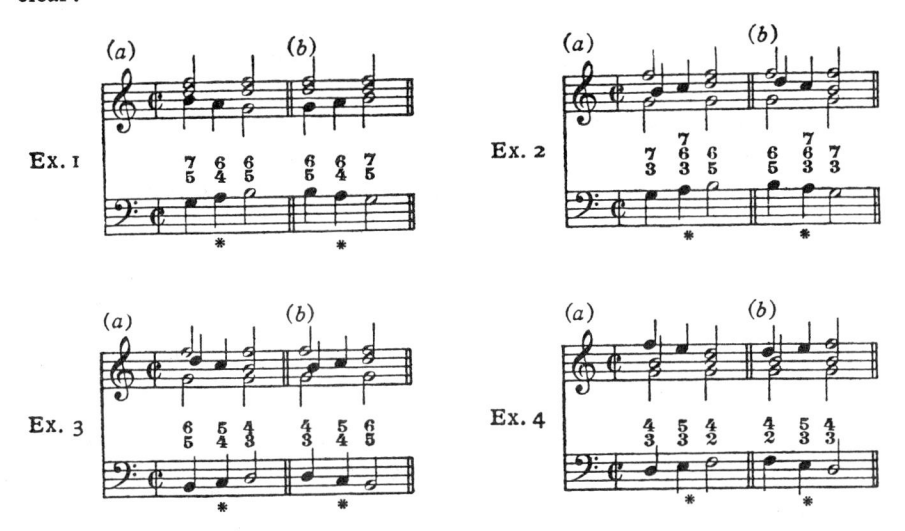

All the figurings in question will be found summarized in the following general example:

§ 9. *Necessary precautions.*

(*a*) When the passage of a chord from its root position to its first inversion, and vice versâ, or from one inversion to another, is not indicated in the figuring, care must be taken to avoid consecutive Octaves. The following examples will suffice to illustrate the point:

Ex. 2 1) [J. S. Bach, *Sonata in C for two Violins and Bass*, Largo, bar 16. B-G. ed., IX, p. 237.]

(*b*) The introduction of transitional notes in an upper part, corresponding to those already present in the Bass, calls for great discretion at all times, but more particularly when more than one instrument (or voice) is being accompanied. In such case the accompanist rarely has the score before him,[2] and the risk of discounting the effect of the principal parts, either by disagreeable clashes of one kind and another, or by meaningless reduplication (perhaps an 8ve below the part in question) is greater in proportion to their number.

The following example, from the same work as the preceding one (*Alla Breve*, bars 69 sq., B-G. ed., IX, p. 234), will serve as an illustration:

Ex. 3

If the beginning of the first (complete) bar be taken as follows:

we get consecutive Fifths $_{a\ g}^{e\ d}$ with the first Violin.

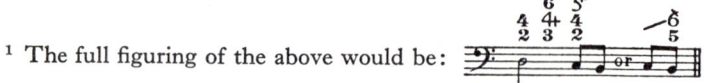

[1] The full figuring of the above would be:

[2] In modern reprints of works with figured Basses (such as the B. G. edition of Bach's works, Joachim and Chrysander's edition of Corelli, &c.) and in a *few* old editions, the score is given. But in playing from contemporary editions of the 'Figured-Bass Age', it is, for the most part, only in the case of Solos, and *very* exceptionally in that of Trios (e.g. Masciti, *Opera Sesta*, which includes a Sonata for Violin, Gamba or Violoncello, and Bass, and Leclair, Sonata for Flute, Gamba, and Bass, included in Book II of the *Sonatas for Violin and Bass*) that the accompanist sees the music which he has to accompany.

If the $\overset{6}{6}$ on *a* in the second (complete) bar be taken as $\overset{6}{\underset{3}{4}}$, and connected with the following $\overset{6}{\scriptscriptstyle 5}$ on ♯*f* by a passing note, as:

the result is a mere duplication (in the lower 8ve) of the ♯*f g* of the 1st Violin.

Such instances might easily be multiplied, but the above will suffice.

CHAPTER XX
PEDAL POINTS

XX
PEDAL POINTS

§ 1. The accompaniment of a Pedal point (Fr. *Point d'orgue*, Germ. *Orgelpunkt*) presents special, and very great, difficulties. A Pedal point, whether on the Dominant or on the Tonic, begins and ends with a chord of which the Pedal is the true Bass, but between these two points there is a series of harmonies, sometimes short and sometimes long, of which the true Bass is the part *next above the Pedal.*

With an ordinary Bass, the chords indicated by the figures can be taken in any position that the player pleases, subject, of course, to such limitations as the laws of harmony impose; but with the Pedal point it is different: from what has been said it will be realized that if the first chord is not taken in such a position that the part which represents the true Bass is immediately above the Pedal (whatever may be the relative position of the two, or more, remaining upper parts), the intentions of the composer are bound to be defeated, even if the resulting series of chords happens to be admissible in itself.

A simple example will make this clear. In Ex. 1 *a* we have the harmony and the figures as they appear over the Pedal, and in Ex. 1 *b* we have the true Bass (the part immediately above the Pedal in Ex. 1 *a*), which Ph. Em. Bach, from whom the example is taken,[1] has figured exactly as it would be figured, were there no Pedal below it:

Ex. 1

Now, it is perfectly evident that, if the upper parts of Ex. 1 *a* are taken in either of the two following positions, the character of the progression will be entirely altered. In order to facilitate comparison, the lowest of the three parts (i.e. the one immediately above the Pedal) has been figured, as in Ex. 1 *b*:

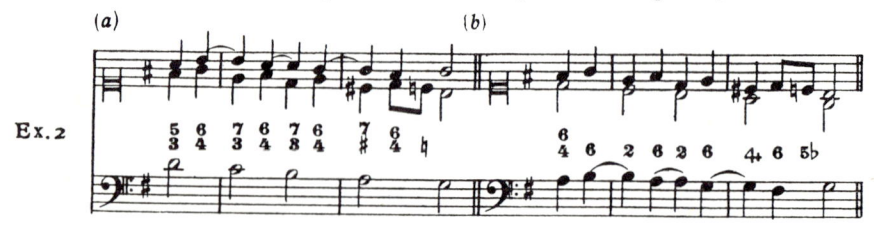

Ex. 2

[1] *Versuch &c.*, Part II, 1762, Ch. 14, § 8, where the example is given, as usual, on a single stave, an Octave lower than here. In Ex. 1 *b* the upper parts have been added in small notes.

XX § 1   PEDAL POINTS   799

Some means, one would have thought, might have been devised by which the accompanist would have been enabled to recognize the position in which the first chords of a Pedal point were intended to be taken;[2] but it is too late to regret what cannot be altered.

§ 2. Besides the difficulty described above, the complexity of the unaccustomed groups of figures which are liable to appear over a Pedal point constitutes, in itself, a very serious obstacle to the player.

In the seventeenth and eighteenth centuries, a competent accompanist was expected to be able to play at sight what was set before him; Ph. Em. Bach alludes to the possibility of having to undertake an accompaniment after only a cursory glance at the part, barely sufficient to reveal the key of the composition.[3] In any such extemporaneous performance, however, it would assuredly have been no disgrace to an accompanist to disregard the figuring of a Pedal point altogether, and to play the Bass only, as though marked *tasto solo*. Indeed, Ph. Em. Bach actually goes so far as to suggest that Pedal points should not be figured at all.

His views on the subject have already been quoted in an earlier chapter of the present work.[4]

Türk expresses himself to much the same effect as Ph. Em. Bach, though, perhaps, not quite so strongly. After giving examples, he writes as follows:[5]

"Whoever does not possess enough skill to play, in similar cases, the harmonies indicated may, perhaps, only play *tasto solo*, or double the Bass (in the lower Octave) and, when the sound is no longer audible, strike the note again at the beginning of a bar. Apart from this, many Pedal points are not figured at all, as it would, after all, not be possible to accompany them throughout, and that without mistakes."

§ 3. This is enough to prove that, in attacking a figured Pedal point, no player need be ashamed to avail himself of any means which may enable him to do so successfully. Above all else, a careful study of the principal parts is necessary, and it may be convenient (as a memorandum for future occasions) to write figures below the Bass (the printed figures being above)—especially at the beginning of the Pedal point—in the order demanded by the position in which the chord in question has to be taken (cf. note 2). For, in spite of what even such authorities as those quoted above may say, it is not to be supposed for a moment that a man so fully occupied as John Sebastian Bach would have spent valuable time in elaborately figuring Pedal points such as, for instance, those in the opening chorus of the St. John Passion, if he had intended the figures to be disregarded.

§ 4. It remains only to give a few short examples which will suffice to show the kind of figuring which may be expected. The first is by Eberlin, and the second (presumably) by Türk, who gives both examples,[6] and figures the part immediately above the Pedal as well as the Pedal itself.

[2] In the example just quoted the figuring of the first chords, $\begin{smallmatrix}5&6\\3&4\end{smallmatrix}$, gives no clue to the position, but, if it had become customary, in such a case, to use not less than three figures (if the harmony was to be in four parts), and (in any case) to arrange them in the order in which it was intended that the intervals in question should be taken $\left(\begin{smallmatrix} 8-\\5\;6\\3\;4 \end{smallmatrix}, \begin{smallmatrix} 5\;6\\3\;4\\8- \end{smallmatrix}, \begin{smallmatrix} 3\;4\\8-\\5\;6 \end{smallmatrix}; \begin{smallmatrix} 8-\\7\;6\\3\;4 \end{smallmatrix}, \begin{smallmatrix} 7\;6\\3\;4\\8- \end{smallmatrix}, \begin{smallmatrix} 3\;4\\8-\\7\;6 \end{smallmatrix}; \&c. \right)$, a great help would have been given.

[3] o.c. Introduction, § 43.   [4] Ch. ii, § 9 c.
[5] *Kurze Anweisung &c.*, 1791, § 195 *ad fin.*, p. 251 sq.
[6] o.c. § 195, pp. 250 sq.

Ex. 3

Ex. 4

In both these examples the two upper staves show, not the accompaniment, but the principal parts.[7]

---

[7] In Ex. 3 the $\frac{9}{4}$ over the Pedal in the first bar must not be taken in the usual way, as $\frac{9}{5}$ (cf. Ch. xvii, § 4); this is one of the cases where Telemann's semicircle, $\frown\!\!\frac{9}{4}$, might have been used with great advantage (cf. Ch. xxiii, 'Varieties of figuring', § 19). The accompaniment of Exx. 3 and 4 might be as follows:

(a)   (b)

The first of the two examples affords an admirable illustration of the need for a careful study of the principal parts. If, instead of effecting the change of position shown on the last quaver of the second bar of (a), the accompanist were to retain the position shown on the penultimate quaver of the same bar, and proceed as follows:

it is obvious that the composer's intentions would not be fulfilled.

XX § 5 PEDAL POINTS 801

The two remaining examples are from Ph. Em. Bach,[8] and are probably intended by him to show how the figures are best to be interpreted by the accompanist, though they may, at the same time, represent the principal parts:

Ex. 5

Ex. 6

[8] o.c. Ch. 24, § 6. In the original, the figured inner part of each example is given separately, and the examples themselves are given, as usual, on a single stave, and (except for the Bass of the first bar and a half of Ex. 5) an Octave lower than here.

[9] In order to bring it to a full close, Bach ends the separate figured inner part as follows:

It is here given *as it appears in the example itself*, but an 8ve higher (cf. note 8).

There are in the original one or two small errors (probably misprints) in the figuring of the Pedal, which have here been corrected. Also, Bach figures the first crotchet (*c*) of the penultimate bar of the figured inner part $\frac{6}{5}$. As the 3 is included in the chord, the ⌒ is superfluous, and has here been omitted.

CHAPTER XXI
INCOMPLETE FIGURING

XXI
INCOMPLETE FIGURING

I. *The omission of accidentals.*

§ 1. Generally speaking, a diminished interval, 3rd, 4th, or 6th, is not assumed, even though in accordance with the key-signature, unless especially indicated in the figuring.

Ph. Em. Bach (*Versuch &c.*, Part II, Cap. 9, I, § 12) gives the following rule:

"Without further indication one takes a major 6th with an augmented 4th (*a*), and a minor 6th with a minor 2nd (*b*); an augmented 4th with an augmented 2nd (*c*), and with an augmented 4th, indicated by a double sharp (4⨯), a major 2nd and major 6th (*d*). The eye is then not bewildered with too many figures."

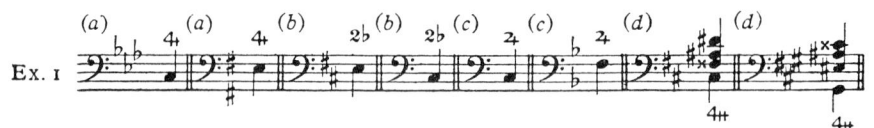

Ex. 1

This rule concerns $^6_4_2$ chords only, but the underlying principle, stated above, applies equally in the following cases of frequent occurrence.

(1) The sharpening of the 3 is rarely indicated:

(*a*) In $^6_3$ or $^6_5$ chords with Bass and minor 3rd accidentally sharpened, as at ** in the following Ex.:

Corelli, *Sonate à Tre*, Opera prima, Sonata IV, Allegro, 2nd section, bars 2–7.

Ex. 2

(*b*) In chords of the diminished 7th in which the Bass and 3rd are accidentally sharpened:

Ex. 3   Leclair, *Sonatas for Violin and Bass*, Bk. IV, Sonata 10, Andante.

Leclair, however, regularly figures the 3rd in contradiction of a previous accidental:

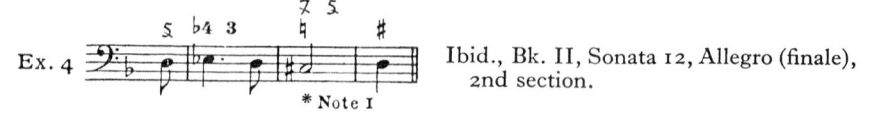

Ex. 4   Ibid., Bk. II, Sonata 12, Allegro (finale), 2nd section.

*Note 1

[1] For the figuring 7 5 see iii, § 2, Ex. 4.

or where the retention of the sharpened 3rd in the following chord makes it desirable in the interests of clearness:

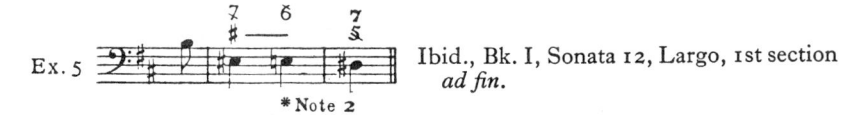

Ex. 5   Ibid., Bk. I, Sonata 12, Largo, 1st section *ad fin.*

*Note 2

rather than:

*Note 3

(2) The accidental sharpening of the 6th is rarely indicated in $^6_3$ chords with augmented 4th:

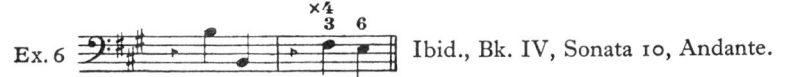

Ex. 6   Ibid., Bk. IV, Sonata 10, Andante.

§ 2. The composers of the seventeenth and early eighteenth centuries commonly assumed the 5th of a chord to be perfect, as at * * in the following Ex. from Matthew Locke's *Melothesia*, London, 1673:

Last bars of an Ex. of 'transition', or passing from one key to another, given in full in Ch. i, § 21 (p. 159), of the present work.

Ex. 7

N.B.—At this period it was not uncommon for the accidentals to be placed, as above, over (or sometimes under) the figures, instead of before or after them.

Ex. 8 A
       B

The above Ex. from Corelli's *Opera Quinta* (12 Sonatas for Violin and Bass), Sonata 3, Allegro, bars 24–30, is given in duplicate, A being from the original edition, Rome, 1700, and B from Estienne Roger's second Amsterdam reprint. The differences in the figuring are instructive as showing a changing

---

[2] Here, as throughout Bk. I of Leclair's Violin Sonatas, $6 = {^6_4_3}$ (Ch. xxiii, §§ 8, 9).

[3] N.B.—In the seventeenth and eighteenth centuries an accidental was regularly assumed to be contradicted unless it was repeated, therefore:

fashion. Apart from the alterations of the harmony in B, $\smash{{}^6_4}$ for $\smash{{}^5_4}$ in the first and last bars and 6 on *c* in the 5th bar, the following differences are to be noted:

(1) The perfect 5th in the 1st and 2nd bars taken for granted in A and figured in B.

(2) The ♭ prefixed to the 3 in the 1st and 2nd bars of A to show that 4 3 is not 'cadential' (= 4 ♯3) as in the last bar (cf. § 3). B omits the ♭.

(3) In the 3rd bar of A the 'leading-note' ♯*d* is left unfigured (cf. III, § 4), but figured in B.

(4) In the same bar, 9, suspended from the 3rd of the previous chord (which, though accidentally sharpened, is itself not figured, cf. § 1), is left without indication of the accidental in A. B has 9.

(5) In the 5th bar of A $\smash{{}^4_\sharp}$ does not, as ordinarily, represent $\smash{{}^6_{\sharp 4}_{\sharp 3}}$, the 4 standing for a tonic pedal against the dominant Triad (cf. IV, § 3, Ex. 5). B omits the 4.

Ambiguity sometimes arises owing to the fact that composers are not always consistent in their practice, especially where details are concerned, as we see from the following three Exx. from Bk. I of Leclair's *Sonatas for Violin and Bass*.

In the first the perfect 5th is figured; in the second it is not figured, but the presence of ♯*c* in the Violin part shows that it is intended; in the third it is indicated only by the general trend of the harmony.

Ex. 9

(a) Sonata 7, Giga, 1st section *ad fin.*

(b) Sonata 6, Allegro, 2nd section *ad fin.*

(c) Ibid., bars 17–20.

§ 3. An instance in which the omission of accidentals is practically confined to the writers of the seventeenth and earlier eighteenth centuries is that of cadences, especially in the minor key, in which the raising of the leading-note was often not indicated.

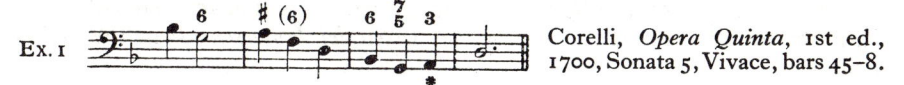

Ex. 1 — Corelli, *Opera Quinta*, 1st ed., 1700, Sonata 5, Vivace, bars 45–8.

N.B.—In this and other similar passages the accidental is supplied in the 3rd and subsequent editions.

Two cases which require special mention are those of a cadential[1] 4 3 and 7 6:

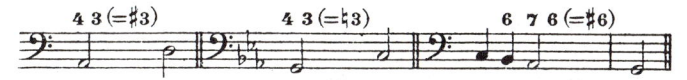

Where the 4 3 was not cadential, i.e. where the Bass did not rise a 4th or fall a 5th, the 3rd was of course major or minor in accordance with the key-signature.

Ex. 2 — A. Scarlatti, 'Principi', Brit. Mus. Add. 14244. 8 a.

In the above Ex. it is only at * * that 4 3 is cadential (3 = ♯3). At † the 4 3 is not cadential, but, the key of G having been established, the major 3rd is possibly intended, in which case it ought strictly to have been figured 4 ♯ (or 4 ♯3), and, in the contrary case, 4 ♭ (or 4 ♭3); but it is in such details that many of the earlier writers left so much to be desired.

Corelli was careful to avoid such ambiguities, as will be seen at * * in the following Exx.:

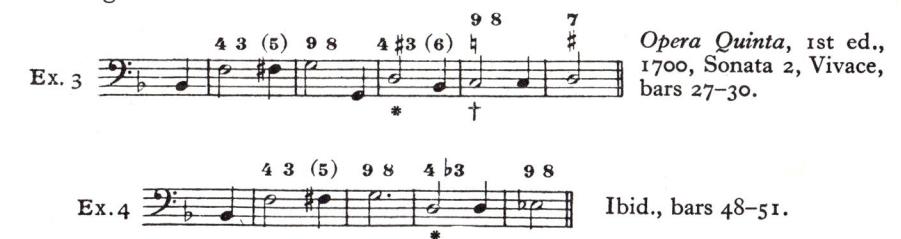

Ex. 3 — *Opera Quinta*, 1st ed., 1700, Sonata 2, Vivace, bars 27–30.

Ex. 4 — Ibid., bars 48–51.

Note especially the 'precautionary' ♮ at † in Ex. 3.

The following quotation from a treatise[2] by Johann Staden, organist of

---

[1] A. Scarlatti ('Per sonare il cembalo', 1715, Brit. Mus. Add. 14244, fol. 39 a) begins his 4th rule as follows: 'When there is a cadence of the 4th and 3rd, the 4th must always be prepared like the two above-mentioned intervals [the 9th and 7th]; and, furthermore, besides the 4th one plays the 5th; and, *if it is a cadence* ("essendo cadenza"), after the 4th one plays the *major* 3rd, save at the pleasure of the composer, who, if he does not wish the 3rd to be major in accordance with the rule, must figure a ♭ or ♮ before the 3rd of the cadence.' Then follows the definition of a cadence.

[2] "Kurzer und einfältiger Bericht für diejenigen, so im *Basso ad Organum* unerfahren, was bei demselben zum Theil in Acht zu nehmen" ('Short and simple account,

St. Sebaldus at Nuremberg, published 1626, is instructive as an instance of idiosyncrasy on the part of a composer in the details of figuring:

"In the matter of the figures and appended signs [i.e. accidentals] I have hitherto found three distinct practices (*dreierlei Unterscheid*) in the Italian *cantiones*.

(1) "In figuring 4 ♯, they ... indicate the major 3rd by ♯:

(2) "In figuring 4 3, some likewise wish to have ... the 3 (without ♯) understood as the major 3rd all the same. Which principle they sometimes extend to 7 6.

"Nota. A practised organist knows that this notation demands the cadences, inasmuch as the bass proceeds a 5th downwards or a 4th upwards. Likewise he recognizes, by the bass note falling a 2nd, where the major 6th is a necessity in view of the 8ve which follows. Albeit this is not an infallible rule, and a composer may occasionally avoid the cadences in the case of the 3rd or 10th, as also in that of the 6th (counting from the Bass, be it understood).

Exempl:

(3) "Some use 4 ♯3 and 7 ♯6 (among them in Italy Giulio S. Petro del Negro) as a proper indication of the major 3rd and 6th, which major 6th is likewise indicated by ♯6 even when not preceded by another figure. In the works of these and other writers I find the ♯ placed *above*[3] the 3 and 6, thus: ♯♯/3 6, ...

"I have, however, myself been pleased to employ this ♯ before 3 (when preceded by another figure [i.e. over the same bass note or its 8ve]) in accordance with the requirements of the Bass, since there are, after all, two kinds of 3rds and 6ths. But with a distinction:

---

for those inexperienced in playing a Thoroughbass on the Organ, of some of the precautions to be observed in so doing'), appended to the Organ part of the author's "Kirchen-Music, Ander Theil, Geistlicher Gesang und Psalmen auf die fürnembsten Fest im Jahr und sonsten zu gebrauchen; von 1, 2, 3, 4, 5, 6 und 7 Stimmen: Dabei etliche auf Violen und andern Instrumenten gericht: Mit einem *Basso ad Organum*", 4° Nürnberg bei Simon Halbmayern, 1626 ('Church Music, Second Part, Sacred Song and Psalms for use on the chief festivals of the year and at other times; in 1, 2, 3, 4, 5, 6, and 7 parts: including some set for viols and other instruments: with a Thoroughbass for the Organ', 4to, Nuremberg, Simon Halbmayer, 1626), and fully described in Ch. i, § 16, of the present work.

[3] Cf. Ex. from Locke's *Melothesia*, § 2, Ex. 7.

XXI 1 § 3   INCOMPLETE FIGURING   809

"When a ♯ or ♭ is found, not followed by a figure, this notation, without figures over the said notes, indicates, ♯ a major, and ♭ a minor 3rd as aforesaid. If, however, the ♯ is followed by a figure, 3 or 6, on the same note, I understand thereby that the Semitonium [4] is required. Just as in the contrary case, where the 3 or 6 stand alone without ♯, the Semitonium is excluded."

Thus, according to the practice of Staden,

(1) 3 or 6, if cadential, *must* be preceded by ♯, *whether accidentally sharpened or not.*

(2) ♯, unaccompanied by the figure 3, merely indicates the accidental sharpening of the 3rd (or possibly in some cases is put as a precaution, even where the major 3rd is diatonic) and does not indicate a cadence.

§ 4. Accidentals were often omitted in stereotyped progressions when the key was clear.

Two cases of frequent occurrence are the omission to figure:

(1) The minor 6th in a $\frac{6}{4}$ chord on the Tonic of minor keys in which the ♭ in question was omitted from the signature (cf. Ch. xxiv, § 1 b): [1]

Key of movement, G minor:

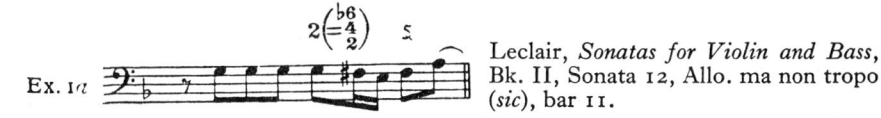

Ex. 1a   Leclair, *Sonatas for Violin and Bass*, Bk. II, Sonata 12, Allo. ma non tropo (*sic*), bar 11.

or, in the case of departure from the original key, on the temporary Tonic: [2]

Ex. 1b   Ibid., bar 39.

(2) The minor 3rd in a $\frac{5}{3}$, $\frac{6}{5}$ or $\frac{7}{5}$ chord on the Subdominant of a minor key, in which, as in the previous case, the ♭ in question is omitted from the signature, as at * * * in the following Ex.:

---

[4] i.e. that the 3rd or 6th should rise a semitone, thus making a cadence, the 'leading note' being called 'Subsemitonium modi' in old treatises.

[1] The absence of the ♭6 in the figuring might be held to indicate that a 'Dorian' 6th was intended, but whereas the latter is somewhat rare, the omission of the ♭6 is very common, and in many cases its presence in the vocal or instrumental parts shows that no 'Dorian' 6th was intended.

[2] A corresponding omission of the ♮ is also found in the sharp keys, in case of a temporary change of key, as in the following Ex.:

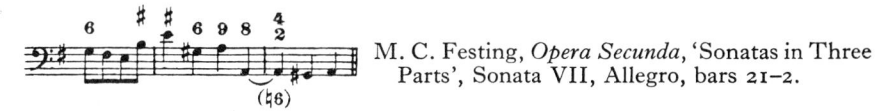

M. C. Festing, *Opera Secunda*, 'Sonatas in Three Parts', Sonata VII, Allegro, bars 21–2.

In the above Ex. the minor 6th of the $\frac{4}{2}$ chord (♮f) is not present in the Violin parts, or it would probably have been included in the figuring. Cf. IV, § 1.

Corelli, *Opera Quinta*, 1st ed., 1700, Sonata 5, Adagio, bars 26-35.

Ex. 2

† Note 3

No doubt the omissions mentioned in this section are in many cases due to carelessness, but in some figured Basses they occur systematically.

(3) The accidentally sharpened leading-note of a minor key (whether it be the key of the movement or only temporary) when the progression of the Bass is such as to render the key unmistakable.

Pietro Locatelli, *Opera Quinta*, VI Sonate a Tre, Sonata 4, Andante, 2nd section, bars 8-10.

Key of movement
C major
Ex. 3

† Note 4

§ 5. An accidental is often omitted from the figuring when the omission is supplied
   (*a*) by the bass note immediately preceding, as § 4, Ex. 2, bars 1 and 7;
   (*b*) by a figure immediately following, as:

Leclair, ibid., bar 28.

Note.—With some composers this figuring would have meant:

Had Leclair intended this, he would have figured:

It will be remembered (cf. § 4, Ex. 1) that the key of the movement is G minor; the ♭ omitted in the figuring of the above Ex. is therefore again the one omitted in the signature.

II. *Accepted optional interpretations of the figuring (Incomplete figuring).*

§ 1. $6 = {6 \atop 4 \atop 3}$. On the Supertonic—or, in the case of modulation, the temporary Supertonic—of either a major or minor key, the figuring 6 (6 ♮6), denoting a major 6th with a minor 3rd, may at the discretion of the accom-

---

[3] At † the accidental is supplied, it being necessary to figure the Triad when followed by another chord on the same bass note; 3 ♯4 would have been misleading.

[4] For ${4 \atop 2} = {7 \atop 4 \atop 2}$ see IV, § 2.

INCOMPLETE FIGURING

panist be taken as $\smash{\overset{6}{\underset{3}{4}}}$, or, in other words, be treated, not as the 1st inversion of the imperfect triad on the 7th degree of the scale, but as the 2nd inversion of a dominant 7th, wherever the latter chord is admissible: i.e. when *either the 4 is present in the preceding chord*, Exx. 1, 2, 3, *or the 3*, Ex. 4 (irrespective of whether the Bass falls to a triad, Exx. 2, 3, 4, or rises to a 1st inversion, Ex. 1), *the 4 in all cases remaining as a part of the next chord*, cf. Ph. Em. Bach, who, in treating the $\smash{\overset{6}{\underset{3}{4}}}$ chord which includes a major 6th, perfect 4th, and minor 3rd (*Versuch*, Part II, Cap. 7, I, § 5), adds: "This chord is sometimes indicated by a mere 6 instead of $\smash{\tfrac{4}{3}}$."[1]

Heinichen (*General-Bass &c.*, 1728, Part I, Cap. 3, § 7, pp. 150–1) gives the rule in a form which would exclude Ex. 4: "In the case of the major 6th in combination with a minor 3rd it is further to be remarked that, instead of the 8ve, one may take the 4, *retaining it from the previous chord*, provided that it can remain stationary as part of the next." He appends a note: "This 4th is styled *4ta irregularis* or *la Quarta irregolare*, because it remains without

---

[1] Later on in the same chapter (II, § 1) Ph. Em. Bach adds: "If, with the major 6th and minor 3rd, one takes the perfect 4th without its being expressly indicated (*a*), one thus sometimes avoids mistakes (*aa*); one remains comfortably in one's position (*b*), without making skips (*c*), and one gets an agreeable progression ('einen guten Gesang') (*d*):

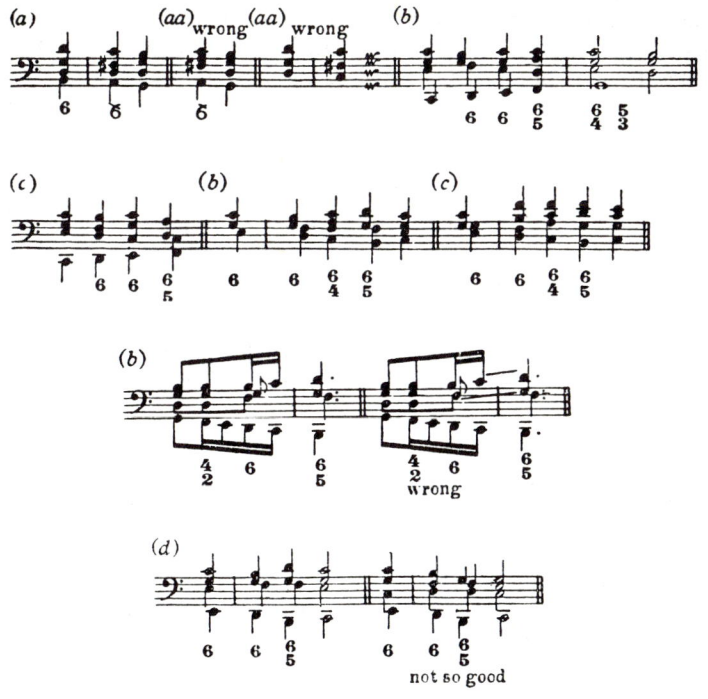

resolution. And it here takes exactly the same liberty as the stationary 7th on a passing note of the Bass; although they are both, 7th and 4th alike, in themselves dissonances requiring resolution, &c."

The conclusion of the rule is given in § 2.

A. Scarlatti disagrees with the authorities above mentioned in one very important point, namely in making a distinction between the cases where the Bass falls to a triad and where it rises to a 1st inversion.

'Per accompagnare il Cembalo ò organo ò altro stromento' ('Accompaniment on the harpsichord, organ or other instrument'), Rule 8, Brit. Mus. Add. 14244, fol. 40 a: ". . . whenever the concord of the major 6th occurs, one adds the 4th above the 3rd of the said concord, because it sounds nice, besides serving to prepare the 5th of the subsequent bass note when the latter falls a tone, *but when it rises a tone* [or semitone] one does not add the aforesaid 4th . . . as in the Ex."

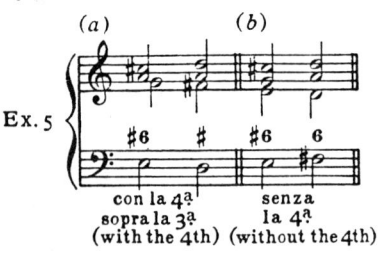

Ex. 5

(a) ♯6 ♯ (b) ♯6 6

con la 4ª   senza
sopra la 3ª   la 4ª
(with the 4th) (without the 4th)

N.B.—Scarlatti gives the Bass only.

A. Scarlatti also furnishes one other point of great interest, as illustrating the traditional practice of his time and country. 'Regole per Principianti' ('Rules for beginners'), Brit. Mus. Add. 14244, fol. 13 a:

"When there is a 7th and 6th [i.e. a 7 6 suspension: he does not say on what degree of the scale, any more than in the Ex. quoted above, but the Exx. make it clear] one takes the 3rd of the bass note either below or above the 7th, and in passing [2] to the 6th one adds the 4th to the 3rd as we see below."

Ex. 6

N.B.—Scarlatti gives the Bass only, but according to his rule the accompaniment is:

[2] In the following instance Ph. Em. Bach takes the 4th *with* the 7th in a 7 6 suspension on the Supertonic, but only as a means of avoiding consecutives in an awkward progression:

7 7 6

Versuch, Part II, Cap. 13, II, § 4, Ex. *g*.

XXI II § 1   INCOMPLETE FIGURING   813

In all the cases mentioned above, the addition of the 4 is optional, and it is to be regretted that there was no means of indicating when its inclusion was definitely not desired. A due discretion must therefore be observed. For instance, in playing from Handel's figured basses, his dislike of the 2nd inversion of the dominant 7th as a chord 'of simple percussion'[3] should be remembered.

In certain cases, however, the inclusion of the 4 is definitely required, as when the Supertonic (actual or temporary), though only figured 6, is preceded by an inversion of the dominant 7th, Ex. 7, and, though in a lesser degree, when it is followed by one, Ex. 8.

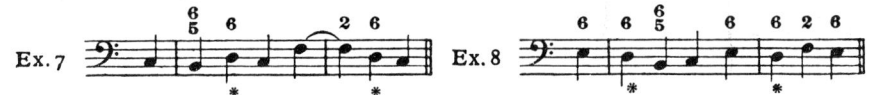

§ 2. $6 = {}^6_4 \left({}^6_3\right)$. A 6 (major 6th and major 3rd) on a Bass falling a semitone to the dominant chord (Triad or 7th) of a minor key†, may, at the discretion of the accompanist, include the augmented 4th, as though figured ${}^4_3 \left({}^{4\sharp}_3\right)$.

Heinichen, continuing the rule of which the first part was quoted in the preceding section, proceeds as follows: "The same thing is in certain instances permissible in the case of the *4ta superflua* [augmented 4th], which, however, in such case is associated with the major 3rd, as the three final Exx. show."

[3] i.e. where the 4, not present in the previous chord, is struck, as instead of being simply retained from the previous chord and remaining as part of the following one like the 'stationary 7th', to which, as we saw, Heinichen compared it.

† There is no doubt that, in major keys also, 6 on the Submediant was often intended to be taken as ${}^6_4_3$.

Schröter has the following Ex., *Deutliche Anweisung zum General-Bass* ('Clear Guide to Thorough-bass'), 1772, § 187 (a), in which, according to his custom, except for the chord in question, he only gives the top part:

Leclair's use of $6 = {}^6_4_3$ in Bk. I of his *Sonatas for Violin and Bass* furnishes an unfailing guide for the use of the chord in parallel passages of his other works in which, under protest, he discontinued this use of 6. See Ch. xxiii ('Varieties of figuring'), § 9.

And he concludes: "In the case of such 6ths, however [i.e. those just mentioned and those treated in § 1], this irregular 4 or 4♯ is not always expressly indicated over the notes; it is rather for the accompanist to see whether he can find it for himself and use it properly...."

A. Scarlatti, 'Principi', Brit. Mus. Add. 14244, fol. 3 a, after giving an Ex.:

Ex. 2a

merely adds, with his usual plea for what 'sounds nice', cf. § 1: "If one adds the major [i.e. augmented] 4th, united with the 3rd, to the aforesaid note, it will have a good effect."

Ex. 2b

N.B.—The figures and accidentals in ( ) are omitted by the transcriber of the MS., only part (if any) of which is autograph.

Ph. Em. Bach, l.c. § 8, in alluding to the practice of using 6 only, where the inclusion of the augmented 4th is intended, says: "The figuring $\frac{4}{3}$ or $\frac{4\sharp}{3}$ is certainly more necessary than in the 5th section [i.e. in the case of 6 on the Supertonic]. It is liable to cause confusion when some people in this case, in the place of the necessary $\frac{4}{3}$, put only 6, or even $\frac{6}{4}$, over the notes."

When the 6 is preceded by a suspended 7th, we have to bear in mind Scarlatti's rule (§ 1), and add the 4 at the moment of resolution:

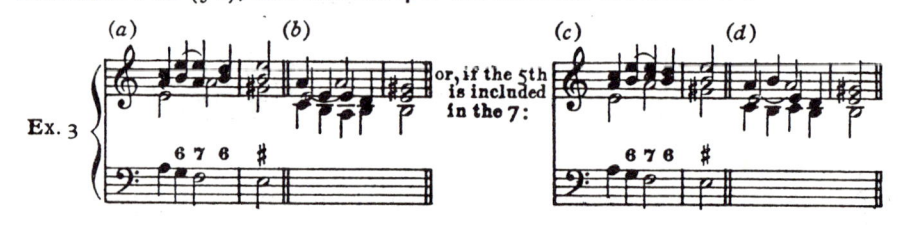

Ex. 3 (a) (b) or, if the 5th is included in the 7: (c) (d)

§ 3. $\overset{6}{6} = \overset{6}{\underset{3}{4}}$. Many composers practised the same economy of figures in the case of the augmented 6th with the augmented 4th and major 3rd ('French Sixth'), figuring the chord with 6 only:

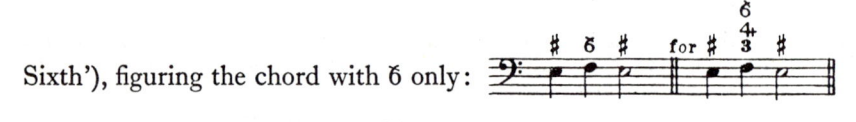

Alluding to this practice, Ph. Em. Bach, l.c. § 11, says: "Many figure this chord inadequately with only 6 and its accidental; it is better to indicate all three intervals over the note."

§ 4. $\overset{6}{6} = \overset{6}{\underset{3}{5}}$. According to G. Ph. Telemann, *Singe-, Spiel- und Generalbass-Übungen* ('Exercises in Singing, Playing, and Thoroughbass'), Hamburg, 1733/4 (reprinted Berlin, 1914), No. 11 g (p. 11), 6 ♮6 on the Supertonic of a minor key can generally be taken as $\overset{6}{\underset{3}{5}}$ ($\overset{\natural 6}{\underset{3}{\flat 5}}$) when *4 is not present* in the music.

"Die 5♭ wird nicht stets geschrieben, sie findet aber allemal bey den 6 6♮ statt, wann die bewegung hinaufwerts in einen weichen ton geschicht, und wann der componist nicht die 4 daselbst (ebenfalls ungezeichnet) angebracht hat, wozu ein gutes vorher lauschendes ohr gehöret. Eine 3 begleitet dieselbe."

("The 5♭ is not always written, but it is always in place when the movement is upwards † to a minor harmony, and when the composer has not introduced the 4 (likewise not figured) in its place; a good ear, that listens for what is coming, is needed. A 3 completes the chord.")

This licence is not mentioned by Heinichen, or Ph. Em. Bach, or in any of the more important works on Thorough-Bass, and it is obvious that great discretion must be used in its employment.

§ 5. In cadences, the 7th, though not indicated in the figuring, may be added to the dominant chord.

A. Scarlatti, 'Regole per Principianti' ('Rules for beginners'), Brit. Mus. Add. 14244, fol. 13 a, Rule 1: "When there is a 4th and a 3rd, take the 5th with the 4th,[1] and it is called a cadence, that is to say, a close; and, in passing to the 3rd, *one touches the 7th as well*, and one must manage, so far as one can, that the 4th and 3rd are on the top, and that there are no other consonances [i.e. 5th or 8ve] above them."

Ph. Em. Bach, *Versuch*, Part II, Cap. 13, II, § 1: "When, in a cadence, and also apart from one, the Bass either rises a degree or leaps to the 4th above or the 5th below, the chord of the 7th can be taken with the penultimate note, even when not indicated, if the note which follows has a Triad over it. In such cases the 5th is usually taken with the 7th (*a*); but if one is afraid of getting too low down with the right hand, one can, in the first of the Exx. (*a*), retain the 8ve instead of the 5th, as (*b*). Not only is a melodious progression ('der gute Gesang') often maintained in this way, but the final Triad [2] retains all its intervals. When the Bass rises a step, one of the intervals of the final Triad [3] often has to be doubled.

Ex. 1

† i.e. when the Supertonic 6th rises to a minor Triad or its 1st inversion instead of being one of a downward series of 6ths, as:

---

[1] Scarlatti's words are 'sopra la 4ᵃ pone la 5ᵃ' ('over the 4th place the 5th'), but the end of the rule makes his meaning clear.

[2] i.e. instead of the 5th being absent and the 8ve of the Bass doubled, as would otherwise be the case in the position shown at (*b*), in which the leading note, being at the top, cannot fall to the 5th of the tonic chord, as in the first of the Exx. *a*.

[3] i.e. whenever the Bass rises a semitone, as in Ex. *c*, in which case the 3rd of the final triad must be doubled, to avoid either (*a*) consecutive 5ths, or (*b*) a downward step of an augmented 2nd on the part of the major 3rd of the dominant chord.

G. M. Telemann, *Unterricht im Generalbass-Spielen* ('Instruction in playing from a Thoroughbass'), Hamburg, 1773, Pt. 3, § 8, p. 104: "Finally: in case of regular final cadences in the Bass ('bassirenden förmlichen Schlusscadenzen'), which consist of a leap to the 5th below or the 4th above with a Triad over each note, one usually strikes the 7th after the 5th or 8ve of the penultimate chord, even where it is not indicated, after which one generally takes the last chord with the 8ve on the top."

Ex. 2 (a) (b)

"There is, however, no obligation in either case, and, if the striking the 7th after the dominant chord ('das Nachschlagen der Septime') would be detrimental to any beauty of the piece accompanied, it is better to omit it. Likewise, if one cannot take the 8ve of the final bass note in the top part without much difficulty, it is better to take the 3rd or 5th instead, more especially if one or more of the vocal or instrumental parts ('mitmusicirenden Stimmen') lie above this 3rd or 5th."

D. G. Türk, *Kurze Anweisung zum Generalbassspielen* ('Short Guide to the art of playing from a Thoroughbass'), Halle and Leipsic, 1791, Cap. 5, I, § 125, gives Exx. in which he carries the licence further than Ph. Em. Bach or G. M. Telemann by taking the 7th with, instead of after, the bass note.

§ 6. According to G. Ph. Telemann, in the little work quoted in § 4, No. 16 *f* and No. 18 *h, i*, in cadences a $^6_5$ chord may be taken on the Subdominant, even when not figured.

Ex. 3 (a) (b)

III. Besides the cases of more or less slovenly figuring to be considered presently (IV), there are those in which the omission of a figure or figures, even if not formally recognized in the text-books, is in itself reasonable. Such cases are:

§ 1. When the figure omitted denotes an interval required for the *preparation of a subsequent discord*, as in the following Exx. The figure omitted is added in ( ) underneath.

Purcell, *Sonnatas of 3 Parts*, 1683, Sonata 2, last movement, bars 26-7.

Ex. 1

XXI III § 1   INCOMPLETE FIGURING   817

Ex. 2 — T. A. Arne, *Opera Terza*, 'VII Sonatas for Two Violins with a Thorough Bass &c.', Sonata 5, Largo, 2nd section, bar 5.

Ex. 3 — M. C. Festing, *Opera Sesta*, 'Six Sonatas for Two Violins and a Bass', Sonata 4, Andante e dolce, bars 5 and 6.

Further instances are mentioned in dealing with the cases where it is necessary to play in 5 parts, Ch. iii, § 4.

§ 2. When the figure omitted denotes an interval *required for the resolution of an antecedent discord*, as in the following Exx.:

Ex. 1 — J.-M. Leclair, Op. 4, 'Six Sonatas for two Violins with a Thorough Bass &c.' (Walsh), Sonata 4, Allegro, bar 32.

M. C. Festing, *Opera Secunda*, 'Twelve Sonatas in Three Parts', Sonata 3, Tempo giusto, bars 9–7 from end.

Ex. 2

Ex. 3 — Ibid., Sonata 7, Andante, bars 9, 10.

Ex. 4 — Leclair, Bk. 4 of *Sonatas for Violin and Bass*, Sonata II, Andante, 2nd section, bars 20–2.

N.B.—The same progression is also frequently figured ♮7 6, ♭7 6. The ♮5 ♭5, *always* being included in the chord of the diminished 7th (even in 3-part harmony), is bound to remain until resolved; therefore in ♮7 6, ♭7 6, the 6 cannot be taken otherwise than as $\begin{smallmatrix}6\\\natural5\end{smallmatrix}$, $\begin{smallmatrix}6\\\flat5\end{smallmatrix}$.

§ 3. When the resolution of an antecedent discord falls upon a passing note of the Bass, and the figures representing notes held over from the previous chord are omitted, as in the following Exx.:

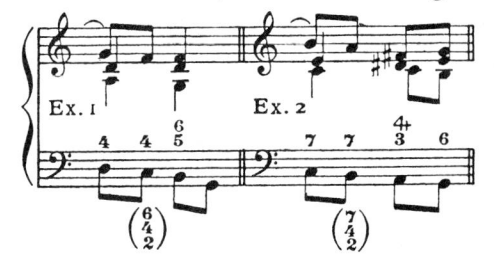

Ex. 1   Ex. 2 — Ph. Em. Bach, *Versuch*, Part II, Cap. 32, § 12, where these Basses are given (an 8ve lower) in a different connexion.

§ 4. In certain cases, especially characteristic of the Italians and their imitators, in which, the progression being clear, the figures are omitted as unnecessary.

Some of the older treatises, e.g. Heinichen, *General-Bass &c.*, 1728, Pt. 2, Cap. 2, give elaborate rules for playing from an *un*figured Bass, though, as Heinichen explains, the occasion ought not to arise except in the case of vocal and instrumental Solos, where the accompanist had the solo part before him over the Bass. Guided by the former, and also by his knowledge of the 'ambitus modi', i.e. of what harmony was natural to the several degrees of the scale and to certain progressions of the Bass, he sometimes had to dispense with figures, though Ph. Em. Bach (*Versuch*, Part II, Cap. 35) emphatically condemns the practice.

The same principle was sometimes applied to a limited extent, even when the accompanist had only the Bass before him, as usually happened except in the case of Solos.[1]

The following are characteristic instances:

(1) The omission of 6 or $^6_5$ over the leading-note actual or temporary:

Bononcini, *XII Sonatas for two Violins and a Bass*, 1732, Sonata 3, Spiritoso, bars 6 and 7

Ex. 1

Ex. 2  Ibid., Sonata 7, Menuet, 2nd section, bars 11 and 12.

In some cases it is impossible to be certain whether 6 or $^6_5$ was intended, but $^6_5$ is certainly always admissible whenever the 5 was present in the previous chord, as on ♯*a* and the following ♯*g* in the 2nd bar of Ex. 1, and on *d* and ♮*b* in the 1st bar of Ex. 2. With regard to the final ♮*b* of Ex. 2, the Violin parts show that $^6_5$ was intended.

(2) The omission of 6 on a bass note rising a semitone to a Triad:

Ex. 3 Corelli, *Opera Quinta*, 1st ed. 1700, Sonata 2, Vivace (finale), bar 49.

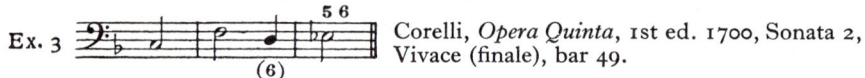

(3) The omission to figure the resolution of a suspension resolving on a different bass note:

Ex. 4 Ibid., Sonata 1, 2nd Adagio, bar 6.

---

[1] There are isolated instances of Trios with the parts printed over the Bass, as e.g. a sonata by Michele Masciti ('il Napolitano') for Violin, Viol da Gamba, and Bass, included, as No. 15, in his *Opera Sesta*, 'Sonate a Violino Solo', and one by Leclair, also for Violin, Viol da Gamba, and Bass, No. 8 in the 2nd book of his *Sonatas for Violin and Bass*. It is no doubt owing to their inclusion among Solos that this method was adopted.

[2] For the omission of the $^6_5$ (♭5 5) on ♯*g* cf. Ex. 2.

(4) The omission to figure the resolution of a suspension over rests:

Ex. 5

Leclair, *Sonatas for Violin and Bass*, Bk. I, Sonata 4, Tempo Gavotta, Altro, 2nd section, bars 8-11.

(5) The omission to figure the resolution of a $\smash{\genfrac{}{}{0pt}{}{6}{\genfrac{}{}{0pt}{}{4}{2}}}$ chord (cf. Ch. i, § 23, note 4).

IV. *Incomplete figurings not recognized by the authorities.*

§ 1. Any attempt to deal exhaustively with the incomplete and misleading figurings to be found in many Basses would be productive of more confusion than enlightenment; there are, however, certain types which it will be well to consider briefly.

Among these are what may be termed 'three-part figurings'. Such figurings do not necessarily imply that the composer desired a three-part accompaniment; but in many cases (though, as we shall see, not in all) they show that, in figuring his Bass, he was intent rather on the notes actually present in the score than on the completion of the harmony.

This is, naturally, more likely to be the case in Trios (for two principal parts and a Bass) than in any other form of composition, and it is from such that the majority of our examples are taken.

There are, however, noteworthy cases in which the incomplete figuring cannot be so accounted for, and in which it can only be regarded as an arbitrary abbreviation, possibly due to haste on the part of the composer. In two examples from the works of no less a person than J. S. Bach, both of them from Trios, the interval omitted in the figuring is *present in the Score* (cf. § 2, Exx. 5 and 8). In both, the figured Bass is believed to be autograph.

A similar example is taken from Antonio Vivaldi's *Sonatas for two Violins and Bass* (§ 2, Ex. 4). In the great majority of cases, however, it will be seen that the composer has simply figured the intervals *actually present in the score*.

§ 2. These misleading figurings are particularly liable to occur over suspended notes in the Bass (whether slurred, as in Exx. 1 and 7, or not, as in Ex. 2), over notes which are really *appoggiaturas* (as in Exx. 3, 9, 10), over changing (i.e. accented passing) notes (as in Exx. 5, 8, 11, 12), and over passing notes (as in Exx. 4 and 6), wherever, in fact, there is a dislocation of the true Bass.

In the examples immediately following (Exx. 1–7) we find $\smash{\genfrac{}{}{0pt}{}{4}{2}}$, $\smash{\genfrac{}{}{0pt}{}{7}{4}}$, 7, 2, as abbreviations of $\smash{\genfrac{}{}{0pt}{}{7}{\genfrac{}{}{0pt}{}{4}{2}}}$, to denote a Triad struck on a note a degree above its true Bass:

$\smash{\genfrac{}{}{0pt}{}{4}{2}} = \smash{\genfrac{}{}{0pt}{}{7}{\genfrac{}{}{0pt}{}{4}{2}}}$ Ex. 1

Corelli, *Opera Quinta*, 1st ed. 1700, Sonata I, Adagio, bars 22, 23.

M. C. Festing, *Opera Secunda*, 1731, Sonata XII,
Largo, 2nd section, bars 2–5.

$\frac{4}{2} = \frac{7}{4}$ Ex. 2

M. C. Festing, *Opera Sesta*, Sonata IV, Poco Allegro, bar 9.

$\frac{4}{2} = \frac{7}{4}$ Ex. 3

N.B.—In this example it will be noticed that the intervals figured (on the first semiquaver of the bar) are, as in the preceding example, those present in the score.

Antonio Vivaldi, *Opera Prima Suonate da Camera a Tre*,
Sonata II, Corrente, 2nd section, bars 15, 16.

$\frac{4}{2} = \frac{7}{4}$ Ex. 4

N.B.—In this example it will be noticed that the interval (7) omitted from the figuring is present in the 2nd Violin part.

XXI IV § 2   INCOMPLETE FIGURING   821

$\frac{7}{4}=\frac{7}{\underset{2}{4}}$ Ex. 5

J. S. Bach, *Sonata in G for two Flutes and Bass*, Presto, bar 9. B.G. ed. IX, p. 270.

N.B.—In this example, too, the interval (2) omitted from the figuring is present in the score.

$7=\frac{7}{\underset{2}{4}}$ Ex. 6

Corelli, *Opera Prima*, Sonata VII, Allegro, bar 8.

$\flat 2=\frac{7}{\underset{\flat 2}{4}}$ Ex. 7 [1]

Leclair, *Sonatas for Violin and Bass*, Book II, Sonata XII, Allegro ma non troppo, bar 39.

In the following example we find $\smash{\frac{7}{5}}$ as the abbreviation of $\smash{\frac{7}{\underset{2}{5}}}$. The chord denoted is $\smash{\underset{3}{\overset{8}{6}}}$ on the Supertonic struck on a changing (i.e. accented passing) note a degree above:

---

[1] For the omission of the accidental on the 5th quaver of the example $\left(2 = \smash{\genfrac{}{}{0pt}{}{\flat 6}{\genfrac{}{}{0pt}{}{4}{2}}}\right)$ see I, § 4, Ex. 1 *a* and *b*.

[Musical example: J. S. Bach, *Sonata in G for Flute, Violin, and Bass*, Vivace, bars 14, 15. B.G. ed. IX, p. 224.]

$\frac{7}{5} = \frac{7}{\substack{5\\2}}$ Ex. 8

In the next example both $\frac{5}{4}$ and $\frac{4}{2}$ occur as abbreviations of $\frac{5}{\substack{4\\2}}$, denoting a $\frac{6}{5}$ chord struck on a note a degree above its true Bass. Both figurings ($\frac{5}{4}$, $\frac{4}{2}$) represent the intervals actually present in the score:

$\frac{4}{2} \& \frac{5}{4} = \frac{5}{\substack{4\\2}}$ Ex. 9

In the following example the figuring $\frac{4}{2}$ is used to represent two different chords: (1) $\frac{5}{\substack{4\\2}}$ (on the first semiquaver), (2) $\frac{7}{\substack{4\\2}}$ (on the ninth semiquaver); but, in both cases, *it gives the notes actually played by the Violins*. The true Bass is as follows:

[Musical example showing the true bass line with figures]

[2] In the suggested accompaniment the crossing of parts will be noticed between the last chord of the second bar and the one which follows. The alternative would be to take the first chord of the third bar in extended harmony, $\genfrac{}{}{0pt}{}{\genfrac{}{}{0pt}{}{g}{c}}{\genfrac{}{}{0pt}{}{d}{g}}$, which is not always convenient with a running Bass.

[3] It will be noticed that the chord figured $\frac{5}{4}$ on the ninth semiquaver (representing $\genfrac{}{}{0pt}{}{6}{\genfrac{}{}{0pt}{}{5}{3}}$ on the following semiquaver *a*) has not the ordinary resolution of a $\frac{6}{5}$ chord. It is really a $\frac{6}{4}$ chord with the 4 delayed by suspension ($\frac{6}{5}\frac{-}{4}$), the suspension resolving, not on its own Bass, but (in root position) on *d*. The inclusion of the 3 is parallel to the inclusion of 5 in 7 6 suspension (cf. Ch. xii, '$\frac{6}{5}$ chords', § 6, 2).

XXI IV § 2   INCOMPLETE FIGURING   823

The first chord of the bar ($^6_5$ on ♯f) is exactly parallel to that on the ninth semiquaver of Ex. 9 (cf. note 3).

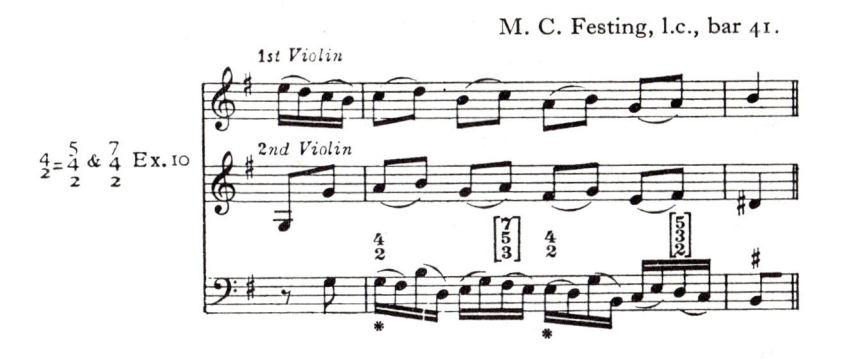

M. C. Festing, l.c., bar 41.

$^4_2 = ^5_4_2 \, \& \, ^7_4_2$ Ex. 10

In the two following examples $^6_4$ stands for $^7_6_4$, the figuring of a $^6_5$ chord struck on a changing (i.e. accented passing) note a degree below the true Bass. In both cases the figuring represents the intervals actually present in the score.

Pergolese, *Twelve Sonatas for Two Violins and a Bass*, Sonata XII, Allegro, bars 65–9.

$^6_4 = ^7_6_4$ Ex. 11

M. C. Festing, *Opera Secunda*, Sonata IX, Allegro, bars 16, 17.

$^6_4 = ^7_6_4$ Ex. 12

§ 3. Other instances of 'three-part figuring'.

Corelli, *Opera Quarta*, Sonata 5, Preludio (Adagio), bars 11 and 12.

Ex. 1

The above Ex. is a particularly instructive one:

(1) We have to do with a very complicated ornamental resolution of the $^5_4$ chord on the 1st quaver of the 1st (complete) bar of the Ex., the tonic chord (E minor) not being reached till the 6th quaver of the following bar, though the 4 resolves on ♯3 on the 4th and 8th quavers of bar 1, the resolution being, in the latter case, discounted by the tonic pedal E in the 1st Violin.

(2) The G on the 2nd quaver of bar 1 is (though reached by leap) really a *passing* note, cf. Ch. xviii, § 1, *i–l*, leaving the rest of the harmony unaltered, and the chords on the 6th quaver of bar 1 and the 2nd quaver of bar 2 (in each case G) are passing concords interposed between two inversions of the same discord.

(3) The major 3rd on the 3rd and 7th quavers (*a*) of bar 1 is due to the upward melodic minor progression of the Violin. In just such a passage some older composers would have had a 'false relation', ♯c in the upward-moving Violin part and ♮c in the downward-moving part.

(4) The 7th quaver of bar 1 (*a*) really requires a $^6_5$ chord rather than a triad, as being another inversion of the preceding unresolved discord $^{4\sharp}_3$ on the 5th quaver (*c*), and on the 3rd quaver, too, a $^6_5$ is more natural, as retaining the suspended 4 at the beginning of the bar.

This gives us the following, as the true harmonic basis of the passage:

Key E minor throughout.

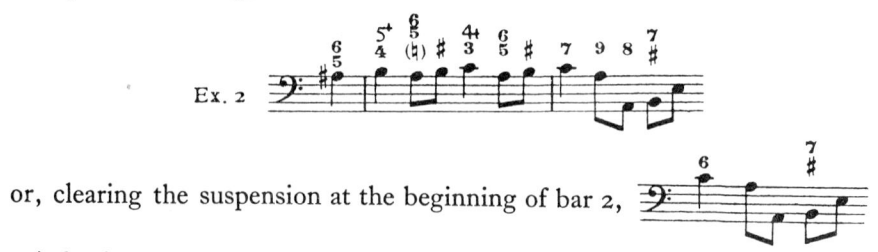

Ex. 2

or, clearing the suspension at the beginning of bar 2,

‡ A 5th part (E) is taken in on the top to gain a higher position, the lower part being immediately dropped, as indicated by the quaver rest. Cf. Ch. iii, § 4, I.

XXI IV § 3   INCOMPLETE FIGURING   825

It is therefore clear that the chord figured $\frac{7}{3}$ (on the 1st quaver of bar 1) can only have 6 as its 4th part. If it were treated as $\genfrac{}{}{0pt}{}{7}{5\genfrac{}{}{0pt}{}{}{3}}$, Ex. 3, it would be anticipating the purposely delayed resolution, and would be inconsistent with the character of the Bass, if we are right in regarding the latter as a passing note.

Ex. 3

The simplest way to figure the passage is: $\genfrac{}{}{0pt}{}{6}{5}\ \genfrac{}{}{0pt}{}{5}{4}\ =$ whereby the unfamiliar combination $\genfrac{}{}{0pt}{}{7}{6\genfrac{}{}{0pt}{}{}{3}}$ is avoided.

Whether a 4-part accompaniment is *desirable* in the earlier part of the passage is another question. The alternative would be

Ex: 4

On comparing this with Ex. 1 it will be seen that it simply reproduces the Violin parts almost note for note, instead of providing an independent harmonic background, which is the proper function of a figured Bass accompaniment; the main objection, however, is that none of the chief authorities (Mattheson, Heinichen, Ph. Em. Bach, &c.) admit such a resolution of a 4 3 suspension.

Whatever the vocal or instrumental parts may do, the canons of the art demand that the accompanist should *hold the 4 till its resolution is reached*.

Corelli, *Opera Quinta*, 1st ed. 1700, Sonata 3,
1st Allegro, bar 28.

Ex. 5

This Ex. is an instance, not of incomplete, but of redundant and misleading figuring, and finds a place here as illustrating what was said in § 1 about the habit of figuring the Bass from the notes present in the score, sometimes at the risk of obscuring the true nature of the harmony.

The chord figured $\smash{\genfrac{}{}{0pt}{}{4}{\sharp}}$ is not a $\smash{\genfrac{}{}{0pt}{}{6}{4}{3}}$ chord at all, as the figuring suggests; the 4 represents the tonic pedal in the Violin part sounding against the dominant chord, exactly as at the end of the 1st bar of the Ex. last discussed.

The 2nd Amsterdam reprint rightly omits the 4.

$\smash{\genfrac{}{}{0pt}{}{7}{2}\genfrac{}{}{0pt}{}{7}{4}} = \smash{\genfrac{}{}{0pt}{}{7}{4}{2}}$. The chord of the dominant 7th suspended as a retardation over the tonic and resolving on the triad of the latter, Ex. 6, is often figured $\smash{\genfrac{}{}{0pt}{}{7}{2}\genfrac{}{}{0pt}{}{8}{3}}$ or $\smash{\genfrac{}{}{0pt}{}{7}{4}\genfrac{}{}{0pt}{}{8}{3}}$ according to which intervals are present in the score, or, sometimes, irrespective of this. Ph. Em. Bach, *Versuch*, Part II, Cap. 16, 1, § 6, regards these abbreviations as in place only when a 3-part accompaniment is expressly desired. The further abbreviation 7 8 he especially condemns, ibid., § 2.

Ex. 6

§ 4. The two cases dealt with in this section and § 5 come under the heading of '3-part figurings', cf. § 1, but are treated separately as having been selected for special condemnation.

$\smash{\genfrac{}{}{0pt}{}{6}{4}} = \smash{\genfrac{}{}{0pt}{}{6}{4}{2}}$. With regard to this figuring Kirnberger, *Kunst des reinen Satzes in der Musik* ('The art of a pure style in musical composition'), Pt. I, 3, Note 34, p. 59, says: 'In a figured Bass it is therefore quite wrong if one figures this chord $\smash{\genfrac{}{}{0pt}{}{6}{4}}$, the 2nd must necessarily be indicated as well.' Nevertheless, on p. 85 (penultimate bar of last Ex.) Kirnberger himself figures the chord in the manner he condemns.

Generally speaking, the figuring in question is found most often where the 2 is not present in the score, and this is on the whole more liable to be the case when the Bass moves down one degree, Ex. 1 *a*, than when the harmony changes on the same bass note, Ex. 1 *b*:

Ex. 1

but an examination of a large number of Exx. from composers who habitually use $\smash{\genfrac{}{}{0pt}{}{6}{4}}$, where $\smash{\genfrac{}{}{0pt}{}{6}{4}{2}}$ *is undoubtedly required* in the accompaniment, reveals so many inconsistencies that it is impossible to establish any rule, as will be seen from the following Exx.

Exx. of $^6_4$ (in trios), where the 2 is present in the score.

Pergolese, *Twelve Sonatas for two Violins and Bass*, Sonata I, Andante, bars 6-10.

Ex. 2

N.B.—In the 1st bar of the Ex. the inclusion of the 2 in the figuring is especially to be desired as there is a strong temptation to take the chord as $^6_4_3$

Ex. 3

M. C. Festing, *Twelve Sonatas in three parts, Opera secunda*, Sonata xii, Allegro, bar 19.

N.B.—In this Ex. the 2 (*d*) in the 1st Violin follows the striking of the chord, but makes the harmony none the less clear.

Exx. of $^4_2$ (in trios) where the 2 is *not* present in the score.

Pergolese, *Twelve Sonatas &c.*, Sonata 4, Allegro, bar 77.

Ibid., Sonata 5, Larghetto, bar 22.

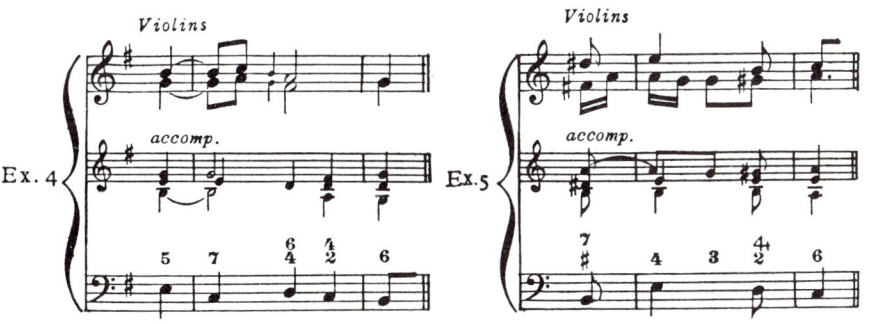

Ex. 4

Ex. 5

In the following Ex., however, from the same composer the only reason for the figuring $^6_{\natural 4}$ instead of $^{\natural 4}_2$ in the 2nd bar of the Ex. seems to be the absence of the 2 in the score. In the previous bar, where the figuring is ♮4♮2, the 2 (♮a) is present in the 1st Violin.

Ex. 6

Ibid., Sonata 3, Allegro (finale), bars 62–3.

In all the Exx. of $\frac{6}{4} = \frac{6}{4}\atop 2$ hitherto given the chord has been that with the augmented 4th, but the usage is by no means confined to these cases, as will be seen from Ex. 7:

Ex. 7

Corelli, *Opera Quinta*, Sonata I, Adagio, bars 25–6.

It is, however, important to realize that the figuring ♯6♯4 ♮6♮4 was sometimes used advisedly in cases where the inclusion of the 2 would have been in place and indeed have seemed more natural.

The following Ex. from Geminiani's Opera 11th, *The Art of Accompaniament* [sic], Part I, Essempio XI (treated in four different ways, pp. 19–21), is highly instructive:

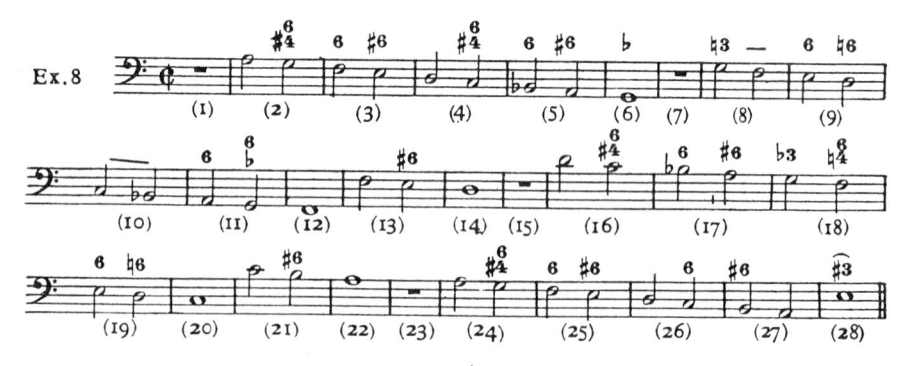

Ex. 8

The chord in question occurs seven times, but Geminiani has figured it (in bars 2, 4, 16, 18, and 24) only where it is necessary to indicate that the 3rd of the previous chord is raised a semitone. In bars 8 and 10 there is a dash, which *should* indicate that the previous harmony is held on unchanged, but in both these cases Geminiani avoids including the 2 in all four versions (1°, 2°, 3°, 4° Modo di suonare L'Antecedente).

Only in *one* instance does he include the 2, namely in bar 24 of the first version:

In most cases he doubles the 6; in one case (bar 4 of the 2nd version) he doubles the Bass, and in other cases he omits the 4th part altogether, or else doubles the 6 in the unison: his method of printing does not enable one to distinguish.

All this goes to prove that, in spite of its inclusion in the one instance, Geminiani did not regard the figuring $\sharp^6_{\sharp 4}$ $^6_{\natural 4}$ as necessarily including the 2 (even in an accompaniment of 4 or more parts and in a progression where its inclusion was in the highest degree natural) but that he regarded its inclusion as *permissible*, at the discretion of the player.

It need hardly be said the 2 must seldom be included in any chord figured $^6_4$ ($\sharp^6_{\sharp 4}$ $^6_{\natural 4}$) except in cases where a $^6_4_2$ chord finds its normal resolution.

Ex. 9

Corelli, *Opera Seconda*, Sonata 7, Giga, 2nd section, bars 8-11.

The 7 on *g* is really a 'stationary' 7th and the $^6_4$ a double appoggiatura. The real progression is:

If therefore a 4-part accompaniment is used, the chord is best taken, not as $^6_{4}_2$, but as $^6_{4}_3$:

Furthermore, when the nature of the progression admits of a chord figured $^\sharp{}^6_4$ $^\natural{}^6_4$ including *either* the 8 *or* the 2, as in Ex. 10, it is better to err on the safe side,

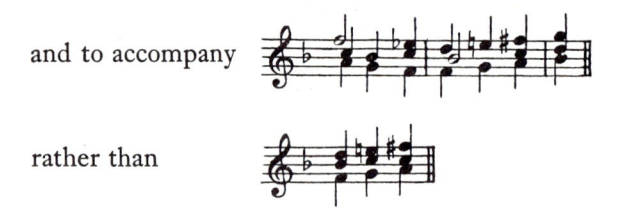

Ex. 10

and to accompany

rather than

§ 5. $^6_4 = ^6_{\substack{4\\3}}$. Ph. Em. Bach (*Versuch*, Part II, Ch. 7, 1, § 4) says:

"In the following Ex. some figurists think that it is enough if they put $^6_4$ after the $^6_5$, as the progression of these two figures is thereby indicated; but a novice might very easily take the 8ve with the $^6_4$ in accordance with the rule for the $^6_4$ chord, instead of the 3rd being a part of it. The figuring in (*b*) is more correct and better in spite of the fact that the eye has a figure the more to take in."

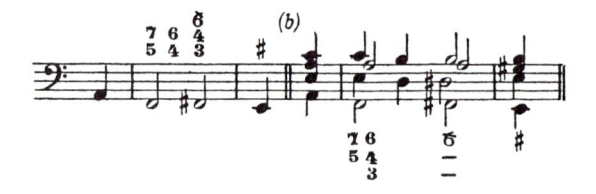

§ 6. (*a*) $^7_4$, as the figuring of a chord of the 7th with suspended 4, stands for (1) $^7_{\substack{5\\4}}$ as Ex. *a*, (2) $^8_{\substack{7\\4}}$ as Ex. *b*.

XXI IV § 6   INCOMPLETE FIGURING   831

Ph. Em. Bach, ibid., Ch. 15, § 3, says: "When our chord is indicated it is of two kinds: (1) it consists of the Seventh, Fifth, and Fourth; (2) of the Seventh, Fourth, and Octave. In both cases the figuring is $^{7}_{4}$. In this instance, too, it would be but little trouble to add the 3rd figure. Matters would be much facilitated for beginners, and the confusion of the chord of the Major Seventh,[1] which is sometimes figured in the same way,[2] would be avoided.

(b) $^{7}_{4}$ = $^{7}_{4\ 3}$ (a Stationary Seventh).

Ph. Em. Bach (ibid., § 13) says: "When, in the case of the passing Seventh [3] in the following Ex., the middle part is intended to move in 3rds with the Bass, while the Fourth remains stationary, some people figure the Bass $^{7}_{4}$, which is not sufficiently clear. The figuring $^{7}_{4\ 3}$ is better.

V. Apart from the types of incomplete figuring hitherto mentioned, there occur, especially in the earlier figured Basses, certain condensed formulae.

§ 1. In cadences.

Matthew Locke, in his *Melothesia*, 1673, Rule 3, gives the following Exx. (on a six-line stave):

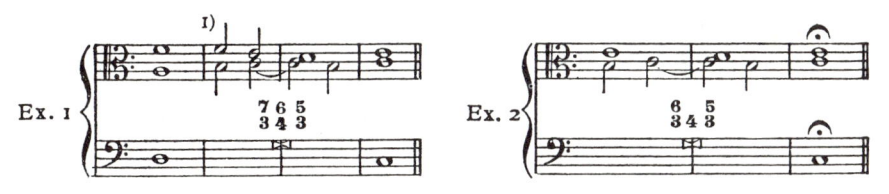

A. Scarlatti, 'Principi', Brit. Mus. Add. 14244, fol. 5 a, gives the rule: "La cadenza lunga viene formata di 3ª e 5ª, 4ª e 6ª, 4ª e 5ª; poi se resolve con la 3ª maggiore, e 7, come l' esempio, e si chiamano lunge, sino che la nota sia una battuta." "The 'long cadence' consists of the 3rd and 5th, the 4th and 6th, the 4th and 5th; it then resolves on the major 3rd and 7th, as in the Ex., and they are called 'long' whenever the note lasts a bar."

---

[1] i.e. the dominant 7th over a tonic pedal.
[2] See Ch. xxiii ('Variety of figuring'), § 14 II, Ex. 7, note 1.
[3] Marpurg, *Handbuch bey dem Generalbasse* ('Handbook of Thoroughbass'), 2nd ed., Berlin, 1762, Abschnitt (Section) I, Absatz (Subsection) IV, § 42, p. 57, rightly protests against the common habit of applying the term 'passing' to this Seventh. He says: "Such Sevenths are generally, though erroneously, called 'passing Sevenths'. Their proper name is 'stationary' or 'unresolving' Sevenths. . . . 'Passing' or 'subsequent' ('durchgehende oder nachschlagende Septimen') are those which occur after a main harmony ('Hauptharmonie') on a stationary Bass and constitute a mere subsidiary harmony ('Nebenharmonie') as: $^{8\ 7}_{9}$ | $^{3}_{c}$.

[1] In the original, by an obvious misprint, as the figure 7 shows, the top note of the 2nd bar of Ex. 1 is d.

[Ex. 3 musical example]

Other Exx. follow with condensed figuring, as Ex. 4:

[Ex. 4 musical example]

Further on, fol. 5 b, he gives Exx., first with full, and then with condensed figuring, in which the 7th, duly prepared, comes at the beginning (as in Ex. 1) as well as the end.

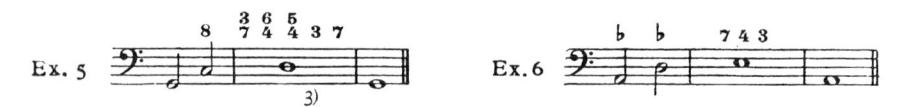

[Ex. 5 and Ex. 6 musical examples]

Further on, fol. 7 a, Scarlatti gives further Exx. with condensed figuring, but with double instead of single figures.

[Ex. 7 musical example]

§ 2. Apart from cadences, abbreviated figurings are often found in the older Basses. In the following Ex., Purcell, *Sonnatas of Three Parts*, 1683, Sonata 3, Canzona, bars 7 and 8, 3 2 = 6 $\frac{4}{2}$:

---

[2] In his 'Regole per principianti' ('Rules for beginners'), ibid., fol. 13 a, Scarlatti directs that in a 4 3 cadence the 4th should, if possible, be in the top part.

[3] The unusual position of the figures, $\frac{3}{7}$ instead of $\frac{7}{3}$ (as also the unnecessary 8 in the previous bar), is probably accidental; but it may also have been a reminder to pupils to get the position which Scarlatti liked with the 4 3 on the top. Cf. note 2.

XXI v § 2   INCOMPLETE FIGURING   833

Ex. to
§ 2

§ 3. The stroke, which usually denotes the retention of the preceding harmony, is sometimes used to save the trouble of figuring a different inversion of the same discord. In the following Exx. the full figuring is given underneath:

Leclair, *Sonatas for Violin and Bass*, Bk. 4, Sonata XI, Gavotta, 2nd section, bar 17.

Ex. 1

Ibid., bar 48.   Ibid., antepenultimate bar.

Ex. 2   Ex. 3

Ibid., Sonata VII, 9th bar from end.

Ex. 4

Schröter, *Deutliche Anweisung zum General-Bass* ('Clear Guide to Thorough-bass'), 1772, comments on the practice as follows: "When after $\frac{6}{5}$, or after $\frac{4}{3}$, or after 7, or after 2, the Bass proceeds to a note present in the previous chord, there arises, instead of the resolution, a different inversion, which, subject to the pace ('nach Beschaffenheit des Mouvements'), is, in its turn,

* * * * For the use of ♯ = ♮ see Ch. xxiv ('Variety of notation'), § 2, and for the omission of 6 over ♯g at ‡ see Ch. xxi, III, § 4 (1).

[1] ♮6 = $\frac{♮6}{4}$. Cf. ii, § 1.
        $\frac{}{3}$

struck in full,[2] although not indicated by special figures. Correct as this rule undoubtedly is, it is much to be desired that composers would adopt a uniform method of figuring. Some put one or more horizontal lines over such inversions, in order thereby to indicate that each inversion is to be struck separately. It has, however, long been customary for such a line to enjoin silence [3] on the right hand. . . . Other composers again put one or more large dots over each inversion, that is to say, when each one is to be struck separately. As the latter method appears to me the most convenient, I shall retain it in the inversions which follow."[4]

In cases like the above mentioned, where an horizontal line is used to connect bass notes representing different intervals of the same chord, it must be borne in mind that, *provided no incorrect progression at the final resolution of the discord is involved*,[5] it is purely a matter of taste whether the original harmony be retained by the right hand, or altered to the respective inversions.

The choice depends largely on the pace of the music, and also upon the nature of the instrument employed, the evanescent tones of the Harpsichord, or even Pianoforte, rendering the retention of a single chord ineffective while on the Organ it may be quite satisfactory. The following Ex., J. S. Bach, *Sonata in E minor for Violin and Bass*, Allemanda *ad fin.*, will illustrate this:

Ex. 5

[2] This, of course, only applies to the Harpsichord with its evanescent tones; on the Organ only one note, or, at the most, two (when an inversion is skipped, as in Exx. 3 and 4), would need to be struck, the remaining intervals, or interval, being sustained.

[3] 'Silence' here means merely that a fresh chord is not struck. On the Harpsichord this would be tantamount to silence, but not on the Organ.

[4] As in the following Ex., l.c. § 189:

[5] Ph. Em. Bach (*Versuch &c.*, Part II, Ch. 32, § 8) gives, among others, the following Exx. (an octave lower on a single stave) in which a different inversion of the previous harmony must be taken, even though not indicated in the figuring, in order to avoid consecutive octaves with the Bass; he says: "One can avoid many mistakes

It will be seen that Bach not only figures each inversion in full, but even the passing notes (the 6 on the 5th quaver of the bar is an appoggiatura) by which he wishes them connected.

Leclair, on the other hand, would probably have figured the passage:

and the accompanist would have been at liberty, either to treat it *exactly as figured by Bach*, passing notes connecting the harmonies being a recognized adornment at the discretion of the player (see Ch. iv, § 3 II *b*), or to retain the original chord:

by effecting an exchange between the upper parts and the passing notes of the Bass." Cf. Ch. xxii, 'Inversion &c.', § 2.

CHAPTER XXII

INVERSION AND TRANSFERENCE OF DISCORD. TRANSFERENCE OF RESOLUTION. *ANTICIPATIO TRANSITUS. CATACHRESIS*

XXII

INVERSION AND TRANSFERENCE OF DISCORD. TRANSFERENCE OF RESOLUTION. *ANTICIPATIO TRANSITUS. CATACHRESIS*

§ 1. There is nothing more characteristic of the free, as opposed to the strict, style than its greater freedom in the treatment of discords, as in the instances treated in the present chapter.

Inversion and transference of discord.

§ 2. Before the resolution of an essential discord inversion may take place, i.e. the Bass may effect an exchange with one or other of the upper parts, passing either from root position to a 1st inversion, from a 1st to a 2nd, a 2nd to a 3rd, or vice versâ as in Ex. 1:

Ex. 1

or the intermediate step may be skipped, as Ex. 2:

Ex. 2

When the transition is either to or from a $\frac{4}{2}$ chord, as in the above Ex., it is obvious that we get not only inversion but *transference of the discord* to or from the Bass.

Apart from this transference, in playing a figured Bass—whatever the vocal or instrumental parts may do—the discord must, except in the case of the dominant and diminished 7ths, remain in the same part, Ex. 3.

Ex. 3

XXII § 2   INVERSION AND TRANSFERENCE OF DISCORD, ETC.   839

In the case of the exceptions named this is not obligatory, Exx. 4 and 5,

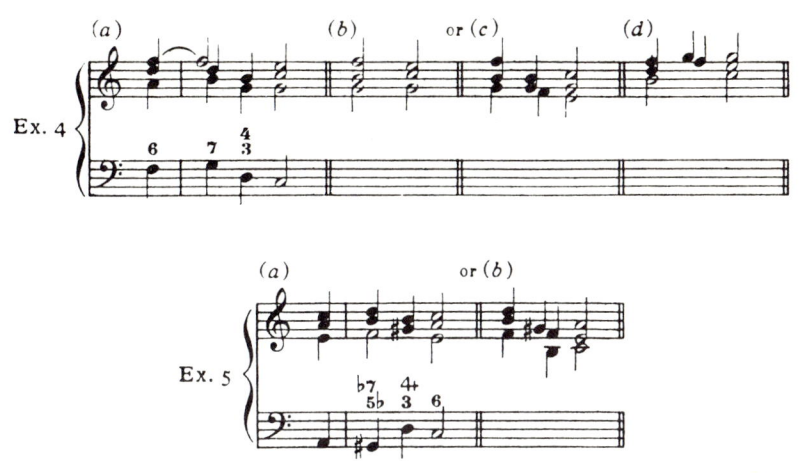

Ex. 4

Ex. 5

but upon general grounds (the avoidance of unnecessary skips and of intervals not tolerated at all in the strict style, as e.g. the augmented 4th in the Alto in Ex. 5 b) it is generally advisable, unless there is some special reason to the contrary, as, for instance, the desire to secure a particular melody in the top part of the accompaniment during the pauses of a solo, or to gain a higher or lower position for the right hand.

Similarly, where transference of the discord, to or from the Bass, takes place, the best progression of the upper parts is usually that which involves least movement, Exx. 6, 7.

Ex. 6

Ex. 7

When, however, instead of falling a degree, the Bass rises, either a minor 7th from a $\frac{7}{5}$ on the Dominant to a $\frac{6}{2}$, or a diminished 7th from the leading note of the minor scale to a $\frac{6}{4}{}_{2}$, contrary motion is sometimes best; especially so when the Bass subsequently falls to other inversions of the same harmony, Exx. 8 and 9, as the passage thereby gains in symmetry.

§ 3. *Transference of the resolution.*

Transference of the resolution takes place when some other part than that in which the discord occurs proceeds to the note on which the latter would normally resolve, leaving the discord itself free to move to some other interval of the chord in question.

It may occur in the case of either an essential discord or a suspension.

The transference may be either:

(1) From one upper part to another, as in Ex. 1:

This kind of transference occurs only in the vocal and instrumental parts, and does not affect the treatment of the accompaniment, in which the discords are resolved in the normal way. It will be noted that in (c) the note of resolution is not heard in its proper octave.

Or (2) from an upper part to the Bass, as Ex. 2:

XXII § 3 INVERSION AND TRANSFERENCE OF DISCORD, ETC.   841

Or (3) from the Bass to an upper part, as in Ex. 3:

Ex. 3

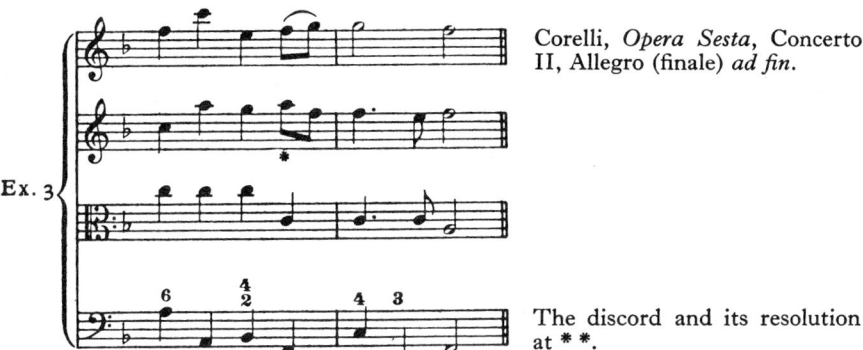

Corelli, *Opera Sesta*, Concerto II, Allegro (finale) *ad fin.*

The discord and its resolution at * *.

N.B.—In the above Ex. the presence of *c* in the Viola part, as well as the figuring $^4_2$, puts the nature of the chord beyond question. Examples may be found, similar in all respects as far as the Bass is concerned, figured $^6_4$ ($^6_{4\natural}$) on the Subdominant. Only an examination of the other parts can determine whether this is careless figuring, $^6_4 = {^6_{4\natural}_2}$ (see Ch. xxi, 'Incomplete figuring', IV, § 4), or whether the 2nd inversion of the imperfect triad on the leading note (of which the Bass is free in its progression, as in the subjoined examples) may be intended.

Corelli, *Opera seconda*, Sonata VI, *Allemanda*, 1st section *ad fin.*

Loeillet, *Opera Secunda*, XII Sonatas in three parts (Walsh), Sonata X, Allegro (finale), 2nd section *ad fin.*

Heinichen, *G-B. &c.*, 1728, Pt. 2, Ch. 1, "On the theatrical resolutions of discords", § 49, defines the matter as follows; after discussing in the preceding section, from which Ex. 1 above is taken, the transference of the resolution between two upper parts, he proceeds:‡ "The transference of the resolution which takes place between an upper part and the Bass is of more importance, and there are in practice two kinds in common use.

"(1) The first and best kind is when both parts make an exchange of the notes on which they would naturally resolve, so that the Bass steals the resolution of the upper part, and vice versâ.

‡ The quotation is abridged in parts.

"For example, the augmented 4th usually resolves on the 6th $\{{bc \atop fe}\}$; instead of this we get $\{{b \diagdown e \atop f \diagup c}\}$. Similarly for $\{{c\ b \atop \sharp f\ g}\}$ we get $\{{c \diagdown g \atop \sharp f \diagup b}\}$.

"(2) The second kind is when the Bass, it is true, steals the resolution of the upper part, but the latter, instead of retaliating, takes a third note of the chord, on which both parts would naturally resolve: e.g. $\{{b \diagdown g \atop f \diagdown c}\}$ for $\{{b\ c \atop f\ e}\}$, $\{{c \diagdown d \atop \sharp f \diagdown b}\}$ for $\{{c\ b \atop \sharp f\ g}\}$."

It will be noticed that Heinichen selects for illustration a discord of which both extremes have a fixed resolution, upward and downward respectively—a *terminus acutus* and *terminus gravis*, according to the old nomenclature. It will also be noticed that the accompanist is in no way concerned with the distinction drawn by Heinichen between the two kinds of transference. The two Exx. given would appear to him as [music] and the natural accompaniment would be [music] the resolution of the Bass being transferred to the Tenor and Alto respectively.

The first of the two progressions is shown in Ex. 3 above, in which the resolution of the Bass is transferred to the 2nd Violin.

§ 4. The cases in which a 7th is allowed to rise, when the Bass proceeds to the note on which it would naturally resolve, are of especial interest, as it is a progression which seems not to have been generally sanctioned till late in the eighteenth century. It will therefore be worth while to pass in review the references made to the subject by some of the chief authorities.

I. Heinichen, *G.-B. &c.*, 1728, in the chapter referred to in the preceding section, makes no mention of a 7th rising *in the figured Bass accompaniment*; in the only examples which he gives of a rising 7th, the transference of resolution is between the vocal or instrumental parts, and does not affect the accompaniment. Cf. § 3 above, Ex. 1.

II. Marpurg, *Handbuch &c.*, Pt. 2, 1757, pp. 101–2, Tab. 4, Figs. 12–15, remarks that the resolution of the 7th on the 8ve of the Bass is unsatisfactory *owing to the resulting hidden 8ves*. He recommends that the progression should be used only in full harmony, and that the 7th should be kept if possible in an inner part. As a remedy for the hidden 8ves he further suggests an arbitrary alteration of the Bass by inserting a 'changing' (or *accented* passing) note, Ex. 1.

XXII § 4 II INVERSION AND TRANSFERENCE OF DISCORD, ETC.

He proceeds to say that "any one whose conscience is not sufficiently elastic for this treatment may proceed as follows", i.e. by an ornamental resolution of the discord, Ex. 2:

Ex. 2

It will be noticed that the 7th in Marpurg's first Ex. is a suspension, and, in the latter, a dominant 7th. *In neither case is there any suggestion that the 7th should rise.*

There is, however, one case in which the 7th *must* rise, i.e. when a 7th on the Supertonic resolves, not on the dominant 7th, but on the 1st inversion of the latter, $^6_5$ on the leading note, which would therefore be doubled if the 7th on the Supertonic resolved downwards.

Marpurg simply disallows the progression.

Giving it in three parts only:

Ex. 3

and in letters instead of notes—'to save copper'[1] as he elsewhere expresses it—he says (ibid., Part 1, 1762, Abschnitt I, Absatz IV, § 42, 12, No. 3, pp. 59–60): "It is fundamentally wrong and irregular,[2] use it who

---

[1] Most of the musical Exx. are engraved on separate plates, while those incorporated in the text are given in a sort of tablature.

[2] From this we must infer that Marpurg would have likewise condemned the resolution of the Supertonic 7th—not, it is true, in root position, but in its 2nd inversion—on $^6_5$ on the leading note in the last bar of the following Ex.‡

Leclair, *Sonatas for Violin and Bass*, Bk. I, Paris, 1723, Sonata VII, Allemanda, 1st section, bars 9–11.

Violin

Accomp:

Bass

The rising of the 3rd in the ♭6 $\left(=\begin{smallmatrix}6\\4\\3\end{smallmatrix}\right)$ on *a* is exactly parallel to the rising of the 7th

---

‡ For the use of ♯ = ♮ in the Violin part and Bass, and of ♭6 = $\begin{smallmatrix}6\\4\\3\end{smallmatrix}$ on the 1st quaver of the last bar, see Ch. xxiv, § 2*b*, and Ch. xxiii, § 8.

844 INVERSION AND TRANSFERENCE OF DISCORD, ETC. XXII §4 II

may! Strict musicians improve this progression, even though the figures prescribe the contrary, by interposing a note of resolution, as follows."

Ex. 3b

in Ex. 3 which Marpurg condemns. The only possibility of 'improving the progression' by 'interposing a note of resolution' would be as follows:

thus making the discord resolve, as in Marpurg's 'improved' version of Ex. 3, on an inversion of the dominant 7th on the same Bass, with subsequent inversion of the harmony and transference of the discord as § 2, Ex. 2.

It must meanwhile be remembered that *f*, the second quaver of the bar, is on a par with the passing quavers in the previous bars and probably not intended to imply a change from a 2nd to a 1st inversion; the progression is substantially

and, if this had been what Leclair actually wrote, as it well might have been, the only possible 'improvement' of the progression, in Marpurg's sense, would involve the Bass itself in the 'interposed resolution'.

Marpurg's point of view is remarkable when we consider that Bk. I of Leclair's Sonatas, published thirty-four years before his own *Handbuch*, was probably known to him, as it was to Ph. Em. Bach, who alludes to it in his *Versuch*.

The temporary adoption of a 5th part in the accompaniment gives a more satisfactory progression; the most natural alternatives would be:

(1)

omitting the 6 from the $^6_5$ on ♮b and with thinly veiled 8ves:

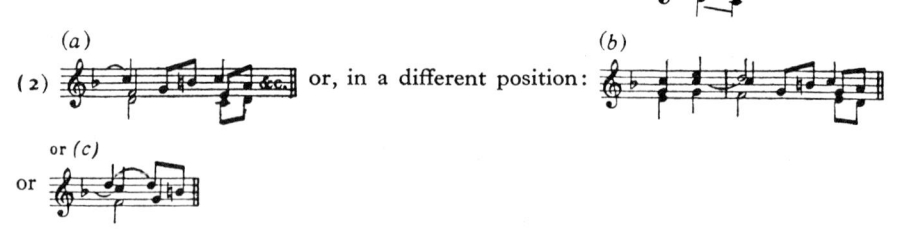

(2) (a) or, in a different position: (b)

or (c)
or

The 'guter Gesang', or smooth and melodious progression, especially of the top part, on which Ph. Em. Bach lays such constant stress, is the criterion which must guide the choice.

III. Ph. Em. Bach, *Versuch &c.*, Part II, 1762, Ch. 1, § 67, gives the following Exx.:

Ex. 4 *(a) (b) (c)* [musical example]

about which he says:

"When the Bass takes a note on which a discord in the right hand ought to resolve, it is called a transference ('Verwechselung') of the resolution; the discord is thereby set free, and leaves the resolution to the Bass. We leave it to composers to avail themselves of this licence in a suitable manner, and here merely make accompanists acquainted with it."

With regard to Ex. 4 *a*, the progression, as far as the rising [3] of the 7th is concerned, is on a par with Ex. 3 which Marpurg so unequivocally condemns; we therefore have an advance on his point of view.

Ex. 4 *b* differs from Ex. 1, in that the 7th is accompanied by the perfect 5th, which makes Marpurg's 'ornamental resolution' impossible, as the latter would result, either (1) in consecutive unisons: [musical example] or (2) in consecutive 5ths with the Bass:

[musical example]

There is also the (unaccented) passing note in the Bass (cf. Ex. 1) which makes the direct downward resolution of the 7th impossible.

[3] The chord figured $\begin{smallmatrix}7\\4\\\sharp\end{smallmatrix}$ may be taken either as $\begin{smallmatrix}7\\5\\\sharp\end{smallmatrix}$: [musical example], or as $\begin{smallmatrix}8\\7\\\sharp\end{smallmatrix}$: [musical example]

In the latter case, however, the 7th, instead of rising, may also fall a 4th: [musical example]

This is more appropriate when it is not in the top part. The progression of the 7th is then the same as in Ex. 4 *c* in which it appears in the 2nd inversion.

In all three cases the ♮g is to be regarded as an *anticipatio transitus* (see § 6) for:

[musical example]

This also applies to the ♭*b* in Ex. 4 *c*: [musical example] for [musical example]

846 INVERSION AND TRANSFERENCE OF DISCORD, ETC. XXII § 4 III

Ph. Em. Bach unfortunately does not indicate the *preparation* of the 7th.

If the complete progression were: [musical example] we should have a genuine suspended 7th, which sometimes included the perfect 5th (Ch. xi, IV, § 2).

If, on the other hand, the progression were: [musical example] we should have the familiar retardation [musical example] disguised by the interposed notes in the Bass. That being so, the natural progression of *a*, the 5th of the dominant chord, is upwards, and it is merely its temporary appearance in the guise of a 7th which suggests the idea of a 'transferred resolution', cf. § 6, Ex. 3.

In Bach's third example, Ex. 4 *c*, [musical example] it will be noticed that the dissonant note *f*, instead of rising a degree, falls a 4th (cf. note 3 above).

For a further example of a rising 7th, given by Ph. Em. Bach, see V *ad fin*.

IV. Kirnberger, who, it will be remembered, was a pupil of J. S. Bach, alludes to the matter only so far as the resolution of the dominant 7th is concerned.

In his (undated) *Grundsätze des General-Basses*, a work intended for beginners, he says (§ 97, p. 45): "It [the 7th] can never resolve on the 8ve of the Bass. For then the progression of the Bass would be a 3rd downwards, e.g. from *g* to *e*, and thus hidden 8ves would arise." He mentions no possibility of the 7th rising.

In his *magnum opus*, *Die Kunst des reinen Satzes &c.*, 1774, Abschnitt (Section) IV. 4, p. 66, he says: "If one passes from the chord of the Seventh, not to the Triad of the fundamental note (*Hauptton*) to which it leads, but to its 1st inversion, the 7th resolves on the 8ve. This resolution is forbidden to all beginners by masters of composition, because hidden 8ves arise thereby. However, we find nevertheless that good harmonists allow 7ths to resolve on the 8ve, by the inversion of the harmony on which the resolution takes place [i.e. when the 7th resolves on a 1st inversion]; but *this always happens in so-called contrary motion* [i.e. the Bass rises a 6th instead of falling a 3rd]." Still no mention of the 7th rising.

Later on, however, Abschnitt VI, p. 99, Kirnberger gives the following

XXII §4 IV INVERSION AND TRANSFERENCE OF DISCORD, ETC. 847

example in which the 7th rises, the resolution being regarded as transferred to the Bass:

Ex. 5

V. Schröter, *Deutliche Anweisung zum General-Bass*, 1772,[4] § 144, end of Ex., gives the following progression:

Ex. 6

of which he says, (*c*), p. 77: "In the 8th bar, where two 7ths follow one immediately after the other, a beginner must not imagine that the upward resolution of the first one is wrong; for this progression is nothing but the inversion of a single $^6_5$ chord (denn diese Tonfolge ist lediglich eine Versetzung des einzeln $^6_5$ = Satzes), as is clear from the eighth bar of the following example."

That is to say, the 7th on *f* is really a $^6_5$, and passes, without first resolving the suspended *e*, to its root position as a $^7_5$ on *d*. The progression is therefore equivalent to

the root progression being

In other words, Schröter explains the progression in question as originating in *ellipse of the resolution* or "*Catachresis*" (see § 8), the same explanation which, as we have seen, Marpurg implied in his correction of Ex. 3, the difference between the two theorists being that Schröter accepts the new development, without deeming 'correction' necessary.

Ph. Em. Bach, *Versuch &c.*, Part II, Ch. 13, II, § 4 *c*, gives the following example:

Ex. 7

---

[4] This work, though not published till 1772, was finished in 1754, as the date at the end shows.

848   INVERSION AND TRANSFERENCE OF DISCORD, ETC. XXII § 4 v

of which he says: "The first 7th over a changing [i.e. accented passing] note rises, because this $\frac{7}{5}$ is in reality a $\frac{6}{4}$ belonging to the following *e*." The root progression is therefore: [musical example]

If, however, instead of semiquavers, the Bass had been

[musical example]

the above explanation would, of course, not have held good; but Schröter's explanation of Ex. 6 would have applied; the progression would have been essentially [musical example] with ellipse of the resolution, the root progression being [musical example]

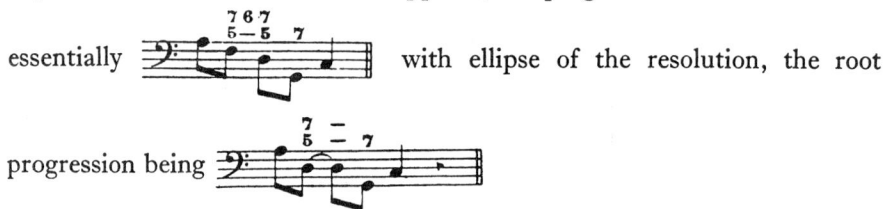

VI. Georg Michael Telemann (grandson of J. S. Bach's well-known contemporary, Georg Philipp Telemann) gives the following Exx., *Unterricht im Generalbass-Spielen*, 1773, Ch. 2, § 8, 6, p. 48:

Ex. 8 [musical example with (a) and (b)]

concerning which he says: "Sometimes the 7th must resolve upwards, namely when, at the moment of resolution, the Bass proceeds to the note, or a note of the same name, as that on which it ought to resolve."

The two Exx. are identical with Exx. 5 and 4 *b* respectively.

VII. Türk, *Kurze Anweisung zum Generalbassspielen*, 1791, § 35, p. 37, gives the following Ex.:

Ex. 9 [musical example]

which is identical with Exx. 5 and 8 *a*; and, in the corresponding section (§ 46, p. 58) of the 1822 edition of the same work, a further example is added, in which the 7th, instead of rising a degree, falls a 4th (cf. note 3 above):

Ex. 10 [musical example]

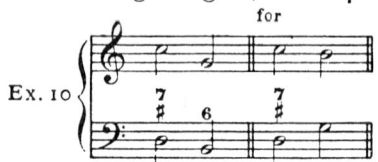

XXII § 4 VII INVERSION AND TRANSFERENCE OF DISCORD, ETC. 849

Thus, the exchange of progression (cf. extract from Heinichen in § 3) is complete.

§ 5. It becomes clear in the light of Schröter's example, § 4, Ex. 6, that, where one 7th follows another on a Bass falling a 3rd, *one or other of them stands for a* $^6_5$.

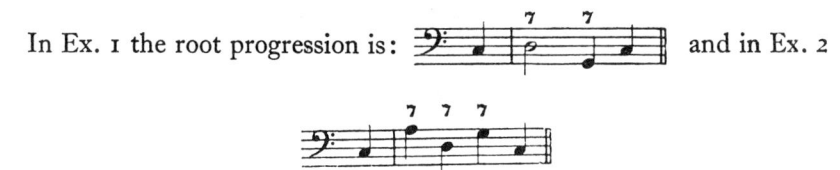

Ex. 1

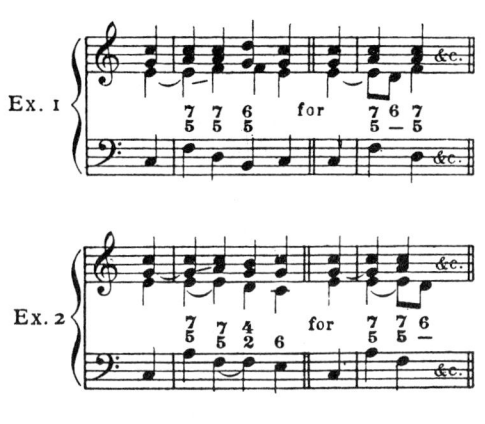

Ex. 2

In Ex. 1 the root progression is: and in Ex. 2

When it is the first of the two 7ths which stands for a $^6_5$, a downward resolution (at the expense of hidden 8ves, unless the Bass rises a 6th instead of falling a 3rd) is possible in four parts:

Ex. 3

but impossible in the contrary case, as the second 7th will lack the 5, which interval must be included in the first 7th, in order to prepare the second.

The alternatives will then be: (1) a 5-part accompaniment with downward resolution of the 7ths, *except where the Bass proceeds to a leading note* (cf. § 4, II), as Ex. 4; or (2) a 4-part accompaniment *with rising 7ths*, each of which will then include the 5th, the 3rd in the previous chord, as Ex. 5.

Ex. 4

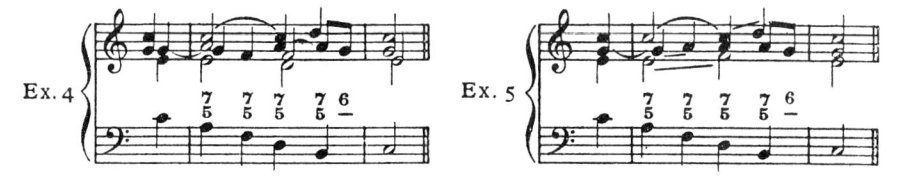

Ex. 5

850   INVERSION AND TRANSFERENCE OF DISCORD, ETC. XXII § 5

It is evident from Exx. 1 and 2 that in such a series of 7ths we have, in a disguised form, the root progression which Kirnberger made the criterion of an essential 7th (cf. Ch. xi, § 1), namely, a Bass rising a 4th or falling a 5th; and if we prolong the series, in a way little likely to be met with in actual practice, as Ex. 6:

we shall find that, *traced to its ultimate origin, every alternate 7th is an unresolved suspension*: , and that the root progression is:

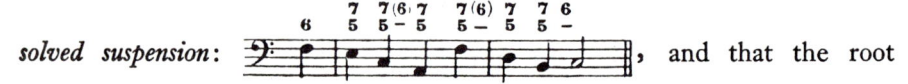

§ 6. The following Exx. of 7ths resolving on a Bass falling a 3rd will serve further to illustrate what has been said in the preceding sections:

Masciti (Napolitano), *Opera Sesta*, Sonata 15, for Violin, Viol da Gamba or Violoncello, and Bass, Largo, bar 12.

A direct downward resolution of the 7th would involve consecutive 8ves with the Bass; the accompaniment may therefore be treated, either as (*a*) (cf. § 4, Ex. 2 *b*), or as (*b*) (cf. ibid., Exx. 4 *b* and 8 *b*), or as (*c*):

N.B.—As in all other Exx., the chords are given in the position in which they are thought to sound best; but, in the absence of any express statement to the contrary, or any obvious reason, as e.g. in Ex. 2 *a*, where consecutive 5ths would result if the (rising) 7th on *b* were in the top part, the position is entirely optional.

XXII § 6 INVERSION AND TRANSFERENCE OF DISCORD, ETC. 851

Loeillet, *Opera Secunda*, XII Sonatas in Three Parts, Sonata 12, for 2 Flutes (traversi) and Bass, Allegro, 1st section *ad fin.*

Ex. 2

The 7 in this Ex. can be treated, either as (*a*) $= \frac{7}{5}\atop{3}$ with upward resolution, in which case, to avoid consecutive 5ths, the 7th must not be in the top part; or as (*b*) $= \frac{8}{7}\atop{3}$ with direct downward resolution; or as (*c*), or, in a different position (*cc*), with ornamental downward resolution.

N.B.—The above Ex. provides a good illustration of the type of mistake which it is not humanly possible always to avoid when accompanying compositions like the above, in which the accompanist has not got the vocal or instrumental parts before him, and more especially, as in the present instance, *when those parts abound in passing, or other ornamental notes, which are not part of the accompanying harmony*.

A very natural variety of (*cc*), and one which would provide a more interesting top part, would unfortunately involve consecutive 5ths * * with the purely ornamental notes ♯*f d* of the second Flute:

852 INVERSION AND TRANSFERENCE OF DISCORD, ETC. XXII § 6

Ph. Em. Bach, *Versuch &c.*, Part II, Ch. 13, II, § 2, Ex. *b*, remarks that the accompaniment, unless it lies above the solo part, [music] must be:

[music] to avoid the consecutive 5ths $\begin{smallmatrix}a&g\\d&c\end{smallmatrix}$, and adds: "This observation seems somewhat far-fetched; but with a slow *tempo* and delicate execution such 5ths are quite audible, and one is therefore bound to avoid them *provided the solo part is given above the Bass.*"

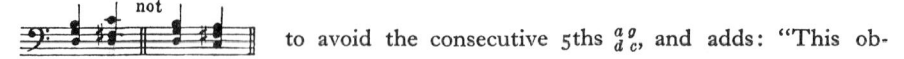

Ex. 3 [music]

Loeillet, *Opera Secunda*, XII Sonatas in Three Parts, Sonata I (for 2 Violins and Bass), Grave, bar 2.

As was pointed out in § 4 in connexion with Ex. 4 *b*, this is hardly to be regarded as an instance of genuine transference of the resolution, as the progression is clearly a sophisticated form of the common retardation:

[music]

The natural progression of the 7th on ♭*b* is therefore upwards, as (*a*); it can, however, also resolve downwards, hidden 8ves being avoided by an 'ornamental resolution', as (*b*); in this case the 3rd of the dominant chord (♯*f*), though, as leading note, it ought to rise, has, if in an inner part, the same licence to drop to the Dominant as in an ordinary cadence.

(*a*) [music]
(*b*) [music]

XXII § 6 INVERSION AND TRANSFERENCE OF DISCORD, ETC.

Leclair, Op. 4 (Walsh), Six Sonatas for 2 Violins and Bass, Sonata I, Allegro, bars 24-5.

Ex. 4

This is a very instructive example. The root progression in the second (complete) bar is: [musical example] in the temporary key of A minor.

It is, however, obscured by the fact that the 7th on *d* (really the minor 9th on *b*) delays its resolution till the dominant harmony is reached.

Thus the progression, instead of being: [musical example] cf. § 5, is:

[musical example]

If Leclair had contemplated a 4-part accompaniment with rising 7ths, he would probably have figured the passage: [musical example] and to treat it as though so figured is a very slight and pardonable liberty, as it gives a much better progression if the 7th over *d* resolves upwards over *b*, thus preparing the imperfect 5th over ♯*g*; if, on the contrary, Leclair's figuring be strictly adhered to, the *c* must not rise:

[musical example]

as its resolution could no longer be regarded as transferred to the Bass.

The alternatives would be, either (1) [musical example] in which, while the 7th on *d* resolves properly, the imperfect 5th on ♯*g* is taken unprepared in a way not strictly in accordance with the rules even of the free style (cf. Ch. xii, § 1), quite apart from the absence of smooth melodic progression ('guter Gesang') on which Ph. Em. Bach so constantly insists; or (2) the temporary adoption of a 5th part: [musical example]

854   INVERSION AND TRANSFERENCE OF DISCORD, ETC. XXII § 6

If, therefore, we take the suggested liberty with the figuring, the accompaniment, in four parts, will be as (*a*); it will be noticed that the position in which the chords are taken is the only one which leaves room for the highest note of the Bass, without exceeding the usual upward compass of the accompaniment:

It is, however, more likely that Leclair contemplated a 5-part accompaniment with all the 7ths resolving downwards, at the expense even of the consecutive 8ves caused by the passing notes in the Bass.

Born 1697, he may well not have accepted the upward resolution of the 7th any more than Marpurg, cf. § 4, 11. Indeed this is highly probable, for we know that Marpurg was largely influenced by Rameau, and it is more than likely that Leclair based his own ideas of harmony on those of his great compatriot and contemporary. Moreover, in the seventeenth and earlier eighteenth centuries, composers were far less sensitive to hidden 8ves than they became later, and even *actual consecutives between an inner part and a florid Bass* were tolerated, as is evident from the following Exx.: ‡

Heinichen, *G.-B. &c.*, 1728, Pt. I, Ch. 4, § 16, p. 273.

‡ Ph. Em. Bach was much more strict, as will be seen from the following example:

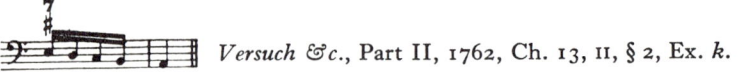

Versuch &c., Part II, 1762, Ch. 13, 11, § 2, Ex. *k*.

of which he says: "Consecutive octaves will result if the 7th is accompanied by the 5th."

The consecutive 8ves could be avoided by allowing the 5th to rise to the 3rd of the following chord; in that case, however, the leading note ♯g would have to rise to *a* instead of dropping to the Dominant, as its note of resolution would otherwise not be present, and the tonic chord would lack the 5th:

the remedy would be a 5-part accompaniment:

If this reasoning be correct, Leclair, whose figurings constantly demand five parts, probably had in mind some such accompaniment as (*b*):

The following points are to be noted: (1) that the chord over *d* in the 2nd bar must be taken in such a position that the 3rd is *above* the 7th, in order to avoid consecutive 5ths $^{c\,b}_{f\,e}$ with the following chord; (2) that this position is gained by taking in an extra part on the top of the preceding chord, and immediately dropping the lower part, as indicated by the rests (cf. Ch. iii, § 4); (3) that this procedure is necessary, as the usual compass of the accompaniment would be exceeded if the first chord of the passage were taken in a higher position with the 5th, *a*, on the top; (4) that, though minims have been used in the above Ex., as making the progression clearer to the eye, on the Harpsichord the full harmony would as a rule be struck on every beat of the bar.

It may be remarked in conclusion that the suggested accompaniment (*a*), even if slightly anachronistic, is far more satisfactory on a modern Piano, and, of course, on the Organ, whereas (*b*) is eminently suited to the Harpsichord.

§ 7. '*Anticipatio transitus*', or the anticipation of a passing note.

This term is somewhat misleading, as the characteristic feature, in the great majority of instances, is not so much the anticipation of a passing note as the *ellipse or suppression of the note from which it is supposed to pass.*

When such is the case, the full designation is *anticipatio transitus per ellipsin.*

This ellipse explains the origin of the unprepared use of the dominant 7th and its inversions in the free style, as well as that of various progressions which at first sight seem irregular.

Heinichen, *G.-B. &c.*, 1728, Pt. 2, Ch. 1, § 14, note *d*, pp. 603-6, gives, among others, the following Exx.:

856 INVERSION AND TRANSFERENCE OF DISCORD, ETC. XXII § 7

In (a) the ellipse and anticipation are in the Bass, in (b) (c) in the upper part, and in (d) (e) in both.

Further on in the same Ch. (§ 42, p. 686), Heinichen gives further Exx. of 'anticipation' in the Bass:

Ex. 2

N.B.—Being, for the moment, concerned with the Bass only, Heinichen disregards the 'anticipation' in the upper part of (c) which should have been figured

He also forgets that the progression [music] in (d) is itself due to *anticipatio transitus*, the progression being [music] or, with passing notes:

Marpurg, *Versuch über die musikalische Temperatur &c.*, § 255, Figs. 26 and 27, gives the following Exx., Ex. 3 a being practically identical with Ex. 2 c:

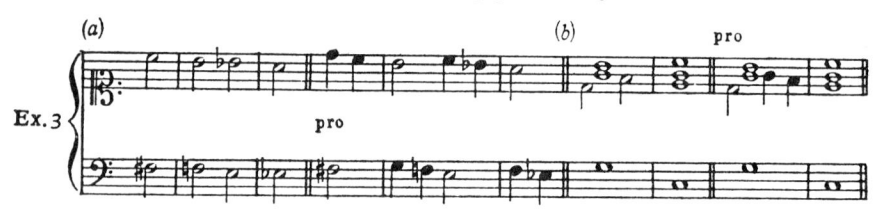

Ex. 3

As was mentioned above, the term *anticipatio transitus* is generally understood to connote the ellipse of the main note (*anticipatio transitus per ellipsin*), but a familiar example of anticipation *without* the ellipse is the resolution of the dominant 7th on the Submediant, which undoubtedly has its origin in a passing note,

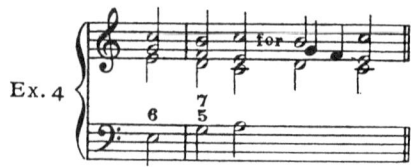

Ex. 4

XXII § 8 INVERSION AND TRANSFERENCE OF DISCORD, ETC. 857

§ 8. *Ellipse of the resolution.*

An apparently incorrect progression of a discord is sometimes due to the ellipse or suppression of the resolution, commonly known as *Catachresis* (καταχρησις = misuse); such a progression is then known as a catachrestic or elliptic resolution.

It will be noticed that *anticipatio transitus per ellipsin* may involve the suppression of a note essential to the resolution of a preceding discord, as § 7, Ex. 2 (*b*) (*c*), and Ex. 3 (*a*); such Exx. might therefore with equal propriety be included in the present section.

Kirnberger, *K. d. r. S. &c.*, Abschnitt (section) V, 3, p. 85, in enumerating the liberties of the free style in the treatment of discords, puts the matter as follows:

"Thirdly, the resolution of the Seventh can actually be passed over; that is to say, the consonant chord resulting from the resolution can be omitted, and another dissonant chord taken at once, of which the dissonance would have been prepared by the chord omitted. Thus, instead of the progression

we can, by omitting the chord marked *, take the following:

Ex. 1

From such instances, in which, owing to this omission, two dissonant chords follow one immediately upon the other, yet other progressions arise through inversions of the harmony, as, for example:

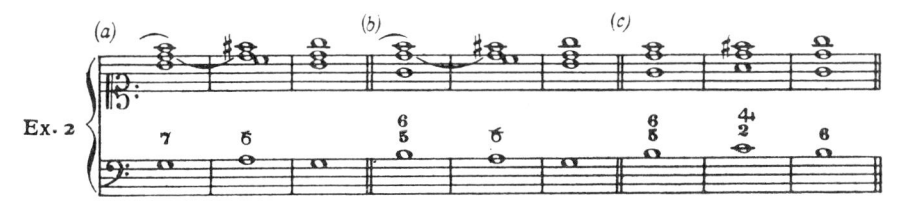

Ex. 2

In other words, the root progression , of which the outstanding feature is the progression of the first 7th a semitone upwards, having once been established, as in Ex. 1, the manner of its origin is forgotten, and

858 INVERSION AND TRANSFERENCE OF DISCORD, ETC. XXII § 8

the same root progression appears in inversions in which the hypothetical connecting link is not so easily supplied.[1]

Heinichen gives some instructive examples of *catachresis* further complicated by transference of the resolution. After illustrating his definition of the latter quoted in § 4, he continues, l.c., § 62:

"It is on this foundation and on this rule that all examples hitherto given are based. But if any one wants to see some examples *in contrarium* it is only necessary to prefix a ♯, either to the Bass of an ordinary transferred resolution, or to some other interval of the chord; if, for instance, one alters the following transferred resolutions as follows: Ex.3

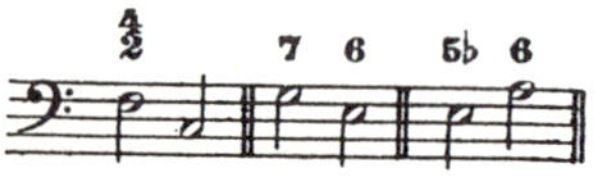

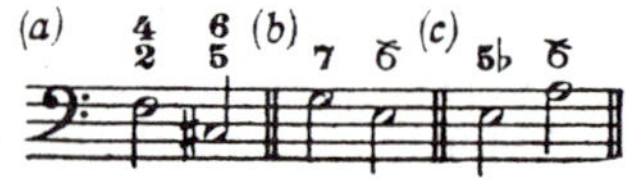

we get in the first example, in place of the previous triad and perfect 5th, an imperfect 5th accompanied by the 6th; accordingly the notes of the chord no longer correspond to the notes $\binom{6}{e}$ on which the resolution would naturally take place. The two last Exx. retain, it is true, the harmony of a Sixth as before, but, as these Sixths have become major, instead of minor as before, the notes of the chord again fail to correspond exactly to the notes $\binom{5}{3}{c}$ and $\binom{5}{3}{\sharp}$ on which the resolution would naturally take place. One must therefore except such examples from the general rule and pass them as good, not only because they resolve properly, but because the chief difference of the transferred intervals is only that of an accidental sharp." (!!)

This extract is given in full as a characteristic example of the slipshod ideas of harmony prevalent at the time, as revealed in the last few lines.

[1] We can, it is true, regard (*c*) as standing for   but, in the case of (*a*), though the progression of each individual part is the same, the hypothetical progression   is much more artificial; we might, it is true, take refuge in   as an alternative, but the root progression will then no longer be the same.

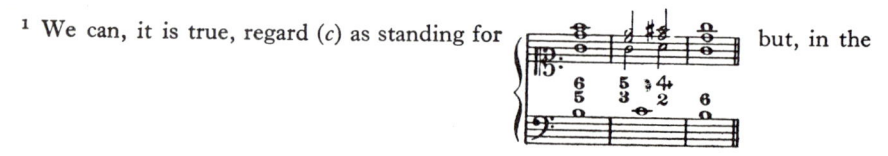

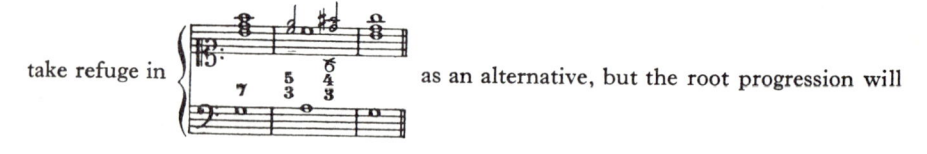

In (*b*) we have to assume the transference of the resolution of the first bass note *b* to an upper part; cf. § 3.

XXII § 8 INVERSION AND TRANSFERENCE OF DISCORD, ETC.

Kirnberger would doubtless have explained the progressions in question by assuming an ellipse of the chords marked * * *.

[musical example]

Such irregular progressions are most often met with in Recitatives,[2] being commonly associated with poignant or dramatic utterances, and belong therefore, not only to the free, but especially to the theatrical style.

Heinichen gives an example, without, however, adding words, of the *catachrestic* progressions [musical example] further modified by transference of the resolution, as used in a Recitative.

Ex. 4 [musical example]

Leclair, *Opera IV*, Six Sonatas for two Violins and Bass, Sonata III, bars 18–19.

Ex. 5 [musical example]

---

[2] Ph. Em. Bach (*Versuch &c.*, Part II, Ch. 38, § 1) says with regard to these abnormal progressions: "Not very long ago Recitatives were, so to speak, crammed with nothing but transferences of the harmony and of the resolution and enharmonic changes (Verwechselungen der Harmonie, der Auflösung und der Klanggeschlechter). A special beauty was sought, generally without the slightest reason, in these harmonic curiosities, and the natural changes of harmony were thought too tame for the Recitative. Thanks be to the sound taste, owing to which unusual harmonies are nowadays only very rarely, and with adequate reason, introduced in Recitatives. The accompanist need not therefore suffer the same anxiety in the performance of the Recitatives of the present sort as formerly."

860   INVERSION AND TRANSFERENCE OF DISCORD, ETC. XXII § 8

The above Ex. furnishes a striking instance of 'ellipse'.
The progression evidently stands for

or, clearing the suspensions:

CHAPTER XXIII
VARIETIES OF FIGURING

XXIII

VARIETIES OF FIGURING

1. § 1. For 1 as an alternative to 8 see s.v. 8, § 12, and 10, 11, 12, 13, 14, § 15.

2. § 2. 2 and 2+ are equivalent to ♯2, and are also used instead of ♮2 to indicate the contradiction of a ♭.[1]

3. § 3. Instead of ♯3 ♮3 ♭3 we commonly find ♯ ♮ ♭, omitting the figure.[2]

In the older figured Basses ♯ and ♭ were used to indicate a major and minor 3rd respectively, even when the 3rd became major by the contradiction of a flat, and minor by the contradiction of a sharp. Niedt, *Musicalische Handleitung*, Hamburg, 1700, Cap. VIII, Regula 3, gives the following Ex.:

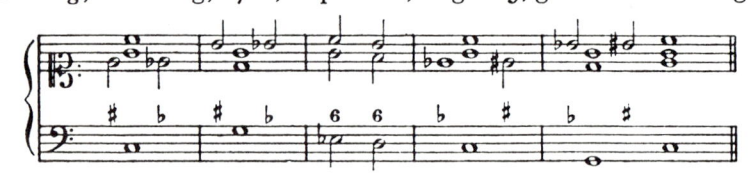

4. § 4. An augmented 4th is indicated, either by ♯4, ×4, or 4+ when augmented by the addition of a sharp, and (except in the earlier Basses) by ♮4 or 4+ when augmented by the contradiction of a flat—or by 4+ in *both* cases.

N.B.—The figuring 4+ (♯4 ×4) is sometimes found even when the augmentation of the interval is not accidental, or where it is due to the accidental lowering of the Bass, as in the Ex. given below.[3]

In all works printed by Roger of Amsterdam we find 4+ = ♭4. This must not be confused with 4+.

5. § 5. Common uses. (1) 5, ♯5, ♭5, 5♭, 5+ are used in all keys to indicate a diminished Fifth, very often irrespective of whether the latter be diatonic

---

[1] N.B.—It is purely a matter of convenience whether the accidental is placed before or after the figure to which it belongs. In the case of double figures the accidental is sometimes found before the one figure and after the other, as ♭7/5♭.

[2] This is probably the reason why, in the case of 3, a stroke through the figure (3 or 3) to indicate the raising of the interval never came into general use. Schröter, however, in the Ex. given below, *General-Bass*, 1772, § 214, uses 3 to indicate an *augmented* 3rd:

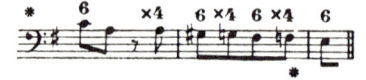

Leclair, *Sonatas for Violin and Bass*, Bk. 2, Sonata I, Allegro, 2nd section, bar 10.

XXIII § 5   VARIETIES OF FIGURING   863

or accidental;[1] 5 (without either stroke or ♭) is so used only when the interval in question is diatonic (Ex. 4), while ♮5 (as the indication of a diminished Fifth) always denotes the contradiction of a ♯, either diatonic (Ex. 2), or accidental (Ex. 3).

(*a*) as an abbreviated equivalent for ♭$^6_5$ (see Ch. xii, § 1).

Wm. Boyce, *XII Sonatas for 2 Violins with Bass*, London, Walsh, 1747. Sonata I, Largo, bars 17-20.

Ex. 1

C. F. Abel, Op. 3, *Six Sonatas for 2 Violins &c.*, London, Sonata IV, Moderato, 2nd section, bar 34.

Ex. 2

Ibid., Andantino, bar 29.

Ex. 3

N.B.—In the first of the two latter Exx. the 5th is accidentally flattened, while in the second the Bass is accidentally sharpened.

Pergolese, *Twelve Sonatas for 2 Violins and a Bass*, London, R. Bremner, Sonata V, Larghetto, bars 18-21.

Ex. 4

Composers sometimes assume that the 5th (whether it actually appears in the figuring or not) is perfect unless the contrary is indicated, as in the two Exx. below:

Leclair, *Sonatas for Violin and Bass*, Bk. I, Paris, 1723, Sonata VI, Allegro.

(In bar 61 it is of course *possible* that Leclair may have intended a false relation between ♯c in the Violin (ascending melodic scale) and ♮ in the accompaniment, but if so he would almost certainly have figured the Bass either 7 or $^7_5$.)

But composers were seldom consistent in these details as the following Ex. shows:

Leclair, ibid., Sonata VII, Giga, Section 1, bar 9.

864   VARIETIES OF FIGURING   XXIII § 5

Antonio Vivaldi, *Suonate da Camera A Tre*, Op. 1, Amsterdam, Roger, Sonata XI, Preludio, 2nd section, bars 4-6.

Ex. 5

It will be noticed that in bar 4 the full figuring $^6_5$ is used.[2]

Giuseppe Valentini, *XII Suonate à Tre*, Op. 5, Amsterdam, Roger, Sonata IV, 'La Garzia', Allegro, 2nd section, bars 15-17.

Ex. 6

The imperfect 5ths † † † † are due to the sharpening of the Bass and those * * are diatonic. For an example of $5 = {}^6_5$ see Ex. 10.

(*b*) As a diminished Triad:

A. Vivaldi, Op. 1, Sonata VI, Preludio, bars 1-3.

Ex. 7

Wm. Boyce, *XII Sonatas &c.*, Sonata I, Fuga, bars 24-8.

Ex. 8

(24)   (25)   (26)   (27)   (28)

The use of ♭5 ♮5 5 = $^6_5$ renders it necessary to watch the course of the harmony very carefully in order to recognize when an imperfect Triad is indicated, as at × and ‡ in the above Ex. As a rule little difficulty will be experienced, if it is remembered that the two chief cases where the 6th must not be included are (1) when in the course of a sequence the 7th degree of a major scale bears a Triad (as at × in the above Ex., the music at that point being in C major), (2) when the bass note figured ♭5 ♮5 5 is the Supertonic of a minor key, as at ‡ of the above Ex., the key at the moment being D minor.

[2] There is no point in which composers are more inconsistent, $^6_5$ and ♭5 occurring at random in the same passage. When two successive notes of a Bass rising by step bear $^6_5$ chords with a diminished 5th in the second one, it is very common to find the first one figured in full as below:

Wm. Boyce, *XII Sonatas*, Sonata I, Fuga, bars 47-9.

[3] In order to avoid 8ves with the Bass, the second quaver of bars 25, 26, 27 must be accompanied as though figured $^4_3$. See Ch. xxi, 'Incomplete figuring', v, § 3, note 5.

XXIII § 5   VARIETIES OF FIGURING   865

Some composers use the figuring $\frac{8}{5}$ to indicate the diminished triad on the 2nd degree of the minor scale.

Leclair, *Sonatas for Violin and Bass*, Bk. I, Paris, 1723.
Sonata VI, Allegro, bar 10.

Ex. 9

In another work Leclair uses $\natural = \flat\frac{6}{5}$ and $\flat 5 = \flat\frac{8}{5}$, * * and † in the following Ex. The Ex. deserves to be given in full.

Leclair, *Six Sonatas for 2 Violins and Bass*, Op. 4,
London, Walsh. Sonata II, Allegro, bars 61–3.

Ex. 10

V⁰ I

V⁰ II

Bass

(61)   (62)   (63)

N.B.—On the last quaver of bar 62 a 5th part must be taken in (see Ch. iii, § 4) doubling the Bass, a temporary 'leading-note'.

(a) (b)

N.B.—At (*a*) the new part is *g*, doubling the Bass, while at (*b*) the bottom part, *d*, 'evaporates' and the *f* proceeds to the ♭*e* of the following chord.

This explanation is necessary, as at first sight the progression of the 2nd and 3rd quavers of bar 63 presents the appearance of 8ves $\begin{smallmatrix}d & \flat e\\ d & \flat e\end{smallmatrix}$ with the Bass.

As a means of distinguishing at a glance between a $\frac{6}{5}$ chord and a diminished Triad, G. P. Telemann invented the sign ⌒, to be placed over the figure, $\overset{\frown}{5}\overset{\frown}{\flat 5}$, to indicate the absence of the 6th. Ph. Em. Bach, *Versuch &c.*, Part II, Ch. 4, § 3, commends the device, but unfortunately it never came into general use.[4]

[4] Ph. Em. Bach uses Telemann's ⌒ throughout the 2nd part of his *Versuch*, both in the case mentioned above, and also to denote the absence of the 3 in a chord figured $\frac{6}{5}$, either by the use of a 3-part accompaniment (Ch. xii, '$\frac{6}{5}$ chords', § 8 (1), Ex. 2), or by doubling the Bass (ibid., § 6 (1), Exx. 1–3), or even the 6 (ibid., Ex. 4). He also uses it in the case of $\frac{8}{6}, \frac{4}{2}$, &c., to denote a 3-part accompaniment (*Versuch &c.*, Part II, Ch. 3, 1, § 19; ibid., Ch. 9, 1, § 15 *et passim*). In short, though not necessarily restricting the accompaniment to three parts, the sign ⌒ always indicates the absence of an interval, not actually specified in the figuring, but one which would ordinarily be included in the chord in question.

G. M. Telemann mentions that his grandfather, the inventor of the sign, never used it in his earlier compositions. *Unterricht im Generalbass-Spielen &c.*, Hamburg, Section (Abschnitt) 2, Cap. 1, § 11, p. 61.

(2) 5✝ is used by some composers instead of ♯5 to indicate a 5 accidentally sharpened.

N.B.—5✝ must not be confused with 5♮ = ♭5.

(*a*) = a perfect 5th:

Giuseppe Valentini, *XII Suonate à Tre*, Op. 5, Amsterdam, Roger. Sonata V, 'la Pacini', Largo, bar 12.

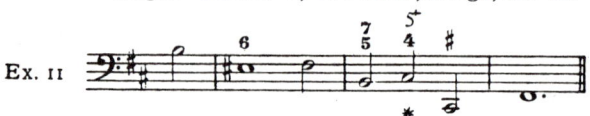

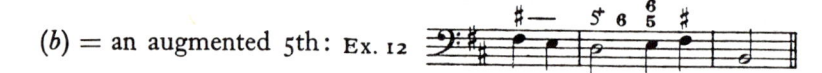

Ex. 11

(*b*) = an augmented 5th: Ex. 12

Ex. 13

G. M. Telemann, *Unterricht im Generalbass-Spielen &c.*, Hamburg, 1773, Section (Abschnitt) 2, Cap. 1, § 5, p. 57.

When a 5th is sharpened by the contradiction of a ♭ the correct figuring is ♮5, but 5✝ is sometimes found. Apropos of this loose usage and the use of ♭ to contradict a ♯, Ph. Em. Bach, *Versuch &c.*, Part II, Cap. 1, § 35, says: "One must not let oneself be puzzled, if some people occasionally put flats (♭) over the [bass] notes, and strokes through the figures instead of the 'B quadratum' (♮). The varying significance of this 'B quadratum', which sometimes flattens and sometimes raises a note, may possibly be responsible for this indiscriminate sort of practice."

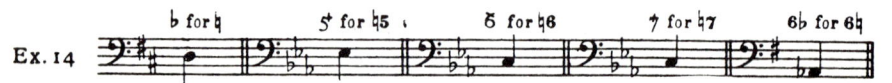

Ex. 14   ♭ for ♮   5✝ for ♮5   6̸ for ♮6   7̸ for ♮7   6♭ for 6♮

"In the case of the imperfect 5th and the diminished 7th, one is more accustomed to their usually appearing with a ♭."

§ 6. Exceptional uses. Normally, as we have seen in the preceding section, a stroke through the *body* of the 5 (5̸) flattens, while a stroke through the top (5✝) sharpens. But exceptional uses occur.

In two different works, printed by different publishers—an important factor in the matter of details of figuring—C. F. Abel, a celebrated player on the Viol da Gamba and composer in the eighteenth century, used the figuring 5̸ in two quite different senses, both entirely at variance with the ordinary practice.

XXIII § 6   VARIETIES OF FIGURING   867

(a) In his *Six Sonatas for two Violins, or a German Flute and Violin, with a Thoroughbass for the Harpsichord*, Opera III, London, printed for the author, Abel uses 5̸, alternating indiscriminately with ⁶₅, to indicate a ⁶₅ chord whether the 5th be diminished or *perfect*.

Thus he uses it repeatedly for a ⁶₅ on the Subdominant.

Sonata I, Minuetto, 1st section, bar 5:   2nd section, bar 19:

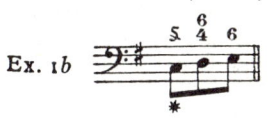

Ex. 1a   Ex. 1b

Sonata III, Adagio, bars 16–18:

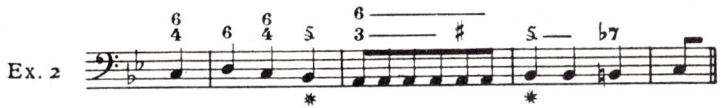

Ex. 2

Note.—Where the 5th is flattened accidentally, or by the contradiction of a preceding accidental, Abel uses 5♮ in sharp keys and 5♭ in flat keys.

(b) In his *Troi (sic) Trios pour le Violon, Violoncelle et Basso*, Amsterdam, chez S. Markordt (no date or opus-number), Abel uses 5̸ to indicate a 5th accidentally *sharpened*!

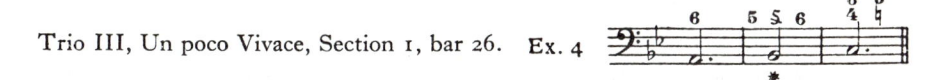

Trio I, Vivace, bar 16. Ex. 3   N.B.—The Violin has ♯d.

Trio III, Un poco Vivace, Section 1, bar 26.   Ex. 4

Note.—In these Trios Abel uses 5♮ 5♭ = ♮⁶₅ ♭⁶₅ (as in the Sonatas) and ⁶₅ in all other cases.

6. § 7. Normal uses. A stroke through the figure (6̸) denotes the rise [1] of a semitone, otherwise indicated by ♯ ♮ [2] (prefixed to, or following the figure), and changes:

(1) a minor into a major 6th:

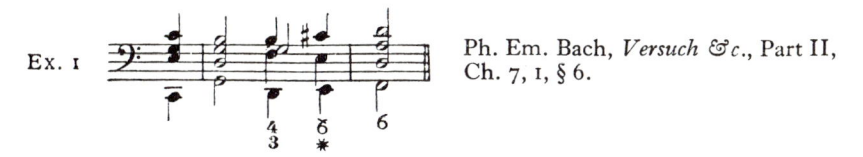

Ex. 1   Ph. Em. Bach, *Versuch &c.*, Part II, Ch. 7, I, § 6.

[1] N.B.—6̸ must not be confused with 6' = ♭6.
[2] Some composers, e.g. Mattheson, *Organisten-Probe*, use 6̸ irrespective of whether the interval is raised by the addition of a sharp or the contradiction of a flat, others use 6̸ in the former case only, and ♮6 in the latter.

(2) a major into an augmented 6th:

Ex. 2 [musical example] Ibid., Ch. 3, 1, § 21.

Note.—It would be interesting to know who first used a stroke to denote the raising, or, in the case of a stroke through the body of a 5 (5̵), the flattening, of an interval. It is not found in Purcell's *Sonnatas of 3 parts*, 1683, or his *Sonatas in 4 parts*, 1697, or in Dr. John Blow's MS. "Rules for playing a Thorough Bass upon Organ and Harpsicon" (Ch. i, § 22), or in the first edition of Corelli's Op. 5, *Sonate a violino e violone o cimbalo*, Rome, 1700, or in A. Scarlatti's MS. 'Principi', Brit. Mus. Add. 14244, or in Gasparini's *L'armonico pratico*, 3rd ed., Venice, 1729. On the other hand, Niedt, *Musicalische Handleitung*, Hamburg, 1700, uses 4̸ = an augmented 4th and 6̸ = a 6th raised by a semitone, while an imperfect 5th is denoted by 5♭ (Cap. IX *ad fin.*, 2nd bar of Ex.). This looks as if 4̸ and 6̸ came into use earlier than 5̵ (= an imperfect 5th), and also as if they came into use earlier in Germany than in Italy.

Ph. Em. Bach, *Versuch &c.*, Part II, Berlin, 1762, Cap. 1, § 39, says: "The practice of using a stroke [i.e. to raise an interval] is familiar and usual everywhere here in Germany. The Italians also have it; it is only the French who diverge in this matter and cause confusion. Look at the figured basses of le Clair, who marked diatonic major intervals, as well as those accidentally minor, both alike with a stroke."

How misleading this was we shall see from the following section on Leclair's use of 6̸. Ph. Em. Bach does not seem to have realized: (1) that the purpose of Leclair's 6̸ (used *only* in the first of his four books of Sonatas for the Violin and Bass) is to denote the presence of the 4 in the chord $\left(6̸ = {6 \atop {4 \atop 3}}\right)$; or (2) that Leclair used 6̸ quite irrespective of whether the 6th in question (major or minor) was diatonic or accidental; or (3) that a stroke through the figure to indicate the raising of an interval by a semitone (quite in accordance with Ph. Em. Bach's own practice) *is* found in the works of French composers early in the eighteenth century, e.g. the Sonatas for Violin and Bass of Senallié le fils, the first book of which was published in Paris in 1710.

§ 8. Leclair's use of $6̸ = {6 \atop {4 \atop 3}}$. In his *Premier Livre de Sonates à Violon Seul avec La Basse Continue*, Paris, 1723, Leclair uses 6̸ to denote a ${6 \atop {4 \atop 3}}$ chord, *whether the 6th be major or minor*. An accidental alteration of the interval is denoted by × (= ♯) ♮ ♭ prefixed to the figure (see Ch. xxiv, § 2 b, 'Accidentals').

Ex. 1 [musical example] Sonata I, Adagio, bars 3 and 4.

Sonata I, Allemande, Allegro, 2nd section, bars 5–9.

Ex. 2 [musical example]

VARIETIES OF FIGURING

Note.—Where an interval of the chord other than the 6 is accidentally altered, the chord is figured in full.

Sonata XII, Largo, 1st section *ad fin.*

Sonata III, Tempo Gavotta, 1st section *ad fin.*

Ex. 3

Sonata XI, Giga, 2nd section, bars 18–22.

Ex. 4

In a short preface ('Avertissement') to his first book of Sonatas Leclair says: 'Le chiffre 6̶ designe l'accord de la Sixte accompagnée de la Tierce et de la Quarte, et nullement la Sixte Majeure, par ce que cette Sixte se trouve naturellement mineure: mais lors qu'elle devient accidentellement majeure ou mineure, on trouve pour lors un ╳ [= ♯] ou un ♭ à coté de ce chiffre 6̶.' This latter statement he modifies by adding a little further on 'Cette petite croix × tient lieu du ╳ parmi les chiffres'. Why Leclair should have used a ╳ in front of a note and a × (denoting exactly the same thing) in front of a figure, it is hard to say. The practice is by no means to be commended as a × was used by some composers to indicate a *double* sharp. See Ch. xxiv, § 3.

Leclair evidently felt the desire to modify the existing system of figuring, for he adds further on: "Je n'ay osé d'avantage épurer ma maniere de chiffrer, crainte de me trop éloigner de l'usage ordinaire: mais il seroit à souhaiter qu'on en donnat par ecrit des régles qu'un chacun voulut bien suivre."

Leclair's use of the 6̶ evidently was not popular, for in the 'Avertissement' to the second book of Violin Sonatas he says, 'J'ay jugé à propos dans ma maniere de chiffrer, de retrancher la petite barre qui designoit l'accord de la petite sixte,[1] quoy que ce fut plus correct: mais l'usage l'emporte sur mon sentiment.'

It was a great pity that he allowed the existing usage to 'outweigh his feelings', for in the 2nd, 3rd, and 4th books of Violin Sonatas he seldom troubled to use the figuring $^4_3$ (perhaps from a sense of pique), except when the 4 or 3 (or both) were accidentally altered.

A careful examination of the passages in the 1st book (*excluding* those cases in which it is *generally* accepted that 4 may be included in the chord though not expressed in the figuring [2]) shows that he must undoubtedly have wished

---

[1] 'la petite sixte' was Rameau's name for a $^6_4_3$ chord, as opposed to 'la grande sixte', the $^6_5$ on the subdominant.

[2] Cf. Ch. xxi, II, § 1.

the 4 included in a great number of chords in books 2, 3, and 4, which he figures with nothing but 6.

The cases in which Leclair used the figure $\stackrel{6}{6} = \stackrel{6}{\stackrel{4}{3}}$ may be divided into two main groups:

(1) In cadences, in which he used the 2nd inversion of a 7th on the Supertonic (i.e. 6 on the Submediant) almost as freely as the familiar 1st inversion, i.e. $\stackrel{6}{5}$ on the Subdominant.

(2) In 7 6 sequences, where he loved to make $\stackrel{7}{\stackrel{5}{3}}$ resolve on $\stackrel{6}{\stackrel{4}{3}}$, thus giving a sequence of essential discords, 2nd inversions alternating with root positions:

Ex. 5

being the same progression as

How thin is the dividing line between so-called essential discords and so-called suspensions!

§ 9. Leclair's 'cadential' use of $\stackrel{6}{6} = \stackrel{6}{\stackrel{4}{3}}$ is, again, of two kinds. In one, and by far the largest, class of Exx. the discordant note of the chord, the 3rd, is *prepared*, like the 5th in the most familiar cadential form of the $\stackrel{6}{5}$ on the subdominant.

Ex. 1   Sonata IV, Allegro, bar 2.

Ex. 2   Sonata II, Corrente, antepenultimate bar.

Ex. 3   Sonata VII, Adagio, penultimate bar.

Ex. 4   Sonata I, Aria (major), 1st section, bar 14.

In another set of Exx. the discord is taken *unprepared*.‡

‡ Compare Ex. 4 with Ex. 5 (from the same movement) and observe in Ex. 5 the 4 3 suspension resolving on the strong beat.

VARIETIES OF FIGURING

Ex. 5 — Ibid., bar 6.

Ex. 6 — Sonata V, Allegro non tropo, bar 2.

Ex. 7 — Sonata X, Allegro, bar 1.

N.B.—In the last 3 Exx. care is necessary to avoid consecutive 5ths. In Ex. 5 the accompaniment (*a*), in which the discord is approached by step, is best; (*b*) and (*bb*) are possible; (*c*) is bad.

(*a*)   (*b*)   (*bb*)   (*c*)

The following are typical Exx. of Leclair's use of $6 = {6 \atop 4 \atop 3}$ in sequences:

Sonata XII, Allegro ma non tropo, bars 53–7.

Ex. 8

Ibid., Largo, 1st section *ad fin.*

Ex. 9

Note.—The chord † is figured in full in order to indicate the augmented 4th.

Sonata II, Giga, bars 5–7.

Ex. 10

Sonata I, Aria (major), 2nd section, bars 9–12.

Ex. 11

N.B.—For the use of ♯ to contradict a flat (diatonic to the key) and of ♭ to contradict a (diatonic) sharp in the above Exx. see Ch. xxiv, § 2 *b*, 'Accidentals'.

A comparison of the passages in Leclair's 1st book of Violin Sonatas in which he uses the figuring $6 = {6 \atop 4 \atop 3}$, as shown in the above Exx., with similar passages in the remaining three books in which he discarded the practice, points strongly to the conclusion that in the latter the figure 6 is often to be interpreted as ${}^6_4{}_3$. It has already been mentioned that in books 2, 3, and 4 Leclair seldom or never used the figuring ${}^4_3$ unless either the 4 or the 3 required an accidental.

Ex. 12

In the preceding Ex. (Bk. 2, Sonata XII, Allegro ma non tropo, bars 28–9) there can be little doubt that Leclair desired some such accompaniment as is given below, taking 6 ※ on the 1st quaver of bar 29 as ${}^6_4{}_3$.

It is not exactly parallel to any of the Exx. of 6 from Bk. 1 given above, but the inclusion of the 4 seems demanded (1) by its presence in the Violin part at *, and (2) by the symmetry of the passage.

7. § 10. Instead of ♯ ♭ ♮ placed next the figure (♯7, ♭7, ♮7 or 7♯, 7♭, 7♮) some composers use a stroke, which, as in the case of 5, denotes either the raising or lowering of the interval according to its position.

According to a common usage a stroke through the top of the figure (⁄7) indicates the raising of the interval by a semitone, while a stroke through the tail (7⁄) indicates that it is lowered to the same extent, irrespective of whether the alteration is 'accidental' or in contradiction of an 'accidental'.‡ When ♭ is used, instead of being placed beside the figure (♭7 or 7♭), it is sometimes drawn through the top (♭̸); in the case therefore of some of the older publishers, e.g. Roger of Amsterdam, who use ⌐ instead of ♭, it is necessary to distinguish carefully between ⁄7 = ♭7 and ⁄7 = ♯7 ♮7, as also between 5⌐ = ♭5 and 5⌐ = ♯5, 6̸ = ♭6, and 6̸ = ♯6.

In the case of a diminished 7th (even when diatonic, as ♭♭ over ♯c when there is a flat in the signature) some composers *invariably* use ♭7, 7♭ or ⁄7, while others use ♮7, 7♮ (instead of ♭7, 7♭) when the 7th is diminished by the contradiction of a sharp, and plain unqualified 7 when it is diatonic.

Here, as in other cases, great inconsistency prevails. An examination of the diminished 7ths in the Violin Sonatas of Leclair shows that the composer

‡ Some composers on the other hand use ⁄7 = ♯7, ⁊ = ♭7, but ♮7 when the 7th is sharpened by the contradiction of a flat or vice versâ. Cf. § 6, note 2.

almost always put a stroke through the tail of the figure to indicate a diminished 7th, and that he *intended* to put ♭ *as well* (♭7̸) when the 7th was '*accidentally*' diminished (by the contradiction of a sharp or otherwise); but he often forgot to prefix ♭ and used 7̸ alone. In the very few cases where he omitted the stroke, ♭7 is used, the diminution of the interval being accidental.

§ 11. Special use of ♮7. In compositions belonging to the earlier part of the eighteenth century ♮7 or 7♮ is sometimes used to indicate a major 7th even when diatonic.

Mattheson, *Grosse General-Bass-Schule*, Hamburg, 1731. 'Mittel-Classe', 'Prob-Stück' 15, bar 41.

The harmony indicated being  In the earlier edition of the same work, the *Organisten-Probe*, Hamburg, 1719, the chord is figured ♮7/5/2, but in the later edition the 5 is corrected to 5̸; there is no likelihood, therefore, of ♮7 being a misprint.

8. § 12. It does not often occur that the figure 8 requires the addition of ♯, ♭, or ♮. Two cases, however, are possible in which it is necessary.

(1) A passing note in an upper part, over a stationary Bass:

Ex. 1

D. G. Türk, *Anweisung &c.*, Halle & Leipsic, 1791, Cap. 4, Abschnitt (section) 2, § 136.

N.B.—Schröter, *Deutliche Anweisung zum General-Bass &c.*, Halberstadt, 1772, Cap. 18, § 210, p. 109, gives ♯8 8 ♯1 1 as alternative figurings, in flat keys ♮8 and ♮1.
G. Ph. Telemann, *Singe-Spiel- und Generalbass-Übungen*, Hamburg, 1733/4, No. 29, says that 1 is very rarely used and that 8 is the ordinary figuring.

(2) A suspension in an upper part over a moving bass:

Ex. 2

‡ (note)

In such a case as this the ♮ (or ♭) is very liable to be omitted.

‡ The full figuring would of course be ♮8 7 / 5 / ♯, but the general practice is to assume that no 3rd in a chord is *diminished* unless it is *expressed* in the figuring. Therefore the

9. § 13. In the use of the stroke 9 differs from 7. Whereas ꝑ and ꝗ represent ♯7 and ♭7 respectively, both ꝗ (as e.g. in Türk's *Generalbass*, 1791, § 25) and ꝗ (as e.g. in Roger's edition of Corelli's *Opera prima, seconda, terza,* and *quarta*) are both equivalent to ♯9, and, like 4̷, 5̷, 6̷, ꝑ, may be used as the equivalent of ♮9 when the interval is raised by the contradiction of a flat. It would not, however, be safe to assert that a stroke through the tail of the figure was *never* used (as in the case of 7) to denote the flattening of the interval (cf. § 6 on the exceptional uses of 5). In playing from Basses printed by Roger of Amsterdam care must be taken not to confuse ꝗ (= ♯9) with ꝗ (= ♭9), the pointed flat ⸜ being drawn through the tail of the figure, and not, as in the case of 5̷, 6̷, ꝑ, through the head.

§ 14. *Cases where 9 and 2 are used interchangeably.*

I. In the figuring of passing and changing (i.e. accented passing) notes.

(a) $\begin{smallmatrix}9\\7\\4\end{smallmatrix}$ instead of $\begin{smallmatrix}7\\4\\2\end{smallmatrix}$.

Ph. Em. Bach gives the following examples (*Versuch &c.*, Part II, 1762, Ch. 1, § 78, and Ch. 13, I, § 19):

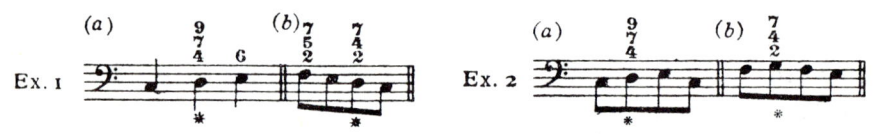

Ex. 1 (a) (b)

Ex. 2 (a) (b)

One is tempted to conclude from them that he used 2 in the cases in which —as in the resolution of a $\begin{smallmatrix}6\\4\\2\end{smallmatrix}$ chord—concord is reached by the *falling of the Bass*, and 9 in the contrary cases, thus following the analogy of chords of the 9th, which resolve by approximation rather than by divergence, though, in their case, it is an upper part, and, in our examples, the Bass which moves.

However, whatever Ph. Em. Bach's practice may have been, this distinction was not generally observed, as will be seen from examples of Heinichen (cf. Ch. xix, 'The figuring of transitional notes', § 5, Ex. 2 b, Ex. 3 b) in which $\begin{smallmatrix}7\\4\\2\end{smallmatrix}$ and $\begin{smallmatrix}9\\7\\4\end{smallmatrix}$, as well as $\begin{smallmatrix}7\\4\end{smallmatrix}$, are used indiscriminately—probably of set purpose, in order to familiarize the student with the different possibilities—to denote the same chord.

(b) $\begin{smallmatrix}9\\7\\5\end{smallmatrix}$ instead of $\begin{smallmatrix}7\\5\\2\end{smallmatrix}$.

Here, again, Ph. Em. Bach appears to use 9 when the Bass rises and 2 when it falls (cf. Exx. 4 a and b), while J. S. Bach uses the two figurings quite indiscriminately. In Ex. 3, in two passages only three bars apart, and both times with a descending Bass, we find $\begin{smallmatrix}9♭\\7\\5\end{smallmatrix}$ and $\begin{smallmatrix}7\\5\\2♭\end{smallmatrix}$ used to denote the same harmony:

---

presence of ♯d and ♮c in the above chord would *generally* be assumed to preclude the presence of ♮f and ♯a respectively, though of course exceptions occur.

In the following Ex. the composer figures the same chord differently in two successive bars, and in both cases contrary to his usual practice; see § 10 *ad fin.*

Leclair, *Troisieme livre de Sonates &c.*, Sonata VIII, Allegro ma non tropo, 2nd section, bars 15–17.

XXIII § 14, I VARIETIES OF FIGURING

J. S. Bach, *Sonata in G for 2 Flutes and Bass*, Presto, bars 87 and 90 (B.-G. ed., IX, p. 272).

Ex. 3

Ph. Em. Bach, *Versuch &c.*, Part II, 1762, Ch. 1, § 75.   Ibid., Ch. 20, § 7 *f.*

Ex. 4*a*   Ex. 4*b*

(*c*) $\frac{9}{5}$ for $\frac{5}{4}$:
   $\frac{4}{}$ $\frac{2}{}$

Ex. 5

J. S. Bach, *Sonata in E minor for Violin and Bass*, Gigue *ad fin.* (B.-G. ed., XLIII, 1, p. 38).

(*d*) $\frac{9}{5}$ for $\frac{5}{3}$ (generally figured $\frac{3}{2}$ unless the 5 requires an accidental):
   $\frac{3}{}$ $\frac{2}{}$

Ex. 6

J. S. Bach, ibid., Allegro ma non tanto, bar 13 (B.-G. ed., IX, p. 263).

II. In retardations.

(*a*) $\frac{9}{7}$ for $\frac{7}{4}$. The chord of the dominant Seventh (with or without the Dominant itself) may be used either (1) as a passing chord over a stationary Bass (Ex. 7 *a*), or (2) as a retardation of the tonic harmony (Ex. 7 *b*, *c*).

Ex. 7   (*a*)   (*b*)   (*c*)

Ph. Em. Bach, *Versuch &c.*, Part II, 1762, Ch. 16, II, § 3.

In the former case (subject to rare exceptions) $\frac{7}{4}$ (often abbreviated $\frac{7}{4}$ or $\frac{7}{2}$, or even 7)[1] is always used, never $\frac{9}{7}$.
   $\frac{4}{}$

In the latter case, however, $\frac{9}{7}$ is not infrequently found, as:
   $\frac{4}{}$

Ex. 8   Ph. Em. Bach, ibid., Ch. 13, II, § 3, Ex. *f* 1.

[1] Ph. Em. Bach (l.c., § 4) condemns abbreviations except when a 3-part accompaniment is to be indicated. Then $\frac{7\ 8}{2\ 3}$ or $\frac{7\ 8}{4\ 3}$ may be used (l.c. § 6). Nevertheless 7 8, and, in a minor key, ♯7 8, ♮7 8 are very frequently to be found.

Only the Bass is given, but the figuring $\genfrac{}{}{0pt}{}{8}{\genfrac{}{}{0pt}{}{3}{3}}$, combined with the recommendation that the accompaniment should be in 5 parts (in order that the tonic chord may not lack the Fifth), shows what is intended, namely:

The 5 of the dominant chord (*b*) is treated as a prepared 9th, and figured and resolved accordingly.

But that this was not in accordance with Ph. Em. Bach's general practice may be inferred from his explanation of the distinction between $\genfrac{}{}{0pt}{}{7}{\genfrac{}{}{0pt}{}{4}{2}}$ and $\genfrac{}{}{0pt}{}{9}{\genfrac{}{}{0pt}{}{7}{4}}$, given with reference to Ex. 7 above. He writes (ibid., l.c. § 4): "One often finds $\genfrac{}{}{0pt}{}{9}{\genfrac{}{}{0pt}{}{7}{4}}$ over the Bass, instead of $\genfrac{}{}{0pt}{}{7}{\genfrac{}{}{0pt}{}{4}{2}}$, as it ought to be according to our method; we shall observe later on that certain cases admit of either figuring. Here we make the distinction, that the major Seventh in conjunction with the Ninth always resolves downwards, and that with the Second, in our chord [i.e. as in Ex. 7], they both rise together. The latter [i.e. the Second], occurring as it does over a stationary Bass, and therefore as a passing note [as in Ex. 7 *a*], or else as a retardation [as in Ex. 7 *b*], has, even as such, the same liberty as in other cases, namely to rise."

This explanation is unsatisfactory, partly because it is inconsistent with Ph. Em. Bach's own occasional practice (as in Ex. 8), but more particularly because what is said about the *major Seventh, in conjunction with the Ninth, resolving downwards* does not apply to the chord under discussion (in which the 7 *invariably rises*), but to such a case as is shown in the following example, in which the chord figured $\genfrac{}{}{0pt}{}{9}{\genfrac{}{}{0pt}{}{7}{4}}$ has a different origin as well as a different resolution:

Ex. 9

The last sentence of the passage quoted above is, of course, intended to explain why the 5 of the dominant chord, when retarded over the Tonic, must not necessarily be regarded and treated as a prepared Ninth.

The natural conclusion seems to be that the figuring $\genfrac{}{}{0pt}{}{9}{\genfrac{}{}{0pt}{}{7}{4}}$ (as opposed to $\genfrac{}{}{0pt}{}{7}{\genfrac{}{}{0pt}{}{4}{2}}$) is to be taken as an indication on the part of the composer that the note in question is to resolve downwards, as:

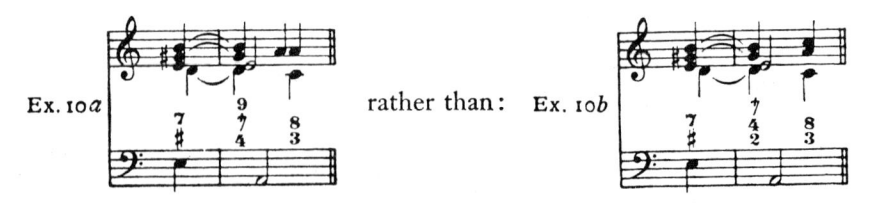

Ex. 10*a*   rather than: Ex. 10*b*

XXIII § 14, II   VARIETIES OF FIGURING   877

(b) $\begin{smallmatrix}9\\7\\6\\(4)\end{smallmatrix}$ for $\begin{smallmatrix}7\\6\\4\\2\end{smallmatrix}$. The chord of the Seventh on the leading note may, like the chord just discussed, be used either (1) as a passing chord over a stationary Bass, or (2) as a retardation (cf. Ch. xv, §§ 7, 8).

The ordinary figuring is $\begin{smallmatrix}7\\6\\4\\2\end{smallmatrix}$, or, in the minor key (in which it most frequently occurs), $\begin{smallmatrix}\sharp 7\\6\\4\\2\end{smallmatrix}, \begin{smallmatrix}\natural 7\\6\\4\\2\end{smallmatrix}, \begin{smallmatrix}7\\6\\4\\2\end{smallmatrix}$.

But 9, instead of 2, is sometimes found, as in the following examples. It will be seen that the 9 in every case *rises* to 3, and is therefore clearly less correct than 2:

Schröter, *Deutliche Anweisung zum General-Bass*, 1772, § 264, p. 148.

Ex. 11

§ 15. 10, 11, 12, 13, 14. When accompaniment from a figured Bass was in its infancy, the figures were taken as denoting only that interval from the Bass which they actually expressed, and not, as later, the same interval *plus* one or more Octaves; e.g. 4 denoted, not, either a 4th or 11th, or even 18th, from the Bass, at the pleasure of the accompanist, but only an actual 4th. When, therefore, it was desired to add an Octave—more was not likely to be required,[1] as it was a fundamental principle to keep the hands close together—to the interval in question, it was necessary to have recourse to the figures 10, 11, 12, 13, 14 to express the 'compound' interval.

The following Exx. from Caccini's *Nuove Musiche*, 1602, and Peri's *Euridice*, 1600, two of the earliest works in which figures are used, illustrate this:

Ex. 1   Caccini, *Nuove Musiche*, Venice, Alessandro Raverii, 1602 (dated at the end 1607, and therefore presumably 2nd ed.), p. 34, last bar. N.B.—This was Caccini's favourite cadence.

Ex. 2   Peri, *Euridice*, 2nd ed., Venice, Alessandro Raverii, 1608, p. 41, 2nd stave, bar 2.

Note the three consecutive unisons at the end, broken only by the dotted note in the voice part.

[2] The unusual arrangement of the figures in Ex. 11 *c* is designed by Schröter to indicate that, *in the major key*, the chord of the Seventh on the leading note must be taken *with the 7 in the upper part*, and so in all its inversions, a rule given by many theorists.
[1] Cavalieri, however, in his *Anima e Corpo*, 1600, goes as far as 18. See Ch. i, § 8.

Ex. 3 Ibid., p. 46, 2nd stave, bar 2.

Ex. 4 Ibid., p. 40, 5th stave, bar 1.

§ 16. The practice of using 'compound' figures to express 'compound' intervals did not long survive, though the tendency to interpret the figures literally did not disappear all at once. In Matthew Locke's *Melothesia*, London, 1673, the principle of using 'simple' figures to express 'compound' intervals is stated in the 1st Rule. "After having perfectly observed the Tone or Key you are to Play on (which is ever known by the last Note of the Bass) with what Notes are properly Flat and Sharp therein, play Thirds, Fifts [*sic*], Eights or their Compounds on all Notes where the following Rules direct not otherwise, or the contrary be not Figured, beginning the Account on the Note you play on and reckoning upward; &c." The 9th Rule runs as follows: "When the Bass is below C fa ut [tenor C] it is better to make your Account from the Octave above the Bass, than otherwise; for the playing of Thirds and Fifts so low will produce rather a confused than Harmonious sound."

This caution shows that the tendency to interpret the figures literally still existed in Locke's time.

At a much later period we occasionally find the figures 10, 11, &c., as well as 1, used, but from a quite different point of view.

Ph. Em. Bach, *Versuch &c.*, Part II, Chap. i, § 22, says: "Firsts, Tenths, Elevenths, and Twelfths are nothing but Octaves, Thirds, Fourths, and Fifths. They are indicated by a 1, 10, 11, 12 and occur for the most part in the free style ['im galanten Styl'] and in a 3-part accompaniment. They are used in order to give a clear indication of the melodic progression of the parts, e.g.:

Ex. 1

[2] The 4 here obviously stands for $\frac{6}{4}$. In the earliest figured Basses, only a single figure was used as a rule. Staden, organist at St. Sebaldus' Church, Nüremberg, added to the Organ-part of his *Kirchen-Music, Ander Theil* [*Second Part*] *&c.*, published at Nüremberg in 1626, a few rules for the performance of a figured Bass which are reprinted in the 12th 'Jahrgang' [annual issue] of the *Allgemeine Musikalische Zeitung* (see Ch. i, § 16). Staden remarks that the "above-mentioned signs (i.e. ♯ and ♭) and figures are sometimes found one above the other" and gives the following cadences, $\frac{6\ 5}{3\ 4\ 4\ 3}$, $\frac{\sharp 7\ 6\ 5}{\sharp 3\ 4\ 4\ \sharp 3}$, $\frac{\sharp 5\ 6\ 5}{\sharp 3\ 4\ 4\ \sharp 3}$ on the Dominant.

XXIII § 16   VARIETIES OF FIGURING

"We see that the progression from 1 to 2 and 2 to 1 is more natural and catches the eye better than if one passed from 8 to 2 and from 2 to 8 (*a*). The same clearness is exhibited in the use of 10, 11, and 12 (*b*).‡

"These compound figures are used, only when the simple figures 7, 8, and 9 either follow or precede them (*c*). This mode of figuring also indicates clearly whether the progression of two parts is to be in 3rds or 6ths (*d*), a matter which in a delicate accompaniment is not always one of indifference."

In the following Ex. of a 4-part accompaniment the use of 10 serves to indicate the best position of the chord, i.e. with the 3rd on the top.

Ex. II   Ibid., Cap. 7, II, § 10.

For the use of $\frac{9}{7}$ rather than $\frac{7}{4}$, cf. § 14, II (cases where 9 and 2 are used interchangeably in retardations).

§ 17. 'Enharmonic' figuring. We occasionally find a figure indicating, not the actual interval required by the harmony, but its enharmonic equivalent.

In the following Ex. we have 6 on ♯*d* instead of ♭7 (♯*b* for ♮*c*).

Ex. 1   Johann Philipp Treiber, *Der accurate Organist im General-Bass*, Arnstadt, 1704, Num. II, penultimate bar.

The usual figuring of the chord * would be ♭7 or ⁊ or 7 or $\frac{7}{5}$, but Treiber, as he explains in his introductory rules, associates ♭7 with a *minor*, and not a diminished, 7th; he would therefore have regarded ♭7 on ♯*d* as indicating not ♮*c* but ♯*c*, and therefore substitutes 6 = ♯*b*.

N.B.—The *position* of the chord, as given above, with the diminished 7th (unprepared) at the top, is dictated by the given melody, the Chorale 'Wer nur den lieben Gott lässt walten', see Ch. ii, § 2. For the doubling of the leading-note in the following chord see Ch. xi, III, § 2, Ex. 2, pp. 560 sq.

A remarkable Ex. of ♭2 for ♯8 is given by Mattheson in the 4th part ('Ober-Classe') of his *Kleine General-Bass-Schule*, 1st 'Aufgabe' (task), § 3.

Ex. 2

‡ The figure 12 does not occur in (*b*). Possibly the first figures in the Ex., $\frac{10}{5}$, though they appear in both the 1st and 2nd editions, are a mistake for $\frac{12}{10}$ as in (*c*).

He repeats the Ex. as below with full figures arranged to show the position in which each chord is to be taken. He remarks that it is easy to see from the key that ♯c, and not ♭d, is intended, but he gives no reason why the chord should not be figured $^{♯8}_{6}$.
$_{4}$

In a note he alludes to the figuring ♯1 as a possibility, but discards it, in order to avoid following Rameau, against whom he indulges in a characteristic tirade, by introducing an 'augmented unison' (*unisonum superfluum*).

In the following Ex. from J. S. Bach (Sonata for Flauto traverso and Continuo in E major, Adagio, penultimate bar, B.-G. ed., XLIII (K.-M., VIII), p. 22) we have an Ex. of ♮4 for ♯3 representing an enharmonic change from ♮f to ♯e.

Ex. 3

§ 18. '*Retrospective*' *figuring*. When the Bass moves by step, a figure sometimes expresses intervals reckoned, not from the note over which it stands, but from the preceding one. In the following Ex. from Purcell's *Sonnatas of 3 Parts*, 1683 (Sonata VII, 1st movement, bar 9) $^{5}_{♯3}$ stands for $^{♯4}_{♯2}$:

A somewhat analogous, and very exceptional, case occurs in the antepenultimate bar of the Presto of J. S. Bach's *Sonata in G major for 2 Flutes and Bass*, B.-G. ed., IX (K.-M., I), p. 273:

The harmony indicated by the $^6_{4\,2}$ over *c* is not struck till the following quaver. The ordinary figuring would have been:

(see Ch. xix, § 5).

Note.—An examination of Bach's autograph might possibly reveal the existence of a stroke connecting the figures with the note to which they belong,

although, according to Kirnberger's testimony, Bach preferred to give changing notes their proper figuring and disapproved of the use of strokes. "It was a maxim of the late Bach (John Sebastian) that people must learn to read figures properly; the value of this maxim is demonstrated especially when three or four notes in semiquavers occur; figuring them with a stroke (whatever there may be in favour of the latter) would be uncertain; whereas Bach's figuring $^7_5$ [as (*a*) above] is better, because the harmony of the note to be struck is indicated at once, besides which, a further advantage is that a copyist is far more likely to place the strokes over the wrong notes by a clerical error than would be the case with Bach's figuring; this being the case, Bach's figuring is far preferable."—*Grundsätze des Generalbasses &c.*, 1781, p. 87.

§ 19. Besides G. P. Telemann's semicircular sign ⌒ already described (§ 5, 1 *b ad fin.*), various devices have been suggested from time to time as a means of making the composer's intentions clearer to the player, but have failed to establish themselves. Thus, Jakob Adlung, in his *Anleitung zu der musikalischen Gelahrtheit*, pp. 643 sq., quoted by G. M. Telemann (*Unterricht im Generalbass-Spielen*, Hamburg, 1773, Abschnitt (Section) 2, Ch. 2, § 10, note, pp. 96–7), suggests placing a small circle o over a Bass note to indicate that no chord is to be struck by the right hand (equivalent, therefore, in significance to the indication *tasto solo* or *t.s.*), while an oblique stroke \ after the o is to show how long the latter remains in operation, as:

Ex. 1

This sign o, if it had come into use, would have been liable to confusion with the o which is sometimes used as an alternative to the figuring of changing (i.e. accented passing) notes, as in Ex. 2 *a* (cf. Ch. xix, 'The figuring of transitional notes', § 5).

Ex. 2

'Magister' Adlung also suggested that the sign ⌇, beginning over a note (or a short rest), should be used to indicate the striking of the chord belonging to the note on which the sign in question ended, as:

Ex. 3

It will be observed that this is merely a variety (and extension) of the usage shown above in Ex. 2 b.

One of the most valuable suggestions was that of Ph. Em. Bach (*Versuch &c.*, Part II, 1762, Ch. 29, § 16), that dots should be used between the figures (exactly as they are used in staff notation) to indicate the duration of the chords, as:

Ex. 4

The adoption of this device would have removed one of the greatest defects of the existing method of figuring.

It is noteworthy that Johann Staden used dots between the figures as an indication of their relative duration, though not in the way suggested by Ph. Em. Bach (cf. Ch. i, § 16, Exx. 4 *a* and *b* and the text immediately preceding).

CHAPTER XXIV
VARIETIES OF NOTATION

XXIV
VARIETIES OF NOTATION

§ 1. *Key-signatures.*

(*a*) Early forms of ♯ and ♭. In music of the seventeenth and early eighteenth centuries, e.g. Purcell's *Sonnatas of III parts*, 1683, Niedt's *Musicalische Handleitung*, 1700, we find 𝄪; and somewhat later, till well on in the eighteenth century, ✕ was the prevailing form. In most cases the sign ♭ was the same as to-day, though some publishers of the eighteenth century, notably Estienne Roger of Amsterdam, used the form ⌐.

In some of his publications, e.g. the second and third editions of Corelli's famous *Opera Quinta*, he uses ⌐ both on the stave and in the figuring, while in others, e.g. Giuseppe Valentini's *XII Suonate à Tre Opera Quinta*, he uses ♭ on the stave and ⌐ in the figuring.

(*b*) A characteristic peculiarity of early key-signatures was the habit of omitting one flat (chiefly in the minor keys), and one sharp (chiefly in the major keys). This practice probably originated with the transposed Doric, Lydian, and Mixolydian modes, in which the Tonics G and ♭B would have one ♭ in the signature, and D one ♯.

Great inconsistency prevailed.

(*c*) Another peculiarity was the habit of putting ♯ or ♭ twice over in the signature for the same note in two different 8ves, so far as the stave permitted.

In Mattheson's *Organisten-Probe*, 1719, 'Mittel-Classe', the 14th 'Prob-Stück' is given in two versions, ♭*e* and ♯*d* minor, respectively. The signatures are as follows: [music example] (omitting ♭*c* and duplicating ♭*b* ♭*a* ♭*g*), [music example] (giving all the sharps and duplicating ♯*f* ♯*g* ♯*a*).

§ 2. *Accidentals.*

(*a*) The earlier composers, e.g. Purcell, *Sonnatas of III parts*, 1683, *Sonatas in 4 parts*, 1697, *did not use* ♮ ('B quadratum') *at all*. They contradicted ♯ with ♭, and ♭ with sharp. Corelli in his *Opera Quinta*, first printed in Rome, 1700, uses ♮ to contradict ♭ (both on the stave and in the figuring), but he *still uses ♭ to contradict ♯*. (For an earlier use of ♮ see p. 121 *inf. sq.*)

In all cases ♯ ♮ ♭, placed immediately before (or after) *any* figure,[1] has

---

[1] Some composers, e.g. Leclair, used × (which properly denotes a *double* sharp) before a *figure* instead of 𝄪. With regard to the position of the accidental, *before* or *after* the figure, there is no fixed rule. Inasmuch as an accidental is always placed before the note which it qualifies, it would, undoubtedly, be more logical to follow the same plan when it is a figure, and not a note, that is affected; and this practice is followed in many Basses, especially, perhaps, those printed in England, France, and Italy. Except in some modern reprints (e.g. the publications of the *Bach-Gesellschaft*) we rarely, if ever, find the accidental placed uniformly *after* the figure; but in many Basses it is placed before some figures and after others. Thus Ph. Em. Bach, in the Second Part of his *Versuch*, always places the accidental *before* 7 and 9,

VARIETIES OF NOTATION

exactly the same significance as when attached to the corresponding note on the stave, though we shall see in the sequel that this method was subject to modification.

(*b*) The earlier practice of contradicting ♯ and ♭ with ♭ and ♯ respectively, and the later practice of using ♮ to contradict ♭, while adhering to ♭ as the contradiction of ♯, were both quite clear and could give rise to no confusion, but certain composers introduced practices of their own, which are liable, until thoroughly mastered, to puzzle the player.

In all four books of his Sonatas for Violin and Bass Leclair adopts, though far from consistently, the following practice, of which the chief characteristic is the difference in the treatment of sharps and flats, according to whether they are *diatonic* or *accidental*, and, as a result of this, the special significance attached to the sign ♮.

A sharp *belonging to the key* was contradicted, as formerly, by ♭, but, contrary to the older practice, was *restored* (on the stave and in the figuring alike) by ♮!

Bk. I, Sonata IX, Sarabanda, 2nd section, bar 14 to end.

Ex. 1

Observe ♮g (in the Violin part) in bar 16 = ♯g in contradiction of ♭g = ♮g in bar 14, and ♮g in the Bass of bar 19 = ♯g in contradiction of the ♭ in the previous bar.[2]

In the key of E major Leclair made an exception in his treatment of ♯*d*, which he contradicted with ♮ and restored with ♯, as though it were an 'accidental'.

In the case of *flats* belonging to the key, Leclair was more arbitrary still.

but *after* 2, 4, 5, 6, as in the figuring ♭7₅♭. The idea was probably to put it where there was most room; it was the practice in some Basses (e.g. in many of the publications of Estienne Roger of Amsterdam) to let the accidental *bisect* the nearest approach to an horizontal stroke presented by the figure in question, as 2♭, 4♭, 5♭, 6♭, ♭7 9♭ (the ♮ being used in the same way, but the ♯ generally replaced by a stroke through the figure); and it may well be that this practice helped to make it seem more natural, even to those who did not follow it—whether composers, printers, or engravers—to place the accidental on the same side of the figure as the said horizontal or obliquely curved stroke.

[2] In the seventeenth and eighteenth centuries an accidental was usually assumed to be contradicted unless it was repeated, but the practice of different composers varied greatly in this respect.

♭B received a sort of preferential treatment. He almost invariably contradicted it with 𝕏, but it was *only in the Bass and in the figuring* that he restored it with a ♮; on the upper stave he used ♭.

In the case of ♭E, he contradicts it sometimes (but on the stave only) with 𝕏, more often with ♮, and always restores it with ♭.

Bk. I, Sonata III, Largo, bars 27-30.

Ex. 2

* ♮ = ♭ in contradiction of ♯ = ♮.

Bk. I, Sonata XI, Giga, 2nd section, bars 14-20.

Ex. 3

♮6 at * indicates ♭B in contradiction of ×4 = ♮B in the previous bar. Observe ♭E contradicted by ♮ in the same bar and by 𝕏 in the following one, and in the Violin part (bars 14 and 15) ♭B contradicted by 𝕏 and restored by ♭ in the following bar.

Note.—For Leclair's use of $6 = {6 \atop {4 \atop 3}}$ see Ch. xxiii, § 8.

To contradict 'accidentals', whether ♯ or ♭, Leclair used ♮.

§ 3. *Notation of double sharps and flats.*

Double sharps and flats were originally indicated by 𝕏𝕏 ♭♭ prefixed to the note or placed next the figure, or, in the case of 3, more commonly instead of it.[1] As a simpler alternative the signs × and β were devised, according to

---

[1] False notation of double sharps and flats (♮g for ♯♯f, &c.) was common in the earlier part of the eighteenth century.

The following Ex. shows the same passage as it appears (*a*), with false notation, in Mattheson's *Organisten-Probe*, 1719 (Pt. I, 'Prob-Stück' [test-piece] 14), and (*b*), with

XXIV § 3 　　　VARIETIES OF NOTATION　　　887

the testimony of Schröter, *Deutliche Anweisung &c.*, 1772, by Mattheson. In his *Organisten-Probe*, 1719, and the 2nd ed. entitled *Grosse General-Bass-Schule*, 1731, Mattheson uses ✕✕ owing to the fact that the printer lacked the type for ✖ ('Mittel-Classe', 14th 'Prob-Stück', footnote), which was therefore evidently the original form of the sign, discarded later in favour of ✕, no doubt on account of its indistinctness, when the horizontal bar of the Maltese cross was *on* one of the lines of the stave. The sign β never found favour. Ph. Em. Bach, *Versuch &c.*, Part II, Ch. 1, § 33: "The large ♭ [viz. Mattheson's β], convenient as it is, never came much into use." More commonly than not, only a *single* ✕ or ♭ was used in addition to the one in the signature, as in the following Ex.:[2]

Corelli, *Opera Quinta*, Sonata XI, Allegro, 2nd section, bars 8-10.

The proper way of contradicting double sharps and flats was by the signs ♮✕ ♮♭, but they were very rarely employed. Ph. Em. Bach, l.c. § 34, says:

amended notation, in the later edition of the same work, published 1731 under the title of *Grosse General-Bass-Schule*.

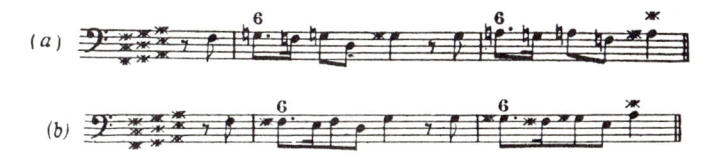

N.B.—In (a) ♮f represents ♯e, even though the latter is in accordance with the key-signature.

[2] We occasionally meet with the sign ✕ to indicate a double sharp as in the following Ex. at (a).

In the *figuring*, however, Leclair uses either ✕ or x (in the latter case adding the 3, which he usually omits) to indicate the doubling of a sharp already present in the signature, as at (b) and (c) in the following Ex.:

Leclair, *Violin Sonatas*, Bk. IV, Sonata IX, Adagio, bars 22-3.

"The signs ♮♭ ♮𝕏 ... are, it is true, not as common in the figuring as exact notation demands. As, however, they may nevertheless occur, we will mention them among the rest, in order that no one may be frightened by them."

A plain ♮ was generally used to contradict double sharps and flats, and very often they were not contradicted at all. It must be remembered that in the seventeenth and eighteenth centuries an accidental did not, as in modern music, hold good for the duration of the bar; unless repeated, it was assumed to be contradicted, though the repetition was often omitted in obvious cases.

§ 4. *Clefs.*

The C clefs are freely employed in figured Basses, and some composers, e.g. Senallié and Festing, use the French Violin clef on the bottom line of the stave. In the following Ex., *Organisten-Probe*, 'Mittel-Classe', Prob-Stück 17, Mattheson uses eight clefs.‡ He points out that the student has really only seven to learn as the contrabass clef (on the top line) reads like the ordinary treble G clef two 8ves lower, and that the French Violin clef reads like the bass clef two 8ves higher!

‡ i.e. all, except the French Violin clef.

** Mattheson must have intended to figure these chords $^6_4$ as otherwise the following 7th is left unprepared.

§ 5. The 'Custos'.

In the seventeenth and eighteenth centuries it was customary to place at the end of each line of music (with leger lines, and with ♯ ♭ ♮ prefixed, if required) the sign ⩘ to indicate the position of the first note of the following line, but without giving any clue to its value.

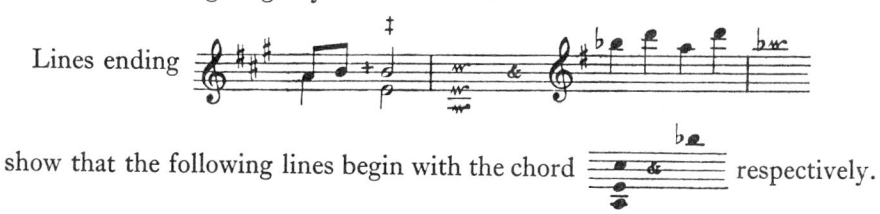

Lines ending [music example] show that the following lines begin with the chord [music example] respectively.

‡ Leclair (from the 2nd book of whose Violin Sonatas the above Exx. are taken) employs + to indicate a shake.

In the figured Bass part the 'custos' is not usually figured. In some editions, however, as in Roger's reprint of Corelli's Op. 1, 2, 3, 4, it is figured throughout, as in the following Ex.:

Corelli, *Opera Seconda*, Sonata XII, Allegro. Estienne Roger and Michael Charles Le Cene, Amsterdam.

the first note of the following line being [music example].

CHAPTER XXV
PRACTICAL HINTS

XXV

PRACTICAL HINTS

§ 1. It may be well to conclude this work with a few practical suggestions for the benefit of those who desire to obtain as early as possible a certain measure of proficiency in playing from a figured Bass.

Those who are by nature highly gifted with a sense of harmony will probably have little difficulty in surmounting the initial obstacle, presented by unfamiliar combinations of figures; but to some this obstacle will, no doubt, appear formidable, and it is for such that these suggestions are intended.

Let it at once be said that an instinct for harmony, denied by nature, may, to a very large extent, be acquired by training, and that there is no training better than constant practice in playing from a Thorough-Bass, a practice which is of the greatest help in acquiring the important faculty of hearing mentally the music read by the eye. One reason for this is the fact that the player is thereby continually forced to realize the identity of any given harmony *taken in different positions* (that is to say, with different arrangements of the upper parts) and mentally to connect the several intervals (thus variously distributed) with each other and with the Bass. Be the reasons what they may, any one who makes the experiment will probably soon become convinced of the fact.

§ 2. Hand in hand with this development of the mental apprehension of combined sound, it is of the first importance, in playing from figures, to develop what may be called "brains in the fingers", namely, a quick and almost automatic response of the muscles to the mental impression derived through the eye; and no one need disdain to avail himself of any means by which this end may the more speedily be attained.

§ 3. Most people, except those who are fortunate enough to be able to rely on their inborn instinct alone, will probably find it helpful to consider carefully the various dispositions of the fingers of the right hand in their relation to certain chords and progressions. It will be enough to indicate briefly what is meant.

We will assume that the student will begin by making himself familiar with the seven fundamental chords and their figurings (including the usual abbreviated forms of the latter), i.e. the Triad with its two inversions $\left(6 = \smash{\substack{8\\6\\3}}, \smash{\substack{6\\3\\6}}, \text{ or } \smash{\substack{3\\6\\3}},\right.$ and $\smash{\substack{6\\4}}$, generally $= \left.\smash{\substack{8\\6\\4}}\right)$, and the Seventh $\left(\smash{\substack{7\\5\\3}} = \smash{\substack{7\\5\\3}} \text{ and } 7 = \smash{\substack{7\\5\\3}} \text{ or } \smash{\substack{8\\7\\3}}\right)$ with its three inversions $\left(\smash{\substack{6\\5}} = \smash{\substack{6\\5\\3}}, \smash{\substack{4\\3}} = \smash{\substack{6\\4\\3}}, \text{ and } 2, \smash{\substack{4\\2}}, 4\!\!\!+, \&\text{c.} = \smash{\substack{6\\4\\2}}, \smash{\substack{6\\4\!\!+\\2}}\right).$

In connexion with the inversions of the Seventh two things will be noticed: (1) that the three upper parts of a $\smash{\substack{4\\3}}$ chord and its resolution (and consequently *the three possible postures of the right hand*) are the same as those of $7 = \smash{\substack{8\\7\\3}}$:

XXV § 3 PRACTICAL HINTS 893

Ex. 1

and (2) that the upper parts of a $\frac{6}{4}$ chord are those of a Triad on the note a degree above the Bass of the $\frac{6}{4}$:
$_{2}$ $_{2}$

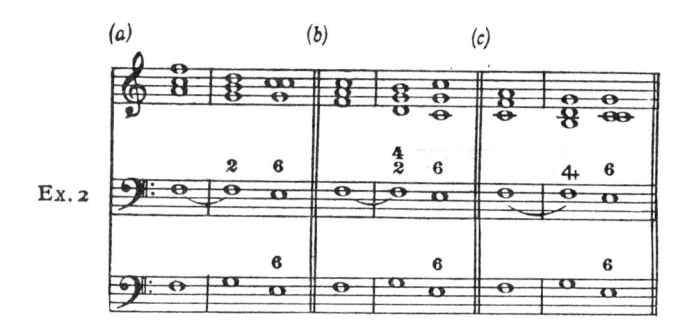

Ex. 2

This hand-consciousness, however, will be of no assistance (but rather the reverse) without a vivid consciousness of the nature of the interval between *at least one* of the upper parts and the Bass: thus, on being confronted with the figuring $\frac{4}{3}$, the "hand-shape" (if such a term may be coined) shown in Ex. 1 *a* must be vividly associated with the interval of a Third (i.e. a Tenth or Seventeenth) between the upper part and the Bass; and so, *mutatis mutandis*, with the two remaining positions. In this way it will be found that, when once the relation between the Bass and whichever interval of a chord happens to be uppermost in the right hand is fully realized, the inner parts will, to a very large extent, take care of themselves.

The same principle, rightly applied, can be made helpful in gaining familiarity with the figurings of suspended discords. It will be seen, for instance, from Ex. 3 on p. 894 that the function of the right hand is the same in 9 8, 7 6 $\left(=\begin{smallmatrix}8&-\\7&6\\3&-\end{smallmatrix}\right)$, and in $\begin{smallmatrix}6&-\\5&4\end{smallmatrix}$.

Similarly, the same upper parts belong to a $\frac{6}{5}$ chord on a Bass rising a degree to a Triad, to $\begin{smallmatrix}9&8\\4&3\end{smallmatrix}$ on the Bass of the same Triad, and to $\begin{smallmatrix}9&8\\7&6\end{smallmatrix}$ on a Bass a Third above the latter (Ex. 4).

Again, when, for one reason or another, $\frac{9}{7}$ has to be taken in five parts $\left(=\begin{smallmatrix}9\\7\\5\\3\end{smallmatrix}\right)$, as e.g. when it resolves on $\frac{6}{5}$, the four "hand-shapes" are those belonging to a chord of the Seventh and its three inversions $\left(\begin{smallmatrix}7\\5\\3\\1\end{smallmatrix},\begin{smallmatrix}6\\5\\3\\1\end{smallmatrix},\begin{smallmatrix}6\\4\\3\\1\end{smallmatrix},\begin{smallmatrix}6\\4\\2\\1\end{smallmatrix}\right)$ taken in four parts (including the Bass) in the right hand, as:

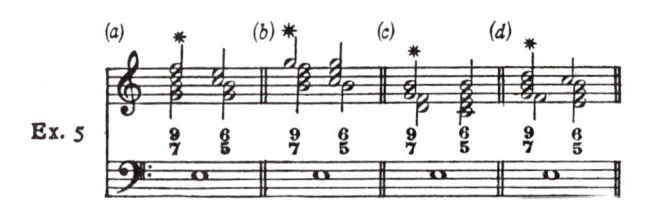

§ 4. It is impossible to exaggerate the importance of becoming thoroughly familiar with all the positions in which the harmony can possibly be taken. In many progressions there is one position which is better and more natural than any other, but the accompanist who is unfamiliar with the others will soon find himself in sore straits; nor must it be forgotten that the use of extended harmony is sometimes indicated, though this may well be left till fair proficiency has been attained in playing the three upper parts in the right hand, and only the Bass in the left. Whether the student finds extended harmony difficult, or not, will depend largely on the nature of his previous training. If he plays certain passages in close harmony, and afterwards transfers the Alto to the left hand (thereby making it the Tenor), he will soon find out what kind of a Bass lends itself to this treatment. As for the "filled-in" accompaniment in an indefinite number of parts in both hands,‡ it is certainly better left alone till the use of four-part harmony, and the correct progression of the individual parts, has been thoroughly mastered.

§ 5. As a means of gaining familiarity with the commoner figurings, and with the different positions of the harmony indicated by them, it is not a bad plan to write down and figure the Bass of a simple sequential passage and gradually elaborate it by the introduction of passing notes, suspensions, &c.

‡ Cf. Ch. iii, § 3.

XXV § 5 PRACTICAL HINTS 895

The longer the passage, the more practice it will afford. The following will serve as an example:

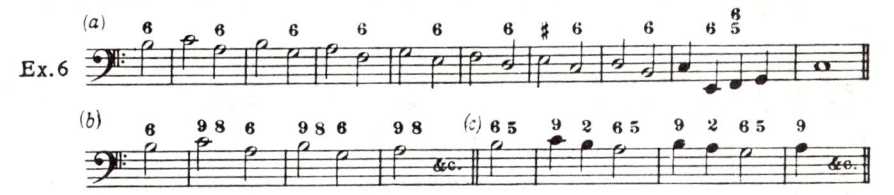

Ex. 6

In Ex. 6 (a) we have the passage in its simplest form; in (b) a suspension is added; in (c) we have the further addition of a passing note both in an upper part and in the Bass. Each form of the Bass should be played in all three possible positions.[1]

In its final form our Bass provides the following exercise:

Ex. 7

[1] The Sixth on the second minim of each bar is to be taken as $\genfrac{}{}{0pt}{}{6}{3}$, the progression of the individual parts remaining the same whether the 6 is doubled in the 8ve or in the unison:

In (a) and (b) the Sixth could, of course, be taken equally well as $\genfrac{}{}{0pt}{}{6}{3}$, the exact pattern of the sequence being broken only at one point *, in order to avoid the progression of an augmented Second:

Even in (c) it is possible, it is true, to take the 6 5 not as $\genfrac{}{}{0pt}{}{6\ 5}{3\ -}$ but as $\genfrac{}{}{0pt}{}{3\ -}{6\ -}$:

(cf. Ch. ix, II, § 3, Exx. 7 d, and 8 d); but for the present purpose it is better to adopt the progression indicated above.

[musical example]

It is better to strike each chord in full, as shown above, rather than to sustain the parts common to two consecutive chords, as the beginner thus better impresses upon his finger-consciousness the nature of the passing harmonies ($^6_5$ and $^4_2$).

Further practice may be obtained by slightly altering the form of the Bass and substituting, first 4 3 (Ex. 8 a), and then $^9_4\,^8_3$ (Ex. 8 b) for the 9 at the beginning of each bar:

Ex. 8 [musical example]

The Basses should then be written out and practised in different keys;[2] the more, the better. It is also a very good thing to transpose them an Octave higher, using the Alto and Tenor clefs, as:

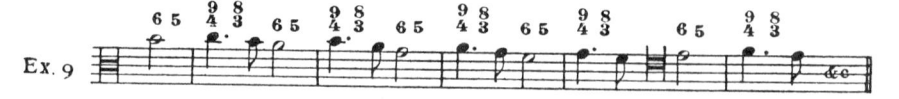

Ex. 9 [musical example]

The following sequence, passing, as it does, through alternate major and

---

[2] In all such exercises, and especially in long sequential passages, the ordinary rules for the *compass* of the accompaniment may be disregarded. The Bass may, of course, be played in Octaves (except when a C clef is prefixed).

XXV § 5   PRACTICAL HINTS   897

minor keys (C major, A minor, F major, D minor, &c.), affords useful practice, and may be prolonged indefinitely:

Ex. 10

The harmony may be varied by substituting 9 8 or $\begin{smallmatrix}9\\4\end{smallmatrix}\begin{smallmatrix}8\\3\end{smallmatrix}$ for 4 3 at the beginning of the second and all subsequent bars.

But let the figuring (1) of the third crotchet, and (2) of the third and fourth crotchets, of each bar be changed from $\begin{smallmatrix}6\\5\end{smallmatrix}$ to 6:

Ex. 11

It will then be found that the harmony can no longer be played in three different positions with exactly the same progression of the individual parts. In (a) it would be highly undesirable, and in (b) impossible; in the latter there is, in fact, only one really satisfactory position, namely, that with the 6 in the upper part. The solution of any difficulties that may arise in experimenting with this example should be found in Ch. ix.

§ 6. An excellent way for a beginner to acquire familiarity with the commoner figurings is by figuring the Basses of simple four-part vocal compositions such as the hymns from Ravenscroft's Psalter and the older German chorales, both of which may be found in any good Hymnal. These Basses, when figured, may be practised in two different ways, (1) without, and (2) with, the composed upper part written above them. The latter exercise is by far the more difficult, as it often involves the alternation between close and extended harmony in order to prepare discords, avoid consecutives,[1] &c., as may be seen from the following examples:[2]

___

[1] The danger of consecutive Fifths arises, in particular, whenever the upper part of two consecutive Triads (or of a Triad followed by $\begin{smallmatrix}7\\5\end{smallmatrix}$) moves in Thirds (Tenths) with the Bass, as in the first two chords of Ex. 12 (a) and the antepenultimate and penultimate chords of (c).

[2] From Türk, *Kurze Anweisung &c.*, 1791, § 214, p. 274.

Ex. 12

§ 7. We will suppose that the student has reached the stage of attempting actual accompaniment, and that he has acquired a copy of, say, Corelli's *Opera Quinta*, the well-known Twelve Sonatas for Violin and Bass. In all cases of doubt or difficulty—and it is idle to pretend that such will not, at first, be of frequent occurrence—he is strongly advised to set out the accompaniment in as many different ways as occur to him, and to weigh carefully the advantages and disadvantages of the different versions.

Ph. Em. Bach attached great importance (as we have already seen)[1] to the adoption from the outset of a severely critical method. First of all, the pupil must play the figured Bass set before him; then he is to set it out on two staves; finally the teacher is to criticize both the performance at the keyboard and also the written version, and the pupil is to give an account of every detail, "why, e.g., this or that note must be where it is, SO and NOT OTHERWISE".

"One cannot", he writes in another place,[2] "practise one's pupils enough in learning the figures.... As soon as one is no longer afraid of any figure, one has all possible liberty to think of the niceties of the accompaniment...."

"One should, therefore, let one's pupils diligently accompany pieces in which, on account of the chromatic harmony occurring therein, the Basses are adequately, that is to say, abundantly, figured. To this end I have used my late Father's figured Basses, with great profit, and without danger to the lives of my pupils. And they are not bad for the fingers either...."

We can imagine the amused smile with which the last two sentences were penned, for some of John Sebastian's Basses are certainly "not bad for the fingers", and, though they may not endanger life, can certainly be relied on to provide food for thought!

There is little that could profitably be added to these suggestions of Philip Emanuel.

Whoever wishes to attain to the highest degree of perfection in the art of accompaniment that his individual musical endowment allows will find a well-nigh inexhaustible field of study, as well as a perennial source of delight, in the figured Basses of John Sebastian Bach.

---

[1] Cf. Ch. v, 'Forbidden progressions', § 2, note 3.
[2] *Versuch* &c., Part II, Ch. 1, §§ 4, 5.

APPENDIX TO CHAPTER I

I. THE TENBURY *SYNTAGMA*

IN all references in these pages to the third volume of the *Syntagma Musicum* of Michael Praetorius the date of publication is given as 1619.

In the Library of St. Michael's College at Tenbury, however, there is a copy of the second and third volumes (bound together, and containing the autograph of G. P. Telemann), each bearing the date 1618. These are, so far as the present writer is aware, the sole survivors of an earlier edition than the well-known one of 1619.

II. *BASSO SEGUENTE*

The term *Basso seguente*, or *Barittono* [sic], is used by Banchieri, and apparently by him alone, to denote that which has been described in § 3 as an 'Organ Bass' (*Basso per Organo*), namely, an instrumental part which follows the vocal Bass *note for note*, and, when the latter is silent, fills the gaps by including whatever happens at the moment to be the *lowest sounding part*.

Kinkeldey (*Orgel und Klavier &c.*, p. 124 sq.) quotes a work of Gio. Piccioni entitled: *Concerti ecclesiastici à 1–8 voci con il suo Basso seguito* (*Venetia, Vincenti*, 1610). The term *Basso seguito*, used by Piccioni, may doubtless be regarded as equivalent to Banchieri's *Basso seguente*, or *Barittono*, as denoting a part which closely *follows* the *lowest* vocal part of the composition.

Banchieri's *Basso seguente* differed from Viadana's *Basso continuo* in two respects: (1) it was *unbarred*, and (2) it was *never independent*, but always closely followed (hence *seguente*) one or other of the voice parts. This latter characteristic was, it is true, shared by many of the *Bassi continui* of Viadana and others, while, on the other hand, these differed from the *Basso seguente* of Banchieri in being barred (*spartiti*).

Banchieri's *Ecclesiastiche Sinfonie detti Canzoni in aria francese per sonare et cantare et sopra un Basso seguente concertare entro l'organo*, Op. 16, 1607, offer an example of the *Basso seguente*. In the preface, quoted *in extenso* by Kinkeldey (o. c., p. 223), Banchieri tells us that, if all four parts of the composition are to be played upon a keyed instrument, it can be barred and put into 'short score' (*si possono spartire & intavolare*), but that, if it is to be performed "with voices and instruments", the Organist must play the *Basso seguente* "with no sort of alteration [i.e. without 'divisions' or other embellishments, which would doubtless be added in the upper parts, as well as, possibly, *in the Bass itself*, in a version for a keyed instrument], but severely and solidly" (*senza alcuna alteratione ma con gravità, & sodezza*). Compare with this injunction the beginning of Viadana's second rule, to the effect that "the Organist is bound to play the Organ part (*Partitura*) simply, and in particular with the left hand" (cf. p. 11, and, for the original version, p. 20).

In the third, greatly enlarged, edition (1614) of his *Cartella musicale* (1st ed. 1601, 2nd ed. 1610, 4th ed. 1615) Banchieri alludes to Viadana, Bianciardi, and Agazzari as having learnedly described "the method to which the Organist must adhere in playing correctly over the *Basso continuo, seguente*, or *Barit-*

tono, whichever we choose to call it" (*il modo che deve tenere l'Organista in suonare rettamente sopra il Basso continuo, seguente ò Barittono che dire lo vogliamo*), and, after giving, and explaining, four examples of how to set a *Basso continuo* to a single vocal part, he concludes: "I commend, however, the barred *Bassi continui*, and in my opinion they answer far better than the *seguenti* [i.e. the unbarred], because the Organist is thus more sure of maintaining the strict time of the *ensemble*" (*Lodo pero & in mio giudicio stanno molto meglio li Bassi continui spartiti che seguenti, per maggiore sicurezza del Organista in condurre rettamente il concerto in battuta*).

III. SAINT-LAMBERT'S MYTHICAL *TRAITÉ* OF 1680

It will be seen from what follows that § 23, describing Saint-Lambert's *Nouveau Traité &c.*, 1707, and thus including it in the period 1600–1700 on the erroneous supposition that it represented a second, slightly enlarged edition of a *Traité* of 1680, belongs, not to the foregoing, but to the next, chapter.

Unfortunately, this knowledge, which the writer owes entirely to the investigations of Professor Van den Borren, Librarian of the *Conservatoire Royal* at Brussels (for whose ever-ready help he cannot adequately express his gratitude), largely supplemented by those of M. Tessier, Secretary-General of the *Societé française de Musicologie* (to whom warm thanks are also due), came too late to permit of any readjustment.

Space does not permit the citation of all the valuable details of confirmatory evidence collected by M. Tessier; the main facts are, briefly, these:

Saint-Lambert's preface to the *Nouveau Traité &c.* (*Paris, Ballard*, 1707), of which the *Bibliothèque nationale* at Paris possesses two copies, contains the following reference to his earlier work, *Les principes du clavecin* (*Paris, Ballard*, 1702):

"Ayant donné cy devant au public un ouvrage sous le titre des principes du clavecin, dans lequel je ne parle que de ce qui regarde les pièces, j'ay cru que le titre ne seroit point assez rempli, *si je n'ajoutois un traité de l'accompagnement*" (the italics are added).

These latter words are not consistent with the assumption that Saint-Lambert had already (in 1680, or at any other time) published a *Traité de l'accompagnement*, an assumption which, in the first instance, rests solely on the authority of Fétis.

The date assigned by the latter to the *Principes du clavecin* is 1697; a palpable error, for the fact that the above-mentioned edition of 1702 was preceded by no earlier one is irrefragably established by Saint-Lambert's own statement in the preface, to the effect that "l'auteur corrigera sur les avis reçus ... *si on en fait une seconde édition*" (the italics are added).

The inclusion of the word *nouveau* in the title of Saint-Lambert's treatise on Accompaniment may well have been suggested by the existence, not of an earlier *Traité* of his own, but of other French treatises on the same subject, to which, indeed, he alludes (without actually naming them), namely, Delair's *Traité d'accompagnement &c., chez l'auteur*, Paris, 1690, and Boyvin's *Traité abrégé de l'accompagnement &c.*, 2nd ed., Paris, 1705. Be that as it may, the work was probably often referred to, for short—as e.g. in an undated catalogue of Roger of Amsterdam (No. 10,872 in the library of the Brussels Conservatoire), which, however, the mention of *Feu* [= the late] Mr *Arcan-*

APPENDIX TO CHAPTER I

gelo Corelli proves to have been printed after 1713—simply as *Traité &c.*, and this may well have led Fétis to assume the existence of two separate works (*Traité* and *Nouveau Traité*); the erroneous dates (*Traité* 1680, *Principes* 1697) do not, unfortunately, stand alone in his works.

It will, then, be seen from the above that the *Traité* of 1680 is a myth, pure and simple, and that, in the *Principes* (1702) and the *Nouveau Traité* (1707), we have two closely related works, forerunners (as regards their subject-matter), in a most remarkable way, of the First and Second Parts of Ph. Em. Bach's famous *Versuch*.

APPENDIX TO CHAPTER V

A. It was shown in Ch. iii, § 10, that in the seventeenth, and early eighteenth, century there was considerably less strictness in the matter of consecutives than at a later period. This is strikingly illustrated by the following example from Corelli (Opera 2^a, Sonata III, Allemanda, bars 3–5), which became the subject of an acrimonious controversy in which many musicians of note were involved (Giov. Paolo Colonna, Antimo Liberati, and others), and of which the records are preserved in the Library of the *Liceo Musicale* at Bologna (for a detailed account see Francesco Vatielli, *Arte e vita musicale a Bologna*, Bologna 1927–, pp. 184 sq., and Nestore Morini, *Notizie di Arcangelo Corelli &c.*, Bologna, 1913, pp. 6 sq.).

In reply to an exceedingly courteous and respectful letter from Padre Matteo Zani (written on behalf of Colonna) Corelli wrote, 17th October 1685, in a highly contemptuous tone. He quoted Francesco Foggia, Antimo Liberati, and Matteo Simonelli as entirely approving the passage, and saying that "whoever found any difficulty did not know the meaning of *legatura* [retardation]".

"If", Corelli writes, "instead of a quaver rest, I had placed a dot, which would be of the same value, after the preceding note, beginners in music, who know no more than the first rules, would not have found any difficulty whatever; but I, wishing the note to be detached and to cease sounding [*che si stacchi e si smorzi la nota*], thinking that it sounded better so, acted as I did."

Corelli, then, regarded the Bass as equivalent to:

N.B.—The semicircle ⌒ over the $\frac{4}{2}$ denotes the absence of the 6 (see Ch. xxiii, § 19).

The assumption that the Fifths are thereby justified is entirely contrary to the teaching of later authorities: Marpurg tells us that Fifths following in the wake of Fourths through the downward progression of the lower part (*Die hinter der Quarte unterwärts nachschlagende[n] Quinten*) can only be used in the middle parts, by which he evidently means between the upper and a middle part (see Ch. v, § 6 *f*, Ex. 30).

Liberati, in a long letter to Colonna, endorses Corelli's assumption of an hypothetical *legatura* in the Bass, but adds that, if this explanation be not accepted, the interposition of the quaver rest is enough to save "the pretended Fifths": he had heard Abbatini (whose pupil Colonna had been) assert that "any atom of a rest is enough to save both Fifths and Octaves", wherefore, "to want to uphold the contrary of this universal practice would be like wanting to check the course of the Danube".

This, again, is entirely contrary to later teaching. Marpurg tells us (*Handbuch &c.*, 1755, pp. 56 and 62; 2nd ed. 1762, pp. 88 and 94) that (with certain exceptions which have no bearing on the present case) the mistake of Octaves and of Fifths "is not made good by the interposition of a short rest", by which, he tells us, we are to understand all rests ranging from the value of a minim in *Allabreve* time to that of a demisemiquaver.

The practical importance to us of this controversy lies largely in the assurance that, in accompanying the passage in question (and analogous ones of approximately the same date), there is no need to have recourse (with very ill effect) to contrary motion, but that Corelli's Fifths can be reproduced in the accompaniment. Three-part harmony is obviously in place, as follows:

B. The preparation of a Ninth by the Octave of the Bass has been mentioned as a practice that was forbidden in the middle of the eighteenth century, though adopted by good composers at an earlier period (see Ch. iii § 10 *a*, Exx. 1–3, and Ch. v, § 4 *e ad fin.*).

It is worth noting that J. S. Bach adhered to a certain extent to the earlier usage, though, in the instances hitherto noticed by the writer, the progression is disguised by a preceding changing, i.e. accented passing, note in the Bass. The following example from the second movement of the Sonata in G major for two Flutes and Bass (assumed by W. Rust to be an earlier version of the

Sonata in the same key for Cembalo and Viola da Gamba) will serve to illustrate the point:

C. (1) Marpurg gives the rule that there must be no consecutive Octaves or Fifths between the last chord of a repeated section of a movement and the first chord, with which it recommences (*Handbuch &c.*, 1755, pp. 60 and 65; 2nd ed., 1762, pp. 92 and 97).

He does not state whether he intends this prohibition to apply to accompaniment as well as to composition, but in any case, it is very certain that no such rule need be observed in accompanying the works of composers of the Corelli period.

(2) He also tells us (o.c., 2nd ed., p. 98) that: One octave may follow another by contrary motion. In harmony of more than four parts this may occur, at a pinch, in slow time and between main notes, but preferably not between extreme parts. When the harmony is thin, the first octave must be a passing note, and the pace brisk (Tab. VI, Fig. 27):

APPENDIX TO CHAPTER XVIII

HEINICHEN's rules for the treatment of quavers moving by step in true (i.e. slow) common time, as opposed to what he calls *Semi-allabreve*, to the effect that each *virtualiter* long quaver (i.e. the first and third of a group of four) bears its own harmony, while the *virtualiter* short ones pass (see Ch. xviii, § 3 c, Ex. 23), unless followed by a leap, in which case they, too, bear a chord (Exx. 25, 26), do not always hold good.

Sometimes, in movements in slow $\frac{4}{4}$ time which have nothing in common with the Overture style, we find the rules apply which Heinichen gives for 'Overture time', slow and fast alike (see § 3 q, r), namely that quavers moving by step are to be treated like semiquavers in true common time (or quavers in *Semi-allabreve*): that is to say, a group of four quavers rising or falling by step passes under the same harmony, unless followed by a leap (or unless the last quaver is figured), in which case *transitus irregularis* is indicated, and the third quaver bears the harmony appertaining to the fourth (see § 3 *d*, Exx. 27, 27 *a*).

Examples might be multiplied, but the following must suffice. In Ex. 1 the minim A in the 1st Violin part makes it certain that the group of four quavers, d', $\sharp c'$, b, a, bears but a single harmony. It is, of course, open to the accompanist to follow the Bass in Thirds (see § 3 *c*, Ex. 24), though the presence of such Thirds in the 2nd Violin part tends to render such a proceeding superfluous; had the composer definitely desired it, he would have figured the Bass as follows:

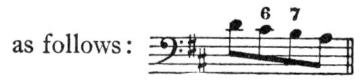

Corelli, Opera 2ᵃ, Sonata VIII, Allemanda, bar 10.

Ex. 1

N.B.—If Corelli intended the sixth quaver, A *, to bear a Triad, instead of being treated as a passing note, it should have been figured (5, $\frac{5}{3}$, or 8).

In Exx. 2 and 3 there can be no doubt that the penultimate quaver * bears the harmony of the one which follows (*transitus irregularis*), in accordance with Heinichen's rule for semiquavers in true $\frac{4}{4}$ time, and for quavers in *Semi-allabreve* and 'Overture time', though he does not expressly mention *transitus irregularis* in connexion with the latter, as far as groups of four quavers are concerned.

Corelli, Opera 2ᵃ, Sonata I, Largo, *ad fin.*

Ex. 2

Corelli, Opera 3ᵃ, Sonata VIII, 2nd Allegro, bars 23, 24.

Ex. 3

In both examples the last four quavers might have been figured as follows:

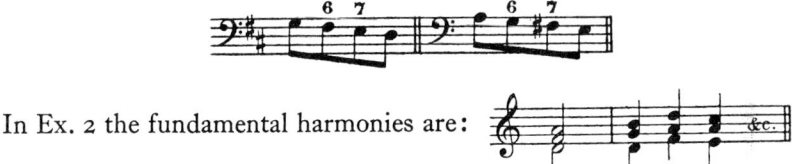

In Ex. 2 the fundamental harmonies are:

This accompaniment, however, has the disadvantage, apart from the somewhat harsh effect, of rising above, and tending to obscure, the principal parts. Though, as a general rule, passing notes which are present in a principal part are best omitted in the accompaniment, more especially if the upper part of the latter happens to coincide with the upper principal part, cases, nevertheless, arise when this principle may be sacrificed with advantage, and it seems not improbable that Ex. 2 may be included among those of which Ph. Em. Bach says that "the accompaniment is identical with the example", i.e. that it simply reproduces the principal parts.

In Ex. 3 it is clearly best to follow the Bass in Thirds, as:

or in three parts:

or

INDEX RERUM

Abbreviations: Ph. Em. B. = Philipp Emanuel Bach, Hein. = Heinichen,
Kirn. = Kirnberger, Mar. = Marpurg, St. L. = Saint-Lambert.

N.B.—*For references omitted in this Index see the Table of Contents.*

accenti: employment of (*Viadana*), 10; defined by Praetorius, 10, n. 2;

Acciaccatura: Heinichen's account based on Gasparini, 251, n. 1; special form of (*Gasparini*), 254; use of in accomp. (*Hein.*), 452 *sq.*;

accidentals: special use of (*Viadana*), 16–18; ♭ in certain cases probably misprint for 6, 18; interval sharpened by ✕ before or *underneath* figure (*Guidotti* [*Cavalieri*]), 48; (and figures) necessity for in *Basso continuo* (*Banchieri*), 88; exceptional position of, 103 & n. 6; ✕, ♭, ♮ (*Sabbatini*), 121 *sq.*; over Bass, economy in use of (*Ebner*), 131 *sq.*; position of in regard to figure (*Locke*), 159 (below Exx.); extended use of ♮ (*St. L.*), 175; omission of in figuring (*St. L.*), 188 *inf. sq.*; various uses of, 884–6; position of (before or after figure), 884, n. 1;

ACCOMPANIMENT: pitch of in relation to principal parts (*Viadana*), 19 *sq.*; full close: a Third above principal part, 46 *sq.*, & nn. 2 & 3; to keep below upper principal part (*Agazzari*), 70; origin of a— from a Bass (*Agazzari*), 72–4; independent of principal parts (*Praetorius*), 97; example of, 97 *sq.*; change of style, 98 *sub* Ex. 3a, N.B. (5); pitch of in relation to voices (*Praetorius*), 98 *inf. sq.*; to be adjusted to number of voices singing, 99; independent of principal parts (*Staden*), 102; pitch of to be adapted to that of voices (*Staden*), 108; pitch in relation to that of high voices (*Staden*), 109; of (*a*) all Bass notes not preceded by sharp, except *B quadro* (*B mi*), (*b*) *B quadro* & all notes preceded by sharp (*Sabbatini*), 111 *inf. sq.*; upward compass of, 112, n. 3; right hand not to go above highest principal part (*Ebner*), 132; of compositions for a single voice (*Penna*), 148–50; on the Organ, general rules for (*Penna*), 150–4; downward compass of (*Locke*), 162, n. 13; Saint-Lambert's definition of, 174; compass of (*St. L.*), 185 (3); licences in (*St. L.*), 195–8; taste in (*St. L.*), 198–202; must generally be simple (*Werckmeister*), 209: its upper part must not continually follow that of the principals, 210: a discord, *though figured*, sometimes best omitted, 210 *sq.*; compass of (*Niedt*), 225, Reg. 2, 226, Reg. 7 & n. 13; interval present in solo part may be omitted, though figured (*Niedt*), 227, Reg. 8; more elaborate during pause in principal parts (*Niedt*), 230 *sup.*; embellishment of, Gasparini's warning against encroachment on Soloist, 251 *sq.*; 'filled-in' (*vollstimmig*), Kirnberger's rules for, 315–17; in 5 or more parts (*Türk*), 322; the instruments used, 326–30; number & distribution of parts, 330–48; forms of described by Heinichen, 332–6; 'filled-in', importance of keeping hands close together, 336 (§ 38), 337, *sub* Ex. 4; 'filled-in', example of (*Hein.*), 343, 4-part version of the same, 343, n. 20, how far Heinichen's principles were generally accepted, 344–6; use of extended harmony, 346–8; temporary adoption of fifth part in 4-part, 349–59; the compass of: A, in itself, 360–4, B, in relation to principal part, 364–73; upper part to be below, rather than above or in unison with, the upper principal part, 364–6; compass of in relation to solo part of low pitch, 366–9; the pitch of in relation (*a*) to discords, (*b*) to successive six-threes in the principal parts, 369–73; how far it should possess independent interest, 382–92; three forms of (*Daube*) 388–90; certain niceties of the, 438–81; definition of good (*Ph. Em. B.*), 439; embellishment of the, two main principles, 439; Ph. Em. Bach's instructions: movement in 3rds (or 10ths) with Bass, 469–71, precautions to be observed, 471 *sq.*, 3rds with Bass alternating with 6ths, 472 *sq.*, a light a— suitable in quick time, 473 *sq.*, skips in the harmony, 474–6, treatment of gaps between slow notes in Bass, passing notes & chords between successive harmonies, 476–81; special cases (*Ph. Em. B.*), 681 *sq.*;

acoustics: interesting question in, 367, n. 7;

Allabreve: (*Hein.*), 721, 724 *sq.*, **764–6**; varieties of, **766–9**;

908   INDEX RERUM

ambitus modi: 166, n. 3; 212, n. 21; 344, n. 24;
Anschlag: dotted, 433-5;
anticipatio transitus: 855 *sq.*; —— *per ellipsin, ibid.*;
anticipation: as an alternative explanation of certain harmonies, 295, n. 1, xiv *ad fin.*, 321 *sup.*, 692, n. 2 *ad fin.*; of the Bass in the right hand, 417-21;
Appoggiatura: in the principal part, the accomp. of, 422-31; use of in accomp. (*Hein.*), 450; double, in Fourths (*Ph. Em. B.*), 706;
Arpa doppia: 72;
arpeggiare: spreading of chords, recommended by Penna, 154 *sup.*;
arpeggios: use of in accomp. (*Hein.*), 457-62;
Arpicordo (see 'Harpsichord'):
arsis: 139, n. 19;
Augmented Second: Penna's use of, 139, n. 21; 140, n. 22;

BASS: doubled in the lower 8ve in cadences (*Bianciardi*), 20, note 14 *ad fin.*; often unfigured where principal part, or parts, are given, 34; rules for playing from unfigured (*Bianciardi*), 75 *sq.*; definition of (*Bianciardi*), 75; to be doubled in the lower 8ve in full closes (*Bianciardi*), 78; passing notes in the (*Bianciardi*), 79; moving by step accompanied with 10ths in upper part (*Bianciardi*), 79; falling a 5th, or rising a 4th, gives rise to accidental in upper parts (*Banchieri*), 86, 87 *inf.*; divisions of (*Sabbatini*), 113; black notes in the (*Sabbatini*), 125 *sq.*; quick notes in the (*Albert*), 129; unfigured, Penna's rules for, 138-42; long notes in (*Penna*), 142 *sq.*; quick notes in (*Penna*), 143 *sq.*; optional addition of in fugal entries (*Penna*), 150, n. 51; quick notes in (*Locke*), 157 (8); quick notes in (*Blow*), 166 [11] *sq.*; unfigured, rules for given by Saint-Lambert, Gasparini & Heinichen, their inadequacy, 192; remarkable rules for unfigured (*St. L.*), 193 *sq.* & nn. 29, 30; modification of by accompanist (*St. L.*), 196; quick notes in (*Niedt*), 229 *sq.*; often unfigured in theatrical & chamber styles, 264; unfigured (*Hein.*), 265-9; quick notes in the B—, 716-77, definition of, 717, n. 3; exceptions to Heinichen's rules for quavers in the, 903-5;
Bass note: accidentally sharpened, employment of the 8ve of (*Ph. Em. B.*) 509, (*Türk*) 510, (*Ph. Em. B.*) 517 *sq.* & n. 4;
Bass voice: accomp. of (*Penna*), 153;

Basse chiffrée: 2;
Bassetgen: 224; 233, n. 19;
Bassetto (Germ. *Basset, Bassett*): treatment of by Agazzari & others (*Praetorius*), example from Viadana, 96; 224; 226, Reg. 7; Niedt's & Heinichen's rules compared, 226, n. 13; Niedt's treatment of *-i*, 232 *sq.* & n. 20; *-i*, 373-81;
Basso continuo or *Bassus continuus* (see also '*Bassus generalis*', 'Thorough-Bass'): 2; defined, 6; opponents of, 80 *sq.*; use of ♮ & ♭, figures, & bar-lines approved by Banchieri, 83; Banchieri's directions for learning to play on, 83-5; how sharpened Sixth may be avoided (*Banchieri*), 87; necessity for accidentals & figures (*Banchieri*), 88; when barred & furnished with accidentals & figures, 'a true epitome of the entire score', 89; rapid spread of from Italy, 92 *sq.*; purpose of (*Praetorius*), 93; B— *continuus* less satisfactory term than B— *generalis* (*Niedt*), 223 & n. 8;
Basso continuato: 6, n. 1;
Basso generale: 6, n. 2;
Basso numerato: 2; 6;
Basso principale: 6, n. 2;
Basso seguente: 899 *sq.*;
Basso seguito: 899;
Bassus ad Organum (see 'Organ Bass'):
Bassus continuus (see '*Basso continuo*'):
Bassus generalis: 6; B— g— *seu continuus*, why so called (*Praetorius*), 93; how to be extracted from vocal Bass (*Praetorius*), 94 *sq.*; on Organ or Lute to be supported by some bass (wind or stringed) instrument, may also be sung (*Praetorius*), 99; etymology & definition (*Niedt*), 223;
Bassus generalis or *Bassus continuus ad Organum*: divergent notation of (Staden), 100;
battere di mano: 139, n. 19;
battuta: Penna's description of, 139, n. 19;
bezifferter Bass: 2;
Bindung: definition of (*Schröter*), 127, n. 2;
Bogenclavier: 327 & n. 3;
broken chords (see 'Chords'):

Cadence: Viadana's rule for *-s*, 11; Exx. (Staden), 12; recommendation (*Werckmeister*), 13; Exx. of $\frac{5\ —}{3443}$, 40, n. 5; striking Ex. (*Monteverde*), 42; *formulae* employed by Cavalieri, 49 *sq.*; *-s* (*Penna*), 145-8; rules for (*Locke*), 155 (3), (*Blow*), 165 *sq.*; 'common' & 'half', sophisticated forms of (*Blow*), 170 [16, 17] *sq.* & nn. 10-13; different forms of (*St. L.*), 183 *sq.*; progression of leading note in a (*St. L.*), 185 (6); different forms & figuring (*Niedt*), 228; apparent discre-

pancy between solo part & figuring in full close (*G. P. Telemann*), 289; disregard of figuring in final -s (*Ph. Em. B.*), 293 & nn. 4, 5;
Catachresis: 857–60;
Cento Concerti (*Viadana*): 2–5;
Ceterone: 72;
changing note (Ital. *nota cambiata*, Germ. *Wechselnote*): 717;
Character Modi: 633;
Chitarrina: 68;
Chitarrone (*Chitarone*): to accompany voice, esp. Tenor (*Caccini*), 42 *sq.*; Cavalieri's use of, 47; 68 & n. 3;
Chords: repercussion of, 109 & n. 16; divided between two hands (*Sabbatini*), 110; repercussion of (*St. L.*), 200 (6), 201 (11, 14); broken (*St. L.*), 200 (7, 8), 201 (14); 'ordinary' (*Werckmeister*), 205, why so called, *ibid.*, n. 5; $^6_4$, Heinichen's remarkable distinction between identical harmonies, 262, n. 13;
Circolo ò Ruota delle Cadenze (*Penna*), 147 *sq.*;
Cither (*cetera*): 68; 72;
clash: between solo part & accomp. (*Caccini*), 46;
clausulae: 'discantisirend', 'altisirend', 'tenorisirend', 'bassirend' (*Werckmeister*), 13; *Modi Ionici*: *cl. principalis, affinalis, minus principalis, finalis* (*Werckmeister*), 14, n. 8; *formales*, in the Ionian & Dorian Modes (*Werckmeister*), 212; *-a principalis et finalis* or *primaria*: *minus principalis* or *secundaria*: *affinalis* or *tertiaria*, 213; *-ae assumptae* & *peregrinae*, 213;
Claves signatae: 212;
Clavichord: use of for accomp., 326 *sq.* & n. 2;
clef: Soprano or Alto in *Bassus ad organum* demands light accomp. (*Staden*), 108; -s in use in a Thorough-Bass (*Niedt*), 224; mastery of all the -s indispensable (*Mattheson*), 272 & n. 3; Ex. (*Mattheson*), illustrating the use of the various -s in a figured Bass, 888;
Close (see also 'Accompaniment' & 'Cadence'): avoidance of full (*Banchieri*), 88, Ex. 10;
Common Chord (see 'Triad'):
compound intervals: figuring of (*Peri, Caccini, Cavalieri*), 34–65 *passim*; (*Praetorius*) 95; (*Staden*) 104; (*Penna*) 135; (*St. L.*) 174 & n. 3; figuring of condemned (*St. L.*), 180; figuring of, 877–9;
CONSECUTIVES (see also 'Fifths' & 'Octaves'): 5ths & 8ves (*Viadana*), 18 *sq.*; Bianciardi's interpretation of rule against, 78, n. 10; avoided by crossing of parts (*Banchieri*), 78 *sq.*, n. 10; forbidden, chiefly between extreme parts (*Penna*), 136; forbidden between extreme parts (*Locke*), 155 (1); not produced by entry of new part (*Mar.*), 160, n. 11; when to be disregarded (*St. L.*), 197; avoided by: (1) contrary motion, (2) alternation with 6th (*Niedt*), 225 *sq.* permissible (except between extreme parts) in 'filled-in' accomp. (*Gasparini*), 252 *inf. sq.*; in Mattheson's Exx., 281 *sq.*; hidden, Schröter's sensitiveness to, 302 *sq.*; permissible in 'filled-in' accomp. *except between extreme parts* (*Hein.*), 334 *sq.* & n. 11; arising through (1) the entry, (2) the disappearance of a part not forbidden (Exx. from *Mar.*), 608, n. 2; cases in which special care is needed (*Ph. Em. B.*), 695; saved by interposition of the smallest rest (*Abbatini*), 902; not saved by interposition of a short rest (*Mar.*), 902; between last & first chord of repeated section forbidden (*Mar.*), 903;
Continuo: word used in two senses, 223, n. 8;
Contralto voice: accomp. of (*Penna*), 153;
contrary motion (see also '*motus contrarius*'): recommended (*Bianciardi*), 78; to avoid consecutives (*Ebner*), 132; recommended (*Penna*), 136; recommended (*Locke*), 157 (10); to avoid consecutives (*Blow*), 163 [2]; to avoid consecutives (*St. L.*), 185 (1);
countersubject: the introduction of in accomp., 389, n. 5, 391 & n. 10;
crossing of parts: in Banchieri's Exx., 85, n. 4; (*St. L.*), 177 *sq.*, nn. 9, 10, & 189; permitted by Kirnberger, 317 *sq.*; (1) to evade consecutives, 392–4, (2) to maintain position of right hand, 394–7; compared with an analogous device, 395, n. 3, 396, n. 7;
custos: 889 *sq.*;

discord (see also 'dissonance'): sometimes omitted, though figured, 39 & n. 4; Caccini's use of unprepared -s, 45 *sq.*; Cavalieri's ditto, 56–8; preparation & resolution of (*Blow*), 165; preparation & resolution of $^6_4$ (*Blow*), 171 [18] & n. 14; Heinichen's classification of -s, 261 *sq.* & nn. 11–13; Kirnberger's classification of, 314; Türk's classification of, 320 *sq.*; Marpurg's theory of, 320, n. 3; resolution of duplicated -s in 'filled-in' accomp. (*Hein.*), 336 *sq.*, anticipated in left hand, 338–42, important reservation, 339, n. 19; inversion of, 838–40; transference of, *ibid.*;

910   INDEX RERUM

dissonance (see also 'discord'): -s & their resolutions (*Penna*), 151 *sq.*; G. M. Telemann's views on, 310;
'Divisions': in Bass, when allowable (*Gasparini*), 252;
dot: after figure as indication of time-value (*Staden*), 105; (*Ph. Em. B.*), 882;
double: sharps & flats, notation of, **886–8**;
doubling (duplication): of leading notes, diatonic or accidental (*Penna*), 153 (Rules 15, 16); Heinichen's remarkable rules based on distinction between intervals naturally & accidentally major, 260 *sq.*; in the *unison* of accidentally sharpened 3rd [leading note] (*Hein., Ph. Em. B., Kirn.*), 551, n. 1; in arpeggio Bass, of a dissonant interval, 640, n. 1;
driving notes: 128, n. 2; in the principal part, the accomp. of, **431–3**;
duplication (see 'doubling'):

Eleventh: (*Niedt*), 232;
ellipse: of the resolution, 857–60;
essential: Seventh (*Kirn.*), 542; discord (*Mar.*), 542 *sq.*;

Falsae: (*Hein.*), 262 *sq.*;
false relation: (*St. L.*), 187, n. 20 *ad fin.*;
Falsetto voices: recommended by Viadana, 19;
Fifth: (or Sixth) on note with accidental ♭ (*Banchieri*), 86; perfect followed by diminished, & vice versâ (*Penna*), 136, n. 11; progression between a perfect & a diminished or augmented (*St. L., Mar., Ph. Em. B.*), 197 *sq.*; diminished, restricted use of (*Gasparini*), 253 & n. 3; diminished, regarded by Mattheson as consonant, 275; imperfect (diminished), inclusion of in chords of the 7th (*Gasparini, Hein., Ph. Em. B.*), 550 *sq.*, 572; (perfect, augmented, imperfect) inclusion of in 7 6 suspensions (*Ph. Em. B.*), 572 *sq.*; sometimes assumed to be perfect unless the contrary is indicated, 863, n. 1;
fifth part: temporary inclusion of, 181, n. 14, **349–59**;
Fifths, consecutive (see also 'Consecutives'): in accomp. (*Viadana*), 18 *inf.*; between voice & *Basso continuo*, 23, n. 1; allowed by Guidotti in accomp., 48; in Ex. of Agazzari, 71; condoned (*St. L.*), 198 (5): examples of (*Mattheson*), 281 *sq.*; G. P. Telemann's sensitiveness to hidden, 286 (3); between principal part & accomp. condoned (*G. P. Telemann*), 286 *sq.*; allowed by Schröter, 304; why

objectionable (*Türk*), 321; arising between successive Sixths in accomp. *below* $\frac{6}{3}$ in principal parts, **371–3**; divergent views on (*Mar., Ph. Em. B., Schröter*), 401–3 & nn. 9–11; unavoidable, between Bass & an upper part of the accomp. (*Leclair, Vivaldi, Corelli*), 404–6; Marpurg's rules, **489–94**; permissible in arpeggios, 494; hidden (*Mar.*), 495 *sq.*; by contrary motion, 496; especial danger of, 634, n. 4; avoidable in only one position, 641 *sq.*, Exx. 1–3; justifiable (*Mar.*), 686;
Figured Bass: 2; 6; addition of to the *Magnum opus musicum* of Orlando di Lasso, 91;
figures: use of by Monodists, 33 *sq.*; Cavalieri's use of triple, 61 *inf.*; not universally adopted, 65–7; (and accidentals) necessity for in *Basso continuo* (*Banchieri*), 88; necessity for (*Praetorius*), 95; details of use of (*Staden*), 101–4; Saint-Lambert's ambiguous use of single: (1) $2=\frac{5}{2},\frac{5}{4}$, (2) $\times 4=\frac{8}{\times 4},\times \frac{6}{3}$, 175 *sq.* & nn. 4, 5; also of double, 179–81; triple, Saint-Lambert's rule for, 181; disregard of (*St. L.*), 189 *inf. sq.* & n. 23; ways of indicating accidental alteration (*Niedt*), 228; theoretically superfluous, sometimes desirable (*Ph. Em. B.*), 730 *sq.*;
figuring: compound intervals denoted, 34 *sq.*; ambiguity of Peri's, 37 *sq.*; of Caccini's, 43; diversity of Cavalieri's, 49; of passing notes (*Cavalieri*), 58–61; special points in Cavalieri's, 61–5; necessity for (*Agazzari*), 68; rules for (*Agazzari*), 69; of compound intervals (*Penna*), 135; incomplete, $4=\frac{6}{2}$ (*Penna*), 144; inadequate (*St. L.*), 175 *sq.* & nn. 5, 6, & 186, n. 19; free interpretation of (*St. L.*), 187 (1) (2); of notes of triple value (*Geminiani, Ph. Em. B.*), 465, n. 3; wrong use of $4\downarrow$, $4\natural=\frac{8}{6},\frac{8}{4\natural}$ (*Ph. Em. B.*), 669, example from Leclair, 671; use of $\frac{9}{7}$ for $\frac{7}{4}$ (*Ph. Em. B.*), 674 *sq.*; incomplete, $\frac{7}{2}=\frac{7}{2}$ (*Schröter*), 708; incomplete, **804–35**; varieties of, **862–82**; 'enharmonic', 879 *sq.*; 'retrospective', 880 *sq.*;
'filling-in': (*St. L.*), 199 (3, 4) & nn. 33–5, 200 (5, 7);
fingering: Penna's, 151 & n. 52;
flat: ♭ misprint for 6 (*Viadana*), 18; ♭ as warning against full close (*Sabbatini*), 122 (8);
forbidden progressions (see 'progression'):
formulae: condensed (*Penna*), 144, **831–5**;

INDEX RERUM

Four-three chords: **628–46**;
fugal entries: treatment of (*Penna*), 150 & n. 51; 373 *sq.* & n. 2;
Fugues: in a Thorough-Bass (*Niedt*), 234;
Füll-Stimmen: 245, n. 6; 274, n. 9;

General Bass (see '*Bassus generalis*'):
gradation of tone: in discords (*Ph. Em. B., Quantz*), **407–14**;
Gravicembalo: as 'instrument of foundation', 68;
groppolo: 47 *sq.*;

hands: to be kept close together (*Penna*), 137; position of (*Penna*), 151 & n. 53;
Handsachen: importance of (*Mattheson*), 272;
harmony: influence of words on, 106, n. 10; inclusion of notes extraneous to the (*Penna*), 145–7, nn. 39 & 41; 'filling in' of the (*Penna*), 150; proper to Bass moving by step (*Locke's* use of progression afterwards forbidden), 156 (6) & n. 5; proper to Bass moving by Thirds (*Locke*), 156 (7); appropriate to the several degrees of the scale (*Hein., Rameau, Gasparini*), 265–7; repercussion of on repeated notes in Bass (*Ph. Em. B.*), 293 *sq.*; extended, use of in accomp., 346–8; fulness to be varied, 348; modifications of the figured h— necessitated by ornaments &c. in the principal part, **421–35**; modification of over passing notes, to avoid consecutives (*Ph. Em. B.*), 727, n. 15;
Harp: 68; 70;
Harpsichord: (*arpicordo*), 70; repercussion of harmony on the, 109, n. 16, 128, 293 *inf. sq.*, 733 *inf. sq.*;
Hülfs-Stimmen: 245, n. 6;

imitation: use of in accomp. (*St. L.*), 201 (12), (*Hein.*), **383–91**;
incoronata: 48;
'Instrument' (Germ.): = Harpsichord or Spinet, 128, n. 4;
'Instruments of foundation': 68; general principles concerning (*Agazzari*), 69 *sq.*; 237;
'Instruments of ornamentation': 68; Agazzari's instructions, 71 *sq.*; Praetorius translates & comments on Agazzari's rules, 99; 237;
Intavolatura (*d'organo*): 8; *d'organo* (*Viadana*), 14, n. 10; disadvantages of (*Agazzari*), 73; unequal staves in, 79, n. 13;
inversion: of discord, 838–40;

Keys: major & minor, circle of (*Blow*), 172 [20] & n. 15; (see also 'Musical Circle');
key-signatures: without, & with ♭ (*per B quadro, per B molle*), 124; change of (*Sabbatini*), 124; Penna's usual practice, 135; inconsistency in (*Niedt*), 235;

leading note: practice in regard to the (*Hein., Mattheson, Ph. Em. B., Kirn.*), 516, n. 3; omission of figuring (6 or $\frac{6}{5}$), 818;
left hand: function of (*Sabbatini*), 112;
legato: style recommended by Penna, 153 *sup.*;
levare di mano: 139, n. 19;
liaison (slurs): over notes in Bass to denote continuance of preceding harmony, 130, n. 7, 178, n. 11, 186, n. 19;
licence: traditional, in the interpretation of certain figures (*St. L.*), 191 *sq.* & n. 25; -s in accompanying (*St. L.*), 195–8;
Lira doppia: 47; 68;
Lirone: 68; 72;
Lute: 68; 70; 72;

'major' & 'minor' notes (*Sabbatini*), 121;
Manacordo: 19, n. 12; 110; 111;
melody: in accomp. (*Hein.*), 453–5;
Melothesia (see 'Locke'):
Modes: knowledge of them necessary (*Werckmeister*), 211 *sq.*;
Modi: ficti, 208, n. 12; *principales* or *authentici*: minus *principales* or *plagales*: *ficti: regulares*, 212;
modulation (transition): (*Locke*), 157, 159; (*Niedt*), 235; (see also 'Musical Circle');
monachina: 47;
mordent: prolonged m— substituted for shake (*Penna*), 146, n. 40; use of in accomp. (*Hein.*), 451 *sq.*;
Motus contrarius (see also 'contrary motion'): (*Werckmeister*), 207 (6) & n. 9;
Musical Circle: Heinichen's, 267–9; Mattheson's, 276 *sq.*;

Neben-Stimmen: 245, n. 6;
Ninth: minor, in cadence (*Penna*), 141 *sq.* & n. 29; wrongly called 'Second' (*Penna*), 151, n. 54; prepared by 8ve of Bass (*Purcell*), 169, n. 9; Saint-Lambert's treatment of, 178 *sq.*; (*Niedt*), 232; rising (*Türk*), 694;
Nona (see 'Ninth'):
nota cambiata (see also 'changing note'): 143, n. 32;
nota cambita: 725, n. 12;
notation: varieties of, **884–90**;

Octave: of ♮B & of sharpened note in Bass (*Sabbatini*), 123; of E in Bass (with ♭ in signature), 124; of Bass rarely taken with a *mi* (*Penna*), 137; of Bass omitted on leading notes (*Penna*), 152 & n. 59; of the Bass to be avoided in upper part (*Penna*), 153 & n. 60; use of -s below (or above) actual Bass, 381 *sq.*; consecutive -s: (*Viadana*), 18 *inf.*, (*Mattheson*), 281 *sq.*, (*Hein.*), 378 *sq.*, (*Mattheson*), 393; increasing sensitiveness to, 397–9; a special case, 399 *sq.*; (*Hein.*), 450, n. 6; (*Marpurg's* rules), 485–7; hidden -s, 487–9; -s by contrary motion, 903;
Organ Bass (*Bassus ad Organum*): early -es, 6–9; addition of to earlier works, 90–2;
Organ: pedals when used (*Viadana*), 15; as 'instrument of foundation', 68; Agazzari's rules, 70 *sq.*;
Organist: Praetorius's advice to, 100; to adapt accomp. to pitch of voices (*Staden*), 108;
Overture Time (*Ouverteur-Tact*): (*Hein.*) 769–74;

Pandora: 68;
partire (*spartire*): 6, n. 3;
Partitio (or *Sectio*) *gravium partium*: 7, n. 3;
Partitura (*Spartitura*): 6;
passages: use of in accomp. (*Hein.*), 455–7;
passaggi: employment of (*Viadana*), 10; defined by Praetorius, 10, n. 3;
passing harmonies: (unfigured) generated by movement of upper (or middle) part in 3rds with Bass (*Hein.*), 734, n. 25; the same, 771;
passing notes: use of in accomp. (*St. L.*), 202 (16); & p. chords, use of in accomp. (*Ph. Em. B.*), 478–81; different forms of, 716–25; difficulty of distinguishing (*Ph. Em. B.*), 731 *sq.*, time-signature (C or $\frac{4}{4}$) insufficient guide, 732, n. 22; different treatment of on Organ & Harpsichord (*Hein.*), 733 *sq.*;
Pedal Point: Ph. Em. Bach's views on the accomp. of -s, 292 *sq.*; -s, **798–801**;
pedals (Organ): use of in Penna's Exx., 140, n. 22, 142, n. 29;
position: of $\frac{7}{5}$ chord on leading note (or sharpened Subdominant), 561 *sq.*, 563, n. 3;
praevenire octavam: 487;
praevenire quintam: 489;
preparation: intervals requiring (*Niedt*), 230–2;
progression: of the 4th, dim. 5th, 7th, 9th, Tritone, augmented 5th, major 6th [with minor 3rd], & major 7th (*St. L.*), 186;
by augmented 2nd or 4th (*Corelli*), 189; forbidden -s, **484–96**; unvocal -s, 571, n. 5;
Promptuarium Musicum (*Schadaeus*): 91;

Quarta irregularis (*Quarta irregolare*): 259, 811 *sq.*;
quavers: in Bass, when to be treated as semiquavers (*Hein.*), 736, 762, 770, 772;

Radix aucta: 225;
—— *diffusa*: 225;
—— *simplex*: 225;
Recitative: dissonances in the accomp. of & their treatment (*Penna*), 148–50; accomp. of (*Hein.*), 267;
Règle de l'Octave (*Regola dell' Ottava*): 280 (cf. also 265–7); Schröter's, 306 *sq.*;
repeated notes: in Bass, treatment of, 774–7;
repercussion (see 'chords', 'harmony', & 'Harpsichord'):
resolution: transference of, 840–2; ellipse of, 857–60;
retardation: consec. 8ves saved by (*Purcell, Mattheson*), 169, n. 9; Schröter's detailed treatment of -s, 304; of major Seventh (& other intervals) over Tonic, **674–82**; harmonies due to r— (suspension), or anticipation, of one or more intervals, **692–714**;
right hand: progression of (*St. L.*), 185 (2); means of gaining fresh position for (*St. L.*), 197;
ripieni dell' organo (*Viadana*): 15, n. 11;
rückende Noten (see 'driving notes'):
Rückung (see also 'driving notes'): definition of (*Schröter*), 128, n. 2;

scale: figuring of the (*Hein., Rameau, Gasparini*), 265–7, (*Mattheson*), 280 *sq.*, (*Schröter*), 307;
Second: wrongly called 'Ninth' (*Penna*), 152, n. 57; progression of augmented S— sometimes to be used, 533;
semitonium minus: 262;
Semitonium modi: 266;
Septima (see 'Seventh'):
Sequence: 6 5 & $\begin{smallmatrix}6\\4\end{smallmatrix}$ $\begin{smallmatrix}5\\3\end{smallmatrix}$ on falling Bass (*Blow*), 168 [13] & nn. 7, 8; 7 6 on rising Bass (*Blow*), 168 [15] & n. 9; 7 6 on falling Bass (*Blow*), 169 *sup.*;
Seventh: rising (*Locke*), 161 & n. 12; struck *after* chord (*Blow*), 165, n. 2; Saint-Lambert's treatment of, 176–8; rising (*St. L.*), 179; rising (*Niedt*), 231; -s, **542–99**; when unprepared (*Mar.*), 545, 547 *sup.*; major -s resolving upwards

over the same Bass, **674–82**; rising -s, **842–55**;
Shake: Penna's extensive use of the, 134; fingering & execution (*Penna*), 138; Penna's use of illustrated, 140–3; in cadences (*Penna*), 145 *sq.*; practice of with both hands, 153 *inf.*; traditional use of in accomp. (*Matteson, St. L.*), 447 *sq.*;
Short Octave: 111; effect of, 122 *sq.*;
signa: 94; 97; 100; 101; in conjunction with *numeri* (*Staden*), 102–4;
signatures (see also 'Table'): Heinichen's Table of, 263; Matteson's criticism of the latter, 276 *sq.*; Matteson's Table of, 278–80; Schröter's Table of, 304–6; G. M. Telemann's Table of, 310 *sq.*;
signum cancellatum: 16; 100, n. 1;
similar motion: when safe (*St. L.*), 185 (4) & n. 17;
sixte: la petite s— & *la grande s—* (*Rameau*), 869, n. 1;
Sixth: on notes of which the Fifth is 'false', i.e. diminished (*Banchieri*), 85 *inf. sq.*; on all notes accidentally sharpened, 86; (or Fifth) on notes with accidental ♭, 86; accidentally major or minor indicated by ✕ ♭ below Bass, 122; with sharpened notes & ♮B in Bass (*Sabbatini*), 123; on E (with ♭ in signature), 124; to be taken with *mi* (*Penna*), 137; with bass notes accidentally sharpened, 137; minor, on what degrees of the scale (*Locke*), 155 (2) & n. 4; (preceded by Seventh) on falling Bass: (1) with major 3rd, (2) with minor 3rd (*Locke*), 156 (4); succession of -s on rising or falling Bass (*St. L.*), 190 *sq.* & n. 24; Niedt's rules, 227 *sq.*; major, with minor 3rd, doubling of (*Hein.*), 261; augmented, Matteson's figuring, 276; successive -s often best in 3 parts only, 331 & n. 4; chords of the, **516–33**; major, with minor 3rd, doubling of (*Ph. Em. B., Schröter, Türk*), 519, n. 7, (*Kirn.*), 523, progression of the, 521; 'Added S—', 622, n. 1; chords with an augmented S—, **684–9**;
Six-five chord: a passing, 528, n. 6; -s, **602–26**;
Six-four chords: **535–40**;
Six-four-three chords (see 'Four-three'):
Six-four-two chords: **648–72**;
slide: dotted, **433**, **435**; use of in accomp. (*Hein.*), 450 *sq.*;
slur: over bass notes indicating retention of harmony (*St. L.*), 178, n. 11, & 186, n. 19;
Soprano: voice, accomp. of (*Penna*), 153;
spartire (see '*partire*'):
Spartitura (see also '*Partitura*'): ='score' (*Agazzari*), 7, n. 3;

stroke: after figures, special use of, 833 *sq.*; through figure, Ph. Em. Bach on the use of, 868, Note; through figures, 872 *sq.*;
Style: Heinichen's distinctions, 263, n. 15; theatrical, irregularities of, legitimate & illegitimate (*Hein.*), 264 *sq.*; strict & free, definitions (*Hein., Kirn.*), 359, n. 11;
superjectio: 149 & n. 47, 454, n. 12;
Suspension (see also 'Retardation'): 7 6 -s on falling Bass (*Ebner*), 133, (*Locke*), 156 (6), (*Blow*), 165, 169; on a rising Bass (*Blow*), 168, (*St. L.*), 177, (*Ph. Em. B* & *J. S. Bach*), 584, (*Schröter*), 585 *sq.*; 9 8 -s on rising Bass (*Kirn.*), 349 *sq.*, 396 *sq.*; suspended Sevenths, **569–92**;
Syncopatio: term used in two senses, 764, n. 65;
syncopiren: ='breaking' (*brechen*), 444, n. 10;

Tablature (French): 91, n. 4;
Tablature (German Organ-): 99, n. 9; drawbacks of (*Werckmeister*), 211; 239;
Table (see also 'Signatures'): of the commonest figurings (*Türk*), 321;
Tasto solo: (*Ph. Em. B.*), 414–17; by temperament: form of advocated Werckmeister, 204, n. 2, 205, n. 3;
tempo maggiore: 139, n. 19;
tempo minore: 139 & n. 19;
Tenor: voice, accomp. of (*Penna*), 153;
terminus: acutus or *gravis*, 204, n. 2*;
Theorbo: 70; 72;
thesis: 139, n. 19;
Third: always major in final chord (*Ebner*), 131, (*Penna*), 141 & n. 27, (*Niedt*), 228; major, doubling of (*Hein.*), 260 *sq.*; diminished (*Hein.*), 262, n. 14; major, doubling of (*Kirn.*), 317; accidentally minor, doubling of vetoed by Kirnberger, 317; minor, doubling of in ⁶⁄₄ on Supertonic (*Kirn.*), 317, n. 10; major, doubling of (*Kirn., Hein.*), 499 & nn. 5, 6; of the Dominant, progression of, 499 *sq.* & n. 7;
Thorough-Bass (see also '*Bassus continuus*'): defined, 6; addition of to completed composition (*Penna*), 150, n. 51; educational value of (*Werckmeister*), 211;
Through-Bass (see Thorough-Bass):
Tierce de Picardie: in final cadence (*Ebner*), 131, (*Niedt*), 228;
Time, triple: G. M. Telemann's views on, 310;
time-values: of chords over sustained Bass, how indicated, 35 & n. 4; of consecutive figures over same Bass (*St. L.*), 181 *sq.*;

tradition: Italian vocal, 729 sq.;
transference: of discord, 838–40; of resolution, 840–2;
Transitional notes: the figuring of, 780–95;
transitus: irregularis, 130, n. 7 ad fin.; 143, n. 32; to the Third (Hein.), 449 & n. 4; regularis & irregularis, 543, n. 2; regularis, 716; in its widest sense, 719; special forms of, 720 sq., 725, nn. 11, 12; irregularis, though no leap (or figure) follows (Hein.), 740, n. 34 (2) (4) (7); irregularis, in the Bass, different methods of indicating, 783–6;
transposition: aids to (St. L.), 185 sup.;
tremblement: use of in accomp. (St. L.), 186 & n. 19; the same, 201 (15) sq.; defined by Couperin, 201, n. 37;
Triad (or Common Chord): **498–503**; figuring, 500 sq.;
Triad, the augmented: **512** sq.;
Triad, the diminished: **506–10**;
Trias harmonica: simplex & aucta, 333; aucta, 498;
trillo: 47 sq.;
Tritone: divergent practice in figuring of the (St. L.), 184 sq. & n. 16; between extreme parts of successive chords (Schröter), 303;

Undecima (see 'Eleventh'):
unison: coincidence of two parts in the (St. L.), 185, n. 18 & 189; the same recommended by Ph. Em. Bach as means of avoiding consecutives, but avoided by G. P. Telemann, 189, n. 22; means of avoiding (G. P. Telemann), 285; term often used to denote the 8ve, 577, n. 1;
Unisoni (all' unisono): (Ph. Em. B.), 414–17;
unisonus superfluus: 273;

Viola (Viol) da (di) gamba: as adjunct to keyed instrument, 237;
Violin: as 'instrument of ornamentation' (Agazzari), 68, 72;
Violoncello: recommended by Ph. Em. Bach as adjunct to keyed instrument, 237; its uses in accomp., 328–30;
Violone: three ways in which it (=Bass Viol) can play with Cembalo (Ortiz), 5 ? 72; as adjunct to keyed instrument, 237;
virtualiter: long or short note, 716 & n. 1;

Wechselnote (see also 'changing note'): 143, n. 32;

zimbelo: 47;
Zugriff: 245, n. 6;

INDEX NOMINUM

ABBATINI (ANTONIO MARIA): regarded consecutives as saved by the smallest intervening rest, 902;
ABEL (CARL FRIEDRICH): exceptional figuring, 866 sq.;
ADLUNG (JAKOB): suggested signs over Bass, 881 sq.;
AGAZZARI (AGOSTINO): emphasizes need for figures, 66 & n. 2, 68; rules for playing on a Bass, 67–74; 82; treatment of *Bassetti*, 96; influence of words on harmony, 106, n. 10; 236, n. 1;
ALALEONA (DOMENICO): 47;
ALBERT (HEINRICH): rules for treatment of Thorough-Bass, **126–31**;
ALBRECHTSBERGER: on ways of avoiding certain consec. 5ths, 404, n. 11;
ANERIO (GIOVANNI FRANCESCO): 90 *inf.*;
ASULA (G. M.): *Organicus Hymnodiae Vespertinae* (1602), 7, n. 3;

BACH (J. S.): reputed author of rules for playing Thorough-Bass, 214 & n. 2; his Basses used by his son, Ph. Em. B., for teaching, 294; his accomp. described by Kittel, 344 sq., by Daube & Mizler, 389, n. 5; example of 7 6 suspension, 575, n. 2, 582, on a rising Bass, 584; adherence to principles of 17th cent., 902 sq.;
BACH (PH. EM.): on necessity for figuring, 67; 'divided accomp.', 110; rule for time-value of two figures over dotted note, 182; on progression of perfect to diminished 5th, 198; *Versuch* &c., 2nd Pt., **290–4**; on compass of accomp., 364, 365 sq.; employment of various kinds of imitation in accomp., 385–8; on crossing of parts, 392; on 8ves with a Bass in broken harmony, 400; intolerance of consec. 5ths, 402; on gradation of tone, 407, 412, n. 23, 413 sq.; good accomp. defined, 439; on certain niceties of the accomp., **468–81**; advice to teachers, 484, nn. 1 & 3; example of Triads, 503; on chords of the Sixth, **527–33**; inclusion of imperfect 5th in chords of the 7th, 551, 572; rules for 7 6 sequences on rising Bass, 583 sq.; distinction between $\frac{7}{4_2}$ & $\frac{9}{4_7}$ on the Tonic, 642; on the accomp. of double appoggiaturas, 672; Exx. of transferred resolution (rising 7th &c.), 845 sq.; Ex. of (apparently) rising 7th, 847 sq.; on abnormal progressions, 859, n. 2; valuable suggestion, 882; methods of instruction, 898;
BANCHIERI (ADRIANO): *Concerti ecclesiastici a 8 voci*, 1595, 6 *inf. sq.*; rules for use of accidentals, 16 sq.; opinion of *Basso continuo*, 81; *Dialogo Musicale*, **82–90**; *Basso seguente* or *Barittono* [sic], 899 sq.;
BASSANO (GIOVANNI): *Bassi per l'organo* (1598) to his Motets, 9;
BIANCIARDI (FRANCESCO): *Breve regola* &c., **74–80**; 82;
BLOW (Dr. JOHN): rising (Dominant) 7th, 161, n. 12; MS. treatise on playing from a 'Through-Bass', **163–72**; 238; crossing of parts, 394; remarkable Ex. of 7 6 sequence on rising Bass, 588 sq.;
BRIDGE (Sir J. F.): account of R. Deering, 92 sq.;
BURNEY (Dr. CHARLES): 'The Beastialities of Dr. Blow', 163;

CACCINI (GIULIO): early use of figures, 2; indicates time-values of chords over sustained Bass, 35; *l'Euridice* & *Le Nuove Musiche*, 36; **42–7**; 236 sq.;
CAMPION (FRANÇOIS): 280;
CAVALIERI [CAUALLIERE] (EMILIO DEL): early use of figures, 2; *Rappresentatione* &c., 36; **47–65**; 236 sq.;
CHARPENTIER (MARC-ANTOINE): figuring of compound intervals, 180;
CHRYSANDER (F.): interpretation of Viadana's 4th rule, 14;
COLONNA (GIOVANNI PAOLO): 901 sq.;
CORELLI (ARCANGELO): uses progression of augmented 2nd & 4th (*St. L.*), 189; taught Gasparini, 250; interesting example of 'stratified' harmony, 380 sq.; controversy about his consecutive 5ths, 901 sq.;
CORSI (JACOPO): 36;
CROCE (GIOVANNI): *Spartidura* [sic] *delli Motetti a otto voci* (1594), 6 sq.;

DAUBE (JOHANN FRIEDRICH): on accomp. of 'soft and delicate passages', 371; description of J. S. Bach's accomp., 389, n. 5;
DEERING (RICHARD): earliest (?) English figured *Basso continuo*, 92 sq.;
DIRUTA (GIROLAMO): opinion of *Basso continuo*, 81;
DOMVIL ALS TAYLOR (SILAS): 154, n. 1;

INDEX NOMINUM

DOWLAND (JOHN): example from, 126, n. 23; example of $^6_4\,^5_3$ on falling Bass, 168, n. 8;

EBNER (WOLFGANG): rules for treatment of a Thorough-Bass, **131–3**;

FOGGIA (FRANCESCO): 901;
FREUDENBERG (FRAÜLEIN VON): 322;
FUX: on consec. 5ths, 490; *nota cambita*, 725, n. 12;

GALLUS (JOSEPH): Organ part to Motets &c., edited by Aurelius Ribrochus (1598), 8 *sq.* & nn. 6, 7;
GASPARINI (FRANCESCO): rules for unfigured Bass, 66 *sq.*; *L'armonico pratico al cimbalo*, **250–5**; inclusion of imperfect 5th in chords of the 7th, 550, 572;
GEMINIANI (FRANCESCO): 'Art of Accompaniment' [*sic*], 242; 438 *sq.*; principles of accomp., **463–8**; peculiar notation, 464, n. 1;
GERBER (HEINRICH NICOLAUS): realization of Albinoni's figured Bass, 575, n. 2;
GIACOMELLI (GIOUANBATTISTA): 36, n. 1;
GIOUANBATTISTA DAL VIOLINO: 36;
GROSSI, LODOVICO (DA VIADANA): 2;
GUIDOTTI (ALESSANDRO): 6, n. 1; rules for interpretation of Cavalieri's figures, 48;

HABERL (F. X.): interpretation of Viadana's 4th rule, 14;
HEINICHEN (JOHANN DAVID): on unfigured Basses, 67; allusion to Saint-Lambert's *Nouveau traité*, 173 *sq.*; H.'s rule for the accomp. of *Bassetti* compared with Niedt's, 226, n. 13; *Neu erfundene und gründliche Anweisung* &c., 255; *Der General-Bass in der Composition*, **255–69**; Schröter's reference to, 298 *sq.*; forms of accomp. described by, **332–6**; comments on rule for upward compass of the accomp., 363 *sq.*; treatment of *Bassetti*, **374–6**; Mattheson's praise, 379; employment of imitation in accomp., **383–5**; on crossing of parts, 392 *sq.*; consecutive 8ves between upper part of accomp. & passing note in Bass, 399; instructions for embellishment of accomp., **448–63**; recommendation of Mattheson's *Organisten-Probe*, 463; inclusion of imperfect 5th in chords of the 7th, 550, 572; rules for quick notes in the Bass, **731–75**; on transference of resolution, 841 *sq.*; Exx. of catachrestic progressions, 858 *sq.*; exceptions to rules for treatment of quavers in (slow) common time, **903–5**;
HERBST (JOHANN ANDREAS): translated & published Ebner's rules, 131;
HOLFELD (HOLEFELD, HOHLFELD): inventor of *Bogenclavier*, 327 & n. 3;

JOACHIM (JOSEPH): 370;

KELLER (GODFREY): 'A Compleat Method' &c., **247–50**;
KELLNER (DAVID): *Treulicher Unterricht im General-Bass* &c., **269** *sq.*; on 8ves with a Bass in broken harmony, 400;
KINKELDEY (OTTO): gives specimens of madrigals with written-out accomp. by Luzzasco Luzzaschi, 34, n. 2; quotes opinions on *Basso continuo*, 81; 899;
KIRNBERGER (JOHANN PHILIPP): *Kunst des reinen Satzes*, 242; *Grundsätze des Generalbasses* &c., **312–18**; retains old German nomenclature of notes, 313; more discriminating than Ph. Em. Bach, 313, n. 3; enumerates liberties characteristic of the free style, 360, n. 11; on crossing of parts, **395–7**; definition of essential 7th, 542; explanation of the progression $^7_5\,^5_3\atop{g\ a}$, 558, *Note*; on Rameau's *Sixte ajoutée*, 622, n. 2; two ways of treating 4 3 sequences, 696 *sq.*; realization of J. S. Bach's figured Bass, **789–92**; resolution of 7th on 8ve of Bass, 846; Ex. of rising 7th, 847;

LANZETTI (SALVATORE): accompanies Veracini on the Violoncello, 328;
LAPI (GIOVANNI): 36;
LASSO (ORLANDO DI): addition of figured Bass to his *Magnum opus musicum*, 91;
LECLAIR (JEAN-MARIE): $^{7\flat}_5$ sequence on rising Bass, 589; peculiar notation, 636 *sq.*; remarkable chord, 687 *sq.*; use of 6 peculiar to, 868 *sq.*; cadential use of $\flat = ^6_{4\atop 3}$, 870 *sq.*;
LIBERATI (ANTIMO): defence of Corelli's consec. 5ths, 901 *sq.*;
LOCKE (MATTHEW): *Melothesia*, **154–63**; examples of rising 7th, 161, n. 12; 238;
LUZZASCHI (see 'KINKELDEY'):

MALTOT: 280;
MANTICA (FRANCESCO): 47;
MARPURG (F. W.): on progression of diminished to perfect 5th, 198 *sup.*; *Handbuch bey dem Generalbasse*, 242;

INDEX NOMINUM

theory of chord-generation, 320, n. 3; on crossing of parts, 393 *sq.*; views on consecutives, 401-3; rules on forbidden progressions, abstract of, **485-96**; definition of essential discord, 542 *sq.*; unprepared 7ths, 545 *sq.*; preparation of 5 in $^6_5$, 602; of 3 in $^4_3$, 628; of Bass in $^6_4_2$, 648; on 7ths resolving on 8ve of Bass, 842 *sq.*; on rising 7th, 843; further rules concerning consecutives, 903;

MATTHESON (JOHANN): rising (Dominant Seventh), 161, n. 12; consec. 8ves saved by retardation in Bass, 169, n. 9; *Kleine General-Bass Schule*, **270-83**; faulty progressions in Exx., 281 *sq.*; Schröter's reference to, 299; praise of Heinichen's *General-Bass*, 379; example of 'stratified' harmony, 380 *sq.*; on embellishment of accomp., 392; examples of crossing of parts, 393, 394 *sq.*; examples & excerpts from *Organisten-Probe*, **440-8**;

MIZLER (LORENZ): his machine for learning Thorough-Bass, 322 *sq.*; description of J. S. Bach's accomp., 389, n. 5;
MONTALVO (DON GRAZIA): 36;
MORINI (NESTORE): 901;
MORTARO: Masses for 3 choirs, 7, n. 3;

NIEDT (FRIDERICH ERHARD): on use of *Tierce de Picardie*, 131; *Musicalische Handleitung* &c. (*Erster Theil*), **213-36**; *Handleitung zur Variation* &c., 213, n. 1; Introduction to *Handleitung*, 215-22; love of coined words, 219, 221, n. 5, 222, n. 7; advice to disregard figures, 229 & n. 16; 238 *sq.*;

ORTIZ (DIEGO): *Tratado de glosas* &c., 5; 236;

PALESTRINA: addition of Organ Bass (*Bassus ad Organum*, *Basso continuo*), both figured & unfigured, to works of, 90 *sq.* & n. 1; Motets with figured Bass (Strozzi, quoted by Praetorius), 95;
PASQUINI (BERNARDO): Gasparini's eulogy of, 250 *sq.*;
PENNA (LORENZO): instructions *per suonare l' Organo ò Clavicembalo sopra la parte*, **133-54**; rules for accomp. of different voices, 369;
PERI (JACOPO): early use of figures, 2; *Le Musiche ... sopra l'Euridice* &c., 36; **36-42**; 236 *sq.*;
PICCIONI (GIOVANNI): 66, n. 1; 899;
PRAETORIUS (MICHAEL): definition of *ac-centi & passaggi*, 10 *sq.*, nn. 2 & 3; *De Basso generali seu Continuo*, **93-100**; 237; earliest known edition of *Tom.* II, III of the *Syntagma*, 899;
PRINTZ: on hidden 8ves, 488;
PURCELL (HENRY): 9th prepared by 8ve of Bass, 169, n. 9, 397 *inf. sq.*;

QUANTZ (JOHANN JOACHIM): *Versuch* &c., 242; quoted by G. M. Telemann, 291 *sq.*; Schröter's laudatory mention of, 299; on compass of accomp., 364 *inf. sq.*; treatment of *Bassetti*, 375, n. 6; on gradation of tone, **407-14**;
QUINTIANI (D. LUCRETIO): 8-part Masses & Motets, 7 *sq.*, n. 3;

RAMEAU (JEAN-PHILIPPE): Mattheson's opinion of his work, 273; Schröter's reference to, 301; *Grande Sixte* or *Sixte ajoutée*, 621 *inf. sq.*;
RIBROCHUS (AURELIUS): editor of early Organ Bass, 8 *sq.*, nn. 6, 7;
RUETTINO: quoted by Gasparini in support of certain consecutives, 253;

SABBATINI (GALEAZZO): special use of accidentals, 16 *sq.*; *Regola facile* &c., **110-26**;
SAINT-LAMBERT (MICHEL DE): rising (dominant) 7th, 161, n. 12; treatise on accomp., **172-202** (but see also 900 *sq.*); *Nouveau traité* &c., Italian trans. of, 173; reprint of, *ibid.*; quoted by Heinichen, *ibid. sq.*; 237 *sq.*; employment of imitation in accomp., 383; the *Traité* of 1680 a myth, 900 *sq.*;
SCARLATTI (ALESSANDRO): MS. treatise, 254 & n. 4; Solo Cantata by, used by Heinichen as example of unfigured Bass, 267; inclusion of 4 & 4+ in $^6_3$ chord, 812, 814;
SCHADAEUS (ABRAHAM): 91;
SCHNEIDER (PROF. MAX): 369;
SCHREYER (JOHANNES): 369;
SCHRÖTER (CHRISTOPH GOTTLIEB): grateful mention of J. P. Treiber, 243; appreciation of Kellner's *Treulicher Unterricht*, 269 *sq.*; *Deutliche Anweisung zum General-Bass* &c., **294-308**; describes origin of his *D. A.*, 295, n. 1; destruction of his MSS., 297 *sq.*; theory of origin of discords, concession to prevalent ideas, 300 *sq.*; classification of Harmony, 301 *sq.*; sensitiveness to hidden consecutives, 302 *sq.*; amusing reminiscence, 307 *sq.*; tolerance of certain consec. 5ths, 304, 403; position of

$^7_5$ chord on seventh degree of major mode, 562; Exx. of 7 6 sequences on rising Bass, 585 sq., warning against taking 7 6 as $^7_5$ $^6_6$, 588; position of $^6_5$ chord ($^5_6$) on 2nd degree of major mode, 611, n. *; on use of 6 = $^6_4$ = $^6_3$, 635; position of $^4_3$ chord ($^3_4$) on 4th degree of major mode, 638; methods of indicating inversions of preceding (figured) harmony, 833 sq.; Ex. of rising 7th explained, 847;
SEIFFERT (PROF. MAX): 283;
SIMONELLI (MATTEO): 901;
SORGE (GEORG ANDREAS): *Vorgemach der musicalischen Composition*, 242; Schröter's reference to, 301;
STADEN (JOHANN): Exx. of cadences (*Tenor, Cantus, Altus*), 12; instructions concerning *Bassus ad organum*, 100–9;

'*Tacitus*': narrative of (*Niedt*), 217–21;
TELEMANN (GEORG MICHAEL): commends Quantz's rules for accomp., 242; description of Ph. Em. Bach's *Versuch*, Pt. 2, 291 sq.; *Unterricht im Generalbass-Spielen* &c., 308–11; Ex. of rising 7th, 848;
TELEMANN (GEORG PHILIPP): permits full closes in the accomp. with the 5 in the upper part, 46, n. 2; frequently closes with the 3 in the upper part, *above the voice* (contrary to Ph. Em. Bach's rule), 47, n. 3; *Singe- Spiel- und Generalbass-Übungen*, 283–90; employment of intervals not figured: 5♭ with (minor) 6, 285, 5♭ with 6̄, 288; sensitiveness to hidden 5ths, 286; takes accomp. above solo part, allows full close with 5th in upper part, augmented 2nd, 287 & nn. 5–7; rule for ambiguous figuring (2 = $^6_4$ or $^5_4$), 288; instances of discords (in solo part) reduplicated in lower 8ve in the accomp., 371, n. 10; on 8ves with a Bass in broken harmony, 400; inclusion of 5 (5♭) in $^6_3$ ($^6♮_3$) chord, 814 sq.; the use of his sign ⌒, 865 sq. & n. 4;
TESSIER (ANDRÉ): 900;
TEVO: on consec. 5ths, 490;
TREIBER (JOHANN PHILIPP): *Der accurate Organist im General-Bass*, 243–7; Schröter's reference to, 298;
TÜRK (DANIEL GOTTLOB): *Kurze Anweisung zum Generalbassspielen*, 318–22; advocates accomp. of bass instruments & voices in the 8ve above, 366 sq. & nn. 6, 7; examples of tolerated consec. 5ths, 492, n. 12; use of figuring $^9_6_4$ instead of $^6_4_2$, 669; Ex. of rising 7th, 848; Exx. showing alternation between close & extended harmony, 898;

VAN DEN BORREN (CHARLES): 900;
VATIELLI (FRANCESCO): 901;
VERACINI (Francesco): accompanied by Lanzetti on the Violoncello, 328 sq.;
VIADANA (LODOVICO GROSSI DA): *Cento Concerti*, 2–5; his *Auertimenti* or Rules, 9–21; specimens of *concerti*, 21–33; 82; reason for V.'s 9th rule, permitting consecutives in the accomp., 85, n. 4; 92; example of his treatment of *Bassetti*, 96; criticism of (*Staden*), 109; 236 sq.;
VINCENTIUS (CASPAR): 91 sq.;
VIVALDI (ANTONIO): $^7_5^6$ sequence on falling Bass, 591;

WERCKMEISTER (ANDREAS): rule for cadences, 13; omission of discord (though figured), 39, n. 4; emphasizes need for figures, 66; *Die nothwendigsten Anmerckungen* &c., 202–13; 238;
WINTERFELD (C. VON): interpretation of Viadana's 4th rule, 14;

ZANI (MATTEO): 901;